TRAVELLERS'
FOREIGN PHRASE BOOK

BY J. O. KETTRIDGE

Dictionary of the French and English Languages. Crown 8vo. 542 pages.

French Idioms and Figurative Phrases. Demy 8vo. 256 pages.

French for English Idioms. Demy 8vo. 288 pages.

French-English and English-French Dictionary of Commercial and Financial Terms, Phrases and Practice. Royal 8vo. 660 pages.

French-English and English-French Dictionary of Financial and Mercantile Terms, Phrases and Practice. Crown 8vo. 256 pages.

French-English and English-French Dictionary of Technical Terms and Phrases used in Civil, Mechanical, Electrical and Mining Engineering, and Allied Sciences and Industries. Royal 8vo. 1160 pages. In two volumes.

TRAVELLERS' FOREIGN

PHRASE BOOK

by

J. O. KETTRIDGE

I rather would entreat thy company
To see the wonders of the world abroad.
—SHAKESPEARE

Twelfth impression

1981
London, Boston and Henley
ROUTLEDGE & KEGAN PAUL LTD.

CONTENTS

(An alphabetical list of contents will be found on pages 270-272.)

CONTENTS

ENGLISH CARDINAL NUMBERS	FRENCH NOMBRES CARDINAUX	GERMAN GRUNDZAHLEN
One.	Un, Une.	Eins ; Einer, Eine, Ein.
Two.	Deux.	Zwei.
Three.	Trois.	Drei.
Four.	Quatre.	Vier.
Five.	Cinq.	Fünf.
Six.	Six.	Sechs.
Seven.	Sept.	Sieben.
Eight.	Huit.	Acht.
Nine.	Neuf.	Neun.
Ten.	Dix.	Zehn.
Eleven.	Onze.	Elf.
Twelve.	Douze.	Zwölf.
Thirteen.	Treize.	Dreizehn.
Fourteen.	Quatorze.	Vierzehn.
Fifteen.	Quinze.	Fünfzehn.
Sixteen.	Seize.	Sechszehn.
Seventeen.	Dix-sept.	Siebzehn.
Eighteen.	Dix-huit.	Achtzehn.
Nineteen.	Dix-neuf.	Neunzehn.
Twenty.	Vingt.	Zwanzig.
Twenty-one.	Vingt et un, e.	Einundzwanzig.
Twenty-two.	Vingt-deux.	Zweiundzwanzig.
Twenty-eight.	Vingt-huit.	Achtundzwanzig.
Thirty.	Trente.	Dreißig.
Forty.	Quarante.	Vierzig.
Fifty.	Cinquante.	Fünfzig.
Sixty.	Soixante.	Sechzig.
Seventy.	Soixante-dix (Septante).	Siebzig.
Seventy-one.	Soixante et onze.	Einundsiebzig.
Seventy-two.	Soixante-douze.	Zweiundsiebzig.
Eighty.	Quatre-vingts (Octante).	Achtzig.
Eighty-one.	Quatre-vingt-un, e.	Einundachtzig.
Eighty-two.	Quatre-vingt-deux.	Zweiundachtzig.
Ninety.	Quatre-vingt-dix (Nonante).	Neunzig.
Ninety-one.	Quatre-vingt-onze.	Einundneunzig.
Hundred.	Cent.	Hundert.
Hundred and one.	Cent un, e.	Hundert[und]eins.
Two hundred.	Deux cents.	Zweihundert.
Five hundred and one.	Cinq cent, un, e.	Fünfhundert[und]eins.
Thousand.	Mille.	Tausend.
Thousand and one.	Mille un, e.	Tausend[und]eins.
Thousand one hundred or Eleven hundred.	Mille cent ou Onze cents.	Tausendeinhundert oder Elfhundert.
Ten thousand. 10,000	Dix mille. 10.000 ou 10 000	Zehntausend. 10 000 oder 10.000
A million.	Un million.	Eine Million.

Note.—On the Continent of Europe : the figure one is generally written with an upstroke ; thus 1 or Λ.

The figure seven is not written as in England 7, but is crossed ; thus 7.

ITALIAN **NUMERI CARDINALI**	SPANISH **NÚMEROS CARDINALES**	DUTCH **HOOFDTELWOORDEN**
◄Uno, Una.	Un, Uno, Una.	Een.
Due.	Dos.	Twee.
Tre.	Tres.	Drie.
Quattro.	Cuatro.	Vier.
Cinque.	Cinco.	Vijf.
◄Sei.	Seis.	Zes.
Sette.	Siete.	Zeven.
Otto.	Ocho.	Acht.
Nove.	Nueve.	Negen.
Dieci.	Diez.	Tien.
◄Undici.	Once.	Elf.
Dodici.	Doce.	Twaalf.
Tredici.	Trece.	Dertien.
Quattordici.	Catorce.	Veertien.
Quindici.	Quince.	Vijftien.
◄Sedici.	Dieciseis.	Zestien.
Diciassette.	Diecisiete.	Zeventien.
Diciotto.	Dieciocho.	Achttien.
Diciannove.	Diecinueve.	Negentien.
Venti.	Veinte.	Twintig.
◄Ventuno, a.	Veintiun, uno, a.	Een en twintig.
Ventidue.	Veintidos.	Twee en twintig.
Ventotto.	Veintiocho.	Acht en twintig.
Trenta.	Treinta.	Dertig.
Quaranta.	Cuarenta.	Veertig.
◄Cinquanta.	Cincuenta.	Vijftig.
Sessanta.	Sesenta.	Zestig.
Settanta.	Setenta.	Zeventig.
Settantuno, a.	Setenta y un, uno, a.	Een en zeventig.
Settantadue.	Setenta y dos.	Twee en zeventig.
◄Ottanta.	Ochenta.	Tachtig.
Ottantuno, a.	Ochenta y un, uno, a.	Een en tachtig.
Ottantadue.	Ochenta y dos.	Twee en tachtig.
Novanta.	Noventa.	Negentig.
Novantuno, a.	Noventa y un, uno, a	Een en negentig.
◄Cento.	Cien, Ciento.	Honderd.
Centuno, a.	Ciento uno, a.	Honderd een.
Duecento.	Doscientos, as.	Twee honderd.
Cinquecentuno, a.	Quinientos uno, as una.	Vijf honderd een.
Mille.	Mil.	Duizend.
◄Mille uno, a.	Mil uno, Mil y un, uno, a.	Duizend een.
Mille e cento.	Mil cien, Mil ciento.	Elf honderd.
Diecimila. 10.000	Diez mil. 10.000	Tien duizend. 10.000
◄Un milione.	Un millòn.	Een millioen.

The figure five is written either as in England **5**, or thus ſ or ʄ. This is frequently joined on in a flowing style to the preceding figure, thus twenty-five may be written 2ſ, 2ʄ, 2ſ, 2ʄ.

ORDINAL NUMBERS	NOMBRES ORDINAUX	ORDNUNGSZAHLEN
First (1st).	Premier (1er), Première (1re).	Erste (1.).
Second (2nd).	Second, e, Deuxième (2e).	Zweite (2.).
Third (3rd).	Troisième (3e).	Dritte (3.).
Fourth (4th).	Quatrième (4e).	Vierte (4.).
Fifth (5th).	Cinquième (5e).	Fünfte (5.).
Sixth (6th).	Sixième (6e).	Sechste (6.).
Seventh (7th).	Septième (7e).	Siebente (7.).
Eighth (8th).	Huitième (8e).	Achte (8.).
Ninth (9th).	Neuvième (9e).	Neunte (9.).
Tenth (10th).	Dixième (10e).	Zehnte (10.).
Eleventh (11th).	Onzième (11e).	Elfte (11.).
Twelfth (12th).	Douzième (12e).	Zwölfte (12.).
Thirteenth (13th).	Treizième (13e).	Dreizehnte (13.).
Fourteenth (14th).	Quatorzième (14e).	Vierzehnte (14.).
Fifteenth (15th).	Quinzième (15e).	Fünfzehnte (15.).
Sixteenth (16th).	Seizième (16e).	Sechzehnte (16.).
Seventeenth (17th).	Dix-septième (17e).	Siebzehnte (17.).
Eighteenth (18th).	Dix-huitième (18e).	Achtzehnte (18.).
Nineteenth (19th).	Dix-neuvième (19e).	Neunzehnte (19.).
Twentieth (20th).	Vingtième (20e).	Zwanzigste (20.).
Hundredth (100th).	Centième (100e).	Hundertste (100.).
Thousandth (1000th).	Millième (1000e).	Tausendste (1000.).

FRACTIONS	FRACTIONS	BRÜCHE
Three fourths or Three quarters.	Trois quarts.	Drei Viertel oder Dreiviertel.
Two thirds.	Deux tiers.	Zwei Drittel.
One (or A) half.	Un demi.	Einhalb, Eine Hälfte.
One (or A) third.	Un tiers.	Ein Drittel.
One (or A) fourth or One (or A) quarter.	Un quart.	Ein Viertel oder Einviertel.
One (or A) fifth.	Un cinquième.	Ein Fünftel.
One and a half.	Un et demi.	Anderthalb oder Einein- halb.
Two and a half.	Deux et demi.	Zweieinhalb.
A [decimal] point (.)	Une virgule [décimale] (,)	Ein Komma [in einer Dezimalzahl] (,)

DIVISIONS OF TIME	DIVISIONS DE L'HEURE	ZEITEINTEILUNG
One in the morning, in the afternoon.	Une heure du matin, de l'après-midi.	Ein Uhr früh, mittags.
Five past two.	Deux heures cinq.	Fünf Minuten nach zwei.
A quarter past three.	Trois heures et quart.	Viertel nach drei oder Viertel vier.
Half past four.	Quatre heures et demie.	Halb fünf.
Twenty to five.	Cinq heures moins vingt.	Zwanzig vor fünf.
A quarter to six in the evening.	Six heures moins le quart du soir.	Viertel vor (oder Dreivier- tel) sechs Uhr abends.
Ten o'clock at night.	Dix heures du soir.	Zehn Uhr abends.
Noon or Midday.	Midi.	Mittag.
Midnight.	Minuit.	Mitternacht.
Half past twelve in the day.	Midi et demi.	Halb eins, mittags.
Half past twelve at night.	Minuit et demi.	Halb eins, nachts.

NUMERI ORDINALI	NÚMEROS ORDINALES	RANGTELWOORD
Primo, a (1°, 1ª) (*feminines of all below end in a*).	Primer (1er), Primero (1°), Primera (1ª).	Eerste (1ste).
Secondo (2°).	Segundo (2°).	Tweede (2de).
Terzo (3°).	Tercero (3°).	Derde (3de).
Quarto (4°).	Cuarto (4°).	Vierde (4de).
Quinto (5°).	Quinto (5°).	Vijfde (5de).
Sesto (6°).	Sexto (6°).	Zesde (6de).
Settimo (7°).	Septimo (7mo).	Zevende (7de).
Ottavo (8°).	Octavo (8vo).	Achtste (8ste).
Nono (9°).	Noveno o Nono (9no).	Negende (9de).
Decimo (10°).	Décimo (10mo).	Tiende (10de).
Undicesimo (11°).		Elfde (11de).
Dodicesimo (12°).		Twaalfde (12de).
Tredicesimo (13°).		Dertiende (13de).
Quattordicesimo (14°).		Veertiende (14de).
Quindicesimo (15°).	*Note.*—The ordinals after 10th are seldom used now, the cardinals being used instead.	Vijftiende (15de).
Sedicesimo (16°).		Zestiende (16de).
Diciassettesimo (17°).		Zeventiende (17de).
Diciottesimo (18°).		Achttiende (18de).
Diciannovesimo (19°).	*Note.*—*All the above ending in o in the masculine gender end in a in the feminine gender.*	Negentiende (19de).
Ventesimo (20°).		Twintigste (20ste).
Centesimo (100°).		Honderdste (100ste).
Millesimo (1000°).		Duizendste (1000ste).

FRAZIONI	FRACCIONES	BREUKEN
Tre quarti.	Tres cuartos.	Drie vierde of Drie kwart.
Due terzi.	Dos tercios.	Twee derde.
Una metà.	Medio, a, La mitad.	Een half, Een halve.
Un terzo.	Un tercio.	Een derde.
Un quarto.	Un cuarto.	Een vierde of Een kwart.
Un quinto.	Un quinto.	Een vijfde.
Uno e mezzo.	Uno y medio, Una y media.	Anderhalf, Anderhalve.
Due e mezzo.	Dos y medio, a.	Twee en een half, halve.
Una virgola [decimale] (,)	Un punto [decimal] (. o ,)	Een [decimale] komma (,)

DIVISIONE DELL'ORA	HORAS DEL DÍA	TIJDVERDELING
All'una del mattino, del pomeriggio.	La una de la mañana, de la tarde.	Een uur 's nachts, 's middags.
Le due e cinque.	Las dos y cinco.	Vijf (minuten) over twee.
Le tre ed un quarto.	Las tres y cuarto.	Kwart over drie.
Le quattro e mezzo.	Las cuatro y media.	Half vijf.
Le cinque meno venti.	Las cinco menos veinte.	Tien over half vijf.
Alle sei meno un quarto di sera.	Las seis menos cuarto de la tarde.	Kwart voor zes 's avonds.
Alle dieci di sera.	Las diez de la noche.	Tien uur 's avonds.
Mezzogiorno.	El mediodía.	Twaalf uur 's middags.
Mezzanotte.	La media noche.	Middernacht.
Mezzo giorno e mezzo.	Las doce y media del día.	Half een 's middags.
Mezzanotte e mezza.	Las doce y media de la noche.	Half een 's nachts.

SEASONS	SAISONS	JAHRESZEITEN
Spring.	Le printemps.	Frühling.
Summer.	L'été.	Sommer.
Autumn.	L'automne.	Herbst.
Winter.	L'hiver.	Winter.
Single summer time.	La simple heure d'été.	Einfache Sommerzeit.
Double summer time	La double heure d'été.	Doppelte Sommerzeit.
Easter.	Pâques.	Ostern.
Good Friday.	Le vendredi saint.	Karfreitag.
Lent.	Le carême.	Fasten[zeit].
Whitsun.	La Pentecôte.	Pfingsten.
Christmas.	Noël.	Weihnachten.

MONTHS OF THE YEAR	MOIS DE L'ANNÉE	MONATE DES JAHRES
January.	Janvier.	Januar.
February.	Février.	Februar.
March.	Mars.	März.
April.	Avril.	April.
May.	Mai.	Mai.
June.	Juin.	Juni.
July.	Juillet.	Juli.
August.	Août.	August.
September.	Septembre *ou* 7bre.	September.
October.	Octobre *ou* 8bre.	Oktober.
November.	Novembre *ou* 9bre.	November.
December.	Décembre *ou* Xbre.	Dezember.

DAYS OF THE WEEK	JOURS DE LA SEMAINE	WOCHENTAGE
Sunday.	Dimanche.	Sonntag.
Monday.	Lundi.	Montag.
Tuesday.	Mardi.	Dienstag.
Wednesday.	Mercredi.	Mittwoch.
Thursday.	Jeudi.	Donnerstag.
Friday.	Vendredi.	Freitag.
Saturday.	Samedi.	Sonnabend *oder* Samstag.

NOTES

[Brackets] enclose words, or parts of words, which can be used or omitted at will.

or

(introduces a virtually synonymous rendering.)

NOTES

Les [crochets] renferment des mots, ou des parties de mots, qu'on peut employer ou omettre à volonté.

ou

ANMERKUNGEN

Worte, oder Wortteile, in [eckigen Klammern] können, je nach Belieben, gebraucht oder fortgelassen werden.

oder

STAGIONI	ESTACIONES	JAARGETIJDEN
◄La primavera.	La primavera.	Het voorjaar, De lente.
L'estate.	El verano.	De zomer.
L'autunno.	El otoño.	Het najaar, De herfst.
L'inverno.	El invierno.	De winter.
Semplice ora estiva.	La hora simple de verano.	De enkelvoudige zomertijd.
◄Doppia ora estiva.	La hora doble de verano.	De dubbele zomertijd.
Pasqua.	Pascua de Resurrección.	Pasen.
Venerdì santo.	El viernes santo.	Goede Vrijdag.
La quaresima.	La cuaresma.	Vasten.
La Pentecoste.	El Pentecostés.	Pinksteren.
◄Natale.	La Navidad.	Kerstmis.

MESI DELL'ANNO	MESES DEL AÑO	MAANDEN VAN HET JAAR
Gennaio	Enero.	Januari.
Febbraio.	Febrero.	Februari.
Marzo.	Marzo.	Maart.
Aprile.	Abril.	April.
◄Maggio.	Mayo.	Mei.
Giugno.	Junio.	Juni.
Luglio.	Julio.	Juli.
Agosto.	Agosto.	Augustus.
Settembre o 7bre.	Se[p]tiembre.	September.
◄Ottobre od 8bre.	Octubre.	Oktober.
Novembre o 9bre.	Noviembre.	November.
Decembre o 10bre.	Diciembre.	December.

GIORNI DELLA SETTIMANA	DÍAS DE LA SEMANA	DAGEN VAN DE WEEK
Domenica.	Domingo.	Zondag.
Lunedì.	Lunes.	Maandag.
◄Martedì.	Martes.	Dinsdag.
Mercoledì.	Miércoles.	Woensdag.
Giovedì.	Jueves.	Donderdag.
Venerdì.	Viernes.	Vrijdag.
Sabato.	Sábado.	Zaterdag.

NOTE	NOTAS	OPMERKINGEN
◄ Le [parentesi angolari] chiudono parole, o parte di parole, che possono adoperarsi od omettersi a volontà.	Las palabras, o partes de palabras, puestas entre [paréntesis angulares] pueden emplearse u omitirse a discreción.	[Haken] omvatten woorden, of gedeelten van woorden, die naar wens gebruikt of weggelaten kunnen worden.
o or *od*	*o* or *u*	*of*

**If the person to whom you are speaking cannot
understand what you say, point to the sentence in
the book, and let him read it in his own language.**

ENGLISH	FRENCH	GERMAN
RAILWAY TRAVEL, LUGGAGE	**VOYAGES EN CHEMIN DE FER, BAGGAGE**	**BAHNREISE, GEPÄCK**
The railway	**Le chemin de fer**	**Die Eisenbahn**
A branch [line].	Une ligne secondaire.	Eine Nebenstrecke.
A narrow-gauge railway.	Un chemin de fer à voie étroite.	Eine Schmalspurbahn.
A mountain railway.	Un chemin de fer de montagne.	Eine Gebirgsbahn.
A rack [and pinion] railway.	Un chemin de fer à crémaillère.	Eine Zahnradbahn.
A cable railway.	Un funiculaire.	Eine Drahtseilbahn.
A train ferry.	Un bac transbordeur.	Eine Eisenbahnfähre.
A tunnel.	Un tunnel.	Ein Tunnel.
An underground railway.	Un chemin de fer souterrain.	Eine Untergrundbahn.
An escalator.	Un escalier roulant.	Eine Rolltreppe.
The station	**La gare**	**Der Bahnhof**
(*the station building*) e.g., Whereabouts is the station ?	La gare, *p. ex.* (=*par exemple*), De quel côté est la gare ?	Der Bahnhof. *z.B.* (=*zum Beispiel*), In welcher Richtung liegt der Bahnhof ?
(*the station regarded as a stopping place*) e.g., I am getting out at the next station.	La station, *p. ex.*, Je descends à la prochaine station.	Die Station. *z.B.*, Ich steige an der nächsten Station aus.
A junction [station].	Une gare d'embranchement.	Ein Knotenpunkt.
A halt (*wayside station*).	Une halte.	Ein Haltepunkt.
Which is the way in, the way out, the way up, the way down ?	Où est l'entrée, la sortie, la montée, la descente ?	Wo ist der Eingang, der Ausgang ? Wo geht es herauf, herunter ?
The booking hall.	Le hall [des guichets].	Die Eingangshalle.
The booking office or The ticket window. (*See subheading* The ticket, *below*.)	Le guichet [de distribution des billets].	Der Schalter.
Is the booking office open ?	Le guichet est-il ouvert ?	Ist der Schalter offen ?
The [ticket] barrier.	Le portillon [d'accès].	Die Sperre.
The booking clerk.	Le receveur.	Der Schalterbeamte.
The luggage office.	Le guichet des bagages.	Die Gepäckaufbewahrung.
The collection, The delivery, of luggage at residence.	L'enlèvement, La livraison, des bagages à domicile.	Gepäckbeförderung von und zur Wohnung.
At railway station, to be called for.	En gare *ou* Gare restante *ou* Bureau restant.	Bahnlagernd.
At owner's risk.	Aux risques et périls du destinataire.	Auf eigenes Risiko.

ITALIAN	SPANISH	DUTCH
VIAGGIO IN FERROVIA, BAGAGLI	**VIAJES EN FERROCARRIL, EQUIPAJES**	**TREINREIZEN, BAGAGE**
La ferrovia	**El ferrocarril**	**De spoorweg**
Una linea secondaria.	Una vía secundaria.	Een zijlijn.
Una ferrovia a scartamento ridotto.	Una vía de trocha angosta.	Een smal spoor.
Una ferrovia di montagna.	Un ferrocarril de montaña.	Een bergspoor.
Una ferrovia a cremagliera.	Un ferrocarril de cremallera.	Een tandradbaan.
◄Una funicolare.	Un funicular.	Een kabelbaan.
Un pontone trasbordatore.	Una barcaza (o Un Pontón) de transbordo.	Een ferry-boot, Een pot.
Un traforo, Una galleria.	Un tunel.	Een tunnel.
Una ferrovia sotterranea.	Un ferrocarril subterráneo.	Een ondergrondse.
Una scala semovente.	Una escalera movible.	Een roltrap.
La stazione	**La estación**	**Het station**
◄La stazione, *per es.* (= *per esempio*), Da che parte è la stazione?	La estación, *p.ej.* (= *por ejemplo*), ¿Por dónde esta la estación?	Het station, *b.v.* (= *bij voorbeeld*), Waar is het station?
La stazione, *per es.*, Io scendo alla prossima stazione.	La estación, *p.ej.*, Me apeo en la próxima estación.	Het station, *b.v.*, Ik stap op het volgende station uit.
Una diramazione ferroviaria.	Un empalme.	Een kruispunt van spoorwegen.
Una fermata.	Un apeadero.	Een halte.
Dov'è l'entrata, l'uscita, Da che parte si sale, Da che parte si scende.	¿Por dónde es la entrada, la salida, la subida, la bajada?	Waar is de ingang, de uitgang, de trap naar boven, de trap naar beneden?
◄Sala per la vendita biglietti.	La sala de expendeduría de billetes.	De hal van het station.
L'ufficio biglietti o Lo sportello dei biglietti.	El despacho de billetes o La taquilla.	Het loket.
È aperto l'ufficio biglietti?	¿Está abierta la taquilla?	Is het loket open?
Il limite di accesso alla piattaforma.	La barrera.	Het toegangshek.
Il bigliettinaio.	El vendedor de billetes.	De man achter het loket.
◄L'ufficio bagagli.	El despacho de equipajes.	Het bagage-bureau.
Il ritiro, la consegna, del bagaglio a domicilio.	La colecta, La entrega, de equipajes a domicilio.	Het aan huis afhalen, afleveren, van bagage.
Fermo stazione, da ritirarsi.	En la estación, para ser recogido(s)	Ter afhaling.
A rischio del mittente.	A riesgo del propietario.	Voor risico van de eigenaar.

I want to register this article [of luggage] for .. What is the charge for registration, for excess weight?	Je veux faire enregistrer ce colis pour .. Quelle est la taxe d'enregistrement, la taxe pour l'excédent de poids?	Ich möchte dieses Gepäckstück nach .. aufgeben. Was kostet das Aufgeben, Wie ist der Tarif für Übergewicht?
Where is the registered luggage [to be found]? I have a registered trunk. Here is the [luggage] ticket.	Où se trouvent les bagages enregistrés? J'ai une malle enregistrée. Voici le bulletin [de bagages].	Wo findet man aufgegebenes Gepäck? Ich habe einen aufgegebenen Koffer hier liegen. Hier ist der Gepäckschein.
The enquiry office.	Le bureau de renseignements.	Die Auskunft.
Is there a boat train between .. and .. ensuring connexion with the ships?	Y a-t-il un train de paquebot entre .. et .. assurant la liaison avec les navires?	Gibt es einen Zug von .. nach .. mit Anschluß an das Schiff?
Is there a relief train?	Y a-t-il un train supplémentaire?	Geht ein Extrazug?
When does summer time begin, end, in .. ?	L'heure d'été quand commence-t-elle, finit-elle, en .. ?	Wann beginnt, endet, die Sommerzeit hier in .. ?
The waiting room.	La salle d'attente.	Der Wartesaal.
Where is the lavatory, the W.C.?	Où est la toilette (ou le cabinet de toilette), le cabinet [d'aisances]?	Wo ist die Toilette, das Klosett?
A time table.	Un horaire.	Ein Fahrplan.
A railway guide (book).	Un indicateur des chemins de fer.	Ein Kursbuch.
Subject to alterations (as a time table).	Sous réserve de modifications.	Änderungen vorbehalten.
The departure platform.	Le quai de départ.	Der Bahnsteig für abfahrende Züge.
Shall I have long to wait for a train to .. ?	Aurai-je à attendre longtemps un train pour .. ?	Werde ich lange auf den Zug nach .. warten müssen?
Is there a non-stop train about 8 o'clock in the morning, in the evening, at 8 a.m., 8 p.m., to .. ? (See 24-HOUR CLOCK SYSTEM, p. 267.)	Y a-t-il un train sans arrêt vers huit heures du matin, du soir, à huit heures, vingt heures, pour .. ?	Gibt es einen durchgehenden Zug ohne Aufenthalt nach .., um etwa acht Uhr morgens, abends, um acht Uhr, zwanzig Uhr?
Is there a through service without change?	Y a-t-il un service direct sans changement?	Gibt es durchgehende Züge ohne Umsteigen?
Does this train run on week days only?	Ce train circule-t-il la semaine seulement?	Verkehrt dieser Zug nur an Wochentagen?
When is the first, the last, train to .. ?	Quand est le premier, le dernier, train pour .. ?	Wann geht der erste, letzte, Zug nach .. ?
Where does this train go to?	Où va ce train?	Wohin fährt dieser Zug?
Does this carriage go through to .. ?	Cette voiture va-t-elle directement à .. ?	Ist dies ein durchgehender Wagen nach .. ?
Is this the through portion for .. ?	Est-ce ici la rame directe pour .. ?	Sind dies die durchgehenden Wagen nach .. ?
Am I right for .. ? or Is this the train for .. ?	C'est (ou Est-ce) bien le train de .. ? C'est (ou Est-ce) le train direction de .. ?	Ist dies der richtige Zug nach .. ?

Io desidero registrare questo collo per . . Qual'è la tassa per la registrazione, per il peso eccessivo ?	Deseo facturar este bulto [de equipaje] para . . ¿ Qué es la tarifa para facturar, para el exceso de peso ?	Ik wil dit stuk laten aantekenen voor . . . Wat zijn de aantekeningskosten, de kosten voor overwicht?
◄ Dove si trova il bagaglio registrato ? Io ho un baule registrato. Ecco lo scontrino del bagaglio.	¿ En dónde se halla el equipaje facturado ? Tengo un baúl facturado. Aquí tiene usted (usually written Vd) el talón.	Waar vindt ik de aangetekende stukken? Ik heb een aangetekende koffer. Hier is het bewijs.
L'ufficio informazioni.	El despacho de informaciones.	Het informatie bureau of Inlichtingen.
C'è un treno tra . . e . . che ha coincidenza coi battelli ?	¿ Hay un tren entre . . y . . que garantiza el enlace con los vapores ?	Is er een boottrein tussen . . . en . . ., die op de boten aansluit?
Vi è un treno supplementare ?	¿ Hay un tren de relieve ?	Is er een extra trein?
Quando comincia, finisce, l'ora d'estate in . . ?	¿ Cuándo se inaugura, Cuándo termina, la hora de verano en . . ?	Wanneer begint, eindigt, de zomertijd in . . .?
◄ La sala d'aspetto.	La sala de espera.	De wachtkamer.
Dov'è la sala di toeletta, il gabinetto ?	¿ Dónde está el lavabo, el excusado ?	Waar is het toilet, de W.C. (pronounce oué, sé)?
Un orario.	Un itinerario.	Een dienstregeling.
Un indicatore ferroviario.	Un guía de ferrocarril.	Een spoorgids.
Soggetto a modificazione.	Sujeto a modificaciones.	Wijzigingen voorbehouden.
◄ Il binario di partenza.	El andén de salida.	Het perron van vertrek.
Dovrò aspettare molto per un treno in partenza per . . ?	¿ Hay mucho tiempo que esperar por el tren para . . ?	Moet ik lang op een trein naar . . wachten?
C'è un treno senza fermata circa le otto della mattina, della sera, alle otto, venti, per . . ?	¿ Hay un tren sin parada para . . a eso de las ocho de la mañana, de la tarde, a las ocho horas, veinte horas ?	Is er een non-stop trein om ongeveer acht uur 's ochtends, 's avonds, om acht uur twintig uur, naar . .?
C'è un servizio diretto senza cambiare ?	¿ Hay un servicio directo sin cambio ?	Is er een directe verbinding zonder overstappen?
Questo treno corre solo nei giorni feriali ?	¿ Marcha este tren solamente los días de semana?	Loopt deze trein alleen op weekdagen?
◄ Quando è il primo, l'ultimo, treno per . . ?	¿ A qué hora sale el primer, el último, tren para . . ?	Hoe laat is de eerste, de laatste, trein naar . .?
Dove va questo treno ?	¿ Adónde va este tren ?	Waar gaat deze trein heen?
Questa vettura va direttamente a . . ?	¿ Va directo este vagón hasta . . ?	Gaat deze wagon rechtstreeks naar . .?
Questa parte del treno va diretta a . . ?	¿ Es esta la porción directa para . . ?	Is dit gedeelte voor . .?
È questo il treno per . . ?	¿ Es este el tren para . . ?	Is dit de goede trein voor . .?

Does this train connect at .. with the train [coming] from .. ?	Ce train correspond-il à .. avec le train [venant] de .. ?	Hat dieser Zug in .. Anschluß an den Zug aus .. ?
Is there a connexion at .. station ?	Y a-t-il une correspondance en gare de .. ?	Hat man Anschluß in .. ?
Is A .., B .., station on the main line ?	La station d'A .., de B .., est-elle sur la grande ligne ?	Liegt A .., B .., an der Hauptstrecke ?
Which is the train for .. ?	Quel est le train pour .. ?	Welches ist der Zug nach .. ?
When does the train for .. start ?	À quelle heure le train pour .. part-il ?	Wann geht der Zug nach .. ab ?
Does this train stop at all stations ?	Ce train s'arrête-t-il à toutes les stations ?	Hält dieser Zug an allen Stationen ?
Does the 5.0 p.m. train stop at .. ?	Est-ce que le train de dix-sept heures s'arrête à .. ?	Hält der siebzehn Uhr Zug in .. ?
I am leaving by the 8.23 a.m. train for ...	Je pars par le train de huit heures vingt-trois pour ..	Ich nehme den Zug um acht Uhr dreiundzwanzig nach ...
I am, My friends are, travelling first [class], second [class].	Je voyage, Mes amis voyagent, en première [classe], en seconde [classe].	Ich reise, Meine Freunde reisen, erster [Klasse], zweiter [Klasse].
Is the train late ? How late is it ?	Le train est-il en retard ? Combien a-t-il de retard ?	Hat der Zug Verspätung ? Wieviel Verspätung hat er ?
When do we get to .. ? When is the train due at .. ?	Quand est-ce que nous arrivons à .. ? Le train quand doit-il arriver à .. ?	Wann sind wir in .. ? Wann soll der Zug in .. sein ?
A break of journey.	Un arrêt en cours de route.	Eine Fahrtunterbrechung.
Can I break the journey ?	Puis-je interrompre mon voyage en cours de route ?	Kann ich die Fahrt unterbrechen ?
Is it forbidden to cross the line ? Where is the footbridge or the subway ?	Est-il défendu de traverser les voies ? Où est la passerelle ou le souterrain ?	Ist es verboten, die Geleise zu überschreiten ? Wo ist der Übergang oder die Unterführung ?
The arrival platform.	Le quai d'arrivée.	Der Bahnsteig für ankommende Züge.
Is the train from .. in yet ?	Le train venant de .. est-il déjà arrivé ?	Ist der Zug aus .. schon da ?
Where does this train come from ?	D'où vient ce train ?	Wo kommt dieser Zug her ?
When does the train [coming] from .. arrive ?	Quand le train [venant] de .. arrive-t-il ?	Wann kommt der Zug aus .. an ?
The cloak room or The left-luggage office.	La consigne.	Die Gepäckaufbewahrung.
The lost property office.	Le bureau des objets égarés ou trouvés.	Das Fundbüro.
I have lost a parcel. I left it in the train. Has it been found ?	J'ai perdu un colis. Je l'ai laissé dans le train. L'a-t-on trouvé ?	Ich habe ein Paket verloren. Ich habe es im Zug gelassen. Ist es gefunden worden ?
The telegraph office.	Le bureau télégraphique.	Das Telegraphenamt.

Ha questo treno coincidenza a . . con il treno [che viene] da . . ?	¿ Hace enlace este tren en . . con el que viene de . . ?	Heeft deze trein in . . aansluiting op de trein uit . . ?
C'è una coincidenza alla stazione di . . ?	¿ Hay enlace en la estación de . . ?	Is er een aansluiting op het station van . . ?
È la stazione A . ., B . ., sulla linea principale ?	¿ Está la estación A . ., B . ., en la línea central ?	Ligt het station van A., B., op de hoofdlijn ?
Qual'è il treno per . . ?	¿ Cuál es el tren para . . ?	Wat is de trein naar . . ?
A che ora parte il treno per . . ?	¿ A qué hora sale el tren para . . ?	Hoe laat vertrekt de trein naar . . ?
Si ferma questo treno a tutte le stazioni ?	¿ Para este tren en todas las estaciones ?	Stopt deze trein aan alle stations?
Si ferma il treno delle diciassette a . . ?	¿ Para en el tren de las diecisiete [horas]?	Stopt de trein van zeventien uur in . . ?
Io parto con il treno delle otto e ventitrè per . . .	Salgo para . . en el tren de las ocho y veintitres.	Ik vertrek met de trein van acht uur drie en twintig naar . .
Io viaggio, I miei amici viaggiano, in prima [classe], in seconda [classe].	Yo viajo, Mis amigos viajan, en primera[clase], en segunda [clase].	Ik reis, Mijn vrienden reizen, eerste [klasse], tweede [klasse]
È in ritardo il treno ? Di quanto è in ritardo ?	¿ Viene on retraso el tren ? ¿ Qué retraso trae ?	Is de trein laat? Hoeveel is hij te laat?
Quando arriviamo a . . ? A che ora dovrebbe arrivare il treno a . . ?	¿ A qué hora llegamos a . . ? ¿ A qué hora debe llegar el tren a . . ?	Hoe laat komen wij in . . aan? Hoe laat hoort de trein in . . aan te komen?
Un'interruzione di viaggio.	Una interrupción de viaje.	Een onderbreking van de reis.
Posso interrompere il viaggio ?	¿ Puedo interrumpir el viaje ?	Kan ik de reis onderweg onderbreken?
È proibito attraversare il binario ? Dov'è il ponticello o il sottopassaggio ?	¿ Se prohibe cruzar la vía ? ¿ Dónde está el puente o el pasaje subterráneo ?	Is het verboden de spoorlijn over te steken? Waar is de voetbrug of de tunnel?
La piattaforma di arrivo.	El andén de llegada.	Het perron van aankomst.
Il treno da . . è già arrivato ?	¿ Ha llegado el tren de . . ?	Is de trein uit . . al binnen?
Da dove viene questo treno ?	¿ De dónde viene este tren ?	Waar komt deze trein vandaan?
Quando arriva il treno [proveniente] da . . ?	¿ A qué hora llega el tren de . . ?	Hoe laat komt de trein uit . . aan?
La consegna [dei bagagli].	La consigna, El depósito de equipajes.	Het bagagedepot.
L'ufficio di oggetti smarriti.	El depósito de artículos perdidos o extraviados.	[Het bureau van] gevonden voorwerpen.
Io ho perduto un pacco. Io l'ho lasciato nel treno. È stato trovato ?	He perdido un bulto. Lo dejé en el tren. ¿ Ha sido encontrado ?	Ik heb een paket verloren. Ik heb het in de trein laten liggen. Is het gevonden?
L'ufficio telegrafico	El despacho de telégrafos.	Het telegraafkantoor.

Where is the refreshment bar *or* room ? (*See* EATING AND DRINKING, *pp.* 130-171.)	Où est le buffet ?	Wo ist der Erfrischungsraum ?
A luncheon basket (*filled*)	Un panier-repas.	Ein Proviantkorb.
An automatic [delivery] machine.	Un distributeur automatique.	Ein Automat.
Can I see the stationmaster ?	Puis-je voir le chef de gare ?	Kann ich den Stationsvorsteher sehen ?
Where is the assistant stationmaster's office ?	Où est le bureau du chef de gare adjoint ?	Wo ist das Büro des zweiten Stationsvorstehers ?
A porter.	Un facteur, Un porteur.	Ein Gepäckträger.
An outside porter.	Un commissionnaire.	Ein Dienstmann.
The guard.	Le conducteur.	Der Zugführer.
The ticket collector.	Le contrôleur.	Der Fahrkartenkontrolleur, Der Schaffner.

The ticket	**Le billet**	**Die Fahrkarte, Das Billett**
A single [ticket].	Un billet simple.	Eine einfache Fahrkarte.
A return [ticket].	Un [billet d']aller et retour.	Eine Rückfahrkarte.
The outward half (*of return ticket*).	Le coupon d'aller.	[Das Billett für] die Hinfahrt.
The return half.	Le coupon de retour.	[Das Billett für] die Rückfahrt.
A ticket available . . days with option of extension of . . days.	Un billet valable . . jours avec faculté de prolongation de . . jours.	Eine Fahrkarte mit . . tägiger Gültigkeit, . . tägige Verlängerung statthaft.
Validity : forty days with extension on request.	Validité : quarante jours avec prolongation sur demande.	Gültigkeit : vierzig Tage, auf Antrag Verlängerung.
A first class ticket.	Un billet de première classe.	Eine Fahrkarte erster Klasse.
A first, A second, A third, [class] single to . . , via . . .	Une première, Une deuxième, Une troisième, [classe] simple pour . . , via . . .	Eins Erster, Eins Zweiter, Eins Dritter, einfach nach . . , über . . .
A book of travel coupons.	Un carnet de voyage.	Ein Fahrkartenheft.
A cheap ticket, available for one day *or* A cheap day return ticket.	Un billet à prix réduit, valable pour un jour, Un billet d'excursion d'un jour.	Eine Tagesrückfahrkarte.
A child's ticket.	Un billet d'enfant.	Eine Kinderfahrkarte.
A circular ticket *or* A tourist ticket.	Un billet circulaire.	Eine Rundreisefahrkarte.
A combined ticket (railway and motor coach).	Un billet combiné (chemin de fer et autocar).	Eine kombinierte Fahrkarte (für Eisenbahn und Autobus).
An excursion ticket.	Un billet d'excursion.	Eine Ausflugskarte.
A family ticket.	Un billet de famille.	Eine Familienfahrkarte.

Dov'è il buffet o il ristorante.	¿Dónde está el bar o la cantina ?	Waar is het buffet?
Un cestino [guarnito].	Una fiambrera.	Een lunchpakket.
Un distributore automatico.	Un distribuidor automático.	Een automaat.
◄Posso vedere il capo stazione ?	¿Puedo ver al jefe de estación ?	Kan ik de stationschef spreken?
Dov'è l'ufficio del vice-capo stazione ?	¿Dónde está el despacho del asistente del jefe de estación ?	Waar is het kantoor van de assistent-stations-chef?
Un facchino.	Un mozo [de estación].	Een kruier.
Un facchino esterno.	Un mozo.	Een pakjesdrager, Een witkiel.
Il conduttore.	El conductor.	De conducteur.
◄Il controllore.	El revisor [de billetes].	De controleur.

Il biglietto	**El billete**	**Het biljet, Het kaartje**
Un biglietto semplice.	Un billete simple.	Een enkele reis.
Un biglietto di andata e ritorno.	Un billete de ida y vuelta.	Een retour.
Il tagliando di andata.	El talón de ida.	De heenreis-helft.
Il tagliando di ritorno.	El talón de vuelta o de regreso.	De retourhelft.
◄Un biglietto valevole .. giorni con facoltà di prolungarlo di .. giorni.	Un billete valedero por .. días con opción de prolongación hasta .. días.	Een kaartje geldig .. dagen met mogelijk-heid van .. dagen verlenging.
Validità : quaranta giorni con facoltà di essere prolungato a richiesta.	Validez: cuarenta días con prolongación al pedirse.	Geldig: veertig dagen met verlenging op aanvrage.
Un biglietto di prima classe.	Un billete de primera clase.	Een eerste klas [kaartje].
Una prima, Una seconda, Una terza, [classe] semplice per .. , via ..	Un billete simple de primera, segunda, tercera, [clase] a .. , via ..	Een eerste, Een tweede, Een derde, klas enkele reis naar .. , via ..
Un libretto di tagliandi.	Un talonario de viaje.	Een boekje met reisbiljetten.
◄Un biglietto a prezzo ridotto, valevole per un giorno, Un biglietto a riduzione di andata e ritorno per la giornata.	Un billete valedero por un día a precio reducido, Un billete de excursión por un día.	Een goedkope dagretour.
Un biglietto per ragazzo.	Un billete para niño.	Een kinderkaartje.
Un biglietto circolare.	Un billete circular.	Een rondreisbiljet.
Un biglietto combinato (ferrovia ed autobus).	Un billete en combinación (ferrocarril y autocar).	Een gecombineerd kaartje (spoorweg en autocar).
Un biglietto di escursione.	Un billete de excursión.	Een excursie kaartje
◄Un biglietto per famiglia.	Un billete de familia.	Een familiebiljet.

A party ticket.	Un billet de groupe.	Eine Sammelfahrkarte.
A platform ticket.	Un billet de quai.	Eine Bahnsteigkarte.
A reserved seat ticket.	Un billet garde-place.	Eine Platzkarte.
A season ticket.	Une carte d'abonnement.	Eine Wochenkarte, Eine Monatskarte, usw (= &c.).
A week-end return ticket available from Friday noon to Tuesday midnight.	Un billet [d']aller et retour de fin de semaine valable du vendredi midi au mardi à vingt-quatre heures.	Eine Wochenendfahrkarte, gültig von Freitag mittag bis Dienstag mitternacht.
Is this ticket out of date?	Ce billet est-il périmé?	Ist diese Fahrkarte verfallen oder abgelaufen?
To book to . . . To book through to . . .	Prendre un billet, (2 or more) des billets, pour.. Prendre un billet direct, des billets directs, pour..	Eine Fahrkarte (Fahrkarten) nach .. lösen. Eine Fahrkarte (Fahrkarten) direkt nach .. lösen.
What is the fare to ..?	Quel est le prix [de la place ou du billet] pour ..?	Was kostet die Fahrt nach ..?
What is the ordinary fare?	Quel est le prix normal?	Wie hoch ist der normale Fahrpreis?
What saving is there in taking a return ticket over two single tickets?	Quelle économie comporte un billet d'aller et retour sur deux billets simples?	Wie groß ist die Differenz zwischen einer Rückfahrkarte und zwei einfachen Fahrkarten?
What is the excess [fare] for change of class to first, the extra fare (or charge) for admission in a Pullman car?	Quel est le supplément [de taxe] pour le déclassement en première, le supplément à payer pour admission dans une voiture Pullman?	Wie hoch ist der Zuschlag für die erste Klasse, der Zuschlag für den Pullman Wagen?
[Show your] tickets, please!	[Présentez] vos billets, s'il vous plaît!	Die Fahrkarten bitte!
I cannot find, I have mislaid, lost, my ticket.	Je ne peux pas trouver, j'ai égaré, perdu, mon billet.	Ich kann meine Fahrkarte nicht finden, ich habe meine Fahrkarte verlegt verloren.

The train, The train journey	**Le train, Le trajet dans le train**	**Der Zug, Die Eisenbahnfahrt**
A day, A night, train.	Un train de jour, de nuit.	Ein Zug, der am Tage verkehrt, Ein Nachtzug.
An express [train], A fast train.	Un [train] express, Un [train] rapide.	Ein Expreß, Ein Schnellzug, Ein D-Zug.
A mail [train].	Un train-poste.	Ein Postzug.
A slow train.	Un train omnibus.	Ein Personenzug.
The front [portion], The back [portion], The middle [portion], of the train.	La tête, La queue, Le milieu, du train.	Die vordersten Wagen, Die hinteren Wagen, Die mittleren Wagen, des Zuges.
The engine or The locomotive.	La machine, La locomotive.	Die Lokomotive.
A railway carriage or coach.	Une voiture (ou Un wagon) de chemin de fer.	Ein Eisenbahnwagen, Ein Wagon.

Un biglietto per comitiva.	Un billete para una partida.	Een gezelschapsbiljet.
Un biglietto di ingresso alla piattaforma.	Un billete de andén.	Een perronkaartje.
Un biglietto per posto riservato.	Un billete de asiento.	Een plaatsbewijs.
Un biglietto d'abbonamento.	Un billete de abono.	Een abonnement.
◄Un biglietto di andata e ritorno di fine di settimana valevole dal mezzogiorno di venerdì alla mezzanotte di martedì.	Un billete de ida y vuelta de fin de semana valedero desde viernes mediodía hasta martes medianoche.	Een retour over het weekeinde geldig van vrijdag twaalf uur 's middags tot dinsdag middernacht.
È scaduto questo biglietto?	¿Está expirado este billete?	Is dit kaartje verlopen?
Prendere un biglietto, biglietti, per .. Prendere un biglietto diretto, biglietti diretti, a ..	Tomar un billete, billetes, hasta . . . Tomar un billete directo, billetes directos, hasta . . .	Een kaartje, Kaartjes, nemen naar ... Een kaartje Kaartjes, rechtstreeks naar .. nemen.
Qual'è il prezzo del biglietto per .. ?	¿Cuánto vale el viaje a ..?	Hoeveel is (of kost) het naar ..?
Qual'è il prezzo normale?	¿Cuánto es el precio normal?	Wat is de normale prijs?
◄Che economia si ottiene col prendere un biglietto di andata e ritorno, invece di due biglietti semplici?	¿Cuánto se ahorra tomando un billete de ida y vuelta en vez de dos billetes ·imples?	Hoeveel spaart men door een retour te nemen in plaats van twee enkele reizen?
Qual'è il supplemento [di tassa] per il cambiamento di classe alla prima, per l'ammissione in una vettura Pullman?	¿Cuánto es el recargo para la transferencia a primera clase, el suplemento para la admisión al Pullman?	Hoeveel moet ik bij betalen om verder eerste klasse te reizen, voor toelating in een Pullmanwagen?
[Mostrino] i loro biglietti, per favore !	¡Los billetes, Señores !	Kaartjes, als 't U belieft!
Non lo posso trovare, non ricordo dove l'ho messo, io ho smarrito, il mio biglietto.	No puedo encontrar, he extraviado, he perdido, mi billete.	Ik kan mijn kaartje niet vinden, ik ben mijn kaartje kwijt, ik heb mijn kaartje verloren.

Il treno, Il viaggio in treno	**El tren, El viaje en el tren**	**De trein, De treinreis**
Un treno di giorno, di notte.	Un tren por la mañana, por la noche.	Een dagtrein, Een nachttrein.
◄Un [treno] espresso, Un treno lampo.	Un tren expreso, Un tren rápido.	Een expres trein, Een sneltrein.
Un [treno] postale.	Un tren correo.	Een posttrein.
Un treno omnibus.	Un tren ómnibus.	Een boemeltrein.
La [parte di] testa, La coda, Il centro, del treno.	La sección delantera, trasera, de en medio, del tren.	Het voorste, laatste, middelste, gedeelte van de trein.
La macchina, La locomotiva.	La máquina, La locomotora.	De locomotief.
◄Una carrozza (od Una vettura) ferroviaria.	Un carruaje (o Un vagón) de ferrocarril.	Een [spoorweg]wagen.

A corridor carriage.	Un wagon à couloir.	Ein Durchgangswagen.
A through carriage.	Une voiture directe.	Ein durchgehender Wagen.
The luggage (or The guard's) van.	Le fourgon à bagages.	Der Gepäckwagen.
Send me a porter, please.	Veuillez m'envoyer un facteur.	Schicken Sie mir bitte einen Träger.
Please get my luggage from the cloak room. Here is the ticket.	Veuillez chercher mes bagages à la consigne. Voici le bulletin.	Wollen Sie bitte mein Gepäck von der Gepäckaufbewahrung holen. Hier ist der Gepäckschein.
My bag is marked R.T.W.	Ma valise est marquée R.T.W. (pronounce erre, té, double vé.)	Auf meinem Koffer steht R.T.W. (pronounce arre, vé.)
Wait for me, us, here, there.	Attendez-moi, -nous, ici, là.	Warten Sie hier, dort, auf mich, uns.
I will take these things with me in the carriage.	Je prendrai ces choses avec moi dans la voiture.	Ich nehme diese Sachen mit in den Wagen.
Put this on the rack.	Mettez ceci dans le filet.	Tun Sie dies ins Gepäcknetz.
A smoking compartment	Un compartiment de fumeurs.	Ein Raucher[abteil].
A non-smoking compartment.	Un compartiment de non-fumeurs.	Ein Nichtraucher[abteil].
A Ladies only compartment.	Un compartiment pour Dames seules.	Ein Damenabteil.
Will you please find me a compartment with a lavatory ?	Cherchez-moi un compartiment avec une toilette, s'il vous plaît.	Würden Sie bitte ein Abteil mit einer Toilette für mich finden.
An engaged compartment.	Un compartiment loué.	Ein reserviertes Abteil.
To engage a seat in advance.	Louer une place d'avance.	Eine Platzkarte bestellen.
Can I book a seat in the 11.45 p.m. for . . ?	Puis-je retenir une place dans le train de vingt-trois heures quarante-cinq pour . . ?	Kann ich eine Platzkarte für den dreiundzwanzig Uhr fünfundvierzig Zug nach . . bestellen ?
Is this compartment full? Is there any room?	Ce compartiment est-il au complet ? Y a-t-il de la place ?	Ist dieses Abteil voll? Ist hier noch Platz?
Excuse me, sir, this seat is mine, is taken.	Pardon, monsieur, cette place est à moi, est occupée.	Entschuldigen Sie, mein Herr, dies ist mein Platz, dieser Platz ist besetzt.
Find me another seat, a corner seat facing the engine, with back to the engine.	Trouvez-moi une autre place, une place de coin face à la machine, face à l'arrière.	Suchen Sie mir einen anderen Platz, einen Eckplatz vorwärts, rückwärts.
Can we have this compartment to ourselves ?	Pouvons-nous rester seuls dans ce compartiment ?	Können wir dieses Abteil für uns allein haben ?
Is there a dining car on this train ? (See EATING AND DRINKING, pp. 130-171.)	Y a-t-il un wagon-restaurant à ce train ?	Hat der Zug einen Speisewagen ?
Steward ! At what time is the first service ?	Garçon ! À quelle heure est le premier service ?	Ober ! Wann ist das erste Mittagessen, Abendessen?

Un vagone con corridoio.	Un vagón de corredor.	Een doorlopende wagen.
Una vettura diretta.	Un vagón directo.	Een doorgaande wagen.
Il bagagliaio.	El furgón de equipajes.	De bagagewagen.
[Mandatemi] un facchino, per piacere.	Haga el favor de llamarme a un mozo.	Stuur me een kruier, als 't U belieft.
◄Per favore, andate a prendere il mio bagaglio al deposito. Ecco lo scontrino.	Haga el favor de recoger mi equipaje de la consigna. Aquí tiene usted el talón.	Haal mijn bagage van het bagagedepot als 't U belieft. Hier is het bewijs.
La mia valigia è marcata con le lettere R.T.W. (*pronounce* erre, tee, doppio vu).	Mi valija lleva las iniciales R.T.W. (*pronounce* eray, té, doble vé).	Mijn tas is gemerkt R.T.W. (*pronounce* erre, té, oué).
Attendetemi, Attendeteci, qui, là.	Espéreme, Espérenos, aquí, allá.	Wacht hier, daar, op me, ons.
Io prenderò con me queste cose nella vettura.	Llevaré estos bultos conmigo en el vagón.	Ik neem deze dingen in de wagen mee.
Mettete questo sulla rete.	Ponga esto en el porta-equipajes.	Zet dit in het net.
◄Uno scompartimento per fumatori.	Un compartamiento de fumadores.	Een rookcoupé.
Uno scompartimento vietato fumare.	Un compartamiento de no fumar.	Een niet-rookcoupé.
Uno scompartimento per Signore.	Un compartamiento de Señoras.	Een Damescoupé.
Volete trovarmi, per favore, uno scompartimento con gabinetto?	Búsqueme un compartamiento con toileta.	Zoek een coupé met een toilet voor mij als 't U belieft.
Uno scompartimento riservato.	Un compartamiento reservado.	Een gereserveerde coupé.
◄Riservare un posto in anticipo.	Alquilar (o Reservar) un asiento por adelantado.	Van tevoren een plaats bespreken.
Posso avere un posto nel treno delle venti tre e quarantacinque per . . ?	¿ Puedo reservar un asiento en el tren de las veintitres y cuarenta y cinco para . . ?	Kan ik een plaats bespreken op de drie en twintig uur vijf en veertig naar . . ?
È questo scompartimento completo ? C'è un posto libero ?	¿ Está completo este compartamiento ? ¿ No hay sitio ?	Is deze coupé vol? Is er nog plaats?
Mi scusi, signore, questo posto è mio, è impegnato.	Dispénseme, señor, este asiento es mío, está ocupado.	Neem mij niet kwalijk, mijnheer, deze plaats is van mij, is bezet.
Trovatemi un altro posto, un [posto di] angolo che guardi la macchina, con le spalle alla macchina.	Búsqueme otro asiento, de rincón de frente a la máquina, de espaldas a la máquina.	Zoek een andere plaats, een hoekplaats voor me, waar ik vooruit rijd, achteruit rijd.
◄Possiamo avere questo scompartimento solo per noi ?	¿ Podemos ocupar este compartamiento para nosotros solos ?	Kunnen wij deze coupé alleen blijven?
C'è un vagone ristorante in questo treno ?	¿ Hay [vagón] comedor (o restaurante) en este tren ?	Is er een restauratie-wagen in deze trein?
Cameriere ! A che ora è il primo pasto ?	¡ Camarero ! ¿ A qué hora es la primera serie ?	Ober! Hoe laat is de eerste lunch, het eerste diner?

A buffet car.	Un wagon-bar.	Ein Büffett-Wagen.
A Pullman [car].	Une voiture Pullman.	Ein Pullman Wagen.
A saloon [car].	Un wagon-salon.	Ein Salonwagen.
Is there a vacant berth in the sleeping car ?	Y a-t-il une place libre dans le wagon-lit ?	Ist im Schlafwagen noch ein Bett frei ?
Take your seats ! or Step in there !	En voiture ! Prenez vos places !	Einsteigen !
Guard ! What is the name of this station, of the next station, of the next stopping place ?	Conducteur ! Comment s'appelle cette station, la prochaine station, le prochain arrêt ?	Schaffner ! Wie heißt diese Station, die nächste Station, der nächste Haltepunkt ?
How long do we stop here ?	Combien d'arrêt ici ?	Wie lange haben wir Aufenthalt ?
Is there time to get out for a few moments ?	Y a-t-il le temps de descendre pour quelques instants ?	Hat man Zeit, für einen Augenblick auszusteigen?
When do we reach . . ?	À quelle heure arrivons-nous à . . ?	Wann kommen wir nach . . ?
Are we at . . (such or such a station)? or Is this . . ?	Sommes-nous à . . ?	Sind wir in . . ?
Do we get out (or alight) here ?	Est-ce que l'on descend ici ?	Müssen wir hier aussteigen?
Do we change [carriages or trains] here for . . ?	Faut-il changer [de wagon ou de train] ici pour . . ?	Müssen wir hier in den Wagen, den Zug, nach . umsteigen?
All change !	Tout le monde descend !	Alles aussteigen !
Pull the communication cord !	Tirez la sonnette d'alarme !	Ziehen Sie die Notleine !
Please open this door.	Ouvrez cette portière, s'il vous plaît.	Würden Sie bitte diese Tür öffnen.
Call a taxi and put my luggage in it.	Appelez un taxi et mettez mes bagages dedans.	Holen Sie eine Taxe und tun Sie mein Gepäck hinein.
Is the Grand Hotel porter here ? Take my luggage.	Le porteur du Grand Hôtel est-il ici ? Prenez mes bagages.	Ist der Portier vom Grand Hotel hier ? Nehmen Sie mein Gepäck.
Is there a railway omnibus between . . and . . ?	Y a-t-il une [voiture de] correspondance entre . . et . . ?	Gibt es einen Bahnhofsomnibus zwischen . . und . . ?

Articles of luggage	Pièces de bagage	Gepäckstücke
Heavy luggage.	Les gros colis.	Schweres Gepäck.
Hand luggage.	Les colis à la main.	Handgepäck.
A forwarding agent.	Un commissionnaire de transports, Un expéditeur.	Ein Spediteur.
An attaché case.	Une mallette.	Ein Stadtköfferchen.
A bag.	Une valise.	Ein Handkoffer.
A box.	Une boîte, Une malle.	Ein Kasten.
A cabin trunk.	Une malle de paquebot, Une malle de cabine.	Ein Kabinenkoffer.
A change of clothes. (For clothes, see pp. 182-189, 126-127, for boots, see pp. 176 -179.)	Des vêtements de rechange.	Kleidungsstücke zum Umziehen.

Una carrozza con buffet.	Un vagón bar.	Een restauratiewagen.
Una vettura Pullman.	Un vagón Pullman.	Een Pullmanwagen.
◄Una vettura salone.	Un coche salón.	Een salonwagen.
C'è un posto libero nel vagone letti?	¿Hay una litera desocupada en el coche dormitorio?	Is er een plaats vrij in de slaapwagen?
In vettura! Prendano i loro posti!	¡Señores viajeros al tren!	Instappen!
Conduttore! Come si chiama questa stazione, la prossima stazione, la prossima fermata?	¡Conductor! ¿Qué es el nombre de esta estación, de la próxima estación, de la próxima parada?	Conducteur! Hoe heet dit station, het volgende station, de volgende halte?
Quanto tempo ci si ferma qui?	¿Cuánto tiempo de parada hay aquí?	Hoe lang blijven wij hier staan?
◄C'è tempo di scendere per pochi momenti?	¿Hay tiempo para apearse unos momentos?	Is er tijd om even uit te stappen?
Quando arriviamo a ..?	¿Cuándo llegamos a ..?	Hoe laat komen wij in aan?
Siamo noi a ..?	¿Estamos en ..?	Zijn we in ..? Is dit ..?
Si scende qui?	¿Bajamos (o Nos apeamos) aquí?	Stappen wij hier uit?
Si cambia qui [vettura o treno] per ..?	¿Cambiamos aquí [de vagón o de tren] para ..?	Stappen wij hier [op een andere wagen, een andere trein] voor .. over?
◄Tutti cambiano!	¡Cambio general!	Iedereen overstappen!
Tirate il campanello d'allarme!	¡Toque el timbre de comunicación!	Trek aan de noodrem!
Per favore, aprite questo sportello.	Haga el favor de abrir esta puerta.	Opent dit portier als 't U belieft.
Chiamate un taxi e caricatevi il mio bagaglio.	Llame un taxi y meta mi equipaje.	Roep een taxi en laad mijn bagage in.
C'è qui il facchino del Grand Hôtel? Prendete i miei bagagli.	¿Está aquí el portero del Gran Hotel? Tome mi equipaje.	Is de portier van het Grand Hotel hier? Neem mijn bagage.
◄C'è un omnibus tra . e .. che fa servizio all'arrivo del treno?	¿Hay un ómnibus de correspondencia entre .. y ..?	Is er een stationsbus tussen .. en ..?

Articoli di bagaglio	**Bultos de equipaje**	**Stukkenbagage**
Bagaglio pesante.	Bultos pesados.	Zware bagage.
Bagaglio a mano.	Bultos de mano.	Lichte bagage.
Uno spedizioniere.	Un expedidor.	Een expediteur.
Una valigetta.	Un maletín.	Een aktentas. -
◄Una sacca.	Una valija.	Een tas, Een valies.
Una scatola.	Una caja.	Een doos.
Una valigia da cabina.	Un baúl de camarote.	Een hutkoffer.
Vestiti di ricambio.	Un cambio de ropa.	Een verschoning.

A dressing case.	Une mallette garnie.	Ein Nécessaire[koffer].
A hamper.	Une malle en osier.	Ein Tragkorb.
A handbag.	Un sac à main.	Eine Handtasche.
A hat box.	Une boîte à chapeau(x).	Eine Hutschachtel.
A hold-all.	Un fourre-tout.	Ein Plaidrolle.
A jewel case (travelling).	Un porte-trésor.	Eine Schmucktasche.
A kit bag.	Un sac à fermoir articulé.	Ein Reisetasche.
A parcel.	Un colis, Un paquet.	Ein Paket.
A pillow.	Un oreiller.	Ein Kissen.
A rucksack.	Un sac de touriste.	Ein Rucksack.
A suit case.	Un porte-habits.	Ein Koffer.
A sunshade or A parasol.	Une ombrelle.	Ein Sonnenschirm.
A tie-on label.	Une étiquette volante.	Ein Gepäckzettel zum Anhängen.
A [travelling] rug.	Une couverture [de voyage], Un plaid.	Eine Reisedecke.
A trunk.	Une malle.	Ein [großer] Koffer.
An umbrella.	Un parapluie.	Ein Schirm.
A [walking] stick.	Une canne [de promenade].	Ein Stock, Ein Spazierstock.
A wardrobe trunk.	Une malle-armoire.	Ein Schrankkoffer.

SEA TRAVEL	VOYAGES SUR MER	SEEREISEN
Maritime terms	Termes maritimes	Seefahrtsausdrücke
The agent of the shipping company.	L'agent de la compagnie de navigation.	Der Vertreter der Schiffahrtsgesellschaft.
An Atlantic liner.	Un [paquebot] transatlantique.	Ein Transatlantik-Dampfer.
A boat or A ship.	Un bateau, Un navire.	Ein Boot, Ein Schiff.
A boat (a ship's boat).	Une embarcation.	Ein Boot.
A boat (a rowing boat).	Un bateau, Un canot.	Ein Boot.
Boat drill.	Les exercices de mise à la mer.	Rettungsübungen.
The bridge (of ship).	La passerelle.	Die Brücke.
A cabin. (See Booking of berths, below.)	Une cabine.	Eine Kabine.
The captain.	Le capitaine.	Der Kapitän.
The deck.	Le pont.	Das Deck.
Bring me a deck chair.	Apportez-moi une chaise de pont.	Bringen Sie mir einen Liegestuhl.
The deck steward.	Le garçon de pont.	Der Decksteward.
The first class (or The main) dining saloon. (See The dining room, pp. 126-129, and EATING AND DRINKING, pp. 130-171.)	La salle à manger des premières [classes].	Der Speisesaal erster Klasse.
The [English] Channel. The Straits of Dover. The Gulf of Lions. The Atlantic [ocean]. The French coast.	La Manche. Le [détroit du] Pas de Calais. Le golfe du Lion. L'[océan] Atlantique. Les côtes de France.	Der Ärmelkanal. Die Strasse von Dover. Der Golf von Lion. Der Atlantik oder Der Atlantische Ozean. Die französische Küste.
A fast boat.	Un bateau express.	Ein schnelles Schiff.
A gangway (shore to ship).	Une passerelle [de service].	Eine Laufbrücke.

Una valigia con necessari di toeletta.	Un neceser [de tocador].	Een reis-necessaire.
◄Un cesto.	Una cesta.	Een [rieten] mand.
Una borsetta.	Una valija de mano.	Een handtas.
Una cappelliera.	Una sombrerera.	Een hoededoos.
Un porta mantelli.	Un envase de lona.	Een plunjezak.
Un portagioie.	Un estuche de joyas.	Een juwelenkistje.
◄Una valigia inglese.	Una maleta inglesa.	Een klerenzak.
Un pacco.	Un paquete, Un envoltorio.	Een pak, Een paket.
Un guanciale, Un cuscino.	Una almohada.	Een kussen.
Un sacco da turista.	Un saco de turista.	Een rugzak.
Una valigia.	Un maletón.	Een handkoffer.
◄Un parasole.	Una sombrilla.	Een parasol.
Un etichetta volante.	Una etiqueta (o Un rótulo) colgante.	Een label.
Una coperta da viaggio.	Una manta de viaje.	Een reisdeken, Een plaid.
Un baule.	Un baúl.	Een koffer.
Un ombrello.	Un paraguas.	Een paraplu.
◄Un bastone [da passeggio].	Un bastón [para andar].	Een stok, Een wandel-stok.
Un baule armadio.	Un baúl armario.	Een kleerkoffer.

VIAGGI PER MARE
Termini marittimi

VIAJES POR MAR
Términos marítimos

ZEEREIZEN
Zeetermen

L'agente della società di navigazione.	El agente de la compañía de vapores.	De agent van de zeevaartmaatschappij.
Un transatlantico.	Un trasatlántico.	Een transatlantische boot.
Un battello.	Un buque, Un navío.	Een boot, Een schip.
◄Un'imbarcazione.	Un bote, Una nave.	Een sloep.
Una barca, Un canotto.	Un bote.	Een boot.
Gli esercizi di salvataggio.	Ejercicios de salvamento.	Reddingsoefeningen.
Il ponte [di comando].	El puente.	De brug.
Una cabina.	Un camarote.	Een hut.
◄Il capitano.	El capitán.	De kapitein.
Il ponte, La coperta.	La cubierta.	Het dek.
Portatemi una sedia a sdraio.	Tráigame una silla de cubierta.	Breng me een dekstoel.
L'inserviente di ponte.	El camarero de cubierta.	De dekbediende.
Il salone da pranzo di prima [classe].	El comedor de primera [clase].	De eerste klas eetzaal.
◄Il Canale della Manica. Lo Stretto di Dover. Il Golfo di Lione. L'[oceano] Atlantico. La costa francese.	La Mancha. El Paso de Calais. El Golfo de Lion. El [oceano] Atlántico. La costa de Francia.	Het Kanaal, Het Nauw van Calais. De Golf van Lion. De Atlantische Oceaan. De Franse kust.
Un battello rapido.	Un vapor rápido.	Een snelle boot.
Un ponticello di sbarco.	Un portalón.	Een loopplank.

A harbour or A port.	Un port.	Ein Hafen.
An outer harbour.	Un avant-port.	Ein Aussenhafen.
A harbour station.	Une gare maritime.	Ein Hafenbahnhof.
The harbour station master.	Le chef de gare maritime.	Der Hafenstationsvorsteher.
A ladies' cabin.	Une cabine pour dames [seules].	Eine Damenkabine.
A lake steamer.	Un vapeur du lac.	Ein Binnenseedampfer.
A life belt. A life boat. A life buoy.	Une ceinture de sauvetage. Un bateau de sauvetage. Une bouée de sauvetage.	Ein Rettungsgürtel. Ein Rettungsboot. Eine Rettungsboje.
A liner.	Un paquebot.	Ein regelmäßig verkehrendes Passagierboot, Ein Fahrgastboot.
The lower deck.	Le pont inférieur.	Das untere Deck.
A mail boat or steamer.	Un paquebot-poste.	Ein Paketboot.
Man overboard!	Un homme à la mer !	Mann über Bord !
A motor ship.	Un navire à moteur.	Ein Motorschiff.
A passenger ship. A passenger steamer.	Un paquebot. Un paquebot à vapeur.	Ein Fahrgastschiff, Ein Fahrgastdampfer.
A pier.	Une jetée.	Eine Landungsbrücke.
A port [hole].	Un sabord, Un hublot.	Ein Bullauge.
The purser.	Le commissaire [de paquebot].	Der Proviantmeister.
A quay or A wharf or A landing stage.	Un quai, Un appontement, Un débarcadère, Un embarcadère, Un ponton.	Ein Kai, Eine Buhne, Eine schwimmende Landungstelle.
The right bank, The left bank, of a river.	La rive droite, La rive gauche, d'un fleuve.	Das rechte Ufer, Das linke Ufer, eines Flusses.
A (small) river (passenger) steamer.	Un bateau-mouche.	Ein Flußdampfer.
A sailor.	Un marin, Un matelot.	Ein Matrose.
A slow boat.	Un bateau omnibus, Un navire lent.	Ein langsames Schiff.
A steamer or A steamboat or A steamship.	Un vapeur, Un bateau à vapeur, Un navire à vapeur, Un steamer.	Ein Dampfer, Ein Dampfschiff.
The steward. Steward ! Come here !	Le garçon de cabine. Garçon ! Venez ici !	Der Steward. Steward ! Können Sie bitte herkommen !
The stewardess. Stewardess !	La femme de chambre. Mademoiselle !	Die Stewardeß. Stewardeß!
A tender (boat).	Une annexe.	Ein Tender, Ein Zubringe-Schiff.
Way down (between decks). Way up.	Descente. Montée.	Herunter. Herauf.

Enquiries

Demandes de reseignements

Anfragen

Where is the shipping company's office ?	Où est le bureau de la compagnie de navigation ?	Wo ist das Büro der Schiffahrtsgesellschaft ?

Un porto.	Un puerto.	Een haven.
Un avamporto.	Un puerto exterior.	Een buitenhaven.
◄Una stazione marittima.	Una estación marítima.	Een havenstation.
Il capo stazione marittima.	El jefe de estación marítima.	De chef van het havenstation.
Una cabina per signore.	Un camarote de señoras.	Den dameshut.
Un vaporetto del lago.	Un vapor de lago.	Een stoomboot die op de meren vaart.
Una cintura di salvataggio. Un battello di salvataggio. Un boa di salvataggio.	Un salvavidas. Una lancha salvavidas. Una boya salvavidas.	Een reddingsgordel. Een reddingboot. Een reddingsboei.
◄Un battello di linea.	Un vapor de línea.	Een stoomboot (van een stoomvaartlijn).
Il ponte inferiore.	La cubierta inferior.	Het benedendek.
Un [piroscafo] postale.	Un vapor correo.	Een mailboot.
Un uomo in mare !	¡ Hombre al agua !	Man over boord!
Una barca a motore.	Un buque motor.	Een motorboot.
◄Un battello passeggeri. Un piroscafo passeggeri.	Un buque de pasajeros. Un vapor de pasajeros.	Een passagiership. Een passagiersstoomboot.
Una gettata.	Un embarcadero.	Een steiger. Een pier.
Un sabordo.	Una ventanilla [de camarote].	Een patrijspoort.
Il commissario.	El contador.	De administrateur [aan boord].
Una banchina, Uno scalo, Uno sbarcatoio galleggiante, Un pontone.	Un muelle, Un dique, Un embarcadero.	Een kade, Een aanlegkade, Een aanlegplaats.
◄La riva destra, La riva sinistra, di un fiume.	La orilla derecha, La orilla izquierda, del río.	De rechteroever, De linkeroever, van een rivier.
Un vaporetto fluviale.	Un [pequeño] vapor de río.	Een binnenvaartuig.
Un marinaio.	Un marinero.	Een zeeman, Een matroos.
Una barca omnibus.	Un vapor ómnibus.	Een langzame boot.
Un vapore, Un piroscafo, Un battello a vapore.	Un vapor, Un buque (o un navío) de vapor.	Een stoomboot, Een stoomschip.
◄Il cameriere di bordo. Cameriere ! Venite qui !	El camarero. ¡ Camarero ! Ven acá !	De steward. Steward! Kom hier!
La cameriera di bordo. Cameriera !	La camarera. ¡ Camarera !	De stewardess. Stewardess! of Juffrouw!
Una nave ausiliaria.	Una escampavía.	Een tender.
Per scendere.	Dirección hacia arriba.	Naar beneden.
Per salire.	Dirección hacia abajo.	Naar boven.

Domande di informazioni	**Informaciones**	**Inlichtingen**
◄Dov'è l'ufficio della società di navigazione ?	¿ Dónde está el despacho de la compañía de vapores ?	Waar is het kantoor van de scheepvaartmaatschappij?

Give me a sailings list, a time table, please.	Donnez-moi, s'il vous plaît, une liste des départs (ou un tableau de marche), un horaire.	Geben Sie mir bitte eine Liste mit den Abfahrtszeiten, einen Fahrplan.
Can I refer to an accommodation plan?	Puis-je consulter un plan des emménagements?	Kann ich einen Schiffsplan sehen?
Is there a boat from here to . . ?	Y a-t-il un bateau d'ici à . . ?	Gibt es ein Schiff von hier nach . . ?
On which days? How many times a day? At what times?	Quels jours? Combien de fois par jour? À quelles heures?	An welchen Tagen? Wie oft am Tage? Zu welchen Zeiten?
Does this ship go direct to . . ?	Ce navire va-t-il directement à . . ?	Geht dies Schiff direkt nach . . ?
At what ports does the boat call? or At what ports does she call? Does the boat call at . . ?	À quels ports [le bateau] fait-il escale? Le bateau fait-il escale à . . ?	In welchen Häfen legt das Schiff an? Legt das Schiff in . . an?
What are the ports of call?	Quels sont les ports d'escale? Quelles sont les escales?	Welches sind die Anlaufhäfen?
When does the next boat leave?	Quand part le prochain bateau?	Wann geht das nächste Schiff?
Is this the quickest route?	Est-ce la route la plus rapide?	Ist dies die schnellste Route?
A cruise. To cruise.	Une croisière. Croiser.	Eine Seereise, Eine Vergnügungsreise zur See. Kreuzen oder Auf einer Seereise sein.
I want to go on a cruise. for a long cruise in the Mediterranean. (For Pleasure trips see BOATING, pp.254-257.)	Je veux faire une croisière, une longue croisière en Méditerranée.	Ich möchte eine Seereise unternehmen, Ich möchte auf eine lange Seereise im Mittelmeer gehen.
Does a chaplain, a lecturer accompany the cruise?	Est-ce qu'un aumônier, un conférencier, accompagne la croisière?	Ist ein Schiffsgeistlicher, ein Vortragender, mit an Bord?
From where does the boat for . . go?	D'où part le bateau pour . . ?	Von wo geht das Schiff nach . . ab?
Take this luggage to the pier, to the pier head, on board.	Portez ces bagages à la jetée, au musoir, à bord.	Bringen Sie dies Gepäck auf den Pier oder auf den Hafendamm, ans Ende des Hafendamms, an Bord.
Is this the boat for . . ?	Est-ce ici le bateau pour . . ?	Ist dies das Schiff nach . . ?
These articles are cabin luggage, those hold luggage.	Ces colis-ci sont des bagages de cabine, ceux-là des bagages de cale.	Diese Sachen sind Kabinengepäck, die hier gehen in den Laderaum.
When do we embark? When must I be on board?	Quand embarquons-nous? Quand faut-il que je sois à bord?	Wann gehen wir an Bord? Wann muß ich an Bord sein?
What would you charge for taking me over to that steamer?	Combien demanderiez-vous pour me conduire à ce vapeur[-là]?	Was verlangen Sie, um mich zu dem Dampfer dort übersetzen?
How long does the boat stop at . . ?	Combien de temps le bateau s'arrête-t-il à . . ?	Wie lange legt das Boot in . . an?
When do we dock?	Quand entrons-nous en bassin?	Wann gehen wir in Dock?

Datemi, per favore, una lista di partenze, un orario.	Haga el favor de darme una lista de salidas, un itinerario.	Geef mij een vertreklijst, een dienstregeling, als 't U belieft.
Posso vedere una pianta delle cabine ?	¿ Puedo consultar un plano del buque ?	Kan ik een plattegrond raadplegen ?
C'è un battello che parte da qui per . . ?	¿ Hay un buque desde aquí con destino a . . ?	Is er een boot van hier naar . . ?
In quali giorni ? Quante volte al giorno ? A che ora ?	¿ En cuáles días ? ¿ Cuántas veces por día ? ¿ A qué horas ?	Op welke dagen ? Hoevaak per dag ? Op welke tijden ?
Questo battello va diretta a . . ?	¿ Va directo este buque hasta . . ?	Gaat deze boot rechtstreeks naar . . ?
A quale porto fa scalo [il battello] ? Fa questo battello scalo a . . ?	¿ En qué puertos hace el buque escala ? ¿ Hace escala en . . ?	Welke havens loopt de boot aan ? of Welke haven loopt hij aan ? Loopt de boot . . aan ?
Quali sono i porti di scalo ?	¿ Cuáles son los puertos de escala ?	Wat zijn de aanloophavens ?
Quando parte il prossimo battello ?	¿ Cuándo sale (o zarpa) el próximo buque ?	Wanneer vertrekt de volgende boot ?
È la linea più rapida ?	¿ Es esta la ruta más rápida ?	Is dit de snelste route ?
Una crociera. Fare una crociera.	Una travesía (o Un viaje) por mar. Navegar.	Een zeereis. Een zeereis maken of Kruisen.
Io voglio fare una crociera, una lunga crociera nel Mediterraneo.	Deseo hacer un viaje de recreo por mar, un viaje largo de recreo en el Mediterráneo.	Ik wil een zeereis maken, een lange zeereis in de Middellandse Zee maken.
Accompagna la crociera un cappellano, un conferenziere ?	¿ Viene un capellán, un conferenciante, con este viaje de recreo ?	Maakt een kapelaan, een hulpprediker, de (zee)-reis mee ?
Da dove parte il battello per andare a . . ?	¿ De dónde zarpa el buque para . . ?	Vanwaar vertrekt de boot naar . . ?
Portate questi bagagli sulla gettata, alla testata del molo, a bordo.	Lleve este equipaje al muelle, al fondo del muelle, a bordo.	Breng deze bagage naar de pier, naar het pierhoofd, aan boord.
È diretta questo battello a . . ?	¿ Es este el buque para . . ?	Is dit de boot naar . . ?
Questi colli sono bagagli da cabina, quelli per la stiva.	Estos bultos son para el camarote, aquellos para la bodega.	Deze stukken bagage zijn voor de hut, die voor het ruim.
Quando ci imbarchiamo ? Quando debbo essere a bordo ?	¿ Cuándo nos embarcamos ? ¿ Cuándo debo estar a bordo ?	Hoe laat gaan wij aan boord ? Hoe laat moet ik aan boord zijn ?
Quanto mi fate pagare per portarmi su quel piroscafo ?	¿ Cuánto me cobra usted por llevarme a ese vapor ?	Hoeveel vraagt U om mij naar dat stoomschip te brengen ?
Che fermata fa il battello a . . ?	¿ Cuánto tiempo para el buque en . . ?	Hoe lang blijft de boot in . . ?
Quando entreremo nel bacino ?	¿ Cuándo entramos en el dique ?	Wanneer dokken wij ?

Please give me a landing ticket.	Veuillez me donner une carte de débarquement.	Geben Sie mir bitte einen Landungsschein.
At what time do we return?	À quelle heure revenons-nous?	Wann fahren wir zurück?

Booking of berths / Pour retenir des places / Platzbestellung

I want to book a passage to . . .	Je veux retenir une place pour . . .	Ich möchte eine Passage nach . . bestellen.
Can I get passage tickets on board?	Puis-je prendre des billets de voyage à bord?	Kann ich die Schiffskarten an Bord lösen?
What is the passage money (or the fare) to . ., first [class], second [class], steerage?	Quel est le prix du passage (ou du voyage) pour . ., en première [classe], en deuxième [classe], dans les entrepons ou à l'avant?	Was kostet die Überfahrt→ erster Klasse, zweiter Klasse, im Zwischendeck, nach . .?
I wrote, I telegraphed, for a berth.	J'ai écrit, J'ai télégraphié, pour retenir une place.	Ich habe schriftlich, telegraphisch, eine Kabine belegt.
A deck cabin, An outside cabin, An inside cabin with two bedsteads, with bath, with shower bath with lavatory and W.C.	Une cabine de pont, Une cabine extérieure, Une cabine intérieure à deux lits, avec bain, avec douche, avec toilette et water-closet.	Eine Deck-Kabine, Eine Aussenkabine, Eine Innenkabine mit zwei Betten, mit Bad, mit Dusche, mit Toilette und Klosett.
A state cabin. State rooms.	Une cabine de luxe. Des appartements de luxe.	Eine Luxuskabine. Luxusräume.
Cabin class.	La classe cabine.	Kabinenklasse.
Tourist class. Tourist third class.	La classe touriste. La classe touriste-troisième.	Touristenklasse, Dritte Touristenklasse.
Have you a single-berth cabin?	Avez-vous une cabine à une [seule] place?	Haben Sie eine einbettige Kabine?
I prefer an upper, a lower, berth (bunk).	Je préfère une couchette supérieure, inférieure.	Ich möchte ein oberes Bett, ein unteres Bett.
How many berths are there in this cabin?	Combien de places y a-t-il dans cette cabine?	Wieviel Betten hat diese Kabine?
Is this berth engaged?	Cette place est-elle retenue?	Ist dieses Bett besetzt?
Can I change berths?	Puis-je changer de place?	Kann ich mein Bett umtau→schen?
Is there a restaurant on board? (See EATING AND DRINKING, pp. 130-171.)	Y a-t-il un restaurant à bord?	Gibt es ein Restaurant an Bord?
Where must one apply to reserve seats in the dining saloon?	Où faut-il s'adresser pour retenir des places à la salle à manger?	Wo kann man Plätze für den Speisesaal bestellen?

On board ship / À bord du navire / An Bord

What is the name of this boat, that headland [there], that island over there?	Comment s'appelle ce bateau, ce promontoire [-là], cette île là-bas?	Wie heißt dieses Schiff, das Vorgebirge dort, die Insel dort drüben?

Per favore, datemi una carta di sbarco.	Haga el favor de darme un billete de desembarque.	Wilt U als 't U belieft een landingskaart geven.
A che ora ritorneremo ?	¿ A qué hora regresamos ?	Hoelaat komen we terug ?

Per riservare i posti — Para reservar plazas — Plaatsbespreking

Io desidero riservare un posto per . . .	Deseo reservar un pasaje para . . .	Ik wil een plaats bespreken naar . . .
Posso io prendere i biglietti di transito a bordo ?	¿ Puedo obtener los billetes de pasaje a bordo ?	Kan ik aan boord plaatsen nemen ?
Qual'è il prezzo del tragitto (o del viaggio) per . . di prima [classe], di seconda [classe], di terza [classe] ?	¿ Cuánto vale el viaje de primera [clase], de segunda [clase], de tercera [clase], para . . ?	Hoeveel is de passage naar . . , eerste klas tweede klas, tussendek ?
Io ho scritto, Io ho telegrafato, per riservare un posto.	He escrito, He telegrafiado, pidiendo una plaza.	Ik heb geschreven, getelegrafeerd, om een plaats te bespreken.
Una cabina di ponte, Una cabina esterna, Una cabina interna a due letti, con bagno, con doccia, con toeletta e ritirata.	Un camarote de cubierta, Un camarote de exterior, Un camarote de interior con dos camas, con baño, con baño de ducha, con lavabo y retrete.	Een dekhut, Een buitenhut, Een binnenhut met twee bedden, met bad, met douche, met toilet en W.C. (pronounce oué, sé).
Una cabina di lusso. Un appartamento di lusso.	Un camarote de lujo. Apartamentos de lujo.	Een luxehut. Een luxe suite.
La classe cabina.	Clase de cabina.	Hutklasse.
La classe turistica. La terza classe turistica.	Clase de turista. Clase de turista de tercera.	Toeristenklas. Toeristenklas derde klasse.
Avete una cabina con un solo posto ?	¿ Hay camarote con una sola litera ?	Heeft U een enkele hut ?
Io preferisco una cuccetta superiore, inferiore.	Prefiero le litera de arriba, de abajo.	Ik geef de voorkeur aan een bovenkooi, een benedenkooi.
Quanti posti ci sono in questa cabina ?	¿ Cuántas literas tiene este camarote ?	Hoeveel kooien zijn er in deze hut ?
E occupato questo posto ?	¿ Está ocupada esta litera ?	Is deze kooi bezet ?
Posso cambiar posto ?	¿ Puedo cambiar de litera ?	Kan ik van kooi veranderen ?
C'è un ristorante a bordo ?	¿ Hay comedor a bordo ?	Is er een restaurant aan boord ?
Dove bisogna rivolgersi per riservare i posti nella sala da pranzo ?	¿ Dónde se reservan plazas para el comedor ?	Waar kan men plaatsen in de eetzaal bespreken ?

A bordo del battello — A bordo del buque — Aan boord van het schip

Come si chiama questo battello, quel promontorio [là], quell'isola [laggiù] ?	¿ Qué es el nombre de este buque, ese promontorio, aquella isla ?	Hoe heet deze boot, die kaap, dat eiland ?

Where is the saloon, the smoking room, the bar?	Où est le salon, le fumoir, le bar?	Wo ist der Salon, der Rauchsalon, die Bar?
How long will the sea journey take? How long shall we be at sea?	Combien de temps durera le trajet maritime? Combien de temps serons-nous sur mer?	Wie lange dauert die Überfahrt? Wie lange sind wir auf See?
Where are we now? When shall we arrive at ..?	Où sommes-nous à présent? Quand arriverons-nous à ..?	Wo sind wir jetzt? Wann sind wir in . . ?
Shall we have a good, a bad, passage, a rough crossing?	Aurons-nous une bonne, une mauvaise, traversée, une traversée mouvementée?	Werden wir eine gute, eine schlechte, eine stürmische Überfahrt haben?
Is the sea rough, smooth?	La mer est-elle agitée, unie?	Ist das Meer bewegt, glatt?
Is bad weather expected?	Prévoit-on du gros temps?	Werden wir schlechtes Wetter haben?
Steward! I am a bad sailor; please look after me.	Garçon! Je suis mauvais marin; veuillez vous occuper de moi.	Steward! Ich werde sehr leicht seekrank; bitte kümmern Sie sich doch etwas um mich.
I feel unwell. I am going to be sick. Bring me a basin, a glass of water.	Je me sens indisposé. Je vais avoir le mal de mer. Apportez-moi une cuvette, un verre d'eau.	Mir ist schlecht. Ich glaube, ich muß mich übergeben. Bringen Sie mir einen Eimer, ein Glas Wasser.
Please ask the steward, the stewardess, to come.	Veuillez prier le garçon de cabine, la femme de chambre, de venir.	Können Sie bitte den Steward, die Stewardeß, holen.
Can I send a message by wireless?	Puis-je envoyer un message par sans-fil?	Kann ich einen Funkspruch senden?
May I (we) go ashore or must I (we) remain on board?	Peut-on descendre à terre ou faut-il rester à bord?	Kann ich (Können wir) an Land gehen oder muß ich (müssen wir) an Bord bleiben?
Do we land in a boat?	Débarquons-nous dans un canot?	Werden wir ausgebootet?
Does the boat remain in the roads or are the passengers transhipped direct from the boat to the train?	Le paquebot reste-t-il sur rade ou les passagers sont-ils transbordés directement du paquebot au train?	Bleibt das Schiff auf der Reede liegen oder können die Fahrgäste direkt von Bord in den Zug steigen?
Is there a bus near the landing stage?	Y a-t-il un omnibus près du débarcadère?	Gibt es einen Omnibus an der Anlegestelle?

AIR TRAVEL   VOYAGES PAR AVION   LUFTREISEN

Aeronautical terms   Termes aéronautiques   Flugausdrücke

An aerodrome or An airfield.	Un aérodrome, Un champ d'aviation.	Ein Flugplatz.
An aeroplane or An airplane or A plane.	Un aéroplane, Un avion.	Ein Flugzeug.
An aircraft.	Un aéronef.	Ein Flugzeug.
An air line.	Une ligne aérienne, Une ligne d'avions.	Eine Fluglinie.

Dov'è il salone, la sala fumatori, il bar?	¿Dónde está el salón, el salón de fumadores, el bar?	Waar is de salon, de rooksalon, de bar?
Quanto durerà il viaggio di mare? Quanto tempo staremo in mare?	¿Cuánto tiempo dura la travesía por mar? ¿Cuánto tiempo estaremos embarcados?	Hoe lang duurt de zeereis? Hoe lang zullen we op zee zijn?
Dove ci troviamo ora? Quando arriveremo a . . ?	¿En dónde estamos ahora? ¿Cuándo llegamos a . . ?	Waar zjin we nu?.. Wanneer komen wij in .. aan?
Avremo una buona, una cattiva, traversata, una traversata burrascosa?	¿Tendremos buena, mala, travesía? ¿Será tempestuosa?	Zullen we een goede, slechte, passage, een woelige overtocht hebben?
È agitato, È tranquillo, il mare?	¿Está el mar revuelto, tranquilo?	Is de zee woelig, glad?
Si prevede un tempo cattivo?	¿Se espera mal tiempo?	Wordt er slecht weer verwacht?
Cameriere! Io sono un cattivo marinaio, per favore, tenete un occhio sopra di me.	¡Camarero! Suelo marearme; haga el favor de atenderme.	Steward! Ik heb slechte zeebenen; zorg voor me als 't je belieft.
Mi sento male. Sto per avere il mal di mare. Portatemi un bacino, un bicchier d'acqua.	Me siento mareado. Voy a vomitar. Tráigame un escupidera, un vaso de agua.	Ik voel me niet lekker. Ik word zeeziek. Breng me een kom, een glas water.
Volete pregare il cameriere, la cameriera, di venire.	Haga el favor de llamar al camarero, a la camarera.	U gelieve de steward, de stewardess, te roepen.
Posso mandare un messaggio per radiotelegramma?	¿Puedo mandar un mensaje por radiotelegrafía?	Kan ik een bericht sturen per draadloze, [telegrafie]?
Posso io (Possiamo noi) scendere a terra o debbo (dobbiamo) restare a bordo?	¿Puedo (Podemos) ir en tierra o he (hemos) de permanecer a bordo?	Mag ik (Mogen wij) aan land gaan of moet ik (moeten wij) aan boord blijven?
Sbarchiamo noi in una barca?	¿Tenemos que desembarcar en un bote?	Gaan wij in een boot aan land?
Rimane il battello nella rada o i passeggeri sono trasbordati direttamente dal battello al treno?	¿Se queda el buque fuera del puerto o se desembarcan los pasajeros directamente del buque al tren?	Blijft de boot op de ree of stappen de passagiers rechtstreeks, van de boot op de trein over?
C'è un omnibus vicino allo sbarcatoio?	¿Hay un ómnibus que sale desde cerca del desembarcadero?	Is er een bus dichtbij de steiger?

VIAGGIO IN AEROPLANO	VIAJES EN AVIÓN	REIZEN PER VLIEGTUIG
Termini aeronautici	**Términos aeronáuticos**	**Luchtvaarttermen**
Un aerodromo, Un campo d'aviazione.	Un aeródromo, Un campo de aviación.	Een vliegveld.
Un aeroplano, Un velivolo.	Un aeroplano, Un avión.	Een vliegtuig, Een vliegmachine.
Un aéreo.	Un aparato aéreo.	Een vliegtuig.
Un'aviolinea.	Una línea de aviación.	Een luchtlijn.

An air liner.	Un avion de ligne [régulière].	Ein fahrplanmäßiges Passagierflugzeug.
An airman.	Un aviateur.	Ein Flieger.
An air mechanic.	Un mécanicien d'avions.	Ein Flugmechaniker. →
An air pilot.	Un pilote d'avions, Un pilote-aviateur.	Ein Flugzeugführer, Ein Pilot.
An air pocket.	Un trou d'air.	Ein Luftloch.
An airport *or* An air station.	Un aéroport, Un port aérien, Une gare aérienne.	Ein Flughafen.
An air ticket.	Un billet aérien.	Eine Flugkarte.
An airway.	Une voie aérienne.	Eine Flugstrecke. →
An airways (*or* An air lines) company.	Une compagnie de navigation aérienne.	Eine Luftfahrtgesellschaft, Eine Luftreederei.
An aviator.	Un aviateur, Une aviatrice.	Ein(e) Flieger(in).
The cockpit.	Le poste de pilotage.	Die Glaskanzel, Der Führer-Sitz.
A hangar.	Un hangar [d'aviation], Un garage [d'aéroplane].	Ein Flugzeugschuppen.
A land official.	Un agent à terre.	Ein Angestellter der Luftfahrtgesellschaft. →
A landing.	Un atterrissage.	Eine Landung.
A landing ground.	Une aire de débarquement.	Ein Landeplatz.
Night flying.	Le vol de nuit.	Nachtfliegen.
A non-stop flight.	Un vol sans escale.	Ein Ohnehaltflug.
A seaplane *or* A hydroplane.	Un hydravion.	Ein Seeflugzeug, Ein Wasserflugzeug. →
A steward (*aeroplane*).	Un steward.	Ein Steward.
To taxi [along the ground] (*Aviation*).	Rouler [sur le sol].	[Über den Flugplatz] rollen.

Enquiries and requests	**Demandes de renseignements et de services**	**Anfragen und Bitten**
How far is the airport from the city *or* the town?	À quelle distance l'aéroport est-il de la ville?	Wie weit ist es vom Flugplatz zur Stadt?
Please take me to .. airport.	Veuillez me conduire à l'aéroport de . . .	Fahren Sie mich bitte zum Flugplatz in . . .
Is there a car service between the company's office and the airport?	Y a-t-il un service automobile entre le bureau de la compagnie et l'aéroport?	Gibt es einen Autobusdienst vom Büro der Luftreederei zum Flugplatz? →
Where does the car (*or* the [motor] coach) for the air station start from?	D'où part le car (*ou* l'autocar) pour l'aéroport?	Von wo geht das Auto (*oder* der Autobus) zum Flugplatz?
Is there an air service (*or* an aeroplane service) to ..?	Y a-t-il un service aérien (*ou* un service d'avion) pour ..?	Gibt es einen Flugdienst nach ..?
A daily service, Sunday excepted *or* A service on week days only.	Un service quotidien, sauf le dimanche, Un service la semaine seulement.	Ein täglicher Dienst, nur an Werktagen.
Please give me a time table, show me a seating	Veuillez me donner un horaire, me montrer un	Geben Sie mir bitte einen Fahrplan, Zeigen Sie

Un aeroplano di linea.	Un avión de línea.	Een lijnvliegtuig.
Un aviatore.	Un aviador.	Een vliegenier.
Un meccanico d'aviazione.	Un mecánico de aviación.	Een mecaniciën.
Un pilota aviatore.	Un piloto de avión, Un piloto aviador.	Een (lucht)piloot.
Un buco d'aria.	Un vacío [de aire].	Een luchtzak.
Un aeroporto.	Una estación (o Un paradero) para aeroplanos.	Een luchthaven.
Un biglietto aviolinea.	Un billete de aviación.	Een vliegticket.
Una via aerea.	Una vía aérea.	Een luchtvaartlijn.
Una società d'aviolinea	Una compañía de navegación aérea.	Een luchtvaartmaat-schappij.
Un aviatore, Una aviatrice.	Un(a) aviador(a).	Een vliegenier, Een vliegenierster.
La carlinga.	La casilla del piloto.	De stuurstoel, De cockpit.
Un'aviorimessa.	Un hangar, Un garaje para aviones.	Een hangar.
Un agente di terra.	Un agente terrestre.	Een luchtvaart beambte.
Un atterraggio.	Un aterrizaje.	Een landing.
Un campo d'atterraggio.	Un campo de aterrizaje.	Een landingsterrein.
Il volo di notte.	Vuelo nocturno.	Het nachtvliegen.
Un volo senza scalo.	Un vuelo sin parada.	Een non-stop vlucht.
Un idrovolante.	Un hidroavión.	Een watervliegtuig.
Uno steward.	Un steward, Un camarero de avión.	Een steward.
Rullare [sulla pista di decollo].	Correr por tierra.	Taxiën.

Informazioni e richieste	Preguntas y solicitudes	Inlichtingen en aanvragen
A che distanza è l'aeroporto dalla città?	¿A qué distancia de la población está el paradero para aviones?	Hoe ver is het vliegveld van de stad?
Per favore, portatemi all'aeroporto di . . .	Haga el favor de conducirme a la estación .. de aviación.	Breng me naar de lucht-haven van .. als 't U belieft.
C'è un servizio automobilistico tra l'ufficio della società e l'aeroporto?	¿Hay un servicio de autos entre el despacho de la compañía y el paradero para aviones?	Is er een autodienst tussen het kantoor van de maatschappij en de luchthaven?
Da dove parte l'automobile (o l'autobus) per l'aeroporto?	¿Desde dónde sale el auto (o el autocar) para el campo de aviación?	Vanwaar vertrekt de bus naar het vliegveld?
C'è un servizio aereo (o un servizio d'aviazione) per . . ?	¿Hay un servicio aéreo (o un servicio de aviones) para .. ?	Is er een luchtdienst naar .. ?
Un servizio quotidiano, eccetto la Domenica, Un servizio solo (o unico) nei giorni feriali.	Un servicio diario, exceptuando los domingos, Un servicio únicamente los días de semana.	Een dagelijkse dienst, zondags uitgezonderd, Een dienst uitsluitend op weekdagen.
Mi dia un orario, per favore, mi mostri una pianta	Haga el favor de darme un horario, muéstreme un	Geef me een dienst-regeling, laat me een

plan.	plan des places.	mir bitte einen Sitzplan.
Is there an aeroplane to-day for . . ?	Y a-t-il un avion aujourd'hui pour . . ?	Geht heute ein Flugzeug nach . . ?
At what time does the aeroplane for . . start?	À quelle heure l'avion pour . . part-il ?	Wann geht das Flugzeug nach . . ?
How many stages are there in the flight?	Combien d'étapes fait-on au cours du vol ?	Wie oft wird der Flug unterbrochen ?
The reservation (or The booking) office (seats).	Le bureau des réservations.	Das Büro für die Flugkartenbestellung.
I want to reserve a seat in the aeroplane leaving to-morrow morning for . .	Je veux réserver une place dans l'avion qui part demain matin pour . . .	Ich möchte einen Platz für das Flugzeug morgen früh nach . . belegen.
Please book one seat, two seats, for me in the aeroplane for . . leaving at eight a.m., at one p.m., at two p.m. (See 24-HOUR CLOCK SYSTEM, p. 267.)	Veuillez me retenir une place, deux places, dans l'avion pour . . qui part à huit heures [du matin], à treize heures, à quatorze heures.	Bitte belegen Sie für mich einen Platz, zwei Plätze, in dem Flugzeug um acht Uhr früh, um dreizehn Uhr, um vierzehn Uhr, nach . . .
What is the ordinary fare?	Quel est le prix normal?	Wie hoch is der normale Fahrpreis?
What saving is there in taking a return ticket over two single tickets?	Quelle économie comporte un billet d'aller et retour sur deux billets simples ?	Wie gross ist die Differenz zwischen einer Rückfahrkarte und zwei einfachen Fahrkarten?
Can I cancel this ticket and claim a refund of the fare?	Puis-je annuler ce billet et réclamer un remboursement du prix du billet ?	Kann ich diese Fahrkarte zurückgeben ? Habe ich einen Anspruch auf Rückvergütung ?
I wish to have this bag at my disposal at each port of call.	Je désire avoir cette valise à ma disposition à chaque escale.	Ich möchte dieses Gepäckstück bei jeder Zwischenlandung greifbar haben.
The outward journey.	Le parcours de l'aller.	Der Hinflug.
The return journey.	Le parcours de retour.	Der Rückflug.
A through connexion.	Une correspondance directe.	Eine direkte Verbindung.
Is the journey free of all charges?	Le voyage est-il net de tous frais?	Gibt es irgendwelche Sondergebühren?
What is the free allowance of luggage or the weight allowed free?	Quelle est la franchise de bagages ou la franchise de poids ?	Wie hoch ist die Freigrenze für Gepäck ?
What are the rates for excess weight of luggage?	Quel est le tarif pour excédent de poids de bagages?	Wie hoch ist die Gebühr für Übergewicht?
At what percentage of the freight rates is excess luggage charged?	À quel pourcentage du tarif de fret les excédents de bagages sont-ils taxés?	Wieviel Prozent des Frachttarifs bezahlt man für Übergewicht?
Does the steward speak English, several languages?	Le steward parle-t-il l'anglais, plusieurs langues ?	Spricht der Steward Englisch, mehrere Sprachen ?
Do you take unaccompanied children?	Prenez-vous des enfants non accompagnés ?	Dürfen Kinder ohne Begleitung mitreisen ?

dei posti.	plano de los asientos.	plattegrond zien als 't U belieft.
◄C'è un aeroplano oggi per . . ?	¿Hay avión hoy para . . ?	Is er vandaag een vliegtuig naar ..?
A che ora parte l'aeroplano per . . ?	¿A qué hora sale el avión para . . ?	Hoe laat vertrekt het vliegtuig naar . . ?
Durante il volo quante tappe ci sono?	¿De cuántos trayectos consiste el viaje?	Hoeveel etappes zijn er op de vlucht?
L'ufficio di prenotazione dei posti.	El despacho de reservaciones para plazas.	Het plaatskaartenbureau.
Io desidero riservare un posto nell'aeroplano che parte domattina per . .	Deseo reservar asiento en el avión que sale mañana por la mañana para . .	Ik wil een plaats bespreken in het vliegtuig, dat morgenochtend naar . . vertrekt.
◄Per favore, riservatemi un posto, due posti, per me nell'aeroplano per . . che parte alle otto di mattina, alle tredici, alle quattordici.	Haga el favor de reservarme un asiento, dos asientos, en el avión que sale para . . a las ocho de la mañana, a las trece horas, a las catorce horas.	Reserveer een plaats, twee plaatsen, voor me in het vliegtuig naar .., dat om acht uur 's ochtends, dertien uur, veertien uur, vertrekt.
Qual'è il prezzo normale?	¿Cuánto es el precio normal?	Wat is de normale prijs?
Che risparmio porta un biglietto di andata e ritorno invece di due semplici?	¿Cuánto se ahorra tomando un billete de ida y vuelta en vez de dos billetes simples?	Hoeveel spaart men uit door een retour te nemen in plaats van twee enkele reizen?
Posso io annullare questo biglietto ed essere rimborsato della spesa?	¿Puedo cancelar este billete y reclamar el reembolso del precio del billete?	Kan ik dit biljet annuleren, aanspraak maken op teruggave van het reisgeld?
Io desidero avere questa valigia a mia disposizione ad ogni scalo.	Deseo tener esta valija a mi disposición en cada escala.	Ik wens deze tas tot mijn beschikking te hebben op iedere landingsplaats.
◄Il percorso di andata. Il percorso di ritorno.	El viaje de ida. El viaje de regreso.	De uitreis. De thuisreis, De terugreis.
Una coincidenza diretta.	Una correspondencia directa.	Een rechtstreekse verbinding.
È il viaggio netto da ogni altra spesa?	¿Es el viaje inclusive de todo[s] gasto[s]?	Is de reis vrij van alle kosten?
Qual'è la franchigia del bagaglio od il peso del bagaglio che ha il beneficio della franchigia?	¿Cuánto es la franquicia de equipaje o la franquicia de peso?	Hoeveel bagage is vrij of Hoeveel bagage mag men gratis meenemen?
◄Qual'è la tariffa per l'eccesso di peso del bagaglio?	¿Qué es la tarifa por exceso de peso de equipaje?	Wat is het tarief voor bagage boven het vrijgestelde gewicht?
Qual'è la percentuale della tariffa di nolo per il peso eccedente?	¿A qué porcentaje sobre los tipos de flete se cobra el exceso de equipaje?	Met welk percentage van de vrachttarieven wordt bagage boven het vrijgestelde gewicht belast?
Parla inglese, parecchie lingue, lo steward?	¿Habla inglés, varios idiomas, el camarero?	Spreekt de bediende Engels, verschillende talen?
Prendete fanciulli non accompagnati?	¿Se llevan niños que no van acompañados?	Neemt U kinderen zonder begeleiding mee?

Are [light] refreshments served on board free of charge?	Des rafraîchissements sont-ils servis gratuitement à bord?	Bekommt man Erfrischungen an Bord gratis?
Are all the meals (breakfasts, lunches, dinners) included in the price of the ticket and served at the best restaurants and hotels of the ports of call on the journey?	Tous les repas (petits déjeuners, déjeuners, dîners) sont-ils compris dans le prix du billet et servis dans les meilleurs restaurants et hôtels des escales du parcours?	Sind alle Mahlzeiten (Frühstück, Mittagessen, Abendessen) im Fahrpreis einbegriffen, und werden sie bei jeder Zwischenlandung in den besten Restaurants und Hotels gereicht?
When we do take off?	Quand décollons-nous?	Wann starten wir?
I should like something to eat, a light meal or a snack. (See EATING AND DRINKING, pp. 130-171.)	Je désire me restaurer, une collation.	Ich würde gern etwas essen, eine Kleinigkeit zu mir nehmen.
Is smoking allowed?	Peut-on fumer?	Ist Rauchen gestattet?
Show me a route map; I want to follow the progress of the machine.	Faites-moi voir une carte de la route; je veux suivre la marche de l'appareil.	Zeigen Sie mir bitte eine Karte unserer Fahrstrecke; ich möchte gern unseren Kurs verfolgen.
I am subject to air sickness. Have you a remedy which will secure me against indisposition?	Je suis sujet, (woman) sujette, au mal de l'air. Est-ce que vous avez un remède qui me prémunira contre l'indisposition?	Ich werde leicht luftkrank. Haben Sie ein Mittel gegen Unpäßlichkeit?
Ask the wireless operator aboard to dispatch this private telegram.	Priez le radiotélégraphiste du bord d'adresser ce télégramme privé.	Bitten Sie den Funker, dieses private Telegramm durchzugeben.
What is the next stopping place?	Quel est le prochain point d'arrêt?	Wo machen wir die nächste Zwischenlandung?
Do we call at .. ?	Fait-on escale à .. ?	Landen wir in .. ?
At what time do we arrive at our destination?	À quelle heure arriverons-nous à notre destination?	Wann kommen wir in .. an?
When do we land at .. ?	Quand atterrirons-nous à .. ?	Wann landen wir in .. ?

CUSTOMS AND PASSPORTS

DOUANE ET PASSE-PORTS

ZÖLLE UND PÄSSE

The customs.	La douane.	Der Zoll.
A customs declaration.	Une déclaration en douane.	Eine Zollerklärung.
A customs officer.	Un agent de la douane, Un douanier.	Ein Zollbeamter.
A customs station.	Un poste de douane.	Ein Zollamt.
A frontier station.	Une gare frontière.	Eine Grenzstation.
A bond note.	Un acquit-à-caution.	Ein Acquit-à-caution, Ein Einfuhrschein.
Where do they examine luggage? or Where does the customs examination take place?	Où fait-on visiter les bagages? Où se fait la visite de la douane?	Wo ist die Zollabfertigung?
Will examination of lug-	La visite des bagages se	Findet die Gepäckkontrolle

Sono i pasti leggeri gratuitamente serviti a bordo ?	¿ Se sirven a bordo refrescos grátis ?	Worden verversingen aan boord gratis verstrekt?
◄Sono tutti i pasti (la colazione, la seconda colazione, il pranzo) inclusi nel prezzo del biglietto e serviti nei migliori ristoranti degli scali del viaggio ?	¿ Están incluidas en el precio del billete todas las comidas (desayunos, almuerzos, comidas) y servidas en los mejores restaurantes y hoteles de los puertos de escala del viaje ?	Zijn alle maaltijden (ontbijt, lunch, diner) in de prijs van het biljet inbegrepen, en worden ze in de beste restaurants en hotels in de landingsplaatsen op de reis geserveerd ?
Quando decolliamo ?	¿ Cuándo desaterrizamos ?	Hoe laat stijgen wij op?
Vorrei mangiare qualche-cosa, un pasto leggero od uno spuntino.	Deseo comer algo, una merienda o un fiambre.	Ik zou graag iets eten, een licht maal of een hapje.
È permesso di fumare ?	¿ Se permite fumar ?	Mag er hier gerookt worden?
Mi mostri una pianta del viaggio ; io desidero seguire l' itinerario dell'apparecchio.	Muéstreme un plano de la ruta ; deseo seguir la marcha del aparato.	Laat mij een routekaart zien; ik wil de vordering van het toestel volgen.
◄Io sono soggetto al mal di aria. Avete qualche rimedio per difendermi contro l'indisposizione ?	Suelo ser víctima del mal de altura. ¿ Tiene usted un remedio para la enfermedad ?	Ik heb last van luchtziekte. Heeft U een middel om te voorkomen dat ik onpasselijk wordt?
Pregate il radiotelegrafista di bordo di spedirmi questo telegramma privato.	Haga el favor de pedirle al radiotelegrafista que me despache este telegrama privado.	Vraag de marconist aan boord dit persoonlijke telegram te versturen.
Qual'è la prossima fermata?	¿ Cuál es el próximo paradero ?	Wat is de volgende plaats die wij aandoen?
Facciamo scalo a . . ?	¿ Hacemos escala en . . ?	Landen wij in . . ?
A che ora arriveremo alla nostra destinazione ?	¿ A qué hora llegamos a destino ?	Hoe laat komen wij in onze bestemming aan?
◄Quando si atterra a . . ?	¿ Cuándo aterrizamos en . . ?	Hoe laat landen wij te . . ?

DOGANA E PASSAPORTI	ADUANAS Y PASAPORTES	DOUANE EN PAS-POORTEN
La dogana.	La aduana.	De douane.
Una dichiarazione in dogana.	Una declaración de aduana.	Een aangifte bij de douane.
Un ufficiale di dogana, Un doganiere.	Un agente de aduana, Un aduanero.	Een douanebeambte.
Una stazione di dogana.	Un despacho de aduana.	Een douane kantoor.
◄Una stazione di frontiera.	Una estación de frontera.	Een grensstation.
Un acquit-à-caution.	Un acquit-à-caution.	Een acquit-à-caution.
Dove si fa (o Dove ha luogo) la visita dei bagagli?	¿ Dónde examinan el equipaje ? ¿ Dónde se hace la inspección del equipaje ?	Waar wordt de bagage onderzocht? Waar vindt het douane-onderzoek plaats?
La visita dei bagagli si fa	¿ Se hace el examen del	Wordt de bagage aan-

CUSTOMS AND PASSPORTS

gage take place on board, in the train, at the frontier, in Paris?	fera-t-elle à bord, dans le train, à la frontière, à Paris?	an Bord, im Zug, an der Grenze, in Paris, statt?
Where is the custom house? Where must I take my luggage to be examined?	Où est la douane? Où dois-je présenter mes bagages pour la visite?	Wo ist das Zollamt? Wo lasse ich mein Gepäck kontrollieren?
This is my bag.	Cette valise est à moi.	Dies ist mein Koffer.
I have nothing to declare.	Je n'ai rien à déclarer.	Ich habe nichts zu verzollen.
I don't think I have anything to declare.	Je ne pense pas avoir rien à déclarer.	Ich glaube, ich habe nichts zu verzollen.
Not that I know of.	Pas que je sache.	Nicht daß ich wüßte.
I have some cigars, a few cigarettes, a little tobacco.	J'ai quelques cigares, quelques cigarettes, un peu de tabac.	Ich habe einige Zigarren, ein paar Zigaretten, etwas Tabak bei mir.
Is this dutiable, duty-free? Does that pay duty, an ad valorem duty?	Ceci est-il passible de droits, franc de tous droits? Cela paie-t-il un droit, un droit ad valorem?	Ist dies zollpflichtig, zollfrei? Muss man hierfür Zoll bezahlen, Wertzoll bezahlen?
All these things have been worn.	Tous ces effets ont été portés.	All diese Sachen sind getragen.
It is for my own use only.	C'est pour mon usage personnel seulement.	Es ist nur für meinen persönlichen Gebrauch.
That is all I have.	C'est tout ce que j'ai.	Das ist alles, was ich habe.
May I take my luggage away?	Puis-je enlever mes bagages?	Kann ich mein Gepäck wegnehmen?
Do you want to examine my passport, my identity card?	Voulez-vous examiner mon passeport, ma carte d'identité?	Wollen Sie meinen Pass, meinen [Personal-]Ausweis, sehen?
Is a visa required?	Un visa est-il exigé?	Braucht man ein Visum?
Where must I apply for a tourist visa? Where are passports visaed?	Où faut-il demander le visa touristique? Les passeports où sont-ils visés?	Wo kann ich ein Touristenvisum beantragen? Wo werden Visen ausgestellt?
Please give me back my passport.	Veuillez me rendre mon passeport.	Kann ich meinen Pass zurückhaben?
How long can I stay in this country without any formality whatever?	Combien de temps puis-je rester dans ce pays sans formalité quelconque?	Wie lange kann ich mich hier in . . ohne jede Formalitäten aufhalten?
I am a British subject.	Je suis sujet (*feminine* sujette) britannique.	Ich bin britischer Staatsangehöriger, (*feminine*) britische Staatsangehörige.
I am a national of a British oversea territory.	Je suis ressortissant (-e) d'un territoire britannique d'outre-mer.	Ich bin Staatsangehöriger eines britischen Überseelandes.
Can you tell me where the British consulate is?	Pouvez-vous me dire où se trouve le consulat britannique?	Können Sie mir sagen, wo das britische Konsulat ist?
I insist on getting in touch with the British consul.	J'insiste pour communiquer avec le consul britannique.	Ich bestehe darauf, mich mit dem britischen Konsul in Verbindung zu setzen.
A pass book (*motor car*	Un carnet de passages en	Ein carnet de passages en

a bordo, nel treno, alla frontiera, a Parigi?	equipaje a bordo, en el tren, en la frontera, en Paris?	boord, in de trein aan de grens, in Parijs, onderzocht?
Dov'è la dogana? Dove debbo portare il bagaglio per la visita?	¿Dónde está el despacho de aduana? ¿Adónde debo llevar mi equipaje para ser examinado?	Waar is het douane- kantoor? Waar moet ik mijn bagage laten onderzoeken?
◀Questa è la mia valigia. Non ho nulla da dichiarare.	Esta valija es mía. No tengo nada que de- clarar.	Deze tas is van mij. Ik heb niets aan te geven.
Io credo che non ho nulla da dichiarare.	No creo tener nada que declarar.	Ik geloof niet, dat ik iets aan te geven heb.
Non per quanto io sappia.	Por lo que yo sepa, no.	Voor zover ik weet niet.
Io ho alcuni sigari, alcune sigarette, un po' di tabacco.	Tengo algunos puros, unos cuantos cigarrillos, un poco de tabaco.	Ik heb wat sigaren, een paar sigaretten, een beetje tabak.
◀È soggetto a dazio, esente da dazio? Si paga per questo il dazio, una tassa ad valorem?	¿Paga esto derechos? ¿Es franco de derechos? ¿Paga eso derechos, un impuesto ad valorem?	Is dit aan invoerrechten onderhevig, vrij van in- voerrechten? Worden daarvoor invoerrechten betaald, ad valorem invoerrechten betaald?
Tutti questi effetti sono stati usati.	Todos estos artículos son usados.	Dit zijn allemaal ge- dragen kleren.
È per solo mio uso per- sonale.	Es para [mi] uso propio únicamente.	Het is uitsluitend voor mijn eigen gebruik.
Questo è tutto che ho.	Es todo lo que tengo.	Dit is alles wat ik heb.
Posso portare via il mio bagaglio?	¿Puedo llevarme mi equi- paje?	Kan ik mijn bagage weghalen?
◀Vuole esaminare il mio passaporto, il mio foglio d'identità?	¿Desea usted examinar mi pasaporte, mi tarjeta de identidad?	Wilt U mijn paspoort, mijn identiteitskaart, onderzoeken?
È necessario un visto?	¿Es necesario un visado?	Is er een visum nodig?
Dove debbo rivolgermi per il visto turistico?	¿Dónde debo ir para pedir un visado de turista?	Waar kan ik een toeris- tenvisum aanvragen?
Dov'è l'ufficio per il visto dei passaporti?	¿Dónde se hace el visado de pasaportes?	Waar worden de pas- poorten gevisserd?
Prego di restituirmi il passaporto.	Haga el favor de devol- verme mi pasaporte.	Geef mij mijn paspoort terug als 't U belieft.
Quanto tempo posso rima- nere in questo paese senza alcuna formalità?	¿Por cuánto tiempo puedo permanecer en este país sin tener que cumplir ninguna formalidad?	Hoe lang kan ik in dit land vertoeven zonder enige formaliteit?
◀Io sono suddito britannico.	Soy súbdito inglés.	Ik ben een Brits onder- daan.
Io sono nativo di terri- torio britannico oltre- mare.	Soy natural de un terri- torio británico de ultramar.	Ik stam uit een overzees Brits gebied.
Sapete dirmi dov'è il consolato britannico?	¿Puede usted indicarme en donde está el consulado británico?	Kunt U mij zeggen waar het Brits consulaat is?
Io insisto di essere messo in comunicazione con il console britannico.	Insisto en comunicar con el cónsul británico.	Ik sta erop met de Britse consul in verbinding te treden.
Un libretto per i transiti	Una libreta de paso de	Een triptiekenboek.

at customs).	douane.	douane.
A customs pass [sheet] *or* A triptyque : A pass sheet is made up of three leaves : a counterfoil, an importation voucher, and an exportation voucher.	Un triptyque *ou* Un carnet-souche de trois feuilles : Le triptyque se compose de trois volants : une souche, un volant d'entrée, et un volant de sortie.	Eine Grenzkarte *oder* Ein Triptik : Das Triptik besteht aus drei Teilen : einem Stammblatt, einem Einfuhrblatt, und einem Ausfuhrblatt.
My car is registered in Great Britain. Here are my national driving papers. Please give me a special permit valid for ten, twenty, days, one month, three months.	Ma voiture est immatriculée en Grande-Bretagne. Voici mes pièces de circulation nationales. Veuillez me donner un laissez-passer spécial valable pour dix, vingt, jours, un mois, trois mois.	Mein Auto ist in Groß-Britannien eingetragen. Hier ist der Führerschein meines Landes. Geben Sie mir bitte eine Sondererlaubnis für zehn, zwanzig, Tage, einen Monat, drei Monate.
Are my papers in order, ready ?	Mes papiers sont-ils en règle, prêts ?	Sind meine Papiere in Ordnung, fertig ?

ROAD TRAVEL

including Motoring, Cycling, Public Conveyances, Tours, Walking, and Camping

VOYAGES SUR ROUTES

REISEN AUF DER LANDSTRASSE

The road

La route

Die Straße

A road, A way. To go to . . by road.	Une route, Un chemin. Aller à . . par la route.	Eine Straße, Ein Weg. Auf der Landstraße nach . . fahren *oder* gehen.
Is there a carriage road from here to . . ? Is the road in good condition ? Is the road fit for traffic, practicable for cycles, for cars ? Which is the best road ?	Y a-t-il une route carrossable d'ici à . . ? La route est-elle en bon état [de viabilité] ? La route est-elle viable, praticable pour les bicyclettes, pour les autos ? Quelle est la meilleure route ?	Gibt es eine Fahrstraße von hier nach . . ? Ist die Straße in gutem Zustand ? Ist die Straße fahrbar, fahrbar für Räder, für Autos ? Welches ist die beste Straße ?
Which is the way to the station ? Can you direct me to the station, direct me to the town hall ?	Quel est le chemin qui conduit à la gare ? Pouvez-vous m'indiquer le chemin de la gare, m'indiquer le chemin pour aller à l'hôtel de ville ?	Welches ist der Weg nach dem Bahnhof ? Können Sie mir den Weg nach dem Bahnhof zeigen, nach dem Rathaus zeigen ?
Which is the shortest way to . . ? Which way did they go ?	Quel est le [chemin le] plus court pour aller à . . ? Quelle direction ont-ils prise ?	Welches ist der kürzeste Weg nach . . ? Welchen Weg sind sie gegangen ?
Is there a direct road from here to . . ? How far are we from the town ? Is it a long way	Y a-t-il une route directe d'ici à . . ? À quelle distance sommes-nous de la ville ? Y	Gibt es eine direkte Straße von hier nach . . ? Wie weit sind wir von der Stadt ? Ist es weit von

doganali.	aduana (para automóvil).	
◄ Una carta di confine o Un trittico [in doganale]: Il trittico è formato da tre volantini : una matrice, un foglietto di entrata, ed un foglietto di uscita.	Un tríptico o Un librillo de tres hojas : El tríptico se compone de tres hojas : un talón, un resguardo de entrada, y otro de salida.	Een triptiek: Een triptiek bestaat uit drie bladen: een souche, een invoerbewijs, en een uitvoerbewijs.
La mia automobile è registrata in Gran Bretagna. Ecco la mia licenza (o il mio permesso) per la circolazione nazionale. La prego di darmi un lascia-passare valido per dieci, venti, giorni, un mese, tre mesi.	Mi automóvil está matriculado en la Gran Bretaña. Aquí tiene usted mis documentos nacionales de circulación. Haga el favor de otorgarme un permiso especial valedero por diez, veinte, días, un mes, tres meses.	Mijn wagen is in Groot-Brittannië ingeschreven. Hier zijn mijn nationale [auto] papieren. Wilt U me een speciale passavant geven, geldig voor tien, twintig, dagen een maand, drie maanden.
Sono le mie carte in regola, pronte ?	¿ Están en regla, Están listos, mis papeles ?	Zijn mijn papieren in orde, klaar?

VIAGGI SU STRADE	VIAJES POR CARRETERA	REIZEN OP DE WEG
La strada	**El camino**	**De weg**
Una strada, Una via.	Una carretera, Un camino.	Een weg.
Andare a .. per strada carrozzabile.	Ir a .. por carretera.	Over de weg naar .. gaan.
◄ C'è una strada carrozzabile da qui fino a .. ?	¿ Hay una carretera desde aquí hasta . ?	Is er een rijweg van hier naar ..?..
È la strada in buono stato ? È la strada adatta per il traffico, è praticabile per le biciclette, per le automobili ? Qual'è la strada migliore ?	¿ Está la carretera en buen estado ? ¿ Está servible para tráfico, viable para bicicletas, para automóviles ? ¿ Cuál es la mejor carretera ?	Verkeert de weg in goede staat. Is de weg berijdbaar, begaanbaar voor fietsen, voor auto's? Wat is de beste weg?
Qual'è la strada per la stazione ? Potete indicarmi la via che porta alla stazione, indicarmi la via che porta al municipio ?	¿ Cuál es el camino de la estación ? ¿ Puede usted dirigirme hacia la estación, indicarme en que dirección está el ayuntamiento ?	Wat is de weg naar het station? Kunt U mij de weg naar het station wijzen, de weg naar het stadhuis wijzen?
Qual'è la via più corta per andare a .. ?	¿ Cuál es el camino más corto para .. ?	Wat is de kortste weg? naar ..?
Quale via hanno essi preso ?	¿ Qué dirección tomaron ?	Welke kant zijn zij opgegaan?
◄ C'è una strada diretta da qui fino a .. ?	¿ Hay camino directo desde aquí hasta ..?	Is er een directe weg van hier naar ..?
Qual'è la distanza da qui alla città? È un lungo	¿ A qué distancia estamos de la población ? ¿ Está	Hoever is het naar de stad? Is het ver van

from here? Are we half-way?	a-t-il une longue course d'ici là? Sommes-nous à moitié chemin?	hier? Haben wir die Hälfte hinter uns?
How far is the cathedral [from here]?	Combien y a-t-il d'ici à la cathédrale?	Wie weit ist der Dom?
I have lost my way. Should I turn back? Can you put me [back] on the right road to ..?	J'ai perdu mon chemin. Dois-je rebrousser chemin? Pouvez-vous me remettre sur la bonne route pour ..?	Ich habe mich verirrt. Soll ich umkehren? Können Sie mir den richtigen Weg nach .. zeigen?
Have you [got] a [road] map? Could I have a look at it for a few moments?	Avez-vous une carte (routière)? Pourrais-je la regarder pour quelques instants?	Haben Sie eine Straßenkarte? Kann ich sie mir einen Augenblick ansehen?
Where does this road lead to? Does this street lead to the old market?	Où conduit cette route? Est-ce que cette rue mène au vieux marché?	Wohin führt diese Straße? Führt diese Straße nach dem alten Markt?
Must I keep to the right or to the left?	Dois-je tenir la droite ou la gauche?	Muß ich mich links oder rechts halten?
Should I bear [to the] right?	Dois-je prendre à droite?	Soll ich rechts herunter gehen?
Must I, we, turn to the right or left, take the next turning to the right, to the left, or go (or keep) straight on?	Faut-il tourner à droite ou à gauche, prendre la première (street) rue, la première (road) route, à droite, à gauche, ou aller tout droit?	Muß ich, Müssen wir, nach rechts oder links einbiegen, die nächste Querstraße rechts herunter gehen, links herunter gehen, oder geradeaus gehen?
A fork (road, etc.). Should I fork right?	Une bifurcation. Dois-je bifurquer à droite?	Eine Gabelung. Soll ich rechts abbiegen?
Is there a sign post (or a finger post) a little farther on, at the crossroads?	Y a-t-il un poteau indicateur un peu plus loin, à la croisée des chemins?	Gibt es ein Stück weiter einen Wegweiser? Ist ein Wegweiser an der Straßenkreuzung?
The roadside. The verge or The side path.	Le bord de la route. L'accotement.	Der Straßenrand. Der Grünstreifen.
The road[way].	La chaussée.	Die Chaussee.
An arterial road.	Une route nationale de grand itinéraire.	Eine Überlandstraße, Eine Fernverkehrsstraße.
An avenue.	Une avenue, Un boulevard, Un cours.	Eine Allee.
A by-pass [road].	Une route d'évitement.	Ein Nebenweg.
A main road.	Un grand chemin, Une grand-route.	Eine Hauptstraße, Eine Hauptverkehrsstraße.
A major road.	Une route de priorité.	Eine Straße erster Ordnung.
A minor road.	Une route secondaire.	Eine Straße zweiter Ordnung.
A motorway or A motor road or A motor highway.	Une autoroute, Une autostrade.	Eine Autostraße.
X. Street.	(La) rue X.	Xstraße.
A bend (in the road).	Un tournant.	Eine Kurve.
A bend (sharp road turn).	Un virage.	Eine scharfe Kurve.
A hairpin bend.	Un virage en épingle a cheveux.	Eine Haarnadelkurve.
A blind alley or A dead end	Une impasse, Un cul-de-sac.	Eine Sackgasse.

tragitto da qui? Siamo a metà strada?	muy lejos? ¿ Estamos a mitad del camino?	hier? Zijn wij halver-wege?
Quanto dista la cattedrale da qui?	¿ A qué distancia [de aquí] está la catedral?	Hoever is de kathedraal van hier?
Io ho smarrito la strada. Debbo tornare indietro? Mi potete rimettere per la diritta via per.. ?	Me he perdido. ¿ Debo regresar? ¿ Puede usted indicarme cuál es la dirección de .. ?	Ik ben de weg kwijt. Moet ik teruggaan? Kunt U me op de goede weg naar .. helpen?
Avete portato con voi una pianta stradale? Posso esaminarla un momento?	¿ Tiene usted un plano de carreteras? ¿ Me deja usted verlo por unos momentos?	Heeft U een wegenkaart? Zou ik er even op kunnen kijken?
◄Dove porta questa strada? Porta questa strada al mercato vecchio?	¿ Adónde conduce este camino? ¿ Va esta calle hacia la antigua plaza?	Waar gaat deze weg heen? Gaat deze straat naar de oude markt?
Devo io prendere la destra o la sinistra?	¿ Debo ir por la derecha o por la izquierda?	Moet ik rechts of links houden?
Devo io prendere a destra?	¿ Debo encaminarme hacia la derecha?	Moet ik rechts afslaan?
Bisogna girare a destra, a sinistra, prendere la pros-sima strada a destra, a sinistra, o andare sempre diritto?	¿ Debo, Debemos, tomar por la derecha o por la izquierda, tomar la próxima vuelta a la derecha, a la izquierda, o seguir hacia delante?	Moet ik, Moeten wij, rechts of links afslaan, de eerste (*street*) straat, de eerste (road) weg, rechts of links afslaan, of rechtuit gaan?
Una biforcazione. Devo prendere a destra?	Una bifurcación. ¿ Debo bifurcar hacia la derecha?	Hier splitst de weg zich. Moet ik rechtsaf?
◄C'è un segnale indicatore un poco più lontano, all'incrocio delle vie?	¿ Hay un poste de guía un poco más allá, en la bifurcación de caminos?	Is er een wegwijzer (*of* een handwijzer) ver-derop; op de twee-sprong, driesprong?
Il margine della strada. Il sentiero laterale [per pedoni].	El borde del camino. La vereda.	De kant van de weg. De berm.
La carreggiata.	La calzada [de la carretera].	Het wegdek.
Una strada nazionale. Un'arteria principale.	Una carretera arterial.	Een rijksweg.
Un viale.	Una avenida.	Een laan.
◄Una strada laterale.	Una ruta de evitación.	Een omgelegde weg.
Una strada maestra.	Una carretera principal, Una granvía.	Een hoofdweg.
Una strada principale.	Una ruta de prioridad.	Een voorrangsweg.
Una strada secondaria.	Una carretera (*o* Una ruta) secundaria.	Een zijweg.
Un'autostrada.	Una ruta para automóviles.	Een autobaan, Een autostrada.
◄La via X.	[La] calle X.	De X.-Straat.
Una curva, Una svolta.	Una curva.	Een bocht.
Una brusca svolta.	Un viraje.	Een scherpe bocht.
Una curva à forcella.	Un viraje [en forma] de horquilla.	Een haarspeldbocht.
Un angiporto.	Un camino sin salida.	Een doodlopende straat.

A concealed turning.	Un virage masqué.	Eine unübersichtliche Kurve.
A hill.	Une côte.	Ein Hügel.
A crossing of streets.	Un croisement de rues.	Eine Straßenkreuzung.
A pedestrian crossing.	Un passage pour piétons.	Ein Übergang für Fußgänger.
A studded crossing.	Un passage clouté, Les clous.	Ein durch Nägel markierter Straßenübergang.
A circus (*roads meeting in city*).	Un rond-point, Un carrefour.	Ein Platz, Ein Straßenknotenpunkt.
A street refuge.	Un refuge pour piétons.	Eine Verkehrsinsel.
The traffic.	La circulation.	Der Verkehr.
The rule of the road.	Le mode de circulation.	Die Verkehrsregelung.
The highway (*or* The road) code.	Le code de la route.	Die Straßenverkehrsordnung.
A policeman.	Un agent [de police], Un gardien de la paix, Un sergent de ville.	Ein Polizist, Ein Schutzmann.
The police station.	Le bureau (*ou* Le poste) de police.	Die Polizei.
The police station (*divisional*).	Le commissariat de police.	Das Polizeirevier.
The traffic police.	La police de la circulation *ou* du roulage.	Die Verkehrspolizei.
A traffic policeman *or* A policeman on point duty.	Un agent pivot.	Ein Verkehrspolizist, Ein Verkehrsschutzmann.
A traffic sign.	Un poteau de signalisation.	Ein Verkehrszeichen.
Drive slowly *or* at walking pace *or* Dead slow (*traffic sign*).	Au pas.	Langsam fahren.
Entry only (*traffic sign*).	Sens unique.	Nur für Einfahrt.
No entry (*traffic sign*).	Sens interdit.	Einfahrt verboten.
No parking (*notice*).	Défense de stationner.	Parken verboten.
No thoroughfare (*vehicles*).	Circulation interdite.	Durchfahrt verboten.
No thoroughfare (*foot passengers*).	Défense de passer, Passage interdit [au public].	Durchgang verboten.
A one-way street, road.	Une rue, Une voie, à sens unique.	Eine Einbahnstraße.
One-way traffic.	La circulation à sens unique.	Einbahnverkehr.
A [traffic] roundabout *or* circus.	Une place à circulation giratoire.	Ein Platz mit Kreisverkehrsregelung.
The traffic lights.	Les signaux lumineux de circulation, Les feux de circulation.	Die Verkehrslichter, Die Verkehrssignale.
Stop, red (*traffic signal*).	Arrêtez, rouge.	Anhalten, rotes Licht.
Caution, amber.	Attention, ambre.	Achtung, gelbes Licht.
Go, green.	Passez, vert.	Freie Fahrt, grünes Licht.
A traffic block.	Un encombrement de voitures.	Eine Verkehrsstauung.
Is it necessary to cross the street, the road, the bridge?	Faut-il traverser la rue, la route, le pont ?	Muß man die Straße, die Brücke, überqueren?
Is there a public con-	Y a-t-il un chalet de	Gibt es hier in der Nähe

◄Una curva occulta.	Una bocacalle oculta.	Een verborgen (of Een blinde) bocht.
Una collina.	Una cuesta.	Een heuvel.
Un incrocio di strade.	Un cruce de calles.	Een kruispunt van straten.
Una strada per pedoni.	Un paso para peatones.	Een oversteekplaats voor voetgangers.
Un passaggio tracciato da chiodi.	Un paso claveteado.	Een spijkerpad.
◄Una rotonda.	Una confluencia de calles.	Een rond plein.
Un salvagente.	Un refugio para peatones	Een vluchtheuvel.
Il traffico.	La circulación, El tráfico.	Het verkeer.
Il regolamento stradale.	El reglamento de circulación.	De verkeersregels.
il codice stradale.	El código de la vía pública.	De verkeersregels.
◄Un poliziotto, Un agente di polizia, Un questurino.	Un vigilante, Un guardia municipal.	Een [politie] agent.
La stazione di polizia.	La prevención.	Het politiebureau.
Il commissariato di polizia.	La comisaria.	Het hoofdbureau van politie.
La polizia di circolazione.	La vigilancia del tráfico.	De verkeerspolitie.
Un agente che regola il traffico.	Un vigilante de tráfico.	Een verkeersagent.
◄Un segnale di traffico.	Un poste (o Un pilar) de guía.	Een verkeersteken.
Andare piano, Andare al passo [d'uomo].	Al paso, A paso lento.	Langzaam [rijden], Voetstaps.
A senso unico.	Entrada de carruajes.	Eenrichtingsverkeer.
Passaggio (o Accesso) interdetto.	Salida de carruajes.	Verboden toegang.
Proibizione di sosta.	Prohibido estacionarse.	Verboden te parkeren.
◄Circolazione interdetta.	Prohibido el paso.	Geen doorgang.
Strada privata.	Prohibido el paso al público.	Geen doorgang.
Una strada a senso unico.	Una calle, Un camino, de dirección única.	Een éénrichtingstraat.
Circolazione in senso unico.	Circulación en dirección única.	Eénrichtingsverkeer.
Una piazza a traffico circolare.	Un redondel, Una plaza de circulación giratoria.	Rondlopend éénrichtingsverkeer.
◄Il semaforo.	Las señales luminosas de la circulación.	De verkeerslichten.
Fermata, rosso.	Pare, rojo.	Halt, rood.
Attenzione, ambra.	Precaución, ámbar.	Waarschuwing, geel.
Avanti, verde.	Adelante, verde.	Ga, groen.
Un traffico ostruito.	Un alto debido a una congestión [de coches].	Een [verkeers]opstopping.
◄Bisogna attraversare la via, la strada, il ponte?	¿Es necesario cruzar la calle, la carretera, el puente?	Moet ik, Moeten wij, de straat, de brug, oversteken?
C'è una ritirata pubblica	¿Hay letrinas públicas por	Is er een openbaar

venience near here? Men (or Gentlemen) [only]. Women (or Ladies) [only].	nécessité près d'ici? Hommes. Dames.	eine Bedürfnisanstalt? Männer oder Herren. Frauen oder Damen.

Types of vehicles	Types de véhicules	Verschiedene Fahrzeuge
An autocycle or A motorized bicycle.	Une bicyclette à moteur, Un vélomoteur.	Ein Fahrrad mit Hilfsmotor.
An automobile.	Une auto[mobile].	Ein Auto[mobil], Ein Kraftwagen.
A [safety] [bi]cycle or A [push] bike.	Une bicyclette, Un vélocipède, Un vélo, Une bécane.	Ein Fahrrad, Ein Sicherheitsfahrrad, Ein Zweirad, Ein Tretfahrrad, Ein Rad.
A car	Une voiture, Une auto[mobile].	Ein Wagen, Ein Auto→[mobil].
A closed car.	Une auto fermée.	Ein geschlossenes Auto.
A fairy cycle.	Une bicyclette pour les tout petits.	Ein Kinder[fahr]rad.
A gentleman's bicycle.	Une bicyclette d'homme.	Ein Herren[fahr]rad.
A lady's bicycle.	Une bicyclette de dame.	Ein Damen[fahr]rad.
A light car.	Une voiture légère.	Ein leichter Wagen. →
A limousine.	Une limousine.	Eine Limousine.
A mail coach (stage).	Une malle[-poste].	Eine Postkutsche.
A motor [bi]cycle or A motor bike.	Une motocyclette, Une moto.	Ein Motorrad.
A motor [car].	Une auto[mobile].	Ein Auto[mobil].
A [motor] coach.	Un [auto]car.	Ein Autobus, Ein Überlandomnibus.
A motor combination	Une motocyclette avec voiturette de côté.	Ein Motorrad mit Beiwagen.
A motor lorry.	Un camion automobile.	Ein Lastauto, Ein Lastkraftwagen.
A motor [omni]bus.	Un autobus.	Ein Autobus, Ein Kraftomnibus.
An open car.	Une auto découverte.	Ein offenes Auto.
A racing car.	Une voiture de course.	Ein Rennwagen. →
A roadster.	Une bicyclette de route, Une [bicyclette] routière.	Ein Tourenrad.
A runabout.	Une voiturette.	Ein Kleinauto, Ein Zweisitzer.
A two-seater, A four-seater, [car].	Une [voiture à] deux, quatre, places.	Ein Zweisitzer, Ein Viersitzer.
A side car.	Une voiturette de côté.	Ein Beiwagen.
A tandem [bicycle].	Un tandem, Une bicyclette tandem.	Ein Tandem. →
A touring car.	Une voiture de tourisme.	Ein Tourenwagen, Ein Sportwagen.
A trailer.	Une remorque, Une baladeuse.	Ein Anhänger.

qui vicino? Uomini. Donne.	aquí cerca? Caballeros. Señoras.	toilet in de nabijheid? Mannen *of* Heren. Vrouwen *of* Dames.
Tipi diversi di veicoli	**Tipos de vehículos**	**Soorten vervoermiddelen**
Una bicicletta con motore ausiliare.	Una bicicleta con motor auxiliar.	Een fiets met hulpmotor.
Un'automobile.	Un auto[móvil].	Een auto[mobiel].
Una bicicletta, Un velocipede.	Una bicicleta, Un velocípedo.	Een rijwiel, Een fiets.
◄Una vettura, Un'automobile, Una macchina.	Un coche, Un auto[móvil].	Een wagen Een auto[mobiel].
Un'automobile chiusa.	Un automóvil cerrado.	Een gesloten auto.
Una biciclettina.	Una bicicleta para niños.	Een kinderfiets.
Una bicicletta per uomo.	Una bicicleta para hombre.	Een herenfiets.
Una bicicletta per signora.	Una bicicleta para señora.	Een damesfiets.
◄Un'automobile leggera.	Un auto ligero.	Een lichte wagen.
Una limousine.	Una limosina.	Een limousine.
Una corriera.	Un coche correo.	Een postkoets.
Una motocicletta.	Una motocicleta.	Een motorfiets.
Un'automobile.	Un auto[móvil].	Een auto[mobiel].
◄Un autobus.	Un autocar.	Een autocar.
Una motocicletta con carozzetta laterale.	Una motocicleta con cochecillo al lado.	Een motorfiets met zijspan.
Un autocarro.	Un autocamión.	Een vrachtauto.
Un autobus.	Un autobús.	Een autobus.
Un'automobile scoperta.	Un auto descubierto.	Een open wagen.
◄Una vettura da corsa.	Un coche de carreras.	Een race-auto.
Una bicicletta robusta da turismo.	Una bicicleta de turismo.	Een reisfiets.
Una vetturetta.	Un cochecito.	Een toerwagentje.
Una vettura a due posti, a quattro posti.	Un coche de dos asientos, de cuatro asientos.	Een twoseater *of* Een tweepersoonsauto, Een vierpersoonsauto.
Un carozzetta laterale.	Un cochecillo al lado.	Een zijspan.
◄Un tandem.	Un tándem, Una bicicleta tándem.	Een tandem.
Una vettura da turismo.	Un auto de turismo.	Een reiswagen.
Un carro rimorchiato.	Un remolque.	Een aanhangwagen.

Motoring	L'automobilisme	Autofahren
(*See also* **The garage**, *pp.* 58-65, *and* MECHANICAL AND ELECTRICAL TERMS, *pp.* 80-105.)		
To motor.	Aller en auto[mobile].	Auto fahren.
A motorist.	Un(e) automobiliste.	Ein(e) Autofahrer(in).
A motor cyclist.	Un(e) motocycliste.	Ein(e) Motorradfahrer(in), Ein(e) K[raft]radfahrer-(in).
Driving (*a conveyance*).	La conduite.	Fahren.
A driving licence.	Un permis de conduire.	Ein Führerschein.
The driving licence fee.	La taxe de circulation.	Die Gebühr für den Führerschein.
A car licence.	Un permis de circulation.	Eine Zulassungsbescheinigung.
The number plate (*car*).	La plaque de police, La plaque matricule, La plaque d'immatriculation.	Das Nummernschild.
An international certificate for motor vehicle. (*See also* CUSTOMS AND PASSPORTS, *pp.* 42-45.)	Un certificat international pour automobile.	Ein internationaler Fahrtausweis.
To drive a car.	Conduire une auto.	Einen Wagen fahren.
Can you drive? Are you going to take the wheel? Does he drive well? *or* Is he a good driver?	Savez-vous conduire? Allez-vous prendre le volant? Est-ce qu'il conduit bien?	Können Sie Auto fahren? Werden Sie am Steuer sitzen? Fährt er gut?
To tune [up] the engine.	Régler le moteur.	Den Motor einstellen.
Starting.	La mise en marche, Le démarrage.	Starten, In Gang bringen, Anlassen.
To start [up] the engine.	Démarrer le moteur.	Den Motor anlassen.
To let in the clutch.	Embrayer.	Einkuppeln.
To declutch.	Débrayer.	Auskuppeln.
To shut off the engine.	Couper le moteur.	Den Motor abstellen.
To drive in first (*or* low) (*or* bottom) gear, in second gear, in third (*or sometimes* top) gear, in fourth (*or* top) gear.	Filer en première [vitesse], en deuxième [vitesse], en troisième [vitesse], en quatrième [vitesse].	Im ersten, zweiten, dritten, vierten, Gang fahren.
To change into second gear.	Passer en deuxième [vitesse].	In den zweiten Gang umschalten.
To put the lever into neutral.	Mettre le levier au point mort.	Den Gangschalthebel auf Leerlauf stellen.
To step (*or* To tread) on the gas (*open the throttle*).	Ouvrir (*ou* Mettre) les gaz, Écraser l'accélérateur.	Gas geben, Auf den Gashebel treten.
To go for a motor run *or* a car ride.	Faire une promenade en auto.	Eine Autofahrt machen.

L'automobilismo	El automovilismo	Automobilisme
Andare in automobile.	Andar en automóvil.	Autorijden.
Un automobilista, (feminine) Un'automobilista.	Un(a) automovilista.	Een autorijder, (feminine) Een autorijdster.
◄Un(a) motociclista.	Un(a) motociclista.	Een motorrijder, Een motorrijdster.
La condotta.	La conducción, El manejo [de coches, etc.]	Het autorijden.
La patente di abilitazione.	Un permiso de conducción.	Een rijbewijs.
La tassa di patente di abilitazione.	El impuesto de circulación.	De rijbewijs leges.
Una licenza di circolazione.	Una matrícula.	Een kentekenbewijs.
◄La targa di riconoscimento.	La placa de la matrícula.	De nummerplaat.
Un certificato internazionale di circolazione.	Un certificado internacional para automóvil.	Een internationaal rijbewijs.
Condurre un'automobile.	Conducir un automóvil.	Chaufferen.
Puoi guidare (o condurre) un'automobile? Vi mettete voi al volante? Conduce esso bene l'automobile? o È un buon automobilista?	¿Sabe usted conducir? ¿Va usted a tomar el volante? ¿Sabe conducir bien?	Kunt U chaufferen? Neemt U het stuur? Chauffeert hij goed?
Regolare il motore.	Poner a punto el motor.	De motor afstellen.
◄La messa in marcia, L'avviamento.	Ponerse en marcha.	Het starten.
Mettere in moto il motore.	Poner el motor en marcha.	De motor starten.
Innestare il giunto.	Embragar.	Dekoppeling inschakelen.
Disinnestare il giunto.	Desembragar.	Debrayeren.
Spegnere il motore.	Parar el motor.	De motor afsluiten.
◄Andare (o Mettere) in prima [velocità], in seconda [velocità], in terza [velocità], in quarta [velocità].	Conducir en primera [marcha], en segunda [marcha], en tercera [marcha], en cuarta o en directa.	In de eerste de tweede, de derde, de vierde, versnelling rijden.
Scambio di velocità in seconda.	Cambiar a segunda marcha.	In de tweede versnelling overschakelen.
Mettere la leva in neutro.	Poner la palanca en neutro.	De versnellings[hef]boom in neutrale stand brengen.
Spingere l'acceleratore.	Oprimir el acelerador, Abrir el difusor.	Gas geven, Op het gaspedaal trappen.
Fare un giro in automobile.	Dar un paseo en automóvil.	Een [auto]ritje maken.

To drive someone home.	Ramener quelqu'un chez lui en voiture.	Jemanden nach Hause fahren.
I will give you a lift [in my car].	Je vous ferai monter [en voiture] avec moi.	Ich nehme Sie [in meinem Auto] mit.
A chauffeur or A driver, A chauffeuse or A driver.	Un chauffeur, Une chauffeuse.	Ein Chauffeur, Ein(e) Autofahrer(in).
An owner-driver.	Un propriétaire-conducteur, Une propriétaire-conductrice.	Ein Herrnfahrer.
To exceed the speed limit.	Dépasser la vitesse légale ou la vitesse réglementaire.	Die zulässige Geschwindigkeit überschreiten.
A road hog.	Un chauffard, Un écraseur.	Ein wilder Fahrer, Ein Kilometerfresser.
Reckless driving.	La conduite à tombeau ouvert, La conduite en chauffard.	Rücksichtsloses (oder Leichtsinniges) Fahren.
A speed (or A police) trap.	Une zone du contrôle de vitesse.	Eine Polizeifalle.
To overtake (or To pass) another car.	[Dé]passer (ou Doubler) (ou Croiser) une autre voiture.	Ein anderes Auto überholen oder einholen oder vorbeifahren.
To hoot.	Corner.	Hupen.
Sound [your] horn !	Cornez !	Hupen Sie !
To cut in (on the road).	Couper.	Schneiden.
I will pull to one side.	Je vais me garer.	Ich werde zur Seite fahren oder Ich werde ausbiegen.
To turn round in a street.	Virer dans une rue.	Auf einer Straße [um]wenden.
Is the road hilly ?	La route est-elle accidentée ? Le chemin est-il à fortes pentes ?	Ist die Straße hüglig oder uneben ?
To climb a hill (of person or machine).	Gravir une côte.	(person) Einen Hügel heraufsteigen. (machine) Einen Hügel herauffahren.
The steering.	La direction.	Das Lenken, Das Steuern.
To apply (or To put on) the brake.	Freiner, Serrer les freins.	Bremsen, Die Bremsen anziehen.
Braking.	Le freinage.	Das Bremsen.
Brakes on.	Freins bloqués.	Mit angezogenen Bremsen.
To skid.	Patiner, Déraper.	Schleudern.
To side-slip.	Déraper.	Schlingern, Schlittern.
To accelerate.	Accélérer.	Beschleunigen.
The speed.	La vitesse, L'allure.	Die Geschwindigkeit.
To reverse.	Faire marche arrière.	Rückwärts fahren.
To dim the headlights.	Mettre les phares en veilleuse, Baisser les phares, Se mettre en code.	Die Scheinwerfer abblenden.
Dimmed lights.	L'éclairage code.	Abgeblendete Scheinwerfer.
To dip the headlights.	Faire basculer (ou Baisser) les phares.	Die Scheinwerfer nach unten richten.

Riportare qualcuno in vettura a casa.	Llevar una persona a su casa en [el] auto.	Iemand naar huis rijden.
Vi farò salire sulla mia automobile.	Le llevaré en el auto.	Ik zal U mee laten rijden.
Un autista, (feminine) Un'autista, Un(a) conducente.	Un chofer, Un conductor, Una conductora.	Een chauffeur, Een chauffeuse.
Un proprietario conducente, Una proprietaria conducente.	Un conductor dueño.	Een eigenaar-chauffeur, Een eigenaar-chauffeuse.
Eccedere la velocità permessa.	Exceder la velocidad permitida.	De snelheidsgrens overschrijden.
Un conducente sconsiderato.	Un automovilista descortés en el uso de la carretera.	Een kilometervreter.
Una condotta incurante.	Conducción peligrosa.	Het roekeloos rijden.
Una zona del controllo di velocità.	Una trampa de la policía contra velocidad excesiva.	Een gecontroleerde snelheidszone.
Raggiungere (o Oltrepassare) un'altra vettura.	Alcanzar (o Pasar) (o Adelantar) otro vehículo.	Een andere auto inhalen of passeren.
Suonare la tromba.	Sonar la bocina.	Toeteren.
Suonate la tromba !	¡ Suene la bocina !	Toeter!
Tagliare.	Intercalarse.	Snijden.
Io mi porterò in un lato.	Tiraré hacia un lado.	Ik zal langs de kant rijden of ik zal keren.
Girare in una strada.	Dar la vuelta en una calle.	In de straat omdraaien of (om)keren.
La strada è in salita ? La strada è accidentata ?	¿ Es muy accidentada la carretera ?	Is de weg heuvelachtig ?
Prendere una salita.	Subir una cuesta.	Een heuvel beklimmen.
La direzione.	La dirección.	Het sturen.
Frenare, Mettere i freni.	Frenar, Aplicar el freno.	Remmen.
Il frenaggio.	El frenaje.	Het remmen.
Freni chiusi.	Frenos fijos.	Remmen geblokkeerd.
Slittare.	Patinar o Deslizar	Slippen.
Slittare lateralmente.	Patinar de costado.	Wegslippen.
Accelerare.	Acelerar.	Gas geven.
La velocità.	La velocidad.	De snelheid.
Cambiare la marcia, Far marcia indietro.	Ir en marcha atrás, Ir en contramarcha.	Achteruitrijden.
Abbassare i fari.	Reducir la intensidad luminosa de los faros.	De koplampen dimmen.
Le luci abbassate o I fari abbassati.	Reducción de la intensidad luminosa de los faros.	Gedimde lampen.
Abbassare i fari.	Enfocar los faros hacia abajo.	De koplampen laten zakken.

Lighting-up time.	L'heure d'allumer.	Die Zeit nach Eintritt der Dunkelheit.
To back into a garage.	Entrer dans un garage en marche arrière.	Im Rückwärtsgang in die Garage fahren.
A car park, A parking place.	Un parc à voitures *ou* pour autos, Un parc de stationnement.	Ein Wagenpark, Ein Park-→ platz.
To park a car.	Parquer une auto.	Einen Wagen parken.
A car-park attendant.	Un gardien d'autos.	Ein Parkplatzaufseher.

Cycling	**Le cyclisme**	**Radfahren** *oder* **Radeln**
(*See also* **The garage**, *pp.* 58-65, *and* MECHANICAL AND ELECTRICAL TERMS, *pp.* 80-105.)		
To go in for cycling.	Faire de la bicyclette *ou* du vélo.	Radfahren als Sport betreiben.
To ride a motor cycle. He is a good rider.	Conduire une motocyclette. Il est bon motocycliste.	Ein Motorrad fahren. Er ist ein guter Motorradfahrer.
To cycle *or* To pedal *or* To bike.	Aller à bicyclette, Pédaler, Aller à vélo *ou* à bécane.	Radfahren, Radeln. →
Cycling shoes.	Des souliers cyclistes.	Radfahrschuhe.
Is there a cycle shed here?	Y a-t-il ici un garage pour bicyclettes?	Gibt es hier einen Radfahrschuppen?
A [bi]cyclist.	Un(e) [bi]cycliste.	Ein(e) Radfahrer(in), Ein(e) Radler(in).
A pillion [seat].	Un siège arrière, Un tansad.	Ein Soziussitz, Ein Tandemsitz.
A pillion rider.	Un passager, Une passagère, de tan-sad.	Ein(e) Mitfahrer(in),→ Ein(e) Soziusfahrer(in).
To back-pedal.	Contre-pédaler, Rétropédaler, Pédaler en rétro.	Rückwärts treten.
A scorcher.	Un pédard.	Ein rücksichtsloser Radfahrer.
To have a spill.	Ramasser une pelle.	Vom Rad fallen.
Can you lend me your pump, a spanner?	Pouvez-vous me prêter votre pompe, une clef?	Können Sie mir Ihre Radfahrpumpe, einen Schraubenschlüssel, leihen?
Is there a shop here which sells spare parts for bicycles?	Y a-t-il ici un magasin qui vend des pièces de rechange pour bicyclettes?	Gibt es hier ein Geschäft,→ wo man Ersatzteile für Räder bekommt?

L'ora d'accendere le luci.	Hora de encender los faros.	De tijd voor het aansteken der lichten, Het invallen der duisternis.
Entrare nell'autorimessa in retromarcia.	Entrar en garaje en contramarcha.	Een garage achteruit binnenrijden.
◄Un posteggio per automobile.	Un parque para automóviles, Un parque de estacionamiento.	Een parkeerterrein.
Parcare un'automobile.	Estacionar un auto[móvil].	Een auto parkeren.
Un custode d'automobili.	Un empleado del parque de estacionamiento.	Een autobewaker.

Ciclismo   El ciclismo   Fietsen

Andare in bicicletta.	Dedicarse al ciclismo.	Fietsen.
Guidare una motocicletta. È un abile motociclista.	Montar en motocicleta. [Él] sabe montar bien.	(Op een) motorfiets rijden. Hij is een goede motorrijder.
◄Andare in bicicletta, Pedalare.	Montar (o Andar) en bicicleta, Pedalear.	Fietsen, Trappen.
Scarpe da ciclista.	Zapatos para ciclista.	Fietsschoenen.
C'è qui una rimessa per biciclette?	¿Hay aquí un garaje (o un depósito) para bicicletas?	Is er hier een fietsenbewaarplants?
Un(a) ciclista.	Un(a) ciclista.	Een fietser Een wielrijder.
Un sedile (o Una sella) di tandem.	Un asiento (o Una silla) de tándem, Una grupera.	Een duo.
◄Un(a) passeggiere al sedile di tandem.	Un pasajero de grupera.	Een duorijder (feminine) Een duorijdster.
Contropedalare.	Frenar con los pedales, Contrapedalear.	Achteruittrappen.
Un pedalista audace.	Un desenfrenado.	Bergkilometervreter.
Rovesciarsi, Cascare.	Sufrir una caida, Pegar un costalazo.	Een tuimeling maken, Vallen.
Potete voi prestarmi la vostra pompa, una chiave per dadi?	¿Quiere [usted] prestarme su bomba de neumáticos, una llave de tuercas?	Kunt U me Uw pomp, een sleutel, lenen?
◄C'è qui un negozio che venda pezzi di ricambio per biciclette?	¿Hay por aquí una tienda que vende piezas de repuesto para bicicletas?	Is er een winkel hier, die fietsonderdelen verkoopt?

The garage	Le garage	Die Garage
(*See also* MECHANICAL AND ELECTRICAL TERMS, *pp.* 80-105.)		
A garage.	Un garage [pour auto(s)], Un auto-garage.	Eine Garage.
Where is there a garage, a good service station ?	Où y a-t-il un garage, une bonne station de service *ou* agence stockiste ?	Wo ist eine Garage, eine gute Tankstelle mit Autodienst ?
A garage keeper *or* owner.	Un garagiste.	Ein Garagenverwalter, Ein Garagenbesitzer.
To garage a car.	Garer une auto.	Ein Auto in die Garage stellen.
To put up a car for the night.	Loger une auto pour la nuit.	Ein Auto für eine Nacht einstellen.
A mechanic.	Un mécanicien.	Ein Mechaniker.
An inspection pit.	Une fosse à visiter.	Ein Garagenschacht.
A garage repair ramp.	Un ponton de visite, Un pont élévateur.	Eine Garagenplattform.
What is the matter ?	Qu'est-ce qu'il y a ?	Was ist mit dem Wagen los ?
I have had a breakdown. My car has overturned in a ditch along the road. Can you send someone ? Will you send for my car immediately. I am in a hurry. I am not in much of a hurry.	J'ai eu une panne. Mon auto s'est renversée dans un fossé le long de la route. Pouvez-vous envoyer quelqu'un ? Voulez-vous faire prendre mon auto immédiatement ? Je suis très pressé. Je ne suis pas très pressé.	Ich habe eine Panne gehabt. Mein Auto hat sich in einem Straßengraben überschlagen. Können Sie jemand hinschicken ? Würden Sie meinen Wagen bitte sofort abholen lassen. Ich bin in großer Eile. Ich habe keine große Eile.
My car has received a bad shock in a head-on collision.	Mon auto a reçu une rude secousse dans une rencontre de front.	Mein Auto ist durch einen direkten Zusammenstoß schlimm zugerichtet worden.
A breakdown car *or* lorry *or* tender.	Une dépanneuse.	Ein Abschleppauto.
A breakdown gang.	Une équipe de secours *ou* de dépannage.	Abschlepp-Personal.
Can you take my car in tow ? How much will you charge ?	Pouvez-vous prendre mon auto à la remorque ? Combien demandez-vous ?	Können Sie meinen Wagen abschleppen ? Was nehmen Sie dafür ?
A tow rope.	Un câble de remorque.	Ein Schleppseil.
The brakes are out of order. Will you please adjust them ?	Les freins sont déréglés. Voulez-vous les mettre au point ?	Die Bremsen sind defekt. Würden Sie sie bitte in Ordnung bringen ?
A rod is bent. Please straighten it.	Une tige est faussée. Veuillez la redresser.	Eine Stange ist verbogen. Wollen Sie sie bitte ausrichten.
The brake cable is broken. Please replace it.	Le câble du frein est cassé. Veuillez le remplacer.	Der Bremskabel ist zerbrochen. Wollen Sie bitte einen Neuen einsetzen.

L'autorimessa, Il garage	El garaje	De garage
Un'autorimessa, Un garage.	Un garaje.	Een garage.
Dove si trova un garage, una buona stazione di servizio ?	¿Dónde hay un garaje, un buen puesto de servicio ?	Waar is een garage, een goed service station?
Un proprietario di autorimessa.	Un propietario de garaje.	Een garagehouder.
Rimettere un'automobile nel garage.	Depositar un auto en garaje	Een auto stallen.
◄Rimettere un'automobile per la notte.	Alojar (o Depositar) un auto por la noche.	Een auto voor de nacht stallen.
Un meccanico.	Un mecánico.	Een monteur.
Una fossa di ispezionamento.	Un foso de inspección.	Een inspectie kuil.
Una piattaforma ascensore per accesso.	Una plataforma ascensora para acceso.	Een smeerbrug.
Che cosa è successo ?	¿ Qué pasa ?	Wat is er aan de hand?
◄Io ho avuto una panna o un guasto. La mia automobile si è rovesciata in un fosso lungo la strada. Mi potete mandare qualcuno ? Volete mandare qualcuno a prendere la mia automobile immediatamente ? Io ho fretta. Io non ho molta fretta.	He sufrido una pana. Se me volcó el auto en una zanja en el camino. ¿ Puede usted mandarme auxilio ? ¿ Quiere usted mandar recoger mi auto inmediatamente ? Tengo prisa. No tengo gran prisa.	Ik heb panne gehad. Mijn auto is in een greppel over de kop geslagen. Kunt U iemand sturen ? Wilt U meteen mijn wagen laten halen. Ik heb haast. Ik heb niet veel haast.
La mia automobile ha ricevuto una forte scossa in seguito a uno scontro.	Mi auto ha sufrido una fuerte sacudida debido a un choque de frente.	Mijn auto heeft een lelijke klap gehad in een botsing met een tegenligger.
Un'automobile per guasti.	Un camión de reparaciones.	Een herstelwagen.
Una squadra di soccorso.	Un equipo de socorro.	Een herstelploeg.
Potete prendere a rimorchio la mia automobile ? Che prezzo mi domandate ?	¿ Puede usted remolcarme el auto ? ¿ Cuánto me cobrará usted ?	Kunt U mijn wagen slepen ? Hoeveel vraagt U daarvoor?
◄Una corda da rimorchio.	Un cable de remolcar.	Een sleeptouw.
I freni sono guasti. Volete regolarli ?	Los frenos están defectuosos. ¿ Quiere usted arreglármelos ?	De remmen zijn niet in orde. Wilt U ze nakijken.
Una verga è piegata. Per favore, raddrizzatela.	Se me ha torcido una barra. ¿ Quiere usted enderezármela ?	Er is een stang verbogen. Wilt U hem rechtbuigen.
La fune del freno si è rotta. Per favore sostituitela.	Se me ha partido el cable del freno. Haga el favor de reemplazármelo.	De remkabel is gebroken. Wilt U die vervangen.

The wheel is buckled.	La roue est voilée.	Das Rad ist verbogen.
Can you locate the rattling?	Pouvez-vous localiser le ferraillement ?	Können Sie feststellen, wo das Klappern herkommt?
There is [a] vibration. This rod vibrates.	Il y a [une] trépidation. Cette tige tremble.	Etwas klappert. Diese Stange zittert.
There is a fault in the brake gear. Will you please rectify it ?	Il y a un défaut dans la timonerie des freins. Voulez-vous le corriger ?	Die Bremsvorrichtung hat einen Defekt. Wollen Sie sie bitte reparieren?
This part does not work [well].	Cette pièce ne fonctionne pas [bien].	Dieser Teil funktioniert nicht [gut].
I want this nut tightened or screwed up.	Je veux faire serrer cet écrou.	Ich möchte diese Schraubenmutter angezogen haben.
Can you loosen this screw, unscrew this nut ?	Pouvez-vous desserrer cette vis, desserrer (ou dévisser) cet écrou ?	Können Sie diese Schraube lockern, diese Schraubenmutter aufschrauben?
I have engine trouble or engine failure.	J'ai une panne de moteur.	Ich habe eine Motorpanne.
There is something wrong with the engine, with the works.	Il y a quelque chose qui cloche dans le moteur. Il y a un défaut de fonctionnement.	Mit dem Motor, mit dem Getriebe, ist etwas nicht in Ordnung.
The engine has seized.	Le moteur a grippé.	Der Motor ist festgefressen oder festgebrannt.
The engine is firing (or running) badly. Please examine it.	Le moteur donne mal ou boite. Veuillez l'examiner.	Der Motor zieht schlecht. Wollen Sie ihn bitte durchsehen.
The engine is overheating.	Le moteur chauffe.	Der Motor läuft sich heiß.
To race (of engine).	S'emballer.	Durchgehen.
I have ignition trouble.	J'ai une panne d'allumage.	Die Zündung meines Wagens ist nicht in Ordnung.
There is a short[-circuit]. A circuit has short-circuited or shorted.	Il y a un court-circuit. Un circuit s'est mis en court-circuit ou a court-circuité.	Irgendwo ist ein Kurzschluß. Eine Leitung hat Kurzschluß.
The engine misfires.	Le moteur rate ou a des ratés [d'allumage].	Der Motor hat Fehlzündung.
A plug is faulty. Will you please change it ?	Une bougie est défectueuse. Voulez-vous la changer ?	Eine Zündkerze ist defekt. Wollen Sie sie bitte auswechseln ?
The engine knocks.	Le moteur cogne ou pilonne.	Der Motor klopft oder klappert.
There is pinking in the cylinder.	Il y a un cliquetis dans le cylindre.	Es klingelt im Zylinder.
To decarbonize an engine.	Décarboniser un moteur.	Verbrennungsrückstände aus dem Motor entfernen.
To charge an accumulator.	Charger un accumulateur.	Einen Akkumulator laden.
To dismantle.	Démonter.	Auseinandernehmen.
There is a leak[age] in this pipe.	Il y a une fuite dans ce tuyau.	Dieses Rohr ist undicht.
The tank leaks.	Le réservoir fuit ou perd.	Der Behälter ist undicht.

La ruota si è incurvata.	La rueda está doblada.	Het wiel is verbogen.
◄Potete voi localizzare il tintinnio ?	¿ Puede usted localizar el rechinamiento ?	Kunt U nagaan waar het gerammel vandaan komt?
C'è una vibrazione. Questa verga vibra.	Hay trepidación. Esta varilla trepida o vibra.	Er trilt iets. Deze stang trilt.
C'è un difetto nel comando dei freni. Volete correggerlo ?	Hay un defecto en el mecanismo del freno. ¿ Quiere usted corregírmelo ?	Er is een fout in de rem. Wilt U die herstellen, als 't U belieft?
Questo pezzo non funziona [bene].	Esta pieza no funciona [bien].	Dit onderdeel werkt niet [goed].
Io voglio che questa madrevite sia stretta.	Esta tuerca necesita atornillarse.	Ik wil deze moer vastgeschroefd hebben.
◄Potete svitare questa vite, svitare questa madrevite ?	¿ Puede usted aflojar este tornillo, desatornillar esta tuerca ?	Kunt U deze schroef wat losser maken, deze moer losschroeven?
C'è qualche guaio (o C'è un guasto) nel motore.	Está defectuoso (o Ha fallado) el motor.	Ik heb motorpech.
C'è qualche cosa che va male nel motore, C'è un difetto nel funzionamento.	Ocurre algo con el motor, Hay algún defecto del mecanismo.	Er is iets niet in orde met de motor, met het mecanisme.
Il motore si è grippato.	El motor se ha atollado.	De motor is vastgelopen.
Il motore funziona male. Per favore, esaminatelo.	El motor funciona mal. Haga el favor de examinarlo.	De motor loopt slecht. Wilt U hem nakijken.
◄La macchina si [sopra]riscalda.	El motor está recalentándose.	De motor loopt warm.
Precipitarsi, Scappare, Sfuggire,	Dispararse, Embalarse, Precipitarse, Lanzarse de carrera.	Doorslaan.
L'accensione è difettosa.	El encendido está defectuoso.	Ik heb last met de ontsteking.
C'è un corto circuito. Un circuito ha avuto un corto circuito.	Hay un cortocircuito. Un circuito se ha establecido directamente.	Er is een kortsluiting.
Il motore ha guasti d'accensione.	El motor ratea.	De ontsteking weigert.
◄Una candela è deficiente. Volete cambiarmela ?	Hay un taco defectuoso. ¿ Quiere hacer el favor de cambiarlo ?	Er hapert iets aan een bougie. Wilt U die verwisselen, als 't U belieft?
Il motore batte.	El motor detona.	De motor klopt.
C'è un clicchettio nel cilindro.	Hay retintín en el cilindro.	Het rammelt in de cylinder.
Decarbonizzare un motore.	Descarbonizar un motor.	Een motor ontkolen.
Caricare un accumulatore.	Cargar un acumulador.	Een accu laden.
◄Smontare.	Desmontar.	Demonteren.
Vi è una fuga nel tubo.	Hay una fuga en este tubo.	Er is een lek in deze pijp.
Il serbatoio spande o perde.	El depósito tiene fuga, El depósito gotea.	De tank lekt.

The pipe is stopped up, is sooted up.	Le tuyau est bouché, est encrassé.	Das Rohr ist verstopft, ist verrußt.
The tyre has burst.	Le pneu a éclaté.	Der Reifen ist geplatzt.
There is a puncture in the tyre.	Il y a une crevaison dans le pneu.	Der Reifen hat ein Loch. →
The tyre has punctured.	Le pneu a crevé.	Der Reifen hat ein Loch bekommen.
The tyre is slack. Please inflate it.	Le pneu est dégonflé. Veuillez le gonfler.	Der Reifen hat nicht genug Luft. Wollen Sie ihn bitte aufpumpen.
My tyre pressure should be about .. kilogrammes per square centimetre. (*See table* TYRE PRESSURE, *p.* 269.)	La pression dans mon pneu (*ou* Le gonflage) doit être environ .. kilogrammes par centimètre carré.	Der Druck in meinem Reifen muß etwa .. Kilogramm pro Quadratzentimeter betragen. Der Reifen muß etwa .. Kilogramm pro Quadratzentimeter Druck haben.
To deflate a tyre.	Dégonfler un pneu.	Die Luft aus einem Reifen herauslassen.
To grease. Greasing.	Graisser. Le graissage.	Schmieren. Schmieren. →
To oil. Oiling.	Huiler. L'huilage.	Ölen. Ölen.
To wash [down] a car.	Laver une voiture.	Einen Wagen waschen.
To clean. Cleaning.	Nettoyer. Le nettoyage.	Reinigen. Reinigung.
To mend. Where can I get a bicycle repaired ? Do you do repairs ? Can you repair this, effect a temporary repair, a makeshift repair, carry out the necessary repairs, give me a makeshift ? How long will the repair take ? Can you do it in an hour ?	Raccommoder. Où pourrais-je faire réparer une bicyclette ? Faites-vous des réparations ? Pouvez-vous réparer ceci, faire une réparation provisoire, une réparation de fortune, faire les réparations nécessaires, me donner un dispositif de fortune ? Combien de temps faudra-t-il pour faire la réparation ? Pouvez-vous la faire en une heure ?	Reparieren. Wo kann ich ein Rad reparieren lassen ? Machen Sie Reparaturen ? Können Sie dies reparieren, eine provisorische Reparatur vornehmen, eine Notreparatur vornehmen, die nötigen Reparaturen vornehmen, es mir notdürftig reparieren ? Wie lange wird die Reparatur dauern ? Können Sie es in einer Stunde machen ?
A repairer.	Un réparateur.	Eine Reparaturwerkstatt.
Petrol *or* Motor spirit.	De l'essence.	Benzin, Kraftstoff, Treibstoff.
I have run out of petrol.	J'ai une panne sèche.	Mir ist das Benzin ausgegangen.
Where can I get some petrol ?	Où puis-je me procurer de l'essence ?	Wo kann ich Benzin bekommen ?
How much per five litres is it ? (*See table, p.* 268.)	C'est combien les cinq litres ?	Was kosten fünf Liter ?
To fill up with petrol.	Faire le plein d'essence.	Mit Benzin füllen.
Please fill up the radiator.	Veuillez faire le plein du radiateur.	Füllen Sie bitte den Kühler.
Is the tank full ?	Le réservoir est-il plein ?	Ist der Behälter voll ?

Il tubo è intasato, è ostruito con fuliggine.	El tubo está atascado, está obstruido con hollín.	De pijp is verstopt, met roet verstopt.
Il pneumatico è scoppiato.	El neumático se ha reventado.	De band is gescheurd.
←C'è un buco nel pneumatico.	El neumático tiene un pinchazo.	Er is een lek in de band.
Il pneumatico è lesionato.	Se ha perforado el neumático.	De band is lek gesprongen.
Il pneumatico si è sgonfiato. Per favore, gonfiatelo.	El neumático está flojo. Haga el favor de hincharlo.	De band is slap. Wilt U hem oppompen.
La pressione nel mio pneumatico deve essere di circa . . kilogrammi per centimetro quadrato.	La presión de mi neumático debe ser alrededor de . . . kilógramos por centímetro cuadrado.	Mijn banddruk hoort ongeveer . . kilogram per vierkante centimeter te zijn.
Sgonfiare un pneumatico.	Deshinchar un neumático.	Een band leeg laten lopen.
←Ingrassare. Dare il grasso.	Engrasar. El engrase.	Smeren, Invetten, Het smeren, Het invetten.
Oliare. La lubrificazione ad olio.	Lubri[fi]car. La lubri[fi]cación.	Oliëen. Het oliën.
Lavare un'automobile.	Lavar un auto.	Een auto wassen.
Pulire. La ripulitura.	Limpiar. La limpieza.	Schoonmaken. Het schoonmaken.
Riparare, Raccomodare.	Reparar, Componer.	Repareren, Herstellen.
←Dove potrei far riparare una bicicletta? Fate voi riparazioni? Potete voi riparare questo, fare una riparazione provvisoria, una riparazione alla meglio, fare le riparazioni necessarie, aggiustare alla meglio? Quanto tempo ci vuole per la riparazione? Potete farmela in un' ora?	En dónde me pueden componer una bicicleta? Se encarga usted de reparaciones? Puede usted arreglarme esto, efectuar una compostura provisional, un remiendo transitorio, efectuar las reparaciones necesarias, hacerme un remiendo provisional? Cuánto tiempo tardará en hacerse la reparación? Puede hacerla en una hora?	Waar kan ik een fiets laten repareren? Repareert U fietsen, auto's? Kunt U dit repareren, tijdelijk repareren, provisorisch herstellen, de nodige reparaties uitvoeren, me een tijdelijk hulpmiddel geven? Hoe-lang hebt U voor de reparatie nodig? Kunt U het in een uur doen?
Un riparatore.	Un reparador.	Een reparateur, Een hersteller.
La benzina.	Gasolina.	Benzine.
Sono mancante di benzina.	Se me ha agotado la gasolina.	Ik heb geen benzine meer.
Dove posso procurarmi della benzina?	¿Dónde puedo obtener gasolina?	Waar kan ik benzine krijgen?
←Quanto costano cinque litri?	¿Cuánto valen los cinco litros?	Hoeveel is het per vijf liter?
Rifornirsi di benzina.	Proveerse de gasolina.	Benzine bijvullen.
Per favore, riempite il radiatore.	Haga el favor de llenarme el radiador.	Wilt U de radiator vullen, als 't U belieft.
È il serbatoio pieno?	¿Está lleno el depósito?	Is de tank vol?

The capacity of my tank is . . litres.	La capacité de mon réservoir est de . . litres.	Mein Behälter faßt Liter.
Empty. To empty.	Vide. Vider.	Leer. Leeren.
A petrol supplier.	Un distributeur d'essence.	Ein Benzinhändler.
A petrol pump.	Une pompe à essence.	Eine Benzinpumpe.
A [petrol] filling station.	Un poste d'essence.	Eine Tankstelle.
Do you keep motor car accessories?	Avez-vous des accessoires pour autos?	Führen Sie Zubehörteile für Autos?
I want a new tyre, a new inner tube. Please put one on, put one in.	Il me faut un nouveau pneu, une nouvelle chambre à air. Veuillez en mettre un, en mettre une.	Ich möchte einen neuen Reifen, einen neuen Schlauch. Wollen Sie bitte einen aufziehen.
An agent or A stockist.	Un stockiste.	Ein Händler.
A motor hire service.	Une location d'autos.	Eine Autovermietung.
I want to hire a car for the day.	Je veux louer une auto pour la journée.	Ich möchte ein Auto für den ganzen Tag mieten.
How much is it for the day, by the hour?	Combien est-ce pour la journée, à l'heure?	Was kostet es pro Tag, pro Stunde?
How many seats are there in the car?	Combien de places y a-t-il dans la voiture?	Wieviele Sitze hat das Auto?
How much will you charge for driving me to . . and [for bringing me] back [here]?	Combien prendrez-vous (ou compterez-vous) pour me conduire à . . et me ramener ici?	Was rechnen Sie für die Fahrt nach . . und zurück?

Public conveyances — Les voitures publiques — Öffentliche Verkehrsmittel

A one-horse conveyance.	Une voiture à un cheval.	Ein Einspänner.
A two-horse conveyance or A carriage and pair.	Une voiture à deux chevaux.	Ein Zweispänner.
A hired car. Price according to arrangement.	Une voiture de [grande] remise. Prix à débattre.	Ein Mietsauto. Preis nach Vereinbarung.
A stage coach.	Une diligence.	Eine Postkutsche.
The driver (motor vehicle).	Le chauffeur, La chauffeuse, Le conducteur, La conductrice.	Der Chauffeur, Der Autofahrer, Die Autofahrerin.
The driver (horse carriage).	Le cocher, La cochère, Le conducteur, La conductrice.	Der Kutscher.
The driver (electric tram).	Le wattman.	Der Straßenbahnführer.
A donkey driver.	Un ânier, Une ânière.	Ein(e) Eseltreiber(in).
To engage (or To hire) a conveyance by distance, by the hour.	Prendre une voiture à la course, à l'heure.	Ein Fahrzeug per Kilometer, per Stunde, bezahlen.
I want to go for a drive.	Je veux faire une promenade en voiture.	Ich möchte eine Spazierfahrt machen.
[Drive me] to the station.	[Conduisez-moi] à la gare.	[Fahren Sie mich] nach dem Bahnhof.
Go on! or Drive on! or Go ahead! or Right, away! (start away).	Allez! ou Marchez! ou En avant! ou En route!	Los!

La capacità del mio serbatoio è di . . litri.	La capacidad de mi tanque es de . . litros.	De inhoud van mijn tank is . . liter.
Vuoto, a. Vuotare.	Vacío, a. Vaciar.	Leeg. Ledigen.
◄ Un distributore di benzina.	Un proveedor de gasolina.	Een benzinehandelaar.
Una pompa per benzina.	Una bomba de gasolina.	Een benzinepomp.
Un posto [di] rifornimento [di] benzina.	Un puesto para gasolina.	Een benzinestation.
Avete voi accessori per automobili?	¿Tiene usted accesorios para automóviles?	Heeft U auto-onderdelen?
Io desidero un nuovo pneumatico, una nuova camera d'aria. Per favore, mettetene uno, una.	Necesito un nuevo neumático, una nueva cámara de aire. Haga el favor de colocármelo, a.	Ik heb een nieuwe band nodig, een nieuwe binnenband nodig. Wilt U er een opzetten, als 't U belieft.
◄ Un agente concessionario.	Un agente, Un almacenista.	Een agent.
Il noleggio d'automobili.	Un servicio de autos de alquiler.	Een autoverhuur-inrichting.
Io desidero noleggiare un' automobile per la giornata.	Deseo alquilar un auto por el día.	Ik wil een wagen huren voor de hele dag.
Quanto è per tutta la giornata, all'ora?	¿Qué es el precio por día, por hora?	Hoeveel is het per dag, per uur?
Quanti posti ci sono nella vettura?	¿Cuántos asientos tiene el auto?	Hoeveel plaatsen zijn er in de wagen?
◄ Quanto volete per portarmi a . . e per riportarmi qui?	¿Cuánto me cobra usted por llevarme a . . y volver a traerme aquí?	Hoeveel vraagt U om mij naar . . te rijden, en terug?

Vetture pubbliche	**Vehículos públicos**	**Openbare vervoermiddelen**
Una vettura a un cavallo.	Un coche de un caballo.	Een wagen met één paard.
Una vettura a due cavalli.	Un coche de dos caballos.	Een wagen met twee paarden.
Una vettura a nolo. Prezzo da convenirsi.	Un coche de alquiler. Precio según convenido.	Een gehuurde wagen. Prijs volgens afspraak.
Una diligenza.	Una diligencia.	Een diligence.
◄ Lo chauffeur o L'autista, La chauffeuse o L'autista.	El chófer, El conductor, La conductora.	De chauffeur, De chauffeuse.
Il cocchiere, Il vetturino.	El cochero, La cochera.	De koetsier, De voerman.
Il conducente.	El conductor.	De trambestuurder.
Un asinaio, Un'asinaia.	Un arriero.	Een ezeldrijver.
Prendere una vettura a[l] percorso, all'ora.	Alquilar un coche por carrera, por hora.	Een vervoermiddel per kilometer, per uur, huren.
◄ Io desidero fare un giro in vettura.	Deseo dar un paseo en coche.	Ik wil een ritje maken.
[Portatemi] alla stazione.	[Lléveme] a la estación.	[Breng me] naar het station.
Andiamo! o Camminate! o Avanti, avanti!	¡Siga! o ¡Marche! o ¡Adelante!	Vooruit!

Go on ! or Drive on ! or Go ahead ! (do not stop, keep going).	Continuez ! ou Allez toujours !	Weiter !
Do not go so fast. Drive slowly, please.	N'allez pas si vite. Allez au pas, s'il vous plaît.	Fahren Sie nicht so schnell. Fahren Sie langsam, bitte.
Go (or Drive) as fast as possible.	Allez aussi vite que possible.	Fahren Sie so schnell wie Sie können.
Stop at the corner.	Arrêtez au coin.	Halten Sie an der Ecke an.
Set me down at the end of this street, at the corner of that street [there], at the corner of those two streets, where you picked me up.	Déposez-moi au bout de cette rue[-ci], au coin de cette rue-là, à l'angle de ces deux rues-là, où vous m'avez pris.	Setzen Sie mich am Ende dieser Straße, an der Ecke der Straße dort, am Treffpunkt der beiden Straßen ab, wo ich eingestiegen bin.
Please pick us up [again] at . . .	Veuillez nous reprendre à . . .	Wollen Sie uns bitte um . . wieder abholen.
Wait for us here, down there.	Attendez-nous ici, là-bas.	Warten Sie hier, dort unten, auf uns.
Go to . . and wait for us there.	Allez à . . et attendez-nous-y.	Fahren Sie nach . . und warten Sie dort auf uns.
To pay one's fare (in a hired conveyance).	Payer [le prix de] sa course.	Den Fahrpreis bezahlen.
What tip does one usually give to the driver ?	Quel pourboire donne-t-on habituellement au cocher ?	Wieviel Trinkgeld gibt man dem Fahrer im allgemeinen ?

Cabs	Les voitures de place	Droschken
A cab. (For taxi [cab] see below.)	Un fiacre, Une voiture [de place].	Eine Droschke.
A cabman.	Un cocher de fiacre.	Ein Droschkenkutscher.
A cab rank.	Une station de fiacres.	Eine Droschkenhaltestelle.
A four-wheeler (cab).	Un fiacre.	Eine Droschke.
A taxi [cab].	Un taxi, Un auto-taxi.	Eine Taxe, Ein Taxi, Ein Taxameter, Eine Autodroschke.
A taxi [cab] driver or A taximan.	Un chauffeur (ou Un conducteur) de taxi.	Ein Taxichauffeur.
The taximeter or The clock.	Le taximètre, Le compteur [de distance].	Der Taxameter, Die Uhr.
Call a cab, a taxi.	Appelez une voiture, un taxi.	Holen Sie eine Droschke, eine Taxe.
Cabby ! Are you disengaged ?	Cocher ! Êtes-vous libre ?	Kutscher ! Sind Sie frei ?
For hire (notice on taximeter).	Libre.	Frei.
What is the total price of the journey showing on the clock ?	Quel est le prix total de la course qui figure sur le compteur ?	Wie hoch ist der Gesamtfahrpreis auf der Uhr ?
Give me your number.	Donnez-moi votre numéro.	Geben Sie mir ihre Nummer.

Ancora avanti !	¡ No pare ! o ¡ Siga adelante !	Rij door!
Non correte tanto. Andate piano, per favore.	No vaya tan de prisa. Vaya despacio.	Niet zo vlug, Rijd langzaam, als 't U belieft.
◄Correte più presto possibile.	Vaya lo más de prisa posible.	Rijd zo snel mogelijk.
Fermatevi all'angolo.	Pare en la esquina.	Stop op de hoek.
Fatemi scendere in fondo a questa strada, all'angolo di quella strada, all'angolo di quelle due strade, dove voi mi avete preso.	Déjeme al final de esta calle, en la esquina de aquella calle, en la esquina de aquellas dos calles, en donde me recogió usted.	Zet me af aan het einde van deze straat, op de hoek van die straat, van die twee straten, waar U me heeft opgepikt.
Per favore, venite a riprenderci a . . .	Haga el favor de volver a recogernos en . . .	Wilt U ons weer te .. oppikken.
Aspettateci qui, laggiù.	Espérenos aquí, allá abajo.	Wacht hier, daarginds, daar op ons.
◄Andate a . . e aspettateci là.	Vaya a . . y espérenos allí.	Ga naar .. en wacht daar op ons.
Pagare il prezzo della corsa.	Pagar [el precio de] la carrera.	De rit betalen.
Quanto di mancia si dà d'ordinario al cocchiere ?	¿ Qué propina se acostumbra darle al cochero ?	Hoeveel fooi geeft men gewoonlijk aan de koetsier, chauffeur?

Vetture di piazza	**Coches de punto**	**Huurrijtuigen**
Una carrozza, Una vettura di piazza.	Un simón.	Een huurrijtuig.
Un cocchiere, Un vetturino.	Un cochero.	Een koetsier.
◄Una stazione di vetture.	Una fila de coches [de punto].	Een standplaats voor huurrijtuigen.
Una carrozza a quattro ruote.	Un carruaje de cuatro ruedas.	Een vigelante.
Un taxi.	Un taxi.	Een taxi.
Un conducente di taxi.	Un chófer de taxi.	Een taxichauffeur.
Il tassametro.	El taxímetro.	De taximeter.
◄Fate venire una carrozza, un taxi.	Llame un simón, un taxi.	Roep een huurrijtuig, een taxi.
Cocchiere ! Siete libero ?	¡ Cochero ! ¿ Está usted libre ?	Chauffeur ! Ben je vrij?
Libero.	Libre.	Vrij.
Qual'è il prezzo totale della corsa segnato nel tassametro ?	¿ A cuánto asciende el precio total que muestra el taxímetro ?	Hoeveel is de totale prijs van de rit op de taximeter?
Datemi il vostro numero.	Deme su número.	Geef me Uw nummer.

Buses and Trams	Les omnibus et Trams	Omnibusse und Straßenbahnen
An omnibus *or* A [']bus. A motor [omni]bus.	Un omnibus. Un autobus.	Ein Omnibus, Ein Bus. Ein Kraftomnibus, Ein Autobus.
A tramway [line].	Un tramway, Une ligne de tramways.	Eine Straßenbahn[linie].
A tram[car].	Un tram[way].	Eine Straßenbahn, Ein Straßenbahnwagen.
A troll[e]y bus.	Un autobus à trolley.	Ein Ob[erleitungsomni]-bus.
The inside *or* The lower deck (*of tram or bus*). To go inside.	L'intérieur. Aller à l'in-térieur.	Innen *oder* Unten *oder* Der untere Wagen. Hinein gehen.
The outside *or* The top [deck] (*of tram or bus*). To go outside *or* on top.	L'impériale. Aller (*ou* Monter) à l'impériale.	Das Oberdeck. Nach oben gehen.
Is there any room inside (*the bus, tram*), room for one on top, room for two, room for three more?	Y a-t-il de la place à l'intérieur, une place à l'impériale, deux places, encore trois places?	Ist unten noch Platz, Ist oben noch ein Platz, Sind noch zwei Plätze, noch drei Plätze, frei?
A stop[ping place] (*tram, etc.*).	Un arrêt, Une station d'arrêt.	Eine Haltestelle.
A motor bus stop.	Un arrêt d'autobus.	Eine Haltestelle für Auto-busse.
A fixed stop (*tram, etc.*). A request stop.	Un arrêt fixe. Un arrêt facultatif.	Eine [feste] Haltestelle. Eine Bedarfshaltestelle.
Full (*notice on tram, etc.*). Is it full inside, on top?	Complet. Est-ce que c'est complet à l'intérieur, à l'impériale?	Besetzt. Ist unten, oben, alles besetzt?
The conductor (*bus, tram, motor coach*).	Le receveur, La receveuse, Le conducteur, La con-ductrice.	Der Schaffner, Die Schaff-nerin.
A ticket inspector *or* A jumper (*on bus, etc.*).	Un contrôleur [mobile].	Ein Fahrkartenkontrolleur.
When is the first, the last, bus to . . ?	Quand est le premier, le dernier, omnibus pour . . ?	Wann geht der erste, der letzte, Bus nach . . ?
How often does the tram[car] run?	Il y a-t-il un tram[way] tous les combien?	Wie oft geht die Straßen-bahn?
Where can I get a bus to . . ?	Où puis-je prendre un omnibus pour . . ?	Wo kann ich einen Bus nach . . bekommen?
How soon will there be another bus? Will there be another [motor] bus soon?	Dans combien de temps viendra-t-il un autre omnibus? Est-ce qu'il viendra bientôt un autre autobus?	Wann geht der nächste Bus? Kommt der nächste Bus bald?
Which [motor] bus should I take for the cathedral?	Quel autobus dois-je prendre pour la cathé-drale?	Mit welchem Autobus kann ich nach dem Dom fahren?
Is that our bus?	Est-ce là notre omnibus?	Ist das unser Autobus?
Does this bus go to . . ? Do you go to . . ?	Cet omnibus va-t-il à . . ? Allez-vous à . . ?	Geht dieser Autobus nach . . ? Fahren Sie nach . . ?
Do you go near Saint John's Church, anywhere near	Allez-vous près de l'Église Saint-Jean, à proximité	Fahren Sie in die Nähe der Sankt Johanneskirche,

Omnibus e Trams	Ómnibus y Tranvía	Bussen en Trams
◄Un [omni]bus. Un autobus.	Un [ómni]bus. Un autobús.	Een bus. Een autobus.
Una tramvia.	Un tranvía, Una línea de tranvías.	Een tramlijn.
Un tramvai.	Un [coche de] tranvía.	Een tram.
Un trollibus.	Un autobús de trole.	Een trollybus.
◄Dentro. Prendere posto dentro o nell'interno.	El interior. Ir en el interior.	Binnenin. Binneningaan.
L'imperiale. Salire nell'imperiale.	El imperial. Subir al imperial.	Bovenop. Bovenop gaan.
C'è posto dentro, posto per uno nell'imperiale, posto per due, ancora tre posti.	¿Hay sitio en el interior, sitio en el imperial para una persona, sitio para dos personas, sitio para tres personas más?	Is er plaats binnenin, plaats voor één persoon bovenop, plaats voor twee, plaats voor nog drie?
Una fermata. Una stazione per le fermate.	Un paradero, Una parada.	Een halte.
Una fermata di autobus.	Un paradero de autobús.	Een bushalte.
◄Fermata obbligatoria. Fermata facoltativa.	Una parada obligatoria. Una parada discrecional.	Een vaste halte. Een halte op verzoek.
Completo. È tutto completo dentro, nell'imperiale?	Completo. ¿Está completo el interior, el imperial?	Vol. Is het binnenin, bovenop, vol?
Il conduttore, Il conducente, La conducente.	El cobrador, La cobradora.	De conducteur, De conductrice.
Un controllore.	Un revisor.	Een controleur.
◄A che ora è il primo, l'ultimo, omnibus per..?	¿A qué hora es el primer, el último, ómnibus para..?	Hoelaat gaat de eerste, de laatste bus naar..?
Quante volte passa il tramvai?	¿Con qué frecuencia marcha el tranvía?	Om de hoeveel tijd rijdt er een tram?
Dove posso prendere un omnibus per..?	¿En dónde puedo tomar el ómnibus para..?	Waar kan ik een bus naar.. nemen?
Fra quanto tempo passerà un altro omnibus? Ci sarà un altro omnibus subito?	¿Cuándo habrá otro ómnibus? ¿Habrá otro autobús pronto?	Over hoeveel tijd komt er weer een bus? Komt er gauw weer een bus?
Quale autobus debbo prendere per la cattedrale?	¿Qué autobús debo tomar para ir a la catedral?	Welke [auto]bus moet ik nemen voor de kathedraal?
◄È quello il nostro omnibus?	¿Es ese ómnibus el nuestro?	Is dat onze bus?
Va questo omnibus a..? Andate voi a..?	¿Va este ómnibus a..? ¿Va usted a..?	Gaat deze bus naar..? Gaat U naar..?
Andate voi vicino alla chiesa di San Giovanni,	¿Pasa usted cerca de la glesia de San Juan, en	Gaat U langs de Sint Jan's Kerk Komt U

the Bourse, through .. Street?	de la Bourse, par la rue ..?	ungefähr in die Nähe der Börse, durch .. Straße?
How far do you go?	Jusqu où allez-vous?	Wie weit fahren Sie?
Where must I, we, change for the Botanical Gardens?	Où faut-il changer [de voiture] pour le Jardin des Plantes?	Wo muß ich, müssen wir, umsteigen, um nach dem Botanischen Garten zu kommen?
Please let me know when we come to .. Street.	Ayez la bonté de m'avertir quand nous arriverons à la Rue ...	Bitte sagen Sie mir, wenn wir nach der .. Straße kommen.
I want to get off (or out) at the station, at the next stop. Is this where I get off?	Je veux descendre à la gare, au prochain arrêt. Est-ce ici que je descends?	Ich möchte am Bahnhof, an der nächsten Haltestelle, aussteigen. Muß ich hier aussteigen?
Please set me down as near X. Street as you can.	Veuillez me déposer aussi près de la Rue X. que possible.	Bitte setzen Sie mich so nahe der Xstraße wie möglich ab.
A [motor] bus [service] map.	Un itinéraire des autobus.	Eine Karte des Autobus-Verkehrs.
A ticket.	Un billet, Un ticket.	Ein Fahrschein, Ein Billett.
Where do we take tickets?	Où prenons-nous des billets?	Wo lösen wir unsere Fahrscheine?
A transfer [ticket] (tram, etc.).	Une correspondance.	Ein Umsteige-Fahrschein.
The fare.	Le prix [de la place ou de la course ou du billet].	Der Fahrpreis, Die Fahrt.
What is the fare there and back or the return fare?	Quel est le prix d'aller et retour?	Was kostet die Hin- und Rückfahrt?
Show me the fare table or the list of fares.	Faites-moi voir le tarif.	Zeigen Sie mir die Fahrpreis-Liste.
A fare stage (bus, etc.).	Une section.	Eine Teilstrecke.
Fares, please!	Places, s'il vous plaît!	Noch jemand ohne Fahrscheine?
[Show your] tickets, please!	[Présentez] vos billets, s'il vous plaît!	Die Fahrschein bitte!

Motor coaches	**Les autocars**	**Überlandomnibusse**
A [motor] coach.	Un [auto]car.	Ein Überlandomnibus, Ein Autobus.
Where is there a motor coach office, please?	Où y a-t-il un bureau d'autocars, s'il vous plaît?	Wo gibt es ein Büro für den Autobusverkehr?
Where is the motor coach station?	Où est la gare d'autocars?	Wo ist der Halteplatz für Autobusse?
A regular motor coach service in connexion with the station, serving the P.L.M. station.	Un service régulier d'autocars en correspondance avec la gare, desservant la gare P.L.M.	Ein Zubringer-Autobusdienst von und nach dem Bahnhof, von und nach dem P.L.M. Bahnhof.
How many daily departures each way are there, when the motor coaches are working?	Combien y a-t-il de départs quotidiens dans chaque sens, en période de fonctionnement des autocars?	Wieviel Autobusse gehen täglich hin und zurück während der Verkehrssaison?

in qualche punto vicino alla Borsa, passando per via . . ?	la proximidad de la Bolsa, por la calle de . . ?	in de buurt van de Beurs, Gaat U door de .. straat?
Fin dove andate ?	¿ Hasta qué punto va usted ?	Hoever gaat U?
Dove debbo io, dobbiamo noi, cambiare per il Giardino Botanico ?	¿ En dónde hay que cambiar para los Jardines Botánicos ?	Waar moet ik, moeten wij, voor de Plantentuin (of Mortus) overstappen?
◄ Per favore, avvisatemi quando arriviamo alla Via. . .	Haga el favor de avisarme en cuanto que lleguemos a la Calle . . .	Wilt U me waarschuwen, als we bij de .. Straat komen?
Io desidero scendere alla stazione, alla prossima fermata. È qui che debbo scendere ?	Quiero bajar en la estación, en la próxima parada. ¿ Es aquí donde bajo ?	Ik wil bij het station, bij de volgende halte, uitstappen. Moet ik hier uitstappen?
Per favore, fatemi scendere il più vicino possibile alla Via X.	Haga el favor de depositarme a lo más cerca posible de la Calle X.	Wilt U me als 't U belieft zo dicht mogelijk bij de Xstraat afzetten.
Un itinerario degli autobus.	Un plano del itinerario de autobús.	Een bustrajectenkaart.
Un biglietto.	Un billete.	Een kaartje.
◄ Dove si prendono biglietti ?	¿ Dónde se toman los billetes ?	Waar nemen we de kaartjes?
Un biglietto di coincidenza.	Un billete de correspondencia.	Een overstapje.
Il prezzo [del biglietto o della corsa].	El precio [del billete o de la carrera].	De prijs, Het tarief.
Qual'è il prezzo di andata e ritorno ?	¿ Qué es el precio de ida y vuelta ?	Hoeveel is het heen en terug?
Fatemi vedere la tariffa o la lista dei prezzi.	Muéstreme la tarifa o la lista de precios.	Laat me de tarieven zien.
◄ Un frazionamento della corsa.	Una sección.	Een rit.
Il prezzo del biglietto, per piacere !	¡ Billetes !	Kaartjes, als 't U belieft!
[Mostrate] i vostri biglietti, per favore !	¡ Señores, los billetes !	Kaartjes, als 't U belieft!

Gli autobus	**Los autocars**	**Touringcars**
Un autobus.	Un autocar.	Een touringcar.
Dove sta un ufficio degli autobus, per favore ?	¿ En dónde hay una agencia de autocars ?	Waar is er een touringcar bureau, als 't U belieft?
◄ Dov'è la stazione degli autobus?	¿ Dónde está la estación de autocars ?	Waar is het touringcar station?
Un servizio regolare di autobus in coincidenza con la stazione, che fa servizio per la stazione P.L.M.	Un servicio corriente de autocar en correspondencia con la estación, que sirve a la estación de la P.L.M.	Een geregelde touringcar dienst met aansluiting op het station van en en naar het P.L.M. station.
Quante partenze ci sono al giorno in ogni senso, quando gli autobus fanno servizio ?	¿ Cuántas salidas diarias hay en cada dirección durante el periodo de funcionamiento del servicio de autocars ?	Hoeveel touringcars vertrekken dagelijks in beide richtingen, wanneer de touringcars lopen?

A [motor] coach tour.	Un circuit en autocar.	Eine Tour (oder Eine Rundfahrt) im Gesellschaftsauto.
Where is the [motor] coach going to-morrow, weather permitting? I should like to make a motor coach sight-seeing tour.	Où l'autocar (ou le car) va-t-il demain, si le temps le permet? J'aimerais faire une promenade d'orientation en autocar.	Wohin fährt das Gesellschaftsauto morgen bei günstigem Wetter? Ich möchte gern eine Rundfahrt im Gesellschaftsauto (oder im Aussichtswagen) unternehmen.
Is the tour conducted by a guide?	Le circuit est-il accompagné par un guide?	Geht die Tour mit einem Führer vor sich?
Can you, Will you, book me a seat in the motor coach for .. to-morrow?	Pouvez-vous, Voulez-vous, me réserver une place dans l'autocar pour .. demain?	Können Sie mir, Wollen Sie mir, für morgen einen Platz in dem Autobus nach .. bestellen?
The booking of seats.	La location de places.	Die Platzbestellung.
A [motor] coach time table.	Un horaire des [auto-]cars.	Ein Autobusfahrplan.
Is the carriage of luggage charged extra?	Le transport des bagages est-il compté en sus?	Muß man für das Gepäck extra bezahlen?
[At] what time does the coach for .. start?	À quelle heure l'autocar pour .. part-il?	Wann fährt der Autobus nach .. ab?
Does the coach stop on the way?	Le car s'arrête-t-il en route?	Hält der Autobus unterwegs?
How long does the coach stop at ..?	Combien de temps le car s'arrête-t-il à ..?	Wie lange hält der Autobus in ..?
Shall we have time to take some refreshments (or a little something) there?	Aurons-nous le temps de nous restaurer (ou de prendre quelque chose) là?	Werden wir Zeit haben, dort einen Imbiß (oder eine Kleinigkeit) (oder etwas) zu uns zu nehmen?
[At] what time do you start back, do you leave for the return journey?	À quelle heure partez-vous pour le retour, partez-vous pour le trajet de retour?	Um wieviel Uhr fahren Sie zurück, treten Sie die Rückfahrt an?
Shall we be back in good time for dinner? We must be back at noon, by four o'clock [at the latest].	Serons-nous de retour bien à temps pour le dîner? Il faut que nous soyons de retour à midi, pour quatre heures [au plus tard].	Werden wir zur Zeit zum Mittagessen zurück sein? Wir müssen um zwölf, [spätestens] um vier zurück sein.

Tours	**Les circuits**	**Touren** oder **Gesellschaftsreisen**
(*For* motor coach tours, *see above. For* cruises, *see pp.* 30-31.)		
A travel agency.	Une agence de voyages.	Ein Reisebüro.
Whereabouts is the tourists' information bureau?	De quel côté est le bureau du syndicat d'initiative?	In welcher Gegend ist das Auskunftsbüro für Touristen?
Where should I apply for	Où faut-il s'adresser pour	Wo kann ich mich über

Un viaggio circolare in autobus.	Una excursión en autocar.	Een tocht per touringcar.
Dove va l'autobus domani, se il tempo lo permette?	¿A dónde va mañana el autocar, siempre que haga buen tiempo?	Waar gaat de touringcar morgen heen, als het weer het toelaat?
←Mi piacerebbe fare un giro in autobus per dare un'occhiata ai monumenti principali.	Me gustaría hacer una excursión en autocar para visitar los puntos de interés.	Ik zou graag een tocht langs de bezienswaardigheden per touringcar maken.
La gita è accompagnata da una guida?	¿Va un cicerone con esta excursión?	Gaat er een gids mee op de tocht?
Potete, Volete, riservarmi per domani un posto nell'autobus che va a ..?	¿Puede usted, Quiere usted, reservarme una plaza en el autocar de mañana para ..?	Kunt U, Wilt U, een plaats voor mij bespreken in de touringcar voor .. morgen?
Le prenotazioni di posti.	La reservación de plazas.	Het plaatsbespreken.
Un orario d'autobus.	Un horario de autocars.	Een dienstregeling van de touringcar.
←Si paga extra pel trasporto del bagaglio?	¿Es el porte de equipaje un cargo adicional?	Moet er voor bagage extra betaald worden?
A che ora parte l'autobus per ..?	¿A qué hora sale el autocar para ..?	Hoe laat vertrekt de touringcar naar ..?
La vettura ha qualche fermata lungo il percorso?	¿Hace alguna parada el autocar durante el trayecto?	Houdt de touringcar onderweg stil?
Quanto tempo si ferma la vettura a ..?	¿Por cuánto tiempo para el autocar en ..?	Hoe lang houdt de touringcar in .. stil?
Avremo tempo di fare lì uno spuntino?	¿Tendremos tiempo para comer (o tomar) algún refresco allí?	Zullen we tijd hebben daar iets te gebruiken?
←A che ora partite per il ritorno, fate anche il servizio di ritorno?	¿A qué hora se sale de regreso, se emprende el viaje de regreso?	Hoe laat rijdt u terug, gaan we weer terug?
Saremo di ritorno in buon tempo per il pranzo? Bisogna essere di ritorno a mezzogiorno, per le quattro [al più tardi].	¿Estaremos de vuelta con tiempo de sobra para comer? Tenemos que estar de vuelta para el mediodía, para las cuatro [a más tardar].	Zullen we op tijd terug zijn voor het middageten? We moeten om twaalf uur, [op zijn laatst] vier uur, terug zijn.

Escursioni / Excursiones / Tochten

Un'agenzia di viaggi.	Una agencia de viajes.	Een reisagentschap.
Dove trovasi l'ufficio di informazioni viaggi? o Dov'è l'ente nazionale italiano turistico (ENIT)?	¿Por dónde está el despacho de informaciones para turistas?	Waar is het V.V.V.?
Dove debbo rivolgermi	¿Adónde debo dirigirme	Waar moet ik inlichtin-

information about excursions, about tours?	des renseignements sur des excursions, sur des circuits?	Ausflüge, über Touren, erkundigen?
Where should I inquire?	Où devrais-je me renseigner?	Wo kann ich mich erkundigen?
An enquiry office.	Un bureau de renseignements.	Ein Auskunftsbüro.
Where are tickets issued? (*For* kinds of tickets and fares, *see pp.* 18-21.)	Où les billets sont-ils délivrés?	Wo werden die Fahrkarten ausgegeben?
Please give me a few particulars about tours in the Riviera, in Switzerland.	Ayez la bonté de me donner quelques indications pour circuits dans la Riviera (*ou* sur la Côte d'Azur), en Suisse.	Geben Sie mir bitte einige Auskünfte über Touren in der Riviera, in der Schweiz.
A conducted tour.	Un circuit accompagné, Une excursion accompagnée.	Eine Gesellschaftsreise mit Führer.
I should like to make a tour in Brittany.	Je désire faire une randonnée en Bretagne.	Ich möchte eine Tour durch die Bretagne machen.
Is the town of A .., of B .., a good excursion centre, a good starting point for interesting walks, for mountain trips, for boat trips? (*For* pleasure boat trips *see pp.* 254-257.)	La ville d'A .., de B .., est-elle un bon centre d'excursions, un bon point de départ pour des promenades intéressantes, pour des courses de montagne, pour des courses en bateau?	Ist die Stadt A .., B .., ein guter Ausgangspunkt für Ausflüge, für interessante Spaziergänge, für Gebirgstouren, für Bootfahrten?
Is the place a summer resort, a winter resort, a health resort, a pleasure resort? Are there any pleasure resorts in the town? (*For* Seaside and Bathing resorts *see pp.* 246-255.)	La localité est-elle une station estivale, une station hivernale, une station climat[ér]ique, une ville d'agrément *ou* une ville où les distractions abondent? Y a-t-il dans la ville des endroits où l'on s'amuse?	Ist der Ort ein Sommeraufenthalt, ein Winteraufenthalt, ein Kurort, ein Vergnügungszentrum? Gibt es in der Stadt irgendwelche Vergnügungsstätten?
Are there many trippers at that holiday resort?	Y a-t-il beaucoup d'excursionnistes à ce centre de villégiature?	Gibt es in diesem Ferienaufenthalt viele Ausflügler?
What is the itinerary of the tour?	Quel est l'itinéraire du circuit?	Wie ist die Tour geplant?
Can the traveller use, at will, the boat or the railway?	Le voyageur peut-il utiliser, à son gré, le bateau ou le chemin de fer?	Kann der Reisende, je nach Wunsch, per Schiff oder per Eisenbahn fahren?
A whole day motor car excursion.	Une excursion en automobile d'une journée entière.	Ein ganztägiger Autoausflug.
An optional half-day excursion.	Une excursion facultative d'une demi-journée.	Ein auf Wunsch halbtägiger Ausflug.
What is the inclusive charge for a combined railway and motor coach tour in Algeria, in Tunis[ia], in Morocco?	Quel est le prix forfaitaire pour un circuit mixte par chemin de fer ou autocar en Algérie, en Tunisie, au Maroc?	Wie hoch ist der Gesamtpreis für eine kombinierte Eisenbahn- und Autobustour durch Algerien, durch Tunis, durch Marokko?

per avere informazioni su escursioni, su gite turistiche?	para obtener informes sobre excursiones, sobre circuitos?	gen vragen omtrent uitstapjes, omtrent tochten?
◄Dove debbo informarmi?	¿En dónde debo pedir informes?	Waar zou ik inlichtingen moeten vragen?
Un ufficio di informazioni.	Un despacho de informaciones.	Een inlichtingenbureau.
Dove si rilasciano i biglietti?	¿En dónde se emiten los billetes?	Waar worden kaartjes verstrekt?
Per favore, datemi qualche particolare intorno alla gita nella Riviera, in Svizzera.	Haga el favor de darme algunos datos sobre excursiones en la Riviera, en Suiza.	Zoudt U mij wat bijzonderheden omtrent tochten in de Riviera, in Zwitzerland, willen geven.
Una gita turistica con guida.	Una excursión acompañada.	Een tocht met een reisleider.
◄Mi piacerebbe fare un giro turistico in Bretagna.	Me gustaría hacer una excursión en Bretaña.	Ik zou graag een tocht in Bretagne maken.
La città di A .., di B .., è un buon centro di escursioni, un buon punto di partenza per fare interessanti passeggiate, per ascensioni in montagna, per gite in battello?	¿Es la población de A .., de B .., un buen centro para excursiones, un buen punto desde donde emprender paseos interesantes, excursiones a las montañas, paseos en bote?	Is de stad A .., B .., een goed centrum voor uitstapjes, een goed uitgangspunt voor interessante wandelingen, voor bergtochten voor boottochten?
È la località una stazione estiva, una stazione invernale, una stazione climatica, un luogo di divertimento? C'è maniera di divertirsi?	¿Es la localidad un lugar de veraneo, un lugar para invernar, un lugar de curación, un lugar de recreo? ¿Hay puntos de reunión en la población?	Is de plaats een zomeroord, een winteroord, een gezondheidsoord, een plezieroord? Zijn er vermakelijkheden in de stad?
Ci sono molti gitanti in quel centro di villeggiatura?	¿Suelen ir muchos excursionistas a ese punto de recreo?	Zijn er veel plezierreizigers in dat vakantieoord?
Qual'è l'itinerario della gita?	¿Cuál es el itinerario de la excursión?	Wat is de reisroute van de tocht?
◄Può il viaggiatore servirsi a piacere del battello o della ferrovia?	¿Puede valerse el viajero, a discreción, del buque o del ferrocarril?	Kan de reiziger naar wens de boot of de trein nemen?
Un'escursione in automobile per tutta la giornata.	Una excursión de un día entero en automóvil.	Een uitstapje per auto dat de hele dag duurt.
Un'escursione facoltativa di mezza giornata.	Una excursión facultativa por medio día.	Een tocht van een halve dag voor wie mee wil.
Qual'è il prezzo complessivo per un viaggio combinato per ferrovia ed autobus in Algeria, in Tunisia, in Marocco?	¿Qué es el precio inclusive para una excursión por ferrocarril y autocar en combinación en Argelia, en Túnez, en Marruecos?	Wat is de totaalprijs voor een gecombineerde trein en autocar tocht in Algerije, in Tunesië, in Marocco?

The outward, The return, journey.	Le trajet [d']aller, [de] retour.	Die Hinreise, Die Rückreise.
How long does the journey take?	Combien de temps le voyage prend-il?	Wie lange dauert die Reise?
A land excursion.	Une excursion à terre.	Ein Ausflug zu Lande.
Are there free days for visiting the Exhibition?	Y a-t-il des journées libres pour la visite de l'Exposition?	Gibt man uns zur Besichtigung der Ausstellung Tage frei?
Independent travel. Can one travel independently?	Le voyage individuel. Peut-on voyager individuellement?	Unabhängiges Reisen. Kann man unabhängig reisen?

Walking, Camping	**La marche, Le camping**	**Wandern, Zelten**
Walk or Walking distance: It is only an hour's walk.	Marche: Il n'y a qu'une heure de marche.	Entfernung zu Fuß: Es ist nur eine Stunde zu Fuß.
To go for a walk.	Faire une promenade [à pied], Se promener.	Einen Spaziergang machen, Spazieren gehen.
To go on foot.	Aller à pied.	Zu Fuß gehen.
Can I walk to .. in an hour? I am a good walker.	Puis-je aller à .. à pied en une heure? Je suis bon marcheur, bonne marcheuse.	Kann ich in einer Stunde nach .. kommen? Ich bin gut zu Fuß oder Ich gehe ziemlich rasch.
We shall have to walk faster, to walk back.	Il nous faudra marcher plus vite, retourner à pied.	Wir müssen schneller gehen, zu Fuß zurückkehren.
Walking.	La marche, La promenade.	Gehen, Wandern.
A walking tour.	Une excursion à pied.	Eine Wanderung, Eine Fußtour.
Walking boots.	Des chaussures de marche.	Wanderschuhe.
A ramble. A week-end ramble in the country.	Une promenade, Une excursion. Une promenade de fin de semaine à la campagne.	Ein Spaziergang, Ein Ausflug. Ein Wochenendausflug auf das Land.
To go for a hike.	Faire une excursion à pied.	Wandern, Eine Wanderung machen.
A hiker.	Un(e) excursionniste à pied.	Ein Wanderer.
Hiking.	Le tourisme pédestre, Les excursions à pied.	Wandern.
A footpath.	Un sentier, Une sente.	Ein Fußweg, Ein Pfad.
A field path.	Un sentier à travers champs, Un chemin passant dans les prairies.	Ein Feldweg.
A bypath or A byway.	Un chemin écarté.	Ein Nebenweg.
I wish to avoid the beaten path.	Je désire éviter le chemin battu.	Ich möchte den viel begangenen Weg vermeiden.
Is there a short cut to the village across the fields?	Y a-t-il un raccourci pour aller au village à travers champs?	Gibt es einen kürzeren Weg nach dem Dorf über die Felder?
Is there a level crossing, a footbridge, a viaduct	Y a-t-il près d'ici un passage à niveau, une passerelle,	Gibt es hier in der Nähe einen Niveauübergang,

Il tragitto di andata, di ritorno.	El viaje de ida, de regreso.	De uitreis, De thuisreis.
◄Quanto tempo prende il viaggio?	¿Cuánto tiempo se tarda en el viaje?	Hoe lang duurt de reis?
Un escursione per terra.	Una excursión por tierra.	Een landreis.
Ci sono dei giorni liberi per visitare l'Esposizione?	¿Hay días libres para visitar la Exposición?	Zijn er vrije dagen voor het bezoeken van de Tentoonstelling?
Il viaggio individuale. Si può viaggiare individualmente?	Viajes individuales. ¿Se puede viajar individualmente?	Reizen op eigen gelegenheid. Kan men op eigen gelegenheid reizen?

La passeggiata, L'accampamento	**De andar, El camping**	**Wandelen, Kamperen**
Camminate: Non c'è che un'ora di cammino.	El trayecto o La caminata: Solo es cosa de una hora a pie.	Afstand of Lopen: Het is slechts één uur lopen.
◄Fare una passeggiata.	Dar un paseo {a pie}, Pasearse.	Een wandeling maken.
Andare a piedi.	Ir a pie.	Te voet gaan.
Posso arrivare a piedi in un'ora a . . ? Io sono un buon camminatore, una buona camminatrice.	¿Puedo ir en una hora a pie hasta . . ? Soy buen peatón.	Kan ik in een uur naar .. lopen? Ik ben een goede wandelaar, (feminine) wandelaarster.
Dovremo camminare più presto, ritornare a piedi.	Tendremos que andar más de prisa, que volver atrás.	We zullen vlugger, terug, moeten lopen.
La camminata, La passeggiata.	La marcha, El paseo.	De wandeling.
◄Un'escursione a piedi.	Una excursión a pie.	Een wandeltocht.
Gli stivali da camminata.	Botas de marchar.	Wandelschoenen.
Una gita. Una gita in campagna a fin di settimana.	Un paseo (o Una excursión) campestre. Una excursión campestre de fin de semana.	Een zwerftocht. Een zwerftocht naar buiten op zaterdag en zondag.
Fare un'escursione a piedi.	Ir de excursión a pie.	Een trektocht maken.
Un(a) gitante a piedi.	Un(a) excursionista (o Un(a) turista) a pie.	Een trekker, (feminine) Een trekster.
◄Il podismo.	El turismo a pie, Excursiones a pie.	Trekken.
Un sentiero. Un viottolo.	Una senda, Una vereda. Una senda a través de una pradera.	Een voetpad. Een pad door de velden.
Un sentiero poco usato, Una stradicciola.	Un sendero.	Een zijpad.
Io desidero evitare la strada battuta.	Deseo evitar el camino más frecuentado.	Ik wil de druk begane wegen vermijden.
◄C'è una scorciatoia per andare al villaggio attraverso i campi?	¿Hay un atajo a través de la pradera que va hasta la aldea?	Is er een kortere binnenweg naar het dorp door de velden?
C'è qui vicino un passaggio a livello, un ponticello,	¿Hay por aquí cerca un paso a nivel, un puente -	Is er een overweg, een voetbrug, een viaduct

across the valley, a ferry, a ferry [boat], near here?	un viaduc à travers la vallée, un passage, un bateau de passage *ou* un bac?	einen Steg, einen Viaduct über das Tal, eine Fähre, ein Fährboot?
To ferry across a, the, river.	Passer l'eau.	Über einen, den, Fluß setzen.
Will you please hail the ferryman?	Voulez-vous héler le passeur?	Wollen Sie bitte den Fährmann rufen?
Is there a ford hereabouts? Where can one ford the river?	Y a-t-il ici près un gué? Où peut-on passer la rivière à gué?	Gibt es hier in der Nähe eine Furt? Wo kann man den Fluß durchwaten?
Do they levy a toll [charge] for crossing this bridge? Whereabouts is the turnpike?	Est-ce qu'on perçoit un péage pour traverser ce pont? De quel côté la barrière se trouve-t-elle?	Muß man hier Brückengeld➤ bezahlen? Wo ist der Schlagbaum?
May one walk along this tow[ing] path?	Peut-on se promener sur ce chemin de halage?	Darf man auf diesem Leinpfad entlanggehen?
Do you think it possible to arrange with a bargee to go down the canal in a barge?	Est-il possible, croyez-vous, de s'entendre avec un marinier pour la descente du canal en chaland?	Glauben Sie, man kann mit einem Bootsmann abmachen, daß er einen im Boot den Kanal herunterfährt?
A mule track.	Une piste muletière.	Ein Mauleselpfad, Ein Saumpfad.
A stile.	Un échalier.	Ein Zaunübergang, Ein Zauntritt.
Are refreshments to be had on the road?	Peut-on se procurer des rafraîchissements en route?	Bekommt man unterwegs➤ Erfrischungen?
To go camping.	Faire du camping.	Zelten gehen.
Is there a camping ground hereabouts?	Y a-t-il un terrain de camping dans ces parages?	Gibt es in dieser Gegend ein Zeltgelände?
A holiday camp.	Un camp de vacances, Un camping.	Ein Ferienlager.
We are going to camp out.	Nous allons camper.	Wir werden im Freien lagern *oder* zelten.
A bell tent. A bivouac tent *or* A bivvy.	Une tente conique. Une tente forme bonnet de police.	Ein Indianerzelt. ➤ Ein Biwakzelt.
A tent pole. A tent peg. A mallet.	Un mât de tente. Un piquet de tente. Un maillet.	Ein Zeltpfahl. Ein Zeltpflock. Ein Holzhammer.
A camp axe.	Une hache de campement.	Eine Lageraxt.
A camp bed.	Un lit de camp.	Ein Feldbett.
A camp stool. A caravan (*house on wheels*). A trailer caravan.	Un [siège] pliant. Une roulotte. Une remorque-roulotte.	Ein Faltstuhl. ➤ Ein Wohnwagen. Ein Anhängewohnwagen.

un viadotto attraverso la valle, un traghetto, una barchetta che fa la traversata ?	cillo, un viaducto a través del valle, un balsadero, un bote de paso ?	over het dal, een veer, een veerpont, hier dichtbij?
Traghettare un, il, fiume.	Barquear (o Cruzar) de una a otra orilla.	De rivier per veer oversteken.
Per favore, volete chiamare il barcaiolo ?	Haga el favor de llamar al balsero.	Wilt U de veerman roepen?
C'è nelle vicinanze un guado ? Dove si può guadare il fiume ?	¿ Hay por aquí un vado ? ¿ Por dónde se puede vadear el río ?	Is er een waadbare plaats hier in de buurt? Waar kan men door de rivier waden?
◄Si paga un pedaggio per attraversare questo ponte ? Da quale parte si trova la barriera ?	¿ Hay que pagar portazgo para atravesar este puente ? ¿ Dónde está la barrera de portazgo ?	Wordt er op deze brug tol geheven? Waar is de tolboom?
Si può camminare lungo questo sentiero di rimorchio ?	¿ Es permitido andar por este camino de sirga ?	Mag men langs dit jaagpad lopen?
Credete possibile che si possa combinare col barcaiolo per scendere il canale in barca ?	¿ Cree usted que será posible llegar a un arreglo con un barquero para bajar por el canal en una barcaza o gabarra ?	Denkt U dat het mogelijk is met een schipper overeen te komen, om het kanaal per vrachtboot af te zakken?
Una pista da mulattiera.	Una pista de mula o de burro.	Een muilezelpad.
Una barriera scalabile.	Una portilla con escalones.	Een overstaphek.
◄Si può avere dei rinfreschi lungo la via ?	¿ Pueden obtenerse refrescos en el camino ?	Kan men op weg verversingen krijgen?
Accamparsi o Fare un accampamento.	Ir de excursión campestre viviendo en tiendas de campaña.	Kamperen gaan.
C'è nelle vicinanze uno spazio libero per l'accampamento ?	¿ Hay por aquí un terreno de camping o un campamento ?	Is er een kampeerterrein hier in de buurt?
Un accampamento per le vacanze.	Un campamento de pasar vacaciones.	Een vakantiekamp.
Noi andiamo per stare in un accampamento.	Vamos a acampar.	Wij gaan kamperen.
◄Una tenda conica.	Una tienda cónica.	Een kegeltent.
Una tenda da bivacco.	Un vivaque.	Een bivaktent.
Un palo da tenda. Un piolo da tenda. Un mazzapicchio.	Un mastil (o Un montante) de tienda. Una clavija de tienda. Un mazo	Een tentpaal. Een haring, Een houten hamer.
Una scure da accampamento.	Una hacha de campamento.	Een kampbijl.
Un letto da campo, Una branda.	Un catre de tijera.	Een kampbed.
◄Una sedia pieghevole.	Un taburete de tijera.	Een vouwstoel.
Un carro-caravana.	Una cabaña sobre ruedas.	Een kampeerwagen.
Un rimorchio caravana.	Una cabaña sobre ruedas a remolque.	Een aanhang-kampeerwagen.

A corkscrew.	Un tire-bouchon.	Ein Korkenzieher.
A ground sheet.	Une toile de sol.	Eine Zeltbahn.
A hammock.	Un hamac.	Eine Hängematte. →
A hurricane lamp. A lamp wick.	Une lanterne-tempête. Une mèche pour éclairage.	Eine Sturmlaterne. Ein Lampendocht.
An oil, A spirit, stove. A stove wick.	Un réchaud à pétrole, à alcool. Une mèche pour chauffage.	Ein Petroleumkocher, Ein Spirituskocher. Ein Ofendocht.
Methylated spirit.	De l'alcool dénaturé, De l'alcool à brûler.	Spiritus, Denaturierter Brennspiritus.
A tin opener.	Un ouvre-boîte.	Ein Büchsenöffner.
A vacuum flask.	Une bouteille isolante.	Eine Isolierflasche. →
A water bottle (*portable*).	Une gourde.	Eine Feldflasche.
See also **Bedroom furniture,** *pp.* 118-123 *and* **Tableware,** *pp.* 142-145.		
Have you any eatables? (*See* EATING AND DRINKING, *pp.* 130-171.)	Avez-vous des commestibles?	Haben Sie irgend etwas Eßbares?

<table>
<tr><td>

MECHANICAL AND ELECTRICAL TERMS, MOTOR AND CYCLE PARTS AND ACCESSORIES, ETC. (*=et cetera*)

</td><td>

TERMES MÉCANIQUES ET ÉLECTRIQUES, ARTICLES ET ACCESSOIRES POUR AUTOS ET BICYCLETTES, ETC. (*= et cætera*)

</td><td>

AUSDRÜCKE AUS DER MECHANIK UND ELEKTRIZITÄT, BESTANDTEILE VON KRAFTWAGEN UND FAHRRÄDERN, ZUBEHÖR, USW. (*= und so weiter*)

</td></tr>
</table>

For phrases see under **The garage,** *pp.* 58-65. (Abbreviations used in this section *Cyc.= Cycle. Mot.=Motor car. Mach.=Machinery.*)		
The accelerator.	L'accélérateur.	Der Beschleuniger.
An accessory.	Un accessoire.	Ein Zubehörteil.
An accumulator.	Un accumulateur, Un accu.	Ein Akkumulator, Ein→ Sammler.
An adjustable spanner.	Une clef à molette, Une clef anglaise.	Ein verstellbarer Schraubenschlüssel.
The admission manifold.	Le collecteur d'admission.	Das Ansaugrohr, Das Saugrohr.
An air pump.	Une pompe à air.	Eine Luftpumpe.
An amp[ere].	Un ampère.	Ein Ampère.
An am[pere]meter.	Un ampèremètre.	Ein Ampèremeter, Ein→ Strommesser.
An anti-dazzle lamp *or* light.	Un phare anti-éblouissant, Un phare-code.	Eine Abblendungslampe.
The armature.	L'induit.	Der Anker.
The asbestos.	L'amiante.	Der Asbest.

Un cavatappi.	Un tirabuzón, Un sacatapones.	Een kurketrekker.
Un telo da campo.	Un tapete impermeable.	Een grondzeil.
◄ Un'amaca.	Una hamaca.	Een hangmat.
Una lanterna inestinguibile. Un lucignolo per lampada.	Una linterna inextinguible. Una mecha para alumbrar.	Een stormlamp. Een lampepit.
Una stufa a petrolio, a spirito. Una calzetta per lampada.	Una estufa (o Un cocinilla) de petróleo, de alcohol. Una mecha para calentar.	Een oliestel, Een spiritusstel. Een pit voor petroleum stel.
L'alcool denaturato, Lo spirito da bruciare.	Aguardiente para quemar, Alcohol metílico.	Spiritus.
Un apri barattolo.	Un abridor de cajas de lata.	Een blikopener.
◄ Una fiasca isolante.	Un frasco aislador.	Een thermosfles.
Una borraccia.	Una botija.	Een veldfles.
Avete dei commestibili?	¿Tiene usted comestibles?	Heeft U eetwaren?

<table>
<tr><td>

TERMINI MECCANICI ED ELETTRICI, ARTICOLI ED ACCESSORI PER AUTOMOBILI E BICICLETTE, ECC.
(= *eccetera*)

</td><td>

TÉRMINOS DE MAQUINARIA Y ELECTRICIDAD, PIEZAS DE AUTOMÓVILES Y DE BICICLETAS, ACCESORIOS, ETC. (= *et cetera*)

</td><td>

MECHANISCHE EN ELECTRISCHE TERMEN, AUTO EN FIETS ONDERDEELEN EN ACCESSOIRES, ENZ. (= *enzoovort*)

</td></tr>
</table>

L'acceleratore.	El acelerador.	Het gaspedaal.
Un accessorio.	Un accesorio.	Een onderdeel.
◄ Un accumulatore.	Un acumulador.	Een accu.
Una chiave ad aperture regolabile, Una chiave inglese.	Una llave de abertura variable, Una llave inglesa.	Een verstelbare schroefsleutel, Een Engelse sleutel.
Il condotto d'aspirazione.	El colector de admisión.	De inlaat verdelingsarm.
Una pompa da aria.	Una bomba de aire.	Een luchtpomp.
Un'ampere.	Un amperio.	Een ampère.
◄ Un amperometro.	Un amperímetro.	Een ampèremeter.
Un faro anti-abbagliamento.	Un faro contra la ceguera.	Een anti-verblinding lamp.
L'indotto.	El inducido.	Het anker.
L'amianto.	El amianto.	Het asbest.

An axle.	Un essieu.	Eine Achse.
An axle cap.	Un bonnet d'essieu.	Eine Achsenkappe. →
The back axle, *see under* The rear axle.		
A back fire.	Un retour de flamme.	Eine Rückzündung.
A back fire [kick].	Un [choc en] retour de manivelle.	Ein Rückschlag.
Backlash.	Du jeu [inutile].	Toter Gang.
A back tyre.	Un pneu [d']arrière.	Ein Hinterreifen.
The back wheel.	La roue [d']arrière.	Das Hinterrad. →
A baffle [plate].	Une chicane.	Eine Prallfläche.
A ball and socket.	Une rotule sphérique.	Ein Kugelgelenk.
Ball bearings.	Le roulement à billes, Des coussinets à billes.	Das Kugellager.
A band brake.	Un frein à ruban *ou* à bande.	Eine Bandbremse.
A battery (*electric*).	Une batterie, Une pile.	Eine Batterie.
The bearings (*Mach.*).	Les coussinets, Le palier, Le roulement.	Das Lager.
The bell (*Cyc.*).	Le timbre.	Die Glocke, Die Klingel.
A belt (*Mach.*).	Une courroie.	Ein Riemen.
A bevel wheel.	Une roue d'angle.	Ein Kegelrad.
The big end (*or* The crank pin end) of connecting rod.	La grosse tête de bielle.	Das Kurbelzapfenende der → Pleuelstange.
A blade for windscreen wiper.	Un balai pour essuie-glace.	Ein Abstreifer eines Scheibenwischers.
The body (*of a car*).	La caisse, La carrosserie.	Der Aufbau, Die Karosserie.
A body builder.	Un carrossier.	Ein Wagenbauer.
The bodywork.	La carrosserie.	Die Karosserie.
A bolt. To bolt.	Un boulon. Boulonner.	Ein Bolzen. Verbolzen. →
The bonnet (*of car*).	Le capot.	Die Haube.
The bore (*as of a cylinder*).	L'alésage.	Die Ausdrehung.
To bore [out].	Aléser.	Ausdrehen.
A box spanner.	Une clef à douille.	Ein Steckschlüssel.
A brake.	Un frein.	Eine Bremse. →
A brake block.	Un patin de frein.	Eine Bremsklotz.
A brake cable.	Un câble de frein.	Ein Bremskabel.
A brake drum.	Un tambour de frein.	Eine Bremstrommel.
The brake gear.	La timonerie des freins.	Die Bremsvorrichtung.
The brake lever.	Le levier du frein.	Der Handbremshebel. →
The brake pedal.	La pédale du frein.	Der Fußbremshebel.
The brake rod.	La tige du frein.	Die Bremsstange.
Brass.	Du laiton, Du cuivre [jaune].	Messing.
A brass (*bearing*).	Un coussinet.	Ein Messinglager.
To braze. Brazing.	Braser. Le brasage.	Hartlöten. Das Hartlöten. →
A brush (*cleaning*).	Une brosse.	Eine Bürste.
A brush (*dynamo*).	Un balai.	Eine Bürste.
A bulb horn.	Une trompe à poire.	Eine Ballhupe.

Un assale, Un asse, Una sala.	Un eje.	Een as.
◄ Un tappo di assale.	Un tapón de eje.	Een asdop.
Un ritorno di fiamma.	Una retrocesso de la llama.	Een terugslaande ontsteking.
Un contraccolpo, Un ritorno di manovella.	Una reculada de la manivela.	Een terugslag [bij het aanzetten der motor.]
Gioco inutile.	Juego inútil.	Dode gang.
Una gomma di dietro.	Un neumático trasero.	Een achterband.
◄ La ruota posteriore.	La rueda trasera.	Het achterwiel.
Una piastra di intercalazione.	Una chicana, Un tabique deflector.	Een brandplaat, Een zeefplaat.
Una rotella.	Una rótula.	Een kogelgewricht.
Un cuscinetto a sfere.	Cojinetes de bolas.	Een kogellager.
Un freno a nastro.	Un freno de cinta.	Een bandrem.
◄ Una batteria, Una pila.	Una batería, Una pila.	Een batterij.
I cuscinetti.	Los cojinetes.	De lagers, De kussens.
Il campanello.	El timbre, El cascabel.	De bel.
Una cinghia.	Una correa.	Een riem.
Un pignone d'angolo.	Un piñón de ángulo.	Een kegelrad.
◄ Il cuscinetto maggiore.	El cojinete mayor de la biela.	Het brede einde van de drijfstang.
Una spazzola [per] paravento.	Una hoja del limpiaparaviento.	Een veger voor ruitewisser.
La cassa.	La carroza.	De carrosserie.
Un fabbricante di carrozzerie.	Un carrocero.	Een carrosseriebouwer.
La carrozzeria.	La carrocería.	De carosserie.
◄ Un bullone. Inchiavardare.	Un perno. Atornillar.	Een bout. Vastklinken.
Il cofano.	El capó.	De kap.
L'alesaggio.	El alesage.	De boring.
Alesare.	Alesar.	Boren.
Una chiave femmina.	Una llave tubular.	Een dopsleutel.
◄ Un freno.	Un freno.	Een rem.
Un ceppo di freno.	Una zapata de freno.	Een remblok.
Una fune di freno.	Un cable de freno.	Een remkabel.
Un tamburo di freno.	Un tambor de freno.	Een remtrommel.
Gli organi di frenaggio.	La timonería del frenado.	De remgearing.
◄ La leva del freno.	La palanca del freno.	De remhandle.
Il pedale del freno.	El pedal del freno.	Het rempedaal.
Il tirante del freno.	La varilla del freno.	De remstang.
L'ottone.	Latón.	Messing, Koper.
Una bronzina.	Un bronce.	Een messinglager.
◄ Saldare a ottone. La saldatura a ottone.	Soldar con latón. Soldadura de latón.	Solderen (met kopersoldeer). Het hardsolderen.
Una spazzola.	Un cepillo.	Een borstel, Een kwast.
Una spazzola.	Una escobilla.	Een borstel.
Una tromba a pera.	Una bocina con pera.	Een toeter.

A bulb shade.	Un cache-ampoule.	Ein Abdeckschirm.
A bumper.	Un pare-chocs.	Ein Stoßfänger. →
A burner.	Un bec, Un brûleur.	Ein Brenner.
A bush (*Mach.*).	Une coquille, Une bague, Une buselure, Un manchon.	Eine Hülse, Eine Büchse, Ein Futter.
A cable.	Un câble.	Ein Kabel.
The camshaft.	L'arbre à cames.	Die Nockenwelle.
A can carrier (*petrol*).	Un porte-bidon.	Ein Benzinkannenhalter. →
Carbonized.	Carbonisé, e.	Verkohlt.
Carburation.	La carburation.	Die Vergasung.
The carburettor, ·ter.	Le carburateur.	Der Vergaser.
The carrying axle.	L'essieu porteur.	Die Tragachse.
A case, Casing.	Un carter (*pronounce* cartère).	Ein Gehäuse, Ein Kasten. →
A cell jar.	Un bac d'éléments.	Ein Elementgefäß.
A chain.	Une chaîne.	Eine Kette.
The chain case.	Le couvre-chaîne.	Der Kettenschutzkasten.
The chain tension.	La tension de la chaîne.	Die Kettenspannung.
A chamois [leather].	Une peau de chamois, Un chamois.	Ein Gemslederlappen, Ein→ Lederlappen.
A change of gear.	Un changement de vitesse.	Ein Gangwechsel.
A change[-speed] gear. (*See also under* speed.)	Un changement de vitesse.	Ein Gangwechselgetriebe.
The chassis.	Le châssis.	Das Fahrgestell.
A cloth (*cleaning*).	Un chiffon.	Ein Lappen.
The clutch.	Le manchon d'embrayage, L'embrayage.	Die Kupplung. →
The clutch pedal.	La pédale d'embrayage.	Der Kupplungshebel.
A cock *or* A tap.	Un robinet.	Ein Hahn.
A coil (*induction*).	Une bobine.	Eine Spule.
A cold chisel.	Un burin (*ou* Un ciseau) à froid.	Ein Kaltmeißel, Ein Hartmeißel.
A collar (*Mach.*).	Un collier.	Ein Ring, Ein Kragen, Ein→ Reifen.
The combustion chamber.	La chambre d'explosion.	Die Explosionskammer.
The compression.	La compression.	Der Druck, Die Kompression.
A cone.	Un cône.	Ein Kegel.
A connecting rod.	Une bielle.	Eine Pleuelstange.
A contact.	Un contact, Une touche.	Ein Kontakt. →
To cool.	Refroidir.	Kühlen.
Cooling.	Le refroidissement.	Kühlung.
Copper wire.	Du fil de cuivre [rouge].	Kupferdraht.
A cotter.	Une clavette, Une cale.	Ein Keil. →
A countershaft.	Un [arbre de] renvoi, Un arbre secondaire.	Ein Vorgelege, Eine Vorgelegewelle.
A coupling.	Un accouplement, Un manchon.	Eine Kupplung, Eine Rohrverschraubung.
A cover (*for spare tyre*).	Une housse.	Ein Schutzüberzug.
A crank.	Une manivelle.	Eine Kurbel.

Un paralume.	Una pantalla para lámpara.	Een lampekap.
◄Un paracolpi.	Un parachoques.	Een bumper.
Un becco, Un beccuccio.	Un quemador, Un mechero.	Een brander.
Una bussola.	Un manguito.	Een bus.
Una fune.	Un cable.	Een kabel.
L'albero dei cammi.	El árbol de levas.	De nokkenas.
◄Un porta-latta.	Un portalatas.	Een drager voor benzine-blikken.
Carbonizzato, a.	Carbonizado, a.	Gecarboniseerd.
La carburazione.	Carburación.	Carburatie.
Il carburatore.	El carburador.	De carburator.
L'assale portabile.	El eje portador.	De draagas.
◄Un carter, Una scattola, Una cassa.	Una caja, Una funda, Una envoltura.	Een kast, Een bus, Een trommel, Een huls.
Un vaso di pila.	Un vaso de pila.	Een batterijglas.
Una catena.	Una cadena.	Een ketting.
Un copricatena.	La funda de la cadena.	Een kettingkast.
La tensione della catena.	La tensión de la cadena.	De strakheid van de ketting.
◄Una pelle di camoscio.	Una gamuza.	Een zeem.
Un cambio di velocità.	Un cambio de velocidad.	Het in een andere ver-snelling schakelen.
Un cambio di velocità.	Un cambio de velocidad.	Een versnellingsbak.
Lo chassis.	El chasis.	Het chassis.
Uno strofinaccio.	Un paño [de limpiar].	Een [poets]lap.
◄L'innesto, L'accoppia-mento, La frizione.	El embrague, El acopla-miento.	De koppeling, De em-brayage.
Il pedale d'innesto.	El pedal del embrague.	Het koppelingspedaal.
Un rubinetto.	Un grifo.	Een kraantje.
Una bobina.	Un carrete.	Een bobine.
Uno scalpello a freddo.	Un buril en frío.	Een koudbeitel.
◄Un collo, Un collare.	Un aro.	Een kraagring.
La camera di combustione.	La cámara de combustión.	De verbrandingsruimte.
La compressione.	La compresión.	De compressie.
Un cono.	Un cono.	Een kegel.
Una biella.	Una biela.	Een drijfstang.
◄Un contatto.	Un contacto.	Een contact.
Raffreddare.	Enfriar.	Koelen.
Il raffreddamento.	Enfriamiento.	De koeling.
Filo di rame.	Alambre de cobre.	Koperdraad.
◄Una bietta, Un cuneo.	Una chaveta.	Een spie.
Un [albero di] rinvio, Un albero secondario.	Un contra-eje, Un árbol secundario.	Een overbrengas, Een tegenas.
Un accoppiamento.	Un acoplamiento.	Een koppeling.
Una custodia, Un copri-pneu.	Una funda.	Een hoes.
Una manovella.	Una manivela.	Een kruk, Een slinger.

The crank (or The pedal) gear (Cyc.).	Le pédalier.	Der Fußantrieb, Das Pedalwerk.
A crank shaft.	Un arbre [à] manivelle, Un [arbre à] vilebrequin.	Eine Kurbelwelle.
A cushion.	Un coussin.	Ein Kissen, Ein Puffer.
Cutting pliers.	Des pinces coupantes.	Eine Beißzange.
A cyclometer.	Un compteur de bicyclette, Un compteur kilométrique.	Ein Zyklometer, Ein Wegmesser.
A cylinder.	Un cylindre.	Ein Zylinder.
A four-cylinder engine.	Un moteur à **quatre** cylindres.	Ein Vierzylindermotor.
A cylinder head.	Une culasse.	Ein Zylinderdeckel.
The dash board (*instrument board*).	La planche de bord, Le tableau [de bord], Le tablier.	Das Armaturenbrett, Die Stirnwand.
The differential [gear].	Le différentiel.	Das Wechselgetriebe, Das Differentialgetriebe.
A direction indicator (*semaphore arm on car*).	Un indicateur de direction, Un signal mécanique.	Ein Richtungszeiger, Ein Winker.
A distributer.	Un distributeur.	Ein Verteiler.
A door (*of a car*).	Une portière.	Eine Tür, Ein Schlag.
A dress guard (Cyc.).	Un garde-jupe.	Ein Kleiderschutz, Ein Kettenschützer.
A drill.	Un foret, Une mèche [à métaux].	Ein Bohrer.
To drill.	Percer, Forer.	Bohren.
The drive (Mach.).	La transmission.	Der Antrieb.
The driving axle.	L'essieu moteur.	Die Triebachse.
A driving mirror.	Un miroir rétroviseur.	Ein Rückschauspiegel.
The driving shaft.	L'arbre moteur.	Die Triebwelle.
A driving wheel.	Une roue motrice.	Ein Triebrad.
A drum (Mach.).	Un tambour.	Eine Trommel.
A dry battery.	Une pile sèche.	Eine Trockenbatterie.
The dumb iron or The spring carrier arm.	La main de ressort.	Die Federhand.
A dynamo.	Une dynamo.	Ein Dynamo.
Electric lighting.	L'allumage électrique.	Elektrisches Licht.
An electric torch.	Une lampe [électrique] de poche, Une torche électrique.	Eine elektrische Taschenlampe.
Emery cloth.	De la toile d'émeri.	Schmirgelleinwand.
The engine.	Le moteur.	Der Motor.
The engine casing.	Le carter (*pronounce cartère*) du moteur.	Der Motorkasten, Das Gehäuse.
The exhaust.	L'échappement.	Der Auspuff.
The exhaust gas[es].	Le[s] gaz d'échappement.	Das Auspuffgas.
The exhaust manifold.	Le collecteur d'échappement.	Der Auspuffsammler.
The exhaust pipe.	Le tuyau d'échappement.	Das Auspuffrohr.
The exhaust valve.	La soupape d'échappement.	Das Auspuffventil.
A fan.	Un ventilateur.	Ein Ventilator.

◄ Il pedaliere.	La transmisión de pedal, El pedal.	De pedaalaandrijving, Het pedaalwerk.
Un albero a manovella, Un albero a gomito.	Un árbol-manivela, Un cigüeñal.	Een krukas.
Un cuscinetto.	Una almohadilla.	Een kussen.
Una pinzetta a taglio.	Alicates de cortar.	Een draadtang.
Un ciclometro, Un contatore chilometrico.	Un ciclómetro, Un contador kilométrico.	Een kilometerteller.
◄ Un cilindro.	Un cilindro.	Een cylinder, Een cilinder.
Un motore a quattro cilindri.	Un motor de cuatro cilindros.	Een vier cylinder motor.
Una culatta di cilindro.	Una culata de cilindro.	Een cylinderdeksel.
Il cruscotto, Il grembiule.	El tablero.	Het dashbord.
Il [mecanismo] differenziale.	La transmisión por diferencial, El diferencial.	Een differentieel.
◄ Un indicatore di direzione.	Un indicador de dirección.	Een richtingwijzer.
Un distributore.	Un distribuidor.	Een stroomverdeler.
Una portella.	Un portezuela.	Een portier.
Un paraveste.	Un guardafaldas.	Een kettingkast.
Un trapano.	Un taladro.	Een boor.
◄ Trapanare.	Taladrar.	Boren.
La trasmissione.	El accionamiento.	De overbrenging.
L'assale motore.	El eje de accionamiento.	De aandrijfas.
Uno specchio retrospettivo.	Un espejo retrovisor.	Een achteruitkijkspiegel. Een autospiegel.
L'albero motore.	El árbol de accionamiento, El árbol motor.	De drijfas.
◄ Una ruota motrice.	Una rueda motrice.	Een drijfwiel.
Un tamburo.	Un tambor.	Een trommel.
Una pila secca.	Una pila seca.	Een droge batterij.
Il magnone di attacco della molla.	La mano de ballesta.	De veerhand.
Una dinamo.	Una dínamo.	Een dynamo.
◄ L'illuminazione elettrica.	Alumbrado eléctrico.	Electrisch licht.
Una lampadina [elettrica] tascabile, Una torcia elettrica.	Una antorcha (o Una hacha) eléctrica.	Een zaklamp, Een zaklantaarn.
Il panno smerigliato.	Paño de esmeril.	Schuurlinnen.
Il motore.	El motor.	De motor.
Il carter (o La scatola) del motore.	La envoltura del motor.	De motorkap.
◄ Lo scappamento, Lo scarico.	El escape.	De uitlaat.
I gas di scarico.	Los gases de escape.	De uitlaatgassen.
Il condotto di scappamento.	El colector de escape.	De uitlaatverdelingsarm.
Il tubo di scarico.	El tubo de escape.	De uitlaatpijp.
La valvola di scappamento.	La válvula de escape.	De uitlaatklep.
◄ Un ventilatore.	Un ventilador.	Een ventilator.

A feeler [gauge].	Un calibre [d'épaisseur] à lames.	Ein Fühler, Ein Taster.
A file. To file.	Une lime. Limer.	Eine Feile. Feilen.
A filter. To filter.	Un filtre. Filtrer.	Ein Filter. Filtrieren.
A fire extinguisher.	Un extincteur d'incendie.	Ein Feuerlöscher.
The fittings.	La garniture.	Die Armatur, Die Ausrüstung.
A flange. Flanged.	Une bride. À bride(s).	Eine Flansche. Umgebogen oder Umgelegt oder Flanschen-.
A float.	Un flotteur.	Ein Schwimmer.
To flood the carburettor.	Noyer le carburateur.	Den Vergaser überschwemmen.
A flywheel.	Un volant [de chasse ou d'entraînement ou de commande].	Ein Schwungrad.
The flywheel casing.	Le carter (pronounce cartère) du volant.	Das Schwungradgehäuse.
A foot brake.	Un frein au pied ou à pédale.	Eine Fußbremse.
A foot rest.	Un repose-pied[s].	Eine Fußstütze.
A foot starter.	Une pédale de mise en marche.	Ein Fußanlasser.
A footwarmer.	Une chaufferette.	Ein Fußwärmer.
Force-feed lubrication.	Le graissage sous pression.	Druckschmierung, Preßschmierung.
A forge. To forge.	Une forge. Forger.	Eine Schmiede. Schmieden.
The fork (Cyc.).	La fourche.	Die Gabel.
A four-wheel brake.	Un frein sur les quatre roues.	Eine Vierradbremse.
The frame (Mot.).	Le châssis, Le bâti, L'ossature.	Der Rahmen.
The frame (Cyc.).	Le cadre.	Der Rahmen.
A frame pump (Cyc.).	Une pompe de cadre.	Eine am Rad befestigte Pumpe.
A free wheel.	Une roue libre.	Ein Freilaufrad.
Friction.	Le frottement, La friction.	Reibung, Friktion.
A friction clutch.	Un embrayage à friction.	Eine Reibungskupplung, Eine Schleifkupplung.
The front axle.	L'essieu [d']avant.	Die Vorderachse.
A front tyre.	Un pneu [d']avant.	Ein Vorderreifen.
The front wheel.	La roue [d']avant.	Das Vorderrad.
The front sprocket wheel (Cyc.).	Le grand pignon, Le pignon pédalier, La roue dentée [d']avant.	Das vordere Kettenrad.
Fuel consumption.	La consommation de combustible.	Kraftstoffverbrauch.
A funnel.	Un entonnoir.	Ein Trichter, Ein Schornstein.
Fur (in tubes, etc.).	Des incrustations, Des dépôts, Du tartre.	Kesselstein.
A fuse (electric).	Un plomb [fusible].	Eine Sicherung.
A gaiter (for punctured tyre).	Une guêtre.	Ein Schutzring.

Le laminette da spessore.	Las tientas de calar.	Een taster.
Una lima. Limare.	Una lima. Limar.	Een vijl. Vijlen.
Un filtro. Filtrare.	Un filtro. Filtrar.	Een filter. Filteren.
Un estintore d'incendio, Uno spengitoio da fuoco.	Un apagador (o Un extintor) de incendios.	Blusapparaat.
◄ Il fornimento, L'armatura.	Las guarniciones.	De onderdelen. De hulpstukken.
Una flangia. A flangia.	Una brida. Con brida.	Een flens. Van flenzen voorzien.
Un galleggiante.	Un flotador.	Een vlotter.
Annegare il carburatore.	Anegar el carburador.	De carburator doen overstromen.
Un volante, Un volano.	Un volante [de regulación].	Een vliegwiel.
◄ Il carter del volante.	La envoltura del volante.	De vliegwielkast.
Un freno a pedale.	Un freno de pedal.	Een voetrem.
Un posa-piedi.	Un soporte para los pies.	Een voetrust.
Un avviatore a pedale.	Un arranque de pedal.	Een voetstarter.
Uno scaldapiedi.	Un calienta-pies, Un calentador [para los pies].	Een voetenwarmer.
◄ La lubrificazione sotto pressione.	Lubrificación a presión.	Het smeren onder druk.
Una fucina. Fucinare, Forgiare.	Una fragua, Una forja. Forjar.	Een smederij. Smeden.
La forcella.	La horquilla.	De vork.
Un freno sulle quattro ruote.	Un freno en las cuatro ruedas.	Een vierwielrem.
Il telaio.	El bastidor.	Het raam, Het frame, Het chassis.
◄ Il telaio, L'intelaiatura.	El cuadro.	Het frame.
Una pompa per telaio.	Una bomba para cuadro.	Een fietspomp die op het frame bevestigd kan worden.
Una ruota libera.	Una rueda libre.	Een freewheel.
La frizione, L'attrito.	Rozamiento.	Wrijving.
Un innesto a frizione.	Un embrague de fricción.	Een slipkoppeling.
◄ L'assale anteriore.	El eje delantero.	De vooras.
Un pneumatico davanti.	Un neumático delantero.	Een voorband.
La ruota davanti.	La rueda delantera.	Het voorwiel.
La ruota dentata grande.	El piñón delantero, El piñón grande.	Het grote kettingrad.
Il consumo di combustibile.	Consumo de combustible.	Brandstofverbruik.
◄ Un imbuto.	Un embudo.	Een trechter.
Le incrostazioni, I residui, I depositi.	Incrustación.	Ketelsteen.
Un fusibile.	Un fusible.	Een zekering.
Una ghetta.	Un forro.	Een [banden]hoes.

A gasket.	Une bague de garniture, Une baderne.	Eine Abdichtung, Eine Flanschendichtung.
A gauge.	Un appareil de mesure, Une jauge ; Un calibre ; Un manomètre.	Eine Lehre, Ein Eichmaß ; Ein Druckmesser.
A gear (*toothed wheels*).	Un engrenage.	Ein Zahnradgetriebe.
The gear (*speed-capacity of bicycle*).	Le développement.	Die Räderübersetzung.
The gear [ratio].	Le rapport de multiplication *ou* de transmission, La multiplication.	Das Übersetzungsverhältnis.
The gear box.	La boîte des vitesses.	Der Getriebekasten.
The gear case.	Le carter (*pronounce* cartère) [des engrenages].	Das Zahnradgehäuse.
The gear lever *or* The change speed lever.	Le levier du changement de vitesses, Le levier des vitesses.	Der Schalthebel.
A gear wheel.	Une roue d'engrenage.	Ein Zahnrad.
Goggles.	Des lunettes [d'automobiliste].	Staubbrille, Autobrille.
The governor (*Mach.*).	Le régulateur.	Der Regler.
Graphite lubrication *or* Graphiting.	Le graissage au graphite, Le graphitage.	Die Graphitschmierung.
Grease. To grease.	La graisse [consistante]. Graisser.	Schmiere, Schmierfette. Schmieren, Fetten.
A grease gun.	Une seringue à graisse *ou* pour huile épaisse.	Eine Hochdruckschmierpresse.
Greasing.	Le graissage.	Schmieren, Fetten.
A grip *or* A handle (*of handlebar*) (*Cyc.*).	Une poignée.	Ein Handgriff.
A hack saw.	Une scie à métaux.	Eine Hacksäge, Eine Kerbsäge.
A hammer.	Un marteau.	Ein Hammer.
A handle (*of car door*).	Une poignée.	Ein Türgriff, Eine Klinke.
A handle (*a hand lever*).	Une manette.	Ein Griff, Ein Hebel.
The handlebar (*Cyc.*).	Le guidon.	Die Lenkstange.
Handlebar tape.	Du ruban pour guidon.	Band für die Lenkstange.
A headlight *or* A head lamp.	Un phare.	Ein Scheinwerfer.
A head-lamp bracket.	Un porte-phare.	Eine Scheinwerfergabel.
A hexagonal nut.	Un écrou à six pans.	Eine sechskantige Mutter.
The hood (*fixed roof of car*).	Le pavillon fixe.	Das feste Verdeck.
The hood (*folding or Cape type*).	La capote, Le pavillon démontable.	Das Verdeck, Das Wagendach.
A horn *or* A hooter.	Un cornet [avertisseur], Un avertisseur.	Eine Hupe, Ein Signal.
A horn *or* A hooter (*reed type*).	Une trompe.	Eine Hupe.
Horse power. (*Note.*—English h.p.= 550 foot pounds per second. Metric h.p.=75 kilogrammetres per second, or .9863 of English h.p.)	Cheval[-vapeur].	Pferdestärke.

Una baderna di giunto guarnitura.	Un aro de empaquedura.	Een beslaglijn.
◄Uno strumento per misurare, Una misura; Un calibro; Un manometro.	Una regla para medir; Un calibrador; Un manómetro.	Een ijkmaat; Een kaliber; Een manometer.
Un ingranaggio.	Un engranaje.	Een gearing.
Lo sviluppo di velocità.	El desenvolvimiento de velocidad.	De overbrenging.
Il rapporto di trasmissione, La multiplicazione.	La relación de la multiplicación.	De overbrengingsverhouding.
La scatola del cambio di velocità.	La caja de velocidades.	De versnellingsbak.
◄Il carter (o La scatola) del cambio di velocità.	La envoltura de engranajes.	De kettingkast, Het versnellingscarter.
La leva di comando.	La palanca de mando.	De ontkoppelingshefboom.
Una ruota d'ingranaggio.	Una rueda de engranajes.	Een tandrad, Een tandwiel.
Gli occhiali da automobilista.	Anteojos, Gafas.	Een stofbril.
Il regolatore.	El regulador.	De regulateur.
◄La lubrificazione a grafite.	El engrase con grafito.	Het grafietsmeren.
Grasso. Ingrassare.	Grasa. Engrasar.	Vet. Invetten, Smeren.
Un ingrassatore a pressione.	Un engrasador por compresión.	Een vetspuit.
L'ingrassamento.	El engrase.	Het invetten. Het smeren.
Una manopola, Un'impugnatura.	Un puño, Una manecilla.	Een handle.
◄Una sega per metalli.	Una sierra para cortar metal.	Een metaalzaag.
Un martello.	Un martillo.	Een hamer.
Una maniglia.	Una perilla.	Een handle.
Una maniglia.	Una manigueta.	Een handvat.
Il manubrio.	El manillar.	Het stuur.
◄Un nastro per manubrio	Cinta para manillar.	Band voor handvaten.
Un faro, Un proiettore.	Un proyector, Un faro.	Een koplamp.
Un porta-faro.	Un porta-faro.	Een koplamphouder.
Un dado esagonale.	Una tuerca exagonal.	Een zeshoekige moer.
Il tetto fisso.	El pabellón fijo.	De dichte kap.
◄La capote, Il mantice, Il soffietto.	La capota, El pabellón móvil.	De opvouwbare kap.
Una cornetta.	Una bocina, Una corneta.	Een claxon.
Una tromba.	Una trompeta.	Een toeter.
Cavallo-vapore.	Potencia, Caballo de fuerza, Caballo vapor.	Paardekracht.

A ten horse [power] (or 10 h.p.) car.	Une [automobile de] dix chevaux[-vapeur] ou 10 chx[-vap.] ou 10 C.V.	Ein zehn Pferdestärke (oder Ein 10 P.S.) Wagen.
A hub.	Un moyeu.	Eine Nabe.
A hub brake.	Un frein sur moyeux.	Eine Nabenbremse.
A hub cap.	Un bouchon de moyeu.	Eine Nabenkappe.
A hub strap (Cyc.).	Un cache-poussière pour moyeu.	Ein Nabenschutz.
To ignite.	(transitive) Allumer ; (intransitive) S'allumer.	Zünden ; Sich entzünden.
The ignition.	L'allumage.	Die Zündung.
Ignition advance or Advanced ignition.	De l'avance à l'allumage.	Frühzündung, Vorzündung.
Ignition retard or Retarded ignition.	Du retard à l'allumage.	Spätzündung, Nachzündung.
The indiarubber.	Le caoutchouc.	Der Gummi, Der Kautschuk.
An induction coil.	Une bobine d'induction.	Eine Induktionsspule.
An inflator.	Un gonfleur, Une pompe [pour pneumatiques].	Eine Reifenpumpe.
The inlet manifold.	Le collecteur d'admission.	Das Ansaugrohr, Das Saugrohr.
The inlet valve.	La scupape d'admission.	Das Einlaßventil.
An inner tube (tyre).	Une chambre à air.	Ein Schlauch.
Insulation.	L'isolement.	Isolierung.
An insulator.	Un isolant.	Ein Isolator.
The intake.	L'admission, La prise.	Der Einlaß.
A jack.	Un cric, Un vérin.	Eine Winde, Ein Heber.
A jet.	Un jet.	Ein Strahl.
The jet (spraying nozzle of carburettor).	Le gicleur.	Die Düse.
A joint.	Un joint.	Ein Gelenk, Eine Fuge.
A key (lock).	Une clef.	Ein Schlüssel.
A key (shaft).	Une clavette, Une cale.	Ein Keil.
A keyway.	Une rainure (ou Un chemin) de clavette.	Ein Keilweg.
A lamp (electric bulb).	Une lampe.	Eine Lampe.
A lamp (lantern).	Une lanterne, Un feu.	Eine Laterne.
A lamp bracket.	Un porte-lanterne.	Ein Laternenhalter.
A layshaft.	Un arbre secondaire.	Eine Vorgelegewelle.
A leaf (of a spring).	Une lame.	Ein Blatt.
Leather.	Du cuir.	Leder.
A lens.	Une lentille.	Eine Linse.
A lever.	Un levier.	Ein Hebel.
The little end (or The crosshead end) of connecting rod.	La petite tête de bielle.	Das Kreuzkopfende der Pleuelstange.
A lock (fastener).	Une serrure.	Ein Schloß.
To lock.	Fermer à clef.	Schließen, Zuschließen.
A lock nut.	Un contre-écrou.	Eine Gegenmutter.
To lubricate.	Lubrifier, Huiler.	Schmieren.
Lubricating oil.	De l'huile de graissage.	Schmieröl.
A luggage carrier or grid.	Un porte-bagages.	Ein Kofferhalter.

Una [automobile] à dieci cavalli o 10 Cav. Vap. o 10 C.V.	Un coche de diez caballos o 10 C.V.	Een auto van tien paardekracht (of van 10 p.k.).
◄ Un mozzo.	Un cubo.	Een naaf.
Un freno sul mozzo.	Un freno sobre cubo.	Een naafrem.
Un tappo di mozzo.	Una tapa de cubo.	Een naafdop.
Un coperchio parapolvere.	Un guarda-polvo.	Een stofdop voor naaf.
Accendere ; Accendersi.	Encender ; Encenderse.	Ontsteken.
◄ L'accensione.	El encendido.	De ontsteking.
L'anticipazione all'accensione.	El avance al encendido.	Vóórontsteking.
Il ritardo all'accensione.	El retardo al encendido.	Náontsteking.
Il cauccìù.	El caucho.	Het rubber, Het gummi.
Un rochetto d'induzione.	Un carrete de inducción.	Een inductiebobine.
◄ Un gonfiatoio, Una pompa d'aria.	Una bomba para inflar.	Een (fiets)pomp.
Il condotto di aspirazione.	El colector de admisión.	De inlaatverdelingsarm.
La valvola di ammissione o di aspirazione.	La válvula de admisión o de aspiración.	De inlaatklep.
Una camera d'aria.	Una cámara de aire.	Een binnenband.
L'isolamento.	Aislamiento.	Isolatie.
◄ Un isolatore.	Un aislador.	Een isolator.
L'ammissione, L'aspirazione.	La admisión, La aspiración.	De toevoer.
Un martinetto, Un cricco.	Un gato.	Een krik.
Un getto.	Un chorro.	Een straal.
L'ugello per spruzzo, Lo spruzzatore.	El inyector.	De sproeier.
◄ Un giunto.	Una junta.	Een las.
Una chiave.	Una llave.	Een sleutel.
Una bietta, Una chiavetta, Un cuneo.	Una chaveta, Una cuña.	Een spie.
Una scanalatura per bietta.	Una ranura de chaveta.	Een spiegat, Een sleuf.
Una lampada.	Una lámpara.	Een lamp.
◄ Un fanale, Una lanterna.	Una linterna, Un farol.	Een lamp.
Un portafanale.	Un porta-farol.	Een lamphouder, Een lamparm.
Un [albero di] rinvio, Un albero secondario.	Un contra-eje, Un árbol secundario.	Een nevenas.
Una lamina, Una foglia.	Una hoja.	Een blad.
Il cuoio.	Cuero.	Leer.
◄ Una lente.	Un lente.	Een lens.
Una leva.	Una palanca.	Een hefboom.
Il cuscinetto minore della biella.	El extremo menor de la biela.	Het smalle einde van de drijfstang.
Una serratura.	Una cerradura.	Een slot.
Chiudere a chiave.	Cerrar con llave.	Sluiten.
◄ Un controdado.	Una contratuerca.	Een contramoer.
Lubrificare.	Lubrificar.	Smeren.
L'olio lubrificante.	Aceite lubrificante	Smeerolie.
Un porta-bagagli	Un portaequipajes.	Een bagagedrager.

A magnet.	Un aimant.	Ein Magnet.
A magneto.	Une magnéto.	Ein Zündmagnet.
A make-and-break.	Un [inter]rupteur.	Ein Stromunterbrecher.
A map.	Une carte.	Eine Karte.
A map holder, with one face celluloid.	Un liseur pour cartes, avec une face celluloïd.	Eine Kartentasche mit Zelluloidwand.
A mascot (on car).	Un fétiche.	Eine Maskotte.
A milled nut.	Un écrou à molette.	Eine geränderte Mutter.
The motor (engine).	Le moteur.	Der Motor.
A mudguard.	Un garde-boue.	Ein Kotflügel, Ein Schutzblech.
A non-skid chain.	Une chaîne antipatinante.	Eine Gleitschutzkette, Eine Schneekette.
A notch.	Un cran.	Eine Kerbe, Eine Furche.
A nut (Mach.).	Un écrou.	Eine Schraubenmutter.
Oil, To oil.	De l'huile. Huiler.	Öl. Schmieren.
An oil can (storage).	Un bidon à huile.	Eine Ölkanne.
An oil can (nozzled).	Une burette [à huile].	Eine Ölspritze.
An oil groove.	Une rainure de graissage, Une patte d'araignée.	Eine Ölnute, Eine Schmiernute.
An oil hole.	Un trou graisseur.	Eine Ölbohrung.
The oil tank.	Le réservoir d'huile.	Der Ölbehälter, Der Öltank.
An oiler (Mach.)	Un graisseur.	Ein Öler.
An outer cover (tyre).	Une enveloppe.	Eine Reifendecke.
The outlet manifold.	Le collecteur d'echappement.	Der Auspuffsammler.
Overheating.	Le surchauffage, Un coup de feu.	Überhitzung.
A panel (body).	Un panneau, Une planche.	Eine Füllungsplatte.
Paraffin [oil].	L'huile de pétrole, Du pétrole à brûler.	Paraffinöl, Petroleum.
To paraffin.	Paraffiner.	Mit Paraffin reinigen.
Parking lights: white in front and red at back.	Feux de position : blanc à l'avant et rouge vers l'arrière.	Standlichter : vorne weiß und hinten rot.
A part (of machinery).	Une pièce.	Ein Teil.
A patch (outer cover).	Un emplâtre.	Eine Mantelmanschette.
A patch (inner tube).	Une pastille.	Ein Flicken.
A pawl.	Un cliquet [d'arrêt], Un chien.	Eine Sperrklinke.
A pedal.	Une pédale.	Ein Fußhebel, Ein Pedal.
Petrol.	De l'essence.	Benzin.
A petrol can or tin.	Un bidon à essence.	Eine Benzinkanne.
A petrol can carrier.	Un porte-bidon.	Ein Benzinkannenhalter.
The petrol pump.	La pompe à essence.	Die Benzinpumpe.
The petrol tank.	Le réservoir d'essence.	Der Benzinbehälter, Der Kraftstoffbehälter.
Pincers.	Des tenailles.	Eine Zange.
A pinion.	Un pignon.	Das Kleinere von zwei ineinandergreifenden Zahnrädern, Ein Ritzel, Ein Triebel.
A pipe.	Un tuyau.	Eine Röhre, Ein Rohr.

Una calamita.	Un imán.	Een magneet.
Una magnete.	Un magneto.	Een ontstekingsmagneet.
Un interruttore.	Un [inter]ruptor.	Een onderbreker.
Una carta.	Un mapa.	Een kaart.
Un porta carta con la facciata in celluloide.	Un portamapa, con ventana de celuloide.	Een kaartenhouder met een celluloid voorzijde.
Un portafortuna.	Una mascota.	Een mascotte.
Un dado molletato.	Una tuerca estriada.	Een gekartelde moer.
Il motore.	El motor.	De motor.
Un parafango.	Un guardabarros.	Een spatbord.
Una catena antisdrucciolevole	Una cadena antideslizante.	Een antislipketting. Een sneeuwketting.
Una tacca, Un incavo.	Una muesca.	Een inkeping, Een kerf.
Un dado.	Una tuerca.	Een moer.
L'olio.	Aceite. Aceitar.	Olie smeren.
Un bidone per olio.	Una lata para aceite.	Een oliekan.
Un oliatore a mano.	Una aceitera.	Een oliekan.
Una scanalatura per l'olio.	Una ranura para aceite, Una pata de araña.	Een oliegroef, Een smeergleuf.
Un buco ingrassatore.	Un orificio para aceite.	Een oliegaatje, Een smeergaatje.
Il serbatoio d'olio.	El depósito de aceite.	De olietank, De oliebak.
Un oliatore.	Un lubri[fi]cador.	Een smeerdop.
Una copertura.	Una cubierta.	Een buitenband.
Il condottore di scappamento.	El colector de escape.	De uitlaatverdelingsarm.
Un colpo di fuoco.	El recalentamiento.	Oververhitting.
Una tavola.	Un panel, Un tablero.	Een paneel.
L'olio di paraffina.	Parafina, Aceite de petróleo.	[Gezuiverde] petroleum, Lichtpetroleum.
Paraffinare.	Aplicar parafina.	Met petroleum schoonmaken.
I fanali di posizione: bianchi anteriori e rossi posteriori.	Lámparas de estacionamiento: blanco delantero y rojo trasero.	Parkeerlichten: wit vóór en rood achter.
Un pezzo.	Una pieza.	Een deel.
Una rappezzatura.	Un emplasto.	Een lap.
Un impiastro di gomma.	Una pastilla.	Een pleister.
Un nottolino [d'arresto].	Un trinquete [de detención].	Een pal, Een klink.
Un pedale.	Un pedal.	Een pedaal, Een trapper.
La benzina.	Gasolina.	Benzine.
Una latta per benzina.	Una lata para gasolina.	Een benzinekan, Een benzineblik.
Un portalatta da benzina.	Un portalatas de gasolina.	Een drager voor benzineblikken.
La pompa per benzina.	La bomba de gasolina.	De benzinepomp.
Il serbatoio (o La cisterna) di benzina.	El depósito de gasolina.	De benzinetank.
Le tanaglie.	Tenazas, Pinzas.	Een nijptang.
Un pignone.	Un piñón.	Een klein tandwiel, Een rondsel.
Un tubo.	Un tubo.	Een pijp, Een buis.

A pipe wrench.	Une clef pour tuyaux.	Ein Rohrschlüssel, Eine Rohrklemme.
The piping.	La tuyauterie.	Die Rohrleitung.
A piston.	Un piston.	Ein Kolben.
A piston ring.	Un segment de piston.	Ein Kolbenring.
Play (*Mach.*).	Du jeu.	Spiel, Spielraum.
A [pair of] pliers.	Une pince, Des pinces.	Eine kleine Zange, Eine Drahtzange.
A [sparking] plug.	Une bougie [d'allumage].	Eine Kerze, Eine Zündkerze.
Pre-ignition *or* Self-ignition.	L'allumage prématuré, L'auto-allumage.	Selbst[ent]zündung.
The pressure.	La pression, La tension, La charge.	Der Druck, Die Spannung.
A pressure drop.	Une perte de charge.	Ein Abfallen des Drucks, Ein Nachlassen der Spannung.
The propeller (*or* The cardan) shaft.	L'arbre de cardan.	Die Triebwelle, Die Kardanwelle.
A pulley.	Une poulie.	Eine Rolle, Eine Riemenscheibe.
A pump.	Une pompe.	Eine Pumpe.
A pump connexion *or* union (*inflation*).	Un raccord de pompe.	Eine Pumpenverbindung.
A quadrant.	Un secteur.	Ein Sektor, Ein Zahnbogen.
The radiator (*cooling*).	Le radiateur.	Der Kühler.
A radiator cover.	Un couvre-radiateur.	Eine Kühlerhaube.
A rag (*cleaning*).	Un chiffon.	Ein Lappen.
A ratchet.	Un rochet.	Ein Klinkwerk, Ein Sperrwerk.
A rat-trap pedal.	Une pédale à scies.	Ein gerifteltes Pedal.
To ream. A reamer.	Aléser, Un alésoir.	Erweitern, Aufreiben. Eine Reibahle.
The rear (*or* The back) axle.	L'essieu [d']arrière, Le pont arrière.	Die Hinterachsbrücke.
The rear (*or* The back) axle casing.	Le carter (*pronounce* cartère) du pont arrière, L'articulation de l'essieu arrière.	Das Hinterachsgehäuse.
A rear brake.	Un frein [d']arrière.	Eine Rückbremse.
A rear red reflector for mudguard.	Un [arrêt de vélo à] feu rouge (*ou* Un cabochon rouge) arrière pour garde-boue.	Ein Katzenauge für Kotflügel.
The rear sprocket wheel (*Cyc.*).	Le petit pignon, La roue dentée [d']arrière.	Das hintere Kettenrad.
A rear "stop" lamp *or* light.	Une lanterne [d']arrière avec signal[isateur] "stop."	Ein rückwärtiges Stopplicht.
To reassemble.	Rassembler.	Wiederzusammensetzen.
A refill (*for torch*).	Une batterie (*ou* Une pile) de rechange.	Eine Ersatzbatterie.
A reflector (*of lamp*). (*Compare* A rear red reflector.)	Un réflecteur.	Ein Reflektor, Ein Rückstrahler.
A repair outfit *or* A [tyre] patch set.	Un nécessaire à réparations *ou* à rapiécer.	Ein Reparaturkasten, Ein Flickkasten.

Una pinza a tubazione.	Una llave de mordaza para tubos.	Een pijpsleutel.
La tubazione.	La tubería.	De pijpen.
◄Uno stantuffo.	Un pistón, Un émbolo.	Een zuiger.
Un anello di stantuffo.	Un aro de pistón.	Een zuigerring.
Gioco.	Juego.	Speling. Speelruimte.
Le pinzette.	Alicates.	Een tang.
Una candela [d'accensione].	Una bujía [de encendido].	Een bougie.
◄L'accensione spontanea o automatica.	Encendido espontáneo o automático.	Zelf-ontsteking, Zelf-ontbranding.
La pressione. Il carico.	La presión.	De druk.
Una perdita di pressione.	Una perdida de presión.	Een verlies van druk.
L'albero a cardano.	El árbol de cardan.	De cardanas.
Una puleggia.	Una polea.	Een [riem]schijf.
◄Una pompa.	Una bomba.	Een pomp.
Un tubo di pompa.	Un tubo flexible para bomba.	Een pompverbinding.
Un settore.	Un sector.	Een kwadrant.
Il radiatore.	El radiador.	De radiator.
Un copri-radiatore.	Una cubierta de radiador.	Een radiatorhoes.
◄Uno straccio.	Un trapo [de limpiar].	Een poetslap.
Un rocchetto, Un arresto.	Una palanca de trinquete.	Een palwerk met tanden.
Un pedale a sega.	Un pedal con dientes.	Een getand pedaal.
Alesare. Un alesatore.	Escariar. Un escariador.	Ruimen. Een ruimer.
La sala posteriore, Il ponte posteriore.	El eje trasero, El puente atrás.	De achteras.
◄La scatola dell'asse posteriore.	La articulación del eje trasero.	De achteraskast.
Un freno posteriore.	Un freno trasero.	Een achterrem.
Un dispositivo a superficie riflettente rossa per parafango posteriore.	Un reflector rojo trasero para guardabarros.	Een reflector voor het spatbord.
La ruota dentata piccola.	La rueda de cadena trasera, El piñon pequeño.	Het kleine kettingrad.
Un fanalino posteriore con segnale " stop."	Una lámpara trasera de " parada."	Een achterlicht, Een stoplicht.
◄Rimettere assieme.	Montar de nuevo.	Opnieuw monteren.
Una pila di ricambio.	Una pila de repuesto.	Een reserve zaklamp batterij.
Un riflettore.	Un reflector.	Een reflector.
Un corredo per riparazioni, Un astuccio per rattoppare.	Un estuche de reparación.	Een reparatiedoos.

A retreaded tyre.	Un pneu rechapé.	Ein neubelegter Reifen.
The reverse (or reversing) gear.	L'appareil de renversement de marche.	Der Rückwärtsgang. →
A revolution.	Un tour, Une révolution.	Eine Umdrehung, Eine Tour.
So many rev[olution]s a (or per) minute.	Tant de tours à la (ou par) minute.	Soundso viele Umdrehungen in der (oder pro) Minute.
The rim (of wheel).	La jante.	Die Felge.
A rim brake.	Un frein sur jantes.	Eine Felgenbremse.
A rivet. To rivet.	Un rivet. River.	Ein Niet. [Ver]nieten. →
A road map.	Une carte routière.	Eine Wegekarte.
A rod.	Une tige.	Eine Stange.
Roller bearings.	Des coussinets à galets, Le roulement à rouleaux.	Rollenlager.
The roof (of car).	Le toit, Le pavillon.	Das Dach.
The rubber.	Le caoutchouc.	Der Gummi, Der Kaut-→ schuk.
A rubber pedal.	Une pédale [en] caoutchouc.	Ein Gummipedal.
Rubber solution.	De la [dis]solution de caoutchouc.	Gummilösung.
Rubber tubing for air valve.	Boyau pour valves.	Ventilschlauch.
A running board.	Un marchepied.	Ein Trittbrett, Ein Laufbrett.
A saddle (Cyc.).	Une selle.	Ein Sattel. →
A saddle spring.	Un ressort de selle.	Eine Sattelfeder.
Safety glass.	Le verre de sûreté.	Splitterfreies Glas.
Scale (in tubes, etc.).	Des incrustations, Des dépôts, Du tartre.	Kesselstein.
A screw. To screw.	Une vis. Visser.	Eine Schraube. Schrauben.
A screwdriver.	Un tournevis.	Ein Schraubenzieher. →
A seat.	Un siège ; Une place.	Ein Sitz.
The seat[ing] (of a car).	La banquette.	Die Sitze.
The seat stem or The saddle pillar (Cyc.).	La tige de selle, Le support de la selle.	Die Sattelstange.
A sector (quadrant).	Un secteur.	Ein Sektor, Ein Zahnbogen.
A self starter.	Un démarreur automatique, Un auto-démarreur, Un moteur de lancement.	Ein Selbstanlasser. →
A shaft.	Un arbre.	Eine Welle.
The shafting.	La transmission [d'arbres].	Die Übersetzung, Die Transmission.
A shock absorber.	Un amortisseur.	Ein Stoßdämpfer.
A side lamp or light.	Une lanterne de côté.	Eine Seitenlampe.
The silencer.	Le silencieux, Le pot d'échappement.	Der Auspufftopf. →
A sliding roof.	Un toit découvrable.	Ein Rolldach, Ein Schiebedach.
A socket.	Une douille.	Eine Hülse, Eine Fassung.
To solder	Souder.	Löten.

Una gomma rinnovata.	Un neumático con periferie renovada.	Een gevulcaniseerde band.
◄ Il meccanismo d'inversione di marcia.	El mecanismo de inversión de giro.	Zijn achteruit.
Un giro.	Una revolución, Una vuelta.	Een omwenteling, Een toer.
Tanti giri al minuto.	Tantas vueltas por minuto.	Zoveel revoluties (of toeren) per minuut.
Il cerchione, La corona.	La llanta, La corona.	De velg.
Un freno sui cerchioni.	Un freno de llanta.	Een velgrem.
◄ Un chiodo da ribadire. Ribadire.	Un remache, Un roblón. Remachar.	Een klinknagel. Klinken.
Una pianta stradale.	Un plano de carreteras.	Een wegenkaart.
Una verga, Un tirante.	Una barra, Una varilla.	Een stang.
Supporto a rulli.	Cojinete de rodillos.	Rollager.
Il tetto.	El techo.	Het dak.
◄ Il caucciù.	El caucho.	Het rubber, Het gummi.
Un pedale di caucciù.	Un pedal de caucho.	Een rubber pedaal.
La soluzione di gomma.	[Di]solución de goma.	Solutie.
Tubetto della valvola.	Tubo de caucho para válvulas.	Ventielslang.
Un marciapiede.	Un estribo.	Een treeplank.
◄ Una sella.	Una silla.	Een zadel.
Una molla da sella.	Un resorte de silla.	Een zadelveer.
Un vetro di sicurezza.	Vidrio de seguridad.	Veiligheidsglas.
Le incrostazioni, I residui, I depositi.	Incrustación.	Ketelsteen.
Una vite. Avvitare.	Un tornillo. Atornillar.	Een schroef. Schroeven.
◄ Un cacciavite.	Un des[a]tornillador.	Een schroevedraaier.
Una sedia.	Un asiento.	Een [zit]plaats.
I sedili.	Los asientos.	De zitplaatsen.
Il portasella.	El soporte de la silla.	De zadelpen.
Un settore.	Un sector.	Een kwadrant.
◄ Un auto-avviatore.	Un arranque automático, Un auto-arrancador.	Een zelf starter.
Un albero.	Un árbol.	Een as.
La trasmissione [ad alberi].	El juego de árboles o de ejes, La transmisión.	De asleiding.
Uno smorzatore di scosse, Un para-urti.	Un amortiguador de choques.	Een schokbreker.
Un fanale laterale.	Un farol lateral.	Een zijlamp, Een stadslicht.
◄ Il silenziatore, La marmitta di scarico.	El silencioso.	De knalpot.
Un tetto mobile.	Un techo amovible.	Een schuifdak.
Una boccola, Un manicotto.	Un enchufe.	Een huls, Een mof.
Saldare.	Soldar.	Solderen.

A soldering iron.	Un fer à souder.	Ein Lötkolben.
The solution (*rubber*).	La [dis]solution.	Die Lösung.
A spanner.	Une clef [à écrous].	Ein Schraubenschlüssel.
A spare [part].	Une pièce de rechange.	Ein Ersatzteil.
A spare petrol can *or* tin.	Un bidon de secours à essence.	Eine Ersatzbenzinkanne.
A spare wheel.	Une roue de secours.	Ein Ersatzrad.
A spark.	Une étincelle.	Ein Funken.
The spark gap.	Le pont d'éclatement *ou* d'allumage.	Die Funkenstrecke, Die Zünderbrücke.
Sparking.	L'allumage.	Zündung.
A sparking plug.	Une bougie d'allumage.	Eine Zündkerze.
A three-speed gear.	Un dispositif à trois vitesses.	Ein Dreiganggetriebe.
A hub with two-speed gear *or* A change-speed [gear].	Un moyeu de multiplication double, Un changement de vitesse.	Eine Doppelübersetzungsnabe.
A speed indicator *or* A speedometer.	Un indicateur (*ou* Un compteur) de vitesse.	Ein Geschwindigkeitsmesser.
A spindle (*cycle wheel*).	Un axe.	Eine Achse.
A spiral spring.	Un ressort à boudin.	Eine Spiralfeder.
A split pin.	Une goupille fendue.	Ein Splint, Ein Schlitzstift.
A spoke.	Un rayon.	Eine Speiche.
The spraying nozzle.	Le gicleur.	Die Spritzdüse.
A spring.	Un ressort.	Eine Feder.
The springing (*Mot.*).	La suspension.	Die Federung.
A sprocket (*or* A chain) wheel (*Cyc.*).	Un pignon de chaîne, Une roue à chaîne.	Ein Kettenrad.
The starter (*Mach.*).	Le démarreur.	Der Anlasser.
A starting handle.	Une manivelle de mise en marche.	Ein Anlasserhebel.
The steering column.	La coloune de direction.	Die Lenksäule.
The steering gear.	Le mécanisme (*ou* L'engrenage) de direction.	Das Lenkgetriebe.
The steering rod.	La barre de direction.	Die Lenkstange.
The steering wheel (*inside car*).	Le volant de direction.	Das Lenkrad, Das Steuerrad.
Stream-lined.	Caréné, e, Profilé, e, Fuselé, e, Effilé, e, [À profil] aérodynamique.	Stromlinienförmig.
A stroke (*movement of the piston*).	Un coup.	Ein Schlag.
A two-stroke, A four-stroke, engine.	Un moteur à deux temps, à quatre temps.	Ein Zweitaktmotor, Ein Viertaktmotor.
The [length of] stroke (*of the piston*).	La course.	Die Hublänge, Der Kolbenweg.
A stud.	Un goujon [prisonnier].	Ein Stift.
Suction.	L'aspiration.	Saugung.
The sump.	La cuvette d'égouttage, Le fond de carter (*pronounce* cartère).	Der Sumpf.
A sun-glare shield.	Un écran anti-éblouissant, Un pare-soleil.	Eine Blendschutzscheibe.
A sunshine roof.	Un toit découvrable.	Ein Rolldach, Ein Schiebedach.

Un saldatoio.	Un soldador.	Een soldeerbout.
◄La soluzione.	La [di]solución.	De solutie.
Una chiave [per dadi].	Una llave [de tuerca].	Een sleutel.
Un pezzo di ricambio.	Una pieza de repuesto.	Een reserve-onderdeel.
Una latta di benzina di riserva.	Una lata de gasolina de repuesto.	Een reservebenzineblik.
Una ruota di ricambio.	Una rueda de repuesto.	Een reservewiel.
◄Una scintilla.	Una chispa.	Een vonk.
Il ponte d'accensione.	El puente de encendido.	De vonkenbrug.
L'accensione.	El encendido.	De ontsteking.
Una candela d'accensione.	Una bujía de encendido.	Een bougie.
Un ingrannaggio a tre velocità.	Un engranaje de tres cambios.	Een drijfwerk met drie versnellingen.
◄Un mozzo a due velocità.	Uno cubo para multiplicación [doble].	Een naaf met een dubbele versnelling.
Un indicatore di velocità.	Un contador de velocidad, Un velocímetro.	Een snelheidsmeter.
Un asse.	Un husillo.	Een as.
Una molla a spirale.	Un resorte en espiral.	Een spiraalveer.
Uno spillo spaccato.	Una chaveta hendida.	Een splitpen.
◄Una razza, Un razzo.	Un rayo.	Een spaak.
L'ugello per spruzzo, Lo spruzzatore.	El inyector.	De sproeier.
Una molla.	Un muelle, Un resorte.	Een veer.
La sospensione.	La suspensión.	De veerophanging.
Un pignone a catena, Una ruota dentata a catena.	Un piñón de cadena.	Een [getand]kettingrad.
◄La messa in moto.	El arranque.	De starter.
Una manovella d'avviamento.	Una manivela de arranque.	Een aanzetslinger.
Il tubo di direzione, La colonna dello sterzo.	La columna de dirección.	De stuurkolom.
Il meccanismo di direzione, Il comando guida.	El mecanismo de dirección.	De stuurbeweging.
La barra di direzione.	La varilla de dirección.	De stuurstang.
◄Il volante di guida.	El volante de dirección.	Het stuur(wiel).
Affusolato, a, Aerodinamico, a.	Afilado, a, Aerodinámico, a.	Gestroomlijnd.
Un colpo.	Un golpe.	Een slag.
Una macchina a due tempi, a quattro tempi.	Un motor de dos tiempos, de cuatro tiempos.	Een tweetakt. Een viertakt, motor.
La corsa.	El recorrido.	De slaglengte.
◄Una vite prigioniera.	Un espárrago, Un perno prisionero.	Een tapbout.
L'aspirazione.	La aspiración.	De zuiging.
Lo scodellino, Il raccoglitore d'olio.	El vaso colector (o El sumidero) de aceite.	De oliebak.
Un parasole.	Una pantalla contra el sol.	Een zonneklep.
Un tetto mobile.	Un techo amovible.	Een schuifdak.

A suspension spring.	Un ressort de suspension.	Eine Tragfeder. →
A switch (*Elec.*).	Un interrupteur.	Ein Schalter.
A tail "stop" lamp *or* light.	Une lanterne [d']arrière avec signal[isateur] "stop."	Ein rückwärtiges Stopplicht.
A tank.	Un réservoir.	Ein Tank, Ein Behälter.
A tappet (*valve*).	Un poussoir, Une tige-poussoir, Un taquet, Un mentonnet.	Ein Ventilstößel.
A terminal.	Une borne.	Eine Polklemme. →
The thread (*of a screw*) (*the worm*).	Le filet, Le pas.	Das Gewinde, Der Schraubengang.
The thread (*the pitch*).	Le pas, Le filetage.	Die Gewindesteigung, Die Ganghöhe.
To thread a screw.	Fileter une vis.	Eine Schraube mit Gewinde versehen.
A throttle.	Un étrangleur.	Eine Drossel.
A thrust [bearing].	Un palier de butée, Une butée.	Ein Drucklager, Ein Widerlager. →
To time the ignition, the valves.	Régler l'allumage, les soupapes.	Die Zündung, Die Ventile, einstellen *oder* regulieren.
The timing gear.	Les engrenages de distribution, La distribution.	Die Zündungseinstellung.
A tip-up (*or* A flap) seat.	Un strapontin.	Ein Klappsitz.
A toe clip.	Un cale-pied[s].	Ein Fußhaken.
A tool.	Un outil.	Ein Werkzeug. →
A tool (*or* A saddle) bag, with tools (*Cyc.*).	Une sacoche garnie.	Eine Werkzeugtasche, mit Garnitur.
A tool box.	Une boîte à outils.	Ein Werkzeugkasten.
A tool outfit.	Une trousse d'outils.	Eine Werkzeuggarnitur.
A tooth (*Mach.*).	Une dent.	Ein Zahn.
A toothed wheel.	Une roue dentée.	Ein Zahnrad. →
A torch (*electric*).	Une lampe de poche, Une torche.	Eine Taschenlampe.
A traffic indicator (*semaphore arm on car*).	Un indicateur de direction, Un signal mécanique.	Ein Richtungszeiger, Ein Winker.
The transmission [gear].	La transmission.	Das Übersetzungsgetriebe.
The tread (*of a tyre*).	La bande de roulement, La semelle, La chape.	Das Laufband, Die Lauffläche.
The tread (*of a wheel*).	La surface de roulement, Le portant.	Die Rollfläche. →
A trouser clip.	Un pince-pantalon.	Eine Hosenklammer.
A tube.	Un tube.	Ein Rohr, Eine Röhre.
A twist drill.	Un foret hélicoïdal.	Ein Spiralbohrer.
A tyre.	Un pneu[matique], Un bandage.	Ein Reifen.
A tyre lever *or* remover.	Un démonte-pneus.	Ein Reifenheber. →
A tyre pump.	Une pompe à pneu.	Eine Reifenpumpe.

◄—Una molla di sospensione.	Un muelle de suspensión.	Een hangveer.
Un interruttore.	Un interruptor.	Een schakelaar.
Un fanalino posteriore con segnale " stop."	Una lámpara trasera de " parada."	Een achterlicht, Een stoplicht.
Un serbatoio, Una cisterna.	Un depósito, Un tanque.	Een tank.
Una palmola d'urto, Un pulsatore.	Una varilla de levantamiento.	Een klepstoter.
◄—Un morsetto.	Un borne.	Een [pool]klem, Een klemschroef.
Il filetto, Il pane.	**La rosca, El filete.**	De draad.
Il passo.	**El paso.**	De spoed, De ganghoogte.
Filettare una vite.	Filetear un tornillo.	Draadsnijden.
Uno strangolamento.	Un estrangulador.	Een smoorklep.
◄—Un cuscinetto di spinta.	Un cojinete de empuje.	Een einddruklager.
Registrare l'accensione, la punteria.	Regular el encendido, las válvulas.	De ontsteking, De kleppen, regelen.
L'ingranaggio di distribuzione.	El tren de la distribución.	De verdeling.
Uno strapontino.	Una bigotera.	Een klapzitting, Een opklapbankje.
Un fermapiede per pedale.	Un estribo.	Een voethaak.
◄—Un ferro, Un utensile.	Una herramienta.	(a single tool) Een werktuig, Een stuk gereedschap; (tools collectively) Gereedschap.
Una borsa, con i ferri.	Un portaherramientas, Una bolsa, con herramientas.	Een gereedschapstas met gereedschap.
Una cassetta per utensili.	Una caja de herramientas.	Een gereedschapskist.
Un necessario da utensili.	Un equipo de herramientas.	Een gereedschapsuitrusting.
Un dente	Un diente.	Een tand.
◄—Una ruota dentata.	Una rueda dentada.	Een tandrad, Een tandwiel.
Una lampadina tascabile, Una torcia.	Una antorcha, Una hacha.	Een zaklamp, Een zaklantaarn.
Un indicatore di direzione.	Un indicador de dirección.	Een richtingwijzer.
La trasmissione.	La transmisión.	De overbrenging.
La striscia di scorrimento.	La banda de rodamiento.	De loopband.
◄—La superficie di scorrimento.	La superficie de rodamiento.	Het rijvlak.
Un fermapantalone.	Un sujetapantalon.	Een broeksknijper.
Un tubo.	Un tubo.	Een buis, Een pijp.
Un trapano elicoidale.	Una broca salmónica, Una mecha en espiral.	Een spiraalboor.
Un pneumatico, Una gomma.	Un neumático.	Een (buiten)band.
◄—Una leva pel pneumatico o per smontare.	Una palanca para desmontar neumáticos.	Een bandenlichter.
Una pompa d'aria per pneumatici.	Un bomba infladora de neumáticos.	Een (fiets)pomp.

MECHANICAL AND ELECTRICAL TERMS

A union.	Un raccord.	Eine Verschraubung, Eine Schlauchverbindung.
A universal (or A cardan) joint or coupling.	Un joint universel, Un cardan.	Ein Kreuzgelenk, Ein Kardangelenk.
The upholstery (of car).	Le capitonnage.	Die Polsterung.
A valve.	Une soupape, Un clapet.	Ein Ventil. ➤
A valve (tyre).	Une valve.	Ein Ventil.
A valve cap (tyre).	Un chapeau (ou Un bouchon) de valve.	Eine Ventilkappe.
The valve gear.	Les engrenages de distribution, La distribution.	Der Ventilantrieb.
A vice.	Un étau.	Ein Schraubstock.
A visor.	Un pare-soleil, Un écran anti-éblouissant.	Eine Blendschutzscheibe. ➤
Voltage . . volts.	Voltage (ou Tension) . . volts.	Spannung . . Volt.
A voltmeter.	Un voltmètre.	Ein Spannungsmesser.
The wall of the cylinder.	La paroi du cylindre.	Die Zylinderwand.
A wallet, with tools.	Une sacoche garnie.	Eine Werkzeugtasche, mit Garnitur.
A washer (for bolt and nut).	Une rondelle.	Eine Unterlegscheibe. ➤
The water chamber.	La chambre à eau.	Die Wasserkammer.
Water-cooled.	À refroidissement d'eau.	Mit Wasserkühlung.
A water jacket.	Une chemise d'eau.	Ein Wassermantel.
To weld.	Souder [au blanc soudant].	Schweißen.
A wheel (running).	Une roue.	Ein Rad. ➤
A wheel (steering).	Un volant.	Ein Rad.
The wheel base.	L'empattement [des essieux].	Der Radstand, Der Achsstand.
A wheel cap.	Un chapeau de roue.	Eine Radkappe.
A wheel jack.	Un lève-roue, Un lève-auto.	Eine Wagenwinde, Ein Wagenheber.
A wick [for lamp].	Une mèche [pour éclairage].	Ein Docht, Ein Lampendocht. ➤
A wind screen.	Un pare-brise.	Eine Windschutzscheibe.
A wind-screen wiper.	Un essuie-glace.	Ein Scheibenwischer.
The winding of a coil.	L'enroulement d'une bobine.	Die Spulenwicklung.
The wings.	Les ailes.	Die Kotflügel, Die Schutzbleche.
A wing lamp.	Une lanterne d'aile.	Ein Kotflügellaterne. ➤
A wing (or A butterfly) nut.	Un écrou à oreilles, Un écrou papillon, Un papillon.	Eine Flügelmutter.
The wire. To wire.	Le fil. Poser les fils.	Der Draht. Eine Leitung legen, Einen Draht ziehen.
A wire edge tyre.	Un pneu à tringles.	Ein Stahlseilreifen, Ein SS=Reifen.
The wiring.	Les fils.	Die Drahtleitung.
A wrench.	Une clef, Un tourne-à-gauche.	Ein Schlüssel. ➤

Un raccordo.	Un manguito de unión.	Een schroefkoppeling.
Un giunto universale, Un giunto cardanico.*	Una junta universal, Un cardan.	Een universaal (of Een cardan) koppeling.
L'imbottitura, La guarnitura.	El almohadillado.	De bekleding.
◄Una valvola.	Una válvula.	Een klep, Een ventiel.
Una valvola.	Una válvula.	Een ventiel.
Un tappo di valvola.	Un tapón de válvula.	Een ventieldop.
La distribuzione.	La distribución.	De overbrenging.
Una morsa.	Un tornillo [de banco, etc.].	Een bankschroef.
◄Un parasole.	Una pantalla contra el sol.	Een zonneklep.
Voltaggio . . volte.	Voltaje . . voltios.	Voltage . . volts.
Un voltametro.	Un voltímetro.	Een voltmeter.
La parete del cilindro.	La pared del cilindro.	De cylinderwand.
Una borsa, con i ferri.	Un portaherramientas, Una bolsa, con herramientas.	Een gereedschapstas. met gereedschap.
◄Una ranella, Una rondella.	Una arandela.	Een onderlegring, Een moerplaatje.
La camera d'acqua.	La cámara de agua.	De watertank.
Con raffreddamento ad acqua.	Enfriamiento por agua.	Met waterkoeling.
Una camicia d'acqua.	Una camisa de agua.	Een watermantel.
Saldare [a caldo bianco sudante].	Soldar [en caliente].	Lassen.
◄Una ruota.	Una rueda.	Een rad, Een wiel.
Un volante.	Un volante.	Een stuur(wiel).
La distanza tra gli assi, L'interasse.	La distancia entre los ejes.	De wielbasis.
Un tappo di ruota.	Una tapa de rueda.	Een wieldop.
Un sollevatore (o Un martinetto) da vettura.	Un levanta-auto.	Een dommekracht, Een krik.
◄Un lucignolo [per lampada].	Una mecha [para lámpara].	Een [lampe]pit.
Un paravento.	Un vidrio corta-viento, Un paravien.	Een windscherm, Een voorruit.
Un netta-ghiaccio.	Un limpia-paraviento.	Een ruitewisser.
L'avvolgimento di una bobina.	El arrollamiento de una bobina.	De bobinewikkeling.
I parafanghi.	Las aletas.	De vleugels.
◄Un fanale di parafango.	Una lámpara montada en la aleta.	Een spatbordlamp.
Un dado ad aletta o a farfalla.	Una tuerca con orejas.	Een vleugelmoer.
Il filo. Posare i fili.	El alambre. Colocar los alambres.	De draad. Een leiding leggen, Een draad trekken.
Un pneumatico a bordi con rinforzo di filo d'acciaio.	Un neumático reforzado con bordes alambrados.	Een draadband.
I fili.	El alambrado.	Het dradennet.
◄Una chiave.	Una llave.	Een sleutel.

LODGING	HÉBERGEMENT	UNTERKUNFT
Establishments, **Enquiries,** **Telephoning**	**Établissements,** **Demandes** **de renseignements,** **Téléphone**	**Gaststätten,** **Anfragen,** **Fernsprecher**
A hotel.	Un hôtel [pour voyageurs].	Ein Hotel.
A hotel serving meals in the establishment itself.	Un hôtel-pension.	Eine Hotel-Pension.
An annex[e].	Une annexe, Une dépendance.	Eine Dependance.
Furnished, Unfurnished, apartments.	Des appartements meublés, non meublés.	Möblierte, **Unmöblierte,** Zimmer.
A boarding house *or* A pension.	Une pension de famille.	Eine Pension, Ein Fremden→heim.
Board and lodging *or* Board-residence.	Le vivre et le couvert, La table (*ou* La nourriture) et le logement, La pension.	Pension mit voller Verpflegung, Vollpension.
A private house letting rooms without board but with cooking facilities.	Une maison particulière louant des chambres sans pension mais avec facilité de cuisine.	Ein Privathaushalt, wo Zimmer ohne Verpflegung aber mit Kochgelegenheit abgegeben werden.
To rent (*or* To take) a house for the season.	Louer (*ou* Prendre) une maison pour la saison.	Ein Haus für die Saison mieten.
A bungalow.	Une maisonnette, Un chalet, Un pavillon.	Ein einstöckiges Landhaus.
A room *or* An apartment.	Une chambre, Une pièce, Un logement.	Ein Zimmer. →
A self-contained flat.	Un appartement indépendant.	Eine selbständige Wohnung.
An estate agent.	Un agent de location.	Ein Grundstückvermittler.
An estate agency *or* office.	Une agence de location, Une agence immobilière.	Eine Grundstückvermittlung.
Have you an eight-roomed villa to let for the season, for the summer holidays; two reception rooms, one sitting room, three bedrooms, kitchen and scullery?	Est-ce que vous avez une villa à huit pièces à louer pour la saison, pour les grandes vacances ; deux salons, un petit salon, trois chambres à coucher, cuisine et lavoir de cuisine?	Haben Sie eine Villa mit acht Zimmern für die Saison, für die Sommerferien, zu vermieten ; zwei Empfangszimmer, ein Wohnzimmer, drei Schlafzimmer, Küche und Abwaschraum?
Is the house detached, semi-detached? Is there main drainage, town (*or* company's) water, gas, electricity, a slot (*or* a prepayment) meter?	La maison est-elle isolée, jumelle? Y a-t-il le tout-à-l'égout, l'eau de la ville, le gaz, l'électricité, un compteur à paiement préalable *ou* un compteur à tire-lire?	Ist das Haus freistehend,→ gehört das Haus zu einem Doppelwohnhaus? Ist es an die Hauptkanalisation angeschlossen, hat es städtische Wasserversorgung, Gas, Elektrizität, einen Münzzähler *oder* einen Gasautomaten, einen Elektrizitätsautomaten?

ALLOGGIO	HOSPEDAJE	HUISVESTING
Stabilimenti, Domande d'informazioni, Telefono	**Establecimientos, Indagaciones, Teléfonos**	**Instellingen, Inlichtingen, Telefoon**

Un albergo.	Un hotel.	Een hotel.
Un albergo-pensione.	Un hotel pensión.	Een hotel-pension.
Un annesso.	Un anexo, Una dependencia.	Een bijgebouw, Een dependance.
Le camere mobiliate, non mobiliate, Gli appartamenti mobiliati, non mobiliati.	Habitaciones amuebladas, sin amueblar.	Gemeubileerde, Ongemeubileerde, kamers.
◄Una pensione di famiglia.	Una casa de huéspedes, Una pensión.	Een pension.
Vitto e alloggio, La pensione.	Mesa y habitación, Cuarto y comida, Pensión.	Kost en inwoning.
Una casa privata che affitta camere senza pensione con uso di cucina.	Una casa particular que alquila habitaciones sin pensión aunque prestando facilidades de cocina.	Een particulier, die kamers verhuurt zonder pension, maar met kookgelegenheid.
Prendere in affitto una casa per la stagione.	Arrendar (o Tomar) una casa para la temporada.	Een huis voor het seizoen huren of nemen.
Una casetta rustica d'un solo piano.	Una casa de un solo piso.	Een bungalow.
◄Una camera, Una stanza, Un locale, Un appartamento.	Una habitación, Un piso, Una pieza.	Een kamer, Een [woon]vertrek.
Un appartamento indipendente.	Un piso independiente.	Een vrije flat.
Un agente di beni immobili.	Un agente arrendatario.	Een makelaar.
Un'agenzia di beni immobili.	Una agencia de arrendamientos.	Een makelaarskantoor, Een woningbureau.
Ha Lei un villino di otto stanze da affittare per la stagione, per le vacanze estive ; due saloni o sale di ricevimento, un salottino, tre camere da letto, una cucina e la retrocucina ?	¿ Tiene usted para alquilar una casa de campo de ocho habitaciones (o piezas) para la temporada, para el veraneo ; dos salones, un saloncito o una alcoba, tres dormitorios, cocina y fregadero ?	Heeft U een villa met acht kamers te huur voor het seizoen, voor de zomervakantie ; twee ontvangkamers, een zitkamer, drie slaapkamers, keuken en bijkeuken ?
◄È la casa isolata, semi-isolata ? C'è un sistema di fognatura, acqua di città, il gas, l'elettricità, un distributore automatico di gas, di elettricità o un contatore a pagamento anticipato ?	¿ Es la casa aislada, medio aislada o gemela ? ¿ Tiene instalación urbana de cañerías, agua, gas, electricidad, vendedor automático de gas, de electricidad o contador de pago anticipado ?	Is het een alleenstaand huis, twee onder een kap ? Is er riolering leidingwater, gas, electriciteit, een muntmeter ?

Rent[al] (as of a house) per month, including linen, crockery and silver.	Prix de location par mois avec linge, vaisselle et argenterie.	Miete pro Monat einschließlich Bett- und Tischwäsche, Geschirr und Silber.
An inn with sleeping accommodation.	Une auberge où l'on peut coucher.	Ein Gasthaus mit Unterkunftsmöglichkeit, Ein Gasthof.
Is there an inn near here where I can put up (or stay) for the night?	Y a-t-il près d'ici une auberge où je puisse descendre pour la nuit?	Gibt es hier in der Nähe ein Gasthaus, wo ich für eine Nacht unterkommen kann?
A roadside inn.	Un cabaret de rencontre, Un tournebride.	Ein Gasthaus an der Landstraße.
A youth hostel.	Une auberge de la jeunesse.	Eine Jugendherberge. →
Can you recommend me a hotel at .., near the station, right in the centre of the town, facing the sea, au the square, the public gardens, on the [sea] front?	Pouvez-vous me recommander à .. un hôtel, près de la gare, en plein centre de la ville, face à la mer, à la place, au jardin public, sur la mer?	Können Sie mir ein Hotel in .., nahe am Bahnhof, direkt im Mittelpunkt der Stadt, mit Aussicht auf die See, den Platz, die öffentlichen Anlagen, an der See, empfehlen?
Is there a good hotel, a comfortable hotel, a big fashionable hotel, a luxury hotel, a first class hotel, a second class hotel, at ..?	Y a-t-il à .. un bon hôtel, un hôtel confortable, un grand hôtel mondain, un hôtel de luxe ou un palace, un hôtel de premier ordre, un hôtel de deuxième ordre?	Gibt es ein gutes Hotel, ein bequemes Hotel, ein großes mondänes Hotel, ein Luxushotel, ein Hotel ersten Ranges, ein Hotel zweiten Ranges, in ..?
Which is the best hotel at ..?	Quel est le meilleur hôtel de ..?	Welches ist das beste Hotel in ..?
At which hotel are you staying? I am staying at the Grand Hotel.	À quel hôtel logez-vous? Je suis descendu au Grand Hôtel.	In welchem Hotel wohnen Sie? Ich wohne im Grand Hotel.
I wish to see the landlord, the landlady, the manager, the manageress.	Je désire voir le propriétaire, la propriétaire, le directeur, la directrice.	Ich möchte den Wirt oder→ den Besitzer, die Wirtin oder die Besitzerin, den Leiter, die Leiterin, sprechen.
The innkeeper or The landlord, The landlady (of an inn).	L'aubergiste.	Der Gastwirt oder Der Besitzer, Die Besitzerin.
Is the hotel open all the year round?	L'hôtel est-il ouvert toute l'année?	Ist das Hotel das ganze Jahr über geöffnet?
Do you take boarders or paying guests?	Prenez-vous des pensionnaires?	Nehmen Sie Gäste auf?
Please give me a latch key.	Donnez-moi, s'il vous plaît, une clef de la maison.	Geben Sie mir bitte einen Hausschlüssel.
Where is the [reception] office?	Où est la réception ou le bureau [de réception]?	Wo ist das Empfangsbüro?→
I am Mr .., Mrs .., Miss .., of (or from) London.	Je suis Monsieur .., Madame .., Mademoiselle .., de Londres.	Mein Name ist Herr .., Frau .., Fräulein .., aus London.
Have you a lock-up garage, a roof garden, a dark	Avez-vous un garage fermé, un jardin sur le toit en	Haben Sie, eine verschließbare Garage, einen Dach-

Prezzo di affitto per mese, inclusa la biancheria, le stoviglie e l'argenteria.	Precio de alquiler mensual, incluso ropa de casa, loza y vajilla de plata.	Huur per maand, linnen, aardewerk en zilver inbegrepen.
Una locanda (o Un'osteria) con camere da letto.	Una posada con dormitorios.	Een herberg met slaap-gelegenheid.
C'è una locanda dove posso pernottare?	¿Hay por aquí cerca una fonda en donde puedo pasar la noche?	Is er een herberg hier dichtbij, waar ik de nacht kan doorbren-gen?
Una locanda sulla strada, Un caffè per ritrovo.	Una posada.	Een herberg langs de weg.
◄Una casa per la gioventù con alloggio.	Una hospedería para la juventud.	Een jeugdherberg.
Potete raccomandarmi un albergo a . ., vicino alla stazione, proprio nel centro della città, che guardi il mare, dia sulla piazza, dia sui giardini pubblici, dia sulla marina?	¿Puede usted recomen-darme un hotel en . ., cerca de la estación, en el centro mismo de la población, frente al mar, a la plaza, a los jardines públicos, en la marina?	Kunt U me een hotel aanbevelen in . ., dichtbij het station, middenin de stad, dat op de zee uitkijkt, dat op het plein uitkijkt, dat op de openbare tuinen uitkijkt, aan de zee?
Vi è un buon albergo, un albergo comodo, un grande albergo di moda, un albergo di lusso, un albergo di prima classe, un albergo di seconda classe, a . . ?	¿Hay un buen hotel, un hotel cómodo, un gran hotel de moda, un hotel de lujo, un hotel de primera clase, un hotel de segunda clase, en . . ?	Is er een goed hotel, een geriefelijk hotel, een groot mondain hotel, een luxe hotel, een eersterangs hotel, een tweederangs hotel, in . . ?
Qual'è il migliore albergo a . . ?	¿Cuál es el mejor hotel en . . ?	Wat is het beste hotel te . . ?
In quale albergo si trova Lei? Mi trovo al Grand Hôtel.	¿En qué hotel para usted? Paro en el Gran Hotel.	In welk hotel logeert U? Ik logeer in het Grand Hotel.
◄Io desidero vedere il proprietario, la proprie-taria, il direttore, la direttrice.	Deseo ver al patrón, a la patrona, al gerente, a la ama de llaves.	Ik wens de huiseigenaar, of de waard, de hospita of de waardin, de directeur, de directrice te spreken.
Il locandiere, La locandiera.	El posadero, **La posa-dera.**	De herbergier of De waard, De waardin.
È l'albergo aperto tutto l'anno?	¿Está el hotel abierto durante todo el año?	Is het hotel het hele jaar door open?
Prendete voi pensionanti in casa?	¿Recibe usted huéspedes o pupilos?	Neemt U pensiongasten of paying guests?
Per favore, datemi una chiave di casa.	Haga el favor de darme una llave de la casa.	Wilt U me een huissleutel geven.
◄Dov'è l'ufficio di ricevi-mento?	¿Dónde está el despacho [del hotel]?	Waar is de receptie?
Io sono il Signor . ., la Signora . ., la Signo-rina . ., di (o prove-niente da) Londra.	Soy el señor . ., la señora . ., la señorita . ., de Londres.	Ik ben mijnheer . ., mevrouw . ., juffrouw . ., uit Londen.
Avete una rimessa a chiave, un giardino sulla	¿Tiene usted un garaje con llave, un jardín de	Heeft U een dichte garage, een daktuin,

room ?	terrasse, une chambre noire ?	garten, eine Dunkelkammer ?
Can you put up my car ?	Pouvez-vous remiser ma voiture ?	Können Sie meinen Wagen unterbringen ?
Is there a smoking room, a reading room, in the hotel ?	Y a-t-il un [salon] fumoir, un salon de lecture, dans l'hôtel ?	Gibt es in dem Hotel einen Rauchsalon, einen Leseraum ?
Please bring me an ash tray.	Veuillez m'apporter un cendrier [de fumeur].	Bringen Sie mir bitte einen Asch[en]becher.
The drawing room.	Le [grand] salon.	Das Gesellschaftszimmer.
The entrance hall.	Le vestibule.	Die Eingangshalle, **Das** Vestibül.
The lounge.	Le hall.	Die Hall.
The hall porter.	Le concierge.	Der Portier.
The carriage attendant (*at hotel, etc.*).	L'aboyeur.	Der Wagenaufseher.
Will you pay the cabman [for me] ? I have no change.	Voulez-vous me payer le cocher ? Je n'ai pas de monnaie.	Wollen Sie bitte beim Kutscher für mich auslegen. Ich habe kein Kleingeld.
Send a page [boy] *or* a messenger.	Faites venir un chasseur *ou* un groom.	Holen Sie einen Boy *oder* einen Boten.
Is there a lift ?	Y a-t-il un ascenseur ?	Gibt es hier einen Fahrstuhl ?
Where is the liftman ?	Où est le garçon de l'ascenseur *ou* le liftman ?	Wo ist der Fahrstuhlführer ?
Where can I wash my hands ?	Où se lave-t-on les mains ?	Wo kann ich mir die Hände waschen ?
Can I have a wash and brush up ?	Puis-je faire un brin de toilette ?	Kann ich mich etwas waschen und abbürsten ?
The lavatory. A ladies' lavatory.	La toilette, Le cabinet de toilette. Une toilette pour dames.	Die Toilette. Eine Damentoilette.
Where is the W.C. *or* the little place ?	Où est le cabinet [d'aisances], le petit endroit ?	Wo ist die Toilette ?
Please send for my luggage.	Veuillez envoyer chercher mes bagages.	Bitte lassen Sie mein Gepäck holen.
I left my luggage in the cloak room of the Central station. Please have it fetched.	J'ai laissé mes bagages en consigne à la gare Centrale. Veuillez les envoyer chercher.	Ich habe mein Gepäck in der Gepäckaufbewahrung des Zentralbahnhofs gelassen. Würden Sie es bitte holen lassen.
Has my luggage come yet ?	Mes bagages sont-ils déjà arrivés ?	Ist mein Gepäck schon da ?
Ask them to have my luggage sent up.	Priez-les de faire monter mes bagages.	Bitten Sie sie, mein Gepäck heraufzuschaffen.
My luggage is ready. Please bring it down. Look sharp ! I am in a hurry.	Mes bagages sont prêts. Veuillez les faire descendre. Vite ! Je suis pressé.	Mein Gepäck ist fertig. Würden Sie es bitte heruntertragen. Rasch ! Ich bin in Eile.
Have my luggage taken to the station, to the boat, to the [motor] coach, to the airport.	Faites porter mes bagages à la gare, au bateau, à l'autocar, à l'aéroport.	Lassen Sie mein Gepäck bitte nach dem Bahnhof, auf das Boot, zum Autobus, nach dem Flugplatz, schaffen.

terrazza, una camera buia ?	azotea, una cámara obscura ?	een donkere kamer?
Avete posto nella rimessa per la mia automobile ?	¿ Puede usted alojarme el auto ?	Kunt U mijn wagen stallen?
C'è nell'albergo una sala per fumare, una sala di lettura ?	¿ Hay un cuarto de fumar, un salón de lectura, en el hotel ?	Is er een rookkamer, een leeszaal, in het hotel?
◄ Per favore, portatemi un portacenere.	Haga el favor de traerme un cenicero.	Breng me een asbak als 't U belieft.
Il salone.	La sala, El salón.	De zitkamer, De voorkamer, De salon.
Il vestibolo, L'ingresso.	El vestíbulo, El zaguán.	De vestibule.
La gran sala.	El salón de descanso.	De binnenhal.
Il portiere.	El conserje.	De portier.
◄ L'incaricato alle vetture.	El lacayo [de coches].	De [trottoir]portier.
Volete pagar voi il vetturino. Non ho cambio.	¿ Quiere usted pagarle al cochero ? No tengo cambio.	Wilt U de chauffeur voor me betalen? Ik heb geen klein geld.
Mandate un messaggiero.	Haga venir un paje o un mensajero.	Stuur een piccolo of een boodschappenjongen.
C'è un ascensore ?	¿ Hay ascensor ?	Is er een lift?
Dov'è il ragazzo dell'ascensore ?	¿ Dónde está el chico del ascensor ?	Waar is de liftjongen?
◄ Dove mi posso lavare le mani ?	¿ Dónde puedo lavarme las manos ?	Waar kan ik mijn handen wassen?
Dove posso lavarmi e pulirmi ?	¿ Puedo lavarme y arreglarme ?	Kan ik me even opknappen?
La sala di toeletta. La sala di toeletta per signore.	El lavatorio. Un gabinete de señoras.	Het toilet. Een damestoilet.
Dov'è la ritirata o il gabinetto ?	¿ Dónde está el retrete o el excusado ?	Waar is de W.C.? (pronounce oué, sé) (is never used; only: de W.C.)
Per favore, mandate a cercare il mio bagaglio.	Haga el favor de hacer que me traigan el equipaje.	Wilt U mijn bagage laten halen.
◄ Io ho lasciato il bagaglio in consegna alla stazione Centrale. Per favore, mandate a cercarlo.	Dejé mi equipaje en la consigna de la estación Central. Haga el favor de hacer traérmelo.	Ik heb mijn bagage in het bagagedepot van het Centraal Station gelaten. Wilt U die laten halen.
Sono già arrivati i miei bagagli ?	¿ Ha llegado mi equipaje ?	Is mijn bagage al aangekomen?
Pregateli di far portar su i miei bagagli.	Pídales que me suban el equipaje.	Vraag hun mijn bagage naar boven te laten sturen.
I miei bagagli sono pronti. Per favore, fateli portar giù. Presto ! Io ho fretta.	Mi equipaje está listo. Haga el favor de bajármelo. Ande ligero que tengo prisa.	Mijn bagage is gereed. Breng die naar beneden. Vlug! Ik heb haast.
Fate portare i miei bagagli alla stazione, sul battello, nell'autobus, nell'aeroporto.	Haga que se me lleve el equipaje a la estación al buque, al autocar, a la estación de aviación.	Laat mijn bagage naar het station brengen, naar de boot, naar het vliegveld.

Can I leave my things here till I return ?	Puis-je laisser ici mes bagages jusqu'à mon retour ?	Kann ich meine Sachen hierlassen, bis ich zurück-komme ?
Give me my key ; number . . .	Donnez-moi ma clef ; numéro . . .	Geben Sie mir meinen Schlüssel ; Nummer. . .
Where must I leave my key ?	Où faut-il laisser ma clef ?	Wo soll ich meinen Schlüssel lassen ?
[At] what time does the hotel close ; or does it remain open all night ?	À quelle heure l'hôtel ferme-t-il ; ou reste-t-il ouvert toute la nuit ?	Um welche Zeit schließt das Hotel ; oder bleibt es die ganze Nacht offen ?
At what time is lunch, dinner ? What are the meal times ?	À quelle heure est le déjeuner [de midi], le dîner ? Quelles sont les heures des repas ?	Wann wird zu Mittag, zu Abend, gegessen ? Wann finden die verschiedenen Mahlzeiten statt ?
I should like to place my valuables in your charge. Please give me a receipt for the packet.	Je désire confier mes valeurs à votre garde. Veuillez me donner un reçu du paquet.	Ich möchte Ihnen gern meine Wertsachen über-geben. Wollen Sie mir bitte eine Quittung für das Paket geben.
Has anyone called to see me ?	Est-on venu me demander ?	Hat irgend jemand nach mir gefragt ?
Come and see me when you are in London.	Venez me voir quand vous serez à Londres.	Besuchen Sie mich doch, wenn Sie in London sind.
What is the time ? or What o'clock is it ?	Quelle heure est-il ?	Wieviel Uhr ist es ?
The writing room.	La salle de correspondance.	Das Schreibzimmer.
Bring me some writing materials, a pen, some ink, some note paper, some envelopes.	Apportez-moi de quoi écrire, une plume, de l'encre, du papier à lettres, des enveloppes.	Bringen Sie mir bitte etwas zum Schreiben, einen Federhalter, Tinte, Brief-papier, ein paar Um-schläge.
I want some [postage] stamps.	Il me faut quelques timbres[-poste].	Ich brauche ein paar Brief-marken.
Is there a posting box (or a letter box) in the hotel ? Where is there a pillar box ?	Y a-t-il une boîte de la poste (ou une boîte aux lettres) à l'hôtel ? Où y a-t-il une borne postale ?	Gibt es im Hotel einen Briefkasten ? Wo gibt es hier einen Briefkasten ?
At what time does the general post office open, close ?	À quelle heure l'hôtel des postes ouvre-t-il, ferme-t-il ?	Wann macht das Haupt-postamt (oder die Haupt-post) auf, zu ?
When is the first, the next, the last, collection, de-livery, [of letters] ?	À quelle heure est la pre-mière, la prochaine, la dernière, levée, distribu-tion, [de lettres] ?	Wann ist die erste, die nächste, die letzte, Lee-rung ? Wann wird die erste, die nächste, die letzte, Post ausgetragen ?
When does the mail from England arrive ? Has the post arrived ? Are there any letters for me, for Mr X. ?	Quand le courrier d'Angle-terre arrive-t-il ? Le courrier est-il arrivé ? Y a-t-il des lettres pour moi, pour Monsieur X. ?	Wann trifft die Post aus England ein ? Ist die Post da ? Sind für mich, für Herrn X., Briefe da ?
Is there another post from England to-day ?	Y a-t-il encore un courrier aujourd'hui venant de l'Angleterre ?	Kommt heute noch eine Postsendung aus England ?

Posso lasciare le mie cose qui finchè non ritorno ?	¿ Puedo dejar mis bultos aquí hasta que vuelva ?	Kan ik mijn bagage tot mijn terugkomst hierlaten ?
Datemi la mia chiave ; numero . . .	Deme mi llave ; número . . .	Geef mij mijn sleutel; nummer …
Dove debbo lasciare la mia chiave ?	¿ Dónde debo dejar mi llave ?	Waar moet ik mijn sleutel laten ?
A che ora si chiude l'albergo ; o rimane aperto tutta la notte ?	¿ A qué hora se cierra el hotel ; o permanece abierto toda la noche ?	Hoe laat gaat het hotel dicht; of blijft het de hele nacht open?
A che ora è la seconda colazione, il pranzo ? Quali sono le ore dei pasti ?	¿ A qué hora es el almuerzo, la comida ? ¿ Cuáles son las horas de las comidas ?	Hoe laat is de lunch *of* de koffietafel, het diner *of* het avondeten ? Wanneer zijn de maaltijden?
Io vorrei depositare presso di Lei i miei valori. Per fávore, mi dia la ricevuta del pacco.	Desearía confiar mis valores a su cargo. Haga el favor de darme un recibo por el paquete.	Ik zou mijn kostbaarheden bij U in bewaring willen geven. Wilt U me een ontvangbewijs voor het pakket geven.
È venuto nessuno a cercarmi ?	¿ Han venido a preguntar por mí ?	Is er iemand geweest om mij te spreken?
Venga a vedermi quando Lei sarà (o Lei si troverà) a Londra.	Venga a verme cuando esté usted en Londres.	Kom me opzoeken als U in Londen bent.
Che ora è ? o Che ore sono ?	¿ Qué hora es ?	Hoe laat is het?
La sala di corrispondenza.	El [salón] escritorio, La sala de correspondencia.	De schrijfkamer.
Portatemi il necessario per scrivere, una penna, dell'inchiostro, della carta da lettere, qualche busta.	Tráigame avíos de escribir, una pluma, tinta, papel [de escribir], sobres.	Breng me wat schrijfbehoeften, een pen, wat inkt, wat schrijfpapier, een paar enveloppen.
Desidero qualche francobollo.	Necesito sellos de correo.	Ik heb een paar postzegels nodig.
C'è una cassetta per lettere nell'albergo ? Dov'è una buca per le lettere ?	¿ Hay un buzón (o un receptáculo para cartas) en el hotel ? ¿ Dónde hay un buzón ?	Is er een brievenbus in het hotel? Waar is er een brievenbus?
A che ora si apre, si chiude, l'ufficio postale centrale ?	¿ A qué hora se abre, se cierra, la central de correos ?	Hoe laat gaat het hoofdpostkantoor open, dicht?
A che ora è la prima, la prossima, l'ultima, levata, distribuzione, [delle lettere] ?	¿ A qué hora es la primera, la próxima, la última, colecta, repartición, de correspondencia ?	Hoe laat is de eerste, de volgende, de laatste, lichting, postbestelling.
Quando arriva il corriere postale dall'Inghilterra ? È arrivata la posta ? C'è qualche lettera per me, per il Signor X.? C'è un'altra posta dall' Inghilterra oggi ?	¿ A qué hora llega el correo de Londres ? ¿ Ha llegado el correo ? ¿ Hay cartas para mí, para el señor X.? ¿ Hay otro correo de Inglaterra hoy ?	Wanneer komt de post uit Engeland aan? Is de post aangekomen? Is er post voor mij, voor de heer X? Komt er nog meer post uit Engeland vandaag?

Am I in time for the London mail? Has the post gone?	Suis-je à temps pour le courrier de Londres? Le courrier est-il parti?	Kann ich noch einen Brief nach London mitgeben? Ist die Post schon weg?
What is the latest time for posting letters for London? or When is the last post for London?	Quelle est l'heure-limite de dépôt des lettres pour Londres?	Bis wann müssen Briefe nach London eingeworfen sein?
Kindly post this letter.	Veuillez mettre cette lettre à la poste.	Würden Sie bitte diesen Brief einwerfen?
Please forward my letters to this address.	Veuillez faire suivre mes lettres à cette adresse.	Würden Sie bitte meine Briefe an diese Adresse nachsenden.
Where can I buy some photographic films?	Où vend-on des pellicules photographiques?	Wo kann ich Fotofilme kaufen?
I want to send a telegram. Have you a telegram form?	Je veux envoyer un télégramme ou une dépêche. Est-ce que vous avez une formule de télégramme?	Ich möchte ein Telegramm aufgeben. Haben Sie ein Telegrammformular?
I want to telephone. Where can one telephone? Where is there a public call office?	Je veux téléphoner. Où peut-on téléphoner? Où y a-t-il une cabine téléphonique publique?	Ich möchte telefonieren. Wo kann man telefonieren? Wo gibt es eine öffentliche Fernsprechstelle?
Ring up Mr X. Put me through to Mr X.	Appelez Monsieur X. [au téléphone]. Mettez-moi en communication avec Monsieur X.	Rufen Sie Herrn X. an. Verbinden Sie mich mit Herrn X.
Am I through?	Est-ce que j'ai la communication?	Bin ich richtig verbunden?
Hold on! or Hold the line!	Ne quittez pas!	Bleiben Sie am Apparat.
The telephone directory.	L'annuaire des abonnés au téléphone.	Das Telefonbuch.
The [call] number. You have given me a wrong number.	Le numéro [d'appel]. Vous m'avez donné un faux numéro.	Die Telefonnummer. Sie haben mich falsch verbunden.
The [telephone] exchange.	Le bureau [central] [téléphonique], Le poste [central] [téléphonique], Le central.	Das Telefonamt.
The Directory Enquiry (*Telephone*).	Le service de renseignements.	Die Auskunft.
The operator.	L'opératrice.	Die Telefonistin, Das Fräulein vom Amt.
To dial a number.	Composer un numéro [sur le disque d'appel].	Eine Nummer wählen.
A local call. Toll. A toll call.	Une communication locale. [Le] régional. Une communication régionale.	Ein Ortsgespräch. Vorortgespräche. Ein Vorortgespräch.
Trunks A trunk call.	L'interurbain, [L']inter. Une communication interurbaine.	Ferngespräche. Ein Ferngespräch.
An international telephone call.	Une communication téléphonique internationale.	Ein Ferngespräch mit dem Ausland; Ein Telefonanruf aus dem Ausland.

Sono in tempo per il corriere postale di Londra? È partita la posta?	¿Estoy a tiempo para alcanzar el correo para Londres? Ha salido ya el correo?	Ben ik op tijd voor de post naar Londen? Is de post vertrokken?
Fino a che ora si possono impostare le lettere per Londra?	¿Qué es la última hora para poder despachar cartas para Londres?	Wanneer kunnen op zijn laatst brieven voor Londen gepost worden?
Favorisca impostarmi questa lettera.	Haga el favor de echarme esta carta al correo.	Wilt U deze brief voor me op de post doen?
◀ Per favore, respinga le mie lettere a questo indirizzo.	Haga el favor de hacer reexpedir mi correspondencia a esta dirección.	Wilt U mijn brieven naar dit adres doorsturen?
Dove posso comprare pellicole fotografiche?	¿Dónde se venden películas fotográficas?	Waar kan ik rolfilms krijgen?
Desidero spedire un telegramma. Avete voi un modulo per telegramma?	Quiero mandar un telegrama. ¿Tiene usted un formulario para telegrama?	Ik wil een telegram sturen. Heeft U een telegramformulier?
Desidero telefonare. Dove si può telefonare? Dove si trova un ufficio telefonico pubblico?	Quiero telefonear. ¿Dónde se puede telefonear? ¿Dónde hay un quiosco [público] de teléfono?	Ik wil telefoneren. Waar kan men telefoneren? Waar is een publieke telefoon-cel?
Chiamate il Signor X. [al telefono]. Mettetemi in comunicazione con il Signor X.	Llame por teléfono al señor X. Póngame en comunicación con el señor X.	Bel de heer X. op. Verbind me met de heer X.
◀ Sono in comunicazione?	¿Estoy en comunicación?	Ben ik verbonden?
Rimanete all'apparecchio o Tenete la comunicazione.	No se aparte del aparato.	Een ogenblikje! of Blijft U even aan het toestel?
L'elenco telefonico.	El anuario de teléfonos.	Het telefoonboek.
Il numero [richiesto]. Mi avete dato un numero sbagliato.	El número [de teléfono]. Me han dado un número equivocado.	Het [telefoon]nummer. U heeft me verkeerd verbonden.
◀ L'ufficio centrale telefonico, Il centralino.	La [oficina] central [de teléfonos].	De [telefoon]centrale.
Il servizio informazioni.	El servicio de informaciones.	De inlichtingendienst.
L'operatrice.	La [chica] telefonista.	De telefoniste, De telefoonjuffrouw.
Comporre un numero.	Telefonear un número con el sistema automático.	Een nummer draaien.
◀ Una chiamata locale.	Una comunicación urbana.	Een lokaal gesprek.
Intercomunale. Una comunicazione intercomunale.	La interurbana. Una comunicación interurbana.	Interlokaal! Een interlokaal gesprek.
◀ Una comunicazione telefonica internazionale.	Una comunicación telefónica internacional.	Een internationaal telefoongesprek.

Number please?	J'écoute.	Nummer bitte?
North two eight seven five, East double O O four, West eight O one three, speaking.	Ici Nord vingt-huit soixante-quinze, Est double zéro, zéro quatre, Ouest quatre-vingts virgule treize.	Hier ist Nord achtundzwanzig fünfundsiebzig, Ost null null null vier, West acht null dreizehn.
R for Robert.	R comme Robert.	R wie Robert.
Hello! *or* Are you there?	Allô!	Hallo!
No reply.	[Ne] répond pas.	Es meldet sich niemand. →
Have you finished? (*said by operator*)	Personne? Personne?	Sprechen Sie noch?
Line engaged.	Ligne pas libre.	Die Leitung ist besetzt.
Call (*or* Wake) me in the morning at eight.	Réveillez-moi à huit heures.	Wecken Sie mich bitte morgen früh um acht.
I wish to make a complaint.	Je désire déposer une plainte.	Ich habe eine Beschwerde vorzubringen.
I shall complain to the manager.	Je me plaindrai au directeur.	Ich werde mich bei der Aufsicht beschweren.

Accommodation in hotels	**Le logement dans les hôtels**	**Hotelunterkunft**
Have you a room, any bedrooms, disengaged, to let?	Avez-vous une chambre libre, des chambres à coucher libres, à louer?	Haben Sie ein Zimmer, Schlafzimmer, frei, zu vermieten?
Have you a room for to-night at about ....?	Avez-vous une chambre pour ce soir pour à peu près .. francs?	Haben Sie für heute Nacht ein Zimmer zu etwa .. Mark frei?
I want (a) a single room, (b) a single-bedded room, (c) a double-bedded room, (d) a room with a double bed, (e) a quiet room on the first floor, (f) a sunny room on the second floor, (g) with hot and cold running water, (h) a well ventilated room, (i) with [private] bathroom adjoining, (j) with dressing room.	Je veux (a) une chambre individuelle, (b) une chambre à un lit, (c) une chambre à deux lits, (d) une chambre avec un lit à deux places, (e) une chambre tranquille au premier étage, (f) une chambre ensoleillée au deuxième étage, (g) avec eau courante chaude et froide, (h) une chambre bien ventilée, (i) avec salle de bain [privée] attenante, (j) avec cabinet de toilette.	Ich möchte (a) ein Einzelzimmer, (b) ein einbettiges Zimmer, (c) ein zweibettiges Zimmer, (d) ein Zimmer mit Doppelbett, (e) ein ruhiges Zimmer im ersten Stock, (f) ein sonniges Zimmer auf dem zweiten Stock, (g) mit fließend warm und kalt Wasser, (h) ein Zimmer mit gutem Durchzug, (i) mit anschließendem Badezimmer, (j) mit Ankleidezimmer.
Could I have a room on the ground floor, on the mezzanine [floor]?	Pourrais-je avoir une chambre au rez-de-chaussée, à l'entresol?	Könnte ich ein Parterrezimmer, ein Hochparterrezimmer, haben?
I want two communicating rooms, a suite [of rooms].	Je voudrais deux chambres communiquantes, un appartement.	Ich möchte zwei zusammenhängende Zimmer, eine Suite. →
A front room, with a balcony.	Une chambre [donnant] sur le devant *ou* sur la rue, avec un balcon.	Ein Vorderzimmer, mit Balkon.
A back room.	Une chambre sur le derrière *ou* sur la cour.	Ein Hinterzimmer.

Il numero per favore ?
Parla Nord ventottosettantacinque, Est doppio zero, zero quattro, Ovest ottanta tredici.

¡Diga! diga!
Norte [número] dos ocho siete cinco, Este cero cero cero cuatro, Oeste ocho cero uno tres.

Nummer, als 't U belieft?
Dit is Noord twee acht zeven vijf, Oost dubbel o o vier, West acht o een drie.

R per Roberto.
Pronto ?
◄ Non rispondono.
Avete finito di parlare?

R de Roberto.
¿Oiga?
No contestan.
¿Ha acabado de hablar?

R van Robert.
Hallo!
Geen antwoord.
Bent U klaar met spreken?

La linea occupata.
Svegliatemi la mattina alle otto.
Io devo sporgere una lagnanza.
◄ Io mi lagnerò col direttore.

Están comunicando.
Llámeme por la mañana a las ocho.
Tengo que dar una queja.
Voy a quejarme al gerente.

In gesprek.
Roep me morgenochtend om acht uur.
Ik wens een klacht in te dienen.
Ik zal me bij de directeur beklagen.

Alloggio negli alberghi

Alojamientos en hoteles

Hotel accommodatie

Avete una camera libera, delle camere da letto libere, da affittare ?

¿Tiene usted una habitación (o una pieza) libre, algunos dormitorios libres, para alquilar ?

Heeft U een kamer, slaapkamers, vrij, te huur?

Avete una camera per questa notte sulle .. lire?

¿Tiene usted una habitación para esta noche por alrededor de .. pesetas ?

Heeft U een kamer voor vannacht voor ongeveer .. gulden?

Desidero (a) una camera per una persona, (b) una camera ad un letto, (c) una camera a due letti, (d) una camera con letto per due persone, (e) una camera tranquilla al primo piano, (f) una camera assolata al secondo piano, (g) con acqua corrente fredda e calda, (h) una camera ariosa, (i) con annessa [privata] sala de bagno, (j) con stanza de toeletta.

Necesito (a) una habitación individual, (b) una habitación con una sóla cama, (c) una habitación con dos camas, (d) una habitación con cama doble, (e) una habitación tranquila en el piso principal, (f) una habitación asoleada en el segundo piso, (g) con agua corriente caliente y fría, (h) una habitación bien ventilada, (i) con cuarto de baño [privado] anexo, (j) con cuarto de tocador.

Ik wens (a) een enkele kamer, (b) een kamer met één bed, (c) een dubbele kamer, (d) een kamer met een dubbel bed, (e) een stille kamer op de eerste verdieping, (f) een zonnige kamer op de tweede verdieping, (g) met warm en koud stromend water, (h) een luchtige kamer, (i) met bijbehorende (privé) badkamer, (j) met een kleedkamer.

Posso avere una camera a pianterreno, sul mezzanino ?
◄ Desidero due camere contigue, un appartamento.

¿Pueden darme una habitación en el piso bajo, en el entresuelo ?
Necesito dos habitaciones comunicadas, una serie de habitaciones o piezas.

Kan ik een kamer op de benedenverdieping, op de bel-étage krijgen?
Ik wens twee ineenlopende kamers, een suite.

Una camera sul davanti, con [un] balcone.

Una habitación frente a la calle, con balcón.

Een kamer aan de voorkant, met een balcon.

Una camera sul dietro.

Una habitación al interior, Un cuarto hacia el patio.

Een kamer aan de achterkant.

A maid's room.	Une chambre de domestique.	Ein Mädchenzimmer.
I should like a room looking on to the garden, the park, the lake, a room facing south, leading on to the veranda[h].	Je voudrais une chambre donnant sur le jardin, le parc, le lac, une chambre au midi, donnant sur la véranda.	Ich möchte gern ein Zimmer mit Aussicht auf den Garten, den Park, den See, ein nach Süden gelegenes Zimmer, mit Ausgang auf die Veranda.
Let me see the room. On what floor is it?	Faites-moi voir la chambre. À quel étage est-elle?	Zeigen Sie mir bitte das Zimmer. In welchem Stock liegt es?
I will take this room. Is it ready? What is the number?	Je prendrai cette chambre. Est-elle prête? Quel est le numéro?	Ich werde dieses Zimmer nehmen. Ist es fertig? Welche Nummer hat es?
I want to change rooms. Mine is too small, too noisy, sunless.	Je désire changer de chambre. La mienne est trop petite, trop bruyante, sans soleil.	Ich möchte mein Zimmer wechseln. Meins ist mir zu klein, zu laut, Meins hat zu wenig Sonne.
Can you give me another room, a larger one, a quieter one?	Pouvez-vous me donner une autre chambre, une plus grande, une plus tranquille?	Können Sie mir ein anderes Zimmer, ein größeres, ein ruhigeres, geben?
This room will do or will suit me.	Cette chambre me convient.	Dieses Zimmer ist mir recht.
I intend to stay the night only, one day, a few days, a week, a fortnight, a month, for some time.	Je compte rester seulement la nuit, un jour, quelques jours, une semaine, une quinzaine, un mois, quelque temps.	Ich habe die Absicht, nur eine Nacht zu bleiben, einen Tag, einige Tage, eine Woche, vierzehn Tage, einen Monat, einige Zeit, zu bleiben.
I am going out. I shall be back at one [o'clock].	Je vais sortir. Je serai de retour à une heure.	Ich gehe jetzt fort. Ich bin um ein Uhr zurück.
I am leaving, I have to leave, very early tomorrow morning, by the seven-thirty train to . . .	Je vais partir, Il me faut partir, demain matin de très bonne heure, par le train de sept heures trente pour . . .	Ich reise ab, Ich muß abreisen, Ich muß morgen sehr früh, mit dem sieben Uhr dreißig Zug nach . . abreisen.
[Go and] get me a taxi [cab], a cab, a carriage.	Allez me chercher un taxi, un fiacre, une voiture.	Holen Sie mir bitte ein Taxi, eine Droschke, einen Wagen.
Is the taxi there?	Le taxi est-il là?	Ist das Taxi da?
I shall walk to the station. Send my luggage on.	Je me rendrai à la gare à pied. Faites suivre mes bagages.	Ich werde zu Fuß nach dem Bahnhof gehen. Lassen Sie mein Gepäck nachschicken.
I shall return here in a week, within a week.	Je reviendrai ici dans huit jours, dans la huitaine.	Ich komme in einer Woche, in acht Tagen, zurück.

The bedroom furniture	**L'ameublement de la chambre à coucher**	**Die Schlafzimmereinrichtung**
An armchair.	Un fauteuil [à bras].	Ein Sessel.
A bed.	Un lit.	Ein Bett.
The bed clothes.	Les draps et couvertures.	Die Bettwäsche.

Una camera per la donna di servizio.	Una habitación de criada.	Een dienstbodekamer.
Io vorrei una camera che dà sul giardino, sui giardini pubblici, sul lago, una camera al sud che dà sulla veranda.	Desearía una habitación frente al jardín, al parque, al lago, una habitación hacia el sur, dando a la galería.	Ik zou graag een kamer willen hebben, die op de tuin, het park, het meer, uitziet, een kamer op het zuiden, een kamer die op de veranda uitkomt.
◄Fatemi vedere la camera A che piano è ?	Déjeme ver la habitación. ¿ En qué piso está ?	Laat mij de kamer zien. Op welke verdieping is zij ?
[Io] avrò questa camera. È pronta ? Che numero è ?	Tomaré esta habitación. ¿ Está lista ? ¿ Qué número tiene ?	Ik neem deze kamer. Is zij gereed ? Wat is het nummer ?
Io desidero cambiare di camera. La mia è troppo piccola, troppo rumorosa, senza sole.	Quiero cambiar de habitación. La mía es demasiado pequeña, demasiado ruidosa, demasiado obscura.	Ik wens van kamer te veranderen. De mijne is te klein, te luidruchtig, zonder zon.
Potete darmi un'altra camera, una più grande, una più tranquilla ?	¿ Puede usted darme otra habitación, una más grande, una más tranquila ?	Kunt U mij een andere kamer geven een grotere, een stillere kamer ?
Questa camera mi conviene.	Esta habitación me servirá o me conviene.	Deze kamer bevalt me.
◄Io conto di rimanere soltanto la notte, un giorno, pochi giorni, una settimana, quindici giorni, un mese, per un po' di tempo.	Me propongo solamente pasar la noche, quedarme sólo un día, unos cuantos días, una semana, quince días, un mes, una temporada.	Ik ben van plan slechts één nacht te blijven, een paar dagen, een week, twee weken, een maand, enige tijd, te blijven.
Io esco. Sarò di ritorno alle una.	Voy a salir. Estaré de vuelta a la una.	Ik ga uit. Ik ben om één uur terug.
Io parto, Io devo partire, domani mattina molto di buon'ora, con il treno delle sette e trenta per ..	Me marcho, Tengo que marcharme, mañana por la mañana [muy] temprano, por el tren de las siete y treinta para . . .	Ik vertrek, Ik moet morgenochtend vroeg, met de trein van zeven uur dertig naar .. vertrekken.
Fate venire un taxì, una carrozza, una vettura.	Vaya a buscarme un taxi, un simón, un coche.	Roep een taxi, een huurrijtuig, een wagen voor me.
È là il taxì ?	¿ Está el taxi ?	Is de tr ¹er ?
◄Io andrò alla stazione a piedi. Fate proseguire il mio bagaglio.	Iré a pie a la estación. Hágame seguir el equipaje.	Ik ga naar het station lopen. Stuur mijn bagage na.
Io sarò di ritorno fra una settimana, entro una settimana.	Regresaré [a esta] a los ocho días, dentro de la semana.	Ik kom hier over een week, binnen de week, terug.

Il mobilio della camera da letto	**Los muebles del dormitorio**	**Het slaapkamer-ameublement**
Una poltrona.	Un sillón, Una butaca.	Een leunstoel.
Un letto.	Una cama.	Een bed.
I lenzuoli.	La ropa de cama.	Het beddegoed.

The bedding.	La literie, La garniture de lit.	Das Bettzeug, Die Betten.→
A bed pan.	Un bassin [de garde-robe].	Ein Stechbecken.
A [bed]room.	Une chambre [à coucher].	Ein Schlafzimmer, Ein Zimmer.
A bed settee.	Un lit de repos.	Ein Schlafsofa.
A bedside rug.	Une descente de lit.	Ein Bettvorleger.
A bedside table.	Une table de chevet, Une table de nuit.	Ein Nachttisch. →
A bedspread.	Un couvre-lit [de parade], Un jeté de lit.	Eine Bettdecke.
A bedstead.	Un [bois de] lit.	Ein Bettgestell.
A blanket.	Une couverture [de laine].	Eine Wolldecke.
The blind.	Le store.	Die Fenstergardine.
The blind (*Venetian*).	La jalousie.	Die Jalousie. →
A bolster.	Un traversin.	Ein Polster.
The carpet.	Le tapis.	Der Teppich.
A chair.	Une chaise.	Ein Stuhl.
A chamber [pot].	Un vase de nuit.	Ein Nachtgeschirr.
A chest of drawers.	Une commode.	Eine Kommode. →
A chesterfield.	Un canapé-divan	Ein großes Schlafsofa.
A cheval glass *or* A full-length mirror.	Une psyché.	Ein großer Drehspiegel.
A coal scuttle.	Un seau à charbon.	Ein Kohleneimer.
A [night] commode.	Une chaise percée.	Ein Nachtstuhl.
A cot for an infant.	Un lit d'enfant, Un berceau pour enfant.	Ein Kinderbett.
A coverlet *or* A counter-pane.	Un couvre-lit.	Eine Steppdecke.
A cupboard.	Une armoire.	Ein Schrank.
A curtain.	Un rideau.	Ein Vorhang, Eine Gardine.
A dressing table.	Une [table de] toilette, Une coiffeuse.	Eine Toilette, Ein Frisiertisch.
A [drinking] glass.	Un verre [à boire].	Ein Glas, Ein Trinkglas. →
An easy chair.	Un fauteuil, Une bergère.	Ein Lehnsessel.
An eider-down.	Un édredon.	Eine Daunendecke.
A feather bed.	Un lit de plume.	Ein Federbett.
A fender.	Un garde-cendre.	Ein Kaminvorsetzer.
A fire guard.	Un garde-feu, Un pare-étincelles.	Ein Kamingitter. →
The fire irons.	La garniture de foyer	Die Kamingeräte, Die Ofengeräte.
The fireplace *or* The hearth.	La cheminée, L'âtre.	Der Kamin.
A fire screen.	Un écran à pied.	Ein Ofenschirm.
A hanging wardrobe *or* cupboard.	Une penderie.	Ein Kleidervorhang.
A hassock.	Un carreau, Un coussin.	Ein Puff. →
A [looking] glass *or* A mirror.	Une glace, Un miroir.	Ein Spiegel.
The mattress.	Le sommier.	Die Matratze.
A mosquito net *or* curtain.	Une moustiquaire.	Ein Moskito-Netz.
A night light.	Une veilleuse.	Ein Nachtlicht.

L'apparechio del letto.	Los colchones y ropa de cama.	De matras en het kussen.
Una padelletta.	Una silleta.	Een po, een ondersteek.
Una camera [da letto].	Un dormitorio, Un cuarto [de dormir].	Een [slaap]kamer.
Un letto a sdraio, Un canapè.	Una cama plegadiza en forma de canapé.	Een rustbank.
Uno scendiletto.	Una alfombrilla.	Een beddekleedje.
Un comodino.	Una mesita de alcoba.	Een nachttafeltje.
Una sopracoperta.	Un cubrecama.	Een sprei.
Un fusto di letto, Una lettiera.	Una cuja.	Een ledikant.
Una coperta [di lana].	Una frazada, Un cobertor de lana.	Een deken.
La cortina.	La persiana.	Het rolgordijn.
La gelosia, La persiana.	La celosía.	De jalouzie. De markies.
Un capezzale.	Un traversero.	Een rolkussen.
Il tappeto.	La alfombra.	Het [vloer]kleed.
Una sedia.	Una silla.	Een stoel.
Un vaso da notte.	Una escupidera, Un orinal.	Een pot.
Un cassettone.	Una cómoda.	Een commode, Een latafel.
Un sofà.	Un canapé, Un sofá.	Een chesterfield.
Una psiche, Uno specchio a bilico.	Un espejo de vestir.	Een lange spiegel.
Un secchio per carbone.	Una carbonera.	Een kolenemmer.
Una seggetta.	Una silla de noche.	Een stilletje.
Una culla, Un lettino per bambino.	Una camilla de niño.	Een kinderbed, Een kinderledikant.
Una coperta da letto.	Un cobertor, Una colcha.	Een dekeprei.
Un armadio.	Una alacena.	Een kast.
Una tenda.	Una cortina.	Een gordijn.
Un tavolo da toeletta.	Un tocador.	Een toilettafel.
Un bicchiere [per bere].	Un vaso [para beber].	Een [water]glas.
Un seggiolone.	Una butaca.	Een luie stoel.
Un piumino.	Un edredón.	Een donzen deken.
Un letto di piume.	Un colchón de plumas.	Een veren bed.
Un paracenere.	Un guardacenizas.	Een haardrand.
Una caminiera.	Un guardafuegos.	Een vuurscherm.
Gli utensili per caminetto.	Los utensilios de a chimenea.	De haardijzers.
Il caminetto, Il focolare.	El hogar.	De haard.
Un parafuoco.	Una mampara de chimenea.	Een haardscherm.
Un guardaroba.	Un guardaropa colgante o de pared.	Een hangkast.
Un cuscino, Una stoia.	Una banqueta, Un cojín.	Een pouffe.
Uno specchio.	Un espejo.	Een spiegel.
Il materasso.	El colchón.	De matras.
Uno zanzariere.	Un mosquitero.	Een muskietenet, klamboe.
Un lumino da notte.	Una mariposa.	Een nachtlichtje.

A [pair of] tongs.	Des pincettes.	Eine Zange. →
A pillow.	Un oreiller.	Ein Kopfkissen.
A poker.	Un tisonnier.	Ein Feuerhaken.
A settee.	Un divan, Une causeuse.	Ein Divan.
A sheet.	Un drap [de lit].	Ein Laken.
A shovel.	Une pelle.	Eine Schaufel. →
A soap dish.	Un plateau à savon.	Ein Seifnapf.
A sun shutter (*outside, slatted*).	Une persienne.	Ein Fensterladen.
A table.	Une table.	Ein Tisch.
A towel.	Une serviette [de toilette], Un essuie-mains.	Ein Handtuch.
A towel horse *or* rail.	Un porte-serviettes, Un séchoir.	Ein Handtuchständer. →
A wardrobe.	Une armoire.	Ein Schrank.
A [wash]basin.	Une cuvette.	Eine Waschschüssel, Ein Waschbecken.
A washstand.	Une toilette, Un lavabo.	Ein Waschtisch.
A water bottle.	Une carafe [de toilette].	Eine Wasserkaraffe.
A water jug *or* A ewer.	Un pot à eau, Un broc de toilette.	Eine Wasserkanne. →

Service / Le service / Bedienung

Service	**Le service**	**Bedienung**
Who is there? Come in!	Qui est là? Entrez!	Wer ist da? Herein!
Send me the chambermaid, the floor maid, the floor waiter.	Envoyez-moi la femme de chambre, la fille d'étage, le garçon d'étage.	Schicken Sie mir bitte das Zimmermädchen, das Flurmädchen, den Flurkellner.
A maid [servant].	Une fille [de service], Une bonne, Une domestique, Une servante.	Ein Hausmädchen, Eine Hausgehilfin.
A servant (*man*).	Un domestique.	Ein Bedienter.
A valet [de chambre] *or* A manservant.	Un valet de chambre.	Ein Diener, Ein Hausdiener. →
I rang for some water.	J'ai sonné pour avoir de l'eau.	Ich habe geläutet, weil ich etwas Wasser haben möchte.
The boots (*person*).	Le garçon d'hôtel, Le valet d'étage.	Der Hausdiener.
Have my shoes cleaned and send them up to me.	Faites cirer mes souliers et faites-les-moi monter.	Lassen Sie bitte meine Schuhe putzen, und schicken Sie sie mir herauf.
These boots are not mine.	Ces bottines ne sont pas à moi.	Diese Stiefel gehören mir nicht.
I want a fire in my room. Please light the fire. Bring some more coal.	Je veux du feu dans ma chambre. Veuillez allumer le feu. Apportez encore du charbon.	Ich möchte gern ein Feuer → in meinem Zimmer haben. Bitte zünden Sie das Feuer an. Wollen Sie bitte mehr Kohlen bringen.

Le molle.	Unas tenazas.	Een tang.
Un guanciale.	Una almohada.	Een kussen.
Un attizzatoio.	Un atizador.	Een pook.
Un divano.	Un diván, Un canapé.	Een divan.
Un lenzuolo.	Una sábana.	Een [bedde]laken.
Una paletta.	Una pala.	Een schep, Een schop.
Un piattino per sapone.	Una jabonera.	Een zeepbakje.
Una persiana.	Una persiana de fuera.	Een zonneluik.
Una tavola.	Una mesa.	Een tafel.
Un asciugamano.	Una toalla.	Een handdoek.
Un porta-asciugamano.	Un toallero.	Een handdoekenrekje.
Un armadio.	Un armario, Un guarda-ropa.	Een kast.
Un lavandino, Un bacino.	Una palangana, Una jofaina.	Een waskom.
Un lavabo.	Un palanganero.	Een wastafel.
Una caraffa.	Una botella [para agua].	Een waterkaraf.
Una brocca.	Un jarro.	Een toiletemmer.

Il servizio	El servicio	Bediening
Chi è? Avanti!	¿Quién es? ¡Adelante!	Wie is daar? [Kom] binnen!
Mandatemi (o Chiamatemi) la cameriera, la cameriera di questo piano, il cameriere di questo piano.	Mándeme la camarera, la doncella, el camarero [del piso].	Stuur het kamermeisje bij mij, het meisje, de kelner, van deze verdieping.
Una cameriera, Una donna di servizio.	Una doncella, Una sirvienta, Una criada.	Een dienstbode, Een dienstmaagd, Een dienstmeisje.
Un domestico.	Un criado.	Een bediende, Een dienaar, Een huisknecht.
Un servitore.	Un valé, Un criado.	Een kamerdienaar, Een knecht.
Io ho sonato per aver dell'acqua.	He tocado el timbre para que me traigan agua.	Ik heb om wat water gebeld.
Il facchino dei piani.	El limpiabotas [de hotel].	De schoenpoetser.
Fate lucidare le mie scarpe e rimandatemele.	Que me limpien los zapatos y que me los hagan subir.	Laat mijn schoenen poetsen en zend ze naar boven.
Questi stivaletti non sono miei.	Estas botas no son [las] mias.	Deze laarzen zijn niet van mij.
Io desidero un fuoco nella mia camera. Per favore, accendetemi il fuoco. Portatemi un po' più di carbone.	Quiero el fuego en mi habitación. Haga el favor de encender la estufa. Tráiga más carbón.	Ik wens een vuur in mijn kamer. Wilt U het vuur aansteken. Breng nog wat kolen.

The radiator. The central heating is too warm.	Le radiateur. Le chauffage central est trop chaud.	Der Heizkörper. Die Zentralheizung ist zu warm.
I am going to bed at once.	Je vais me coucher [tout] de suite.	Ich gehe sofort zu Bett.
I want another pillow, another blanket, a hot-water bottle.	Je voudrais un oreiller de plus, une couverture de plus, une boule d'eau chaude.	Ich möchte noch ein Kissen, noch eine Decke, eine Wärmeflasche.
You will bring me up some hot water at seven [o'clock].	Vous me monterez de l'eau chaude à sept heures.	Sie werden mir bitte um sieben etwas heißes Wasser bringen.
Bring me some more cold water, some shaving water, some drinking water, a bottle of water, some soap, a clean towel, a candle.	Apportez-moi encore de l'eau froide, de l'eau chaude pour me raser, de l'eau potable, une carafe d'eau, du savon, une serviette propre, une bougie.	Bringen Sie mir bitte noch➤ etwas kaltes Wasser, etwas Wasser zum Rasieren, etwas Trinkwasser, eine Karaffe mit Wasser, etwas Seife, ein sauberes Handtuch, eine Kerze.
Can you lend me a clothes brush?	Pourriez-vous me prêter une brosse à habits?	Können Sie mir eine Kleiderbürste leihen?
Where is the bathroom?	Où est la salle de bain[s]?	Wo ist das Badezimmer?
Is there a bath disengaged?	Y a-t-il une baignoire libre?	Ist irgendein Badezimmer frei?
When can I have a bath?	Quand pourrai-je prendre un bain?	Wann kann ich ein Bad nehmen?
I want [to take] a hot bath, a tepid bath, a cold bath, a foot bath, a shower bath.	Je voudrais [prendre] un bain chaud, un bain tiède, un bain froid, un bain de pieds, un bain-douche.	Ich möchte ein heißes Bad,➤ ein lauwarmes Bad, ein kaltes Bad, ein Fußbad, eine Dusche.

For Spa bathing, *see pp.* 254-255.

The bath plug is missing.	Il manque la soupape du bain.	Der Badewannenstöpsel ist nicht da.
My clothes are wet, My boots are wet, please dry them.	Mes habits sont mouillés, Mes chaussures sont mouillées, faites-les sécher.	Meine Kleider sind durchnäßt, Meine Schuhe sind naß geworden, wollen Sie sie bitte trocknen.
Have you seen my gloves? I think I left them here.	Avez-vous vu mes gants? Je crois que je les ai laissés ici.	Haben Sie meine Handschuhe gesehen? Ich glaube, ich habe Sie hiergelassen.
I have some things to be washed, to be sent to the laundry.	J'ai du linge à blanchir, à envoyer à la blanchisserie.	Ich habe ein paar Sachen zum Waschen, Ich möchte ein paar Sachen in die Waschanstalt geschickt haben.
When can you let me have them back? To-morrow? I must have them back by Saturday.	Quand pouvez-vous me les rendre? Demain? Il me faut les ravoir pour samedi.	Wann kann ich sie zurück➤ haben? Morgen? Ich muß sie bis Sonntag zurückhaben.
Please iron these things for me.	Veuillez me repasser ce linge.	Würden Sie mir bitte diese Sachen plätten?

Il radiatore. Il riscaldamento centrale è troppo caldo.	El calorífero. La calefacción está dando demasiado calor.	De radiator. De centrale verwarming is te warm.
Io vado a letto subito.	Voy a acostarme en seguida.	Ik ga meteen naar bed.
Io desidero un altro guanciale, un'altra coperta di lana, una borsa d'acqua calda.	Necesito otra almohada, otra frazada, un calientapiés.	Ik wens nog een kussen, nog een deken, een warme kruik.
Mi porterete l'acqua calda alle sette.	Me traerá usted el agua caliente a las siete.	U brengt me wat warm water boven om zeven uur.
◄ Portatemi ancora un poco d'acqua fredda, l'acqua calda per radermi, l'acqua da bere, una bottiglia d'acqua, una saponetta, un asciugamano pulito, una candela.	Tráigame más agua [fría], agua de afeitar, agua de beber, un frasco de agua, jabón, una toalla limpia, una vela.	Breng mij nog wat koud water, wat scheerwater, wat drinkwater, een karaf water, een schone handdoek, een kaars.
Potete portarmi una spazzola per panni?	¿Puede usted prestarme un cepillo de ropa?	Kunt U mij een klerenborstel lenen?
Dov'è la sala da bagno?	¿Dónde esta el cuarto de baño?	Waar is de badkamer?
C'è un bagno libero?	¿Hay un baño desocupado?	Is er een bad vrij?
Quando posso avere un bagno?	¿Cuándo podré tomar un baño?	Wanneer kan ik een bad nemen?
◄ Io desidero [avere] un bagno caldo, un bagno tiepido, un bagno freddo, un bagno ai piedi o un pediluvio, una doccia.	Quiero tomar un baño caliente, un baño tibio, un baño frio, un baño de pies, un baño de ducha o una ducha.	Ik wens een warm bad, een lauw bad, een koud bad, een voetbad, een douche, te nemen.
Al bagno manca il tappo.	Se ha extraviado el tapón del baño.	Er is geen badstop.
I miei vestiti sono bagnati, I miei stivaletti sono bagnati, per favore, asciugateli.	Está mojada mi ropa, están mojadas mis botas, haga el favor de secármela(s).	Mijn kleren zijn nat, Mijn schoenen zijn nat, laat ze drogen.
Avete visto i miei guanti? Io credo d'averli lasciati qui.	¿Ha visto usted mis guantes? Creo que me los dejé aquí?	Heeft U mijn handschoenen gezien? Ik geloof, dat ik ze hier heb laten liggen.
Io ho qualche cosa da far lavare, da mandare alla lavanderia.	Tengo alguna ropa que lavar, que mandar al lavado.	Ik heb een paar kleren voor de was, om naar de wasserij te sturen.
◄ Quando potrete rimandarmeli? Domani? È necessario che io li riabbia per sabato.	¿Cuándo pueden devolvérmela? ¿Mañana? Necesito tenerla para el sábado.	Wanneer kan ik ze terugkrijgen? Morgen? Ik moet ze zaterdag terughebben.
Per favore, stiratemi queste cose.	Haga el favor de plancharme esta ropa.	Wilt U deze kledingstukken voor me strijken.

The washing list or The laundry list	La liste de blanchissage	Die Wäscheliste
A brassière.	Un soutien-gorge.	Ein Büstenhalter.
Cami-knickers.	Une chemise-culotte.	Eine Hemdhose.
Combinations.	[Une] combinaison.	Combinations.
A [day] shirt (man's).	Une chemise de jour.	Ein Hemd, Ein Oberhemd.→
A dress shirt.	Une chemise de soirée.	Ein Frackhemd.
A frock.	Une robe, Un costume.	Ein Kleid.
A handkerchief.	Un mouchoir.	Ein Taschentuch.
A night dress or gown (woman's).	Une chemise de nuit.	Ein Nachthemd.
A night dress case.	Une enveloppe pour chemise de nuit.	Ein Pyjamaschoner. →
A night shirt (man's).	Une chemise de nuit.	Ein Nachthemd.
A [pair of] pants or drawers (men's).	Un caleçon.	Ein Paar Unterhosen, Ein Paar Beinkleider.
Panties or Knickers.	[Une] culotte, Un pantalon.	Ein Paar Schlüpfer.
Pyjamas or A suit of pyjamas or A sleeping suit.	Pyjama, Un pyjama, Une combinaison de nuit.	Pyjamas, Ein Pyjama, Ein Schlafanzug.
A shirt collar (detached).	Un faux col de chemise.	Ein Kragen. →
A skirt.	Une jupe.	Ein Rock.
A slip.	Un jupon.	Ein Unterrock.
Socks, A pair of socks.	[Des] chaussettes, Une paire de chaussettes.	Socken, Ein Paar Socken.
A soft collar (detached).	Un faux col souple.	Ein weicher Kragen.
Stockings.	[Des] bas.	Strümpfe. →
An [under]vest.	Un gilet [de dessous].	Eine Unterweste.
A white [evening] waistcoat.	Un gilet [de soirée] blanc.	Eine Frackweste.

The dining room or The coffee room	La salle à manger	Der Speisesaal
Early morning tea.	Le thé pris au réveil.	Tee vor dem Frühstück.
The breakfast.	Le déjeuner [du matin], Le premier déjeuner, Le petit déjeuner.	Das Frühstück.
I should like some breakfast.	Je voudrais prendre quelque chose pour déjeuner.	Ich möchte gern frühstücken.→
A plain breakfast.	Un petit déjeuner simple.	Ein einfaches Frühstück.
I shall take coffee in my room every day at eight.	Je prendrai du café dans ma chambre tous les jours à huit heures.	Ich möchte jeden Morgen um acht Kaffee auf mein Zimmer haben.
A meat breakfast.	Un déjeuner à la fourchette.	Ein Gabelfrühstück.
I should like some cold meat, some ham and eggs, for breakfast.	Je désire au déjeuner de la viande froide, du jambon aux œufs.	Ich möchte etwas kaltes Fleisch, Setzeier mit Schinken, zum Frühstück.
To breakfast.	Déjeuner.	Frühstücken.→
The lunch[eon].	Le déjeuner [de midi].	Das Mittagessen.

La lista della biancheria	La lista de ropa para lavar	De waslijst
Un reggi-petto.	Un corpiño.	Een bustehouder.
Una camicia-mutande.	Una camisa calzón (*de seda u otro género fino*).	Een chemise-enveloppe.
Una combinazione.	Una camisa calzón (*de algodón, lana, o punto*).	Een hemdbroek.
◄Una camicia da giorno.	Una camisa [de hombre].	Een overhemd.
Una camicia da sera.	Una camisa de frac.	Een wit overhemd [voor avondtenue].
Un abito.	Un vestido de señora, Un túnico.	Een jurk, Een japon.
Un fazzoletto.	Un pañuelo.	Een zakdoek.
Una camicia da notte.	Una camisa de dormir.	Een nachtjapon.
◄Una busta per camicia da notte.	Una funda para camisa de dormir.	Een pyjamazak.
Una camicia da notte.	Una camisa de dormir.	Een nachthemd.
Un paio di mutande, Le mutande.	Un par de calzoncillos.	Een onderbroek.
I calzoni corti.	Calzones [de señora].	Een directoire, Een broek.
Un [costume] pigiama.	Un pijama, Un traje de dormir.	Een pyjama.
◄Un colletto staccato.	Un cuello [de camisa].	Een boord.
Una sottana.	Una falda.	Een rok.
Una gonnella.	Una enagua, Un zagalejo.	Een onderjurk.
I calzini, Un paio di calzini.	Calcetines, Un par de calcetines.	Sokken, Een paar sokken.
Un colletto morbido.	Un cuello flexible.	Een slappe boord.
◄Le calze.	Medias.	Kousen.
Una camiciuola.	Una camiseta.	Een borstrok, Een hemd.
Un gilè bianco da sera.	Un chaleco blanco de frac.	Een wit vest [voor avondtenue].

La sala da pranzo	El comedor	De eetzaal *of* De eetkamer
Il tè alle prime ore del mattino.	El té de madrugada.	Vroege thee op bed.
La colazione.	El desayuno.	Het ontbijt.
◄Io vorrei avere qualche cosa a colazione.	Desearía un desayuno.	Ik zou graag wat ontbijt hebben.
Una colazione semplice.	Un desayuno sencillo.	Een eenvoudig ontbijt.
Io prenderò il caffè nella mia camera ogni mattina alle otto.	Tomaré café en mi habitación todos los días a las ocho.	Ik wens iedere dag om acht uur koffie op mijn kamer.
Una colazione alla forchetta.	Un almuerzo.	Een Engels ontbijt.
Vorrei per colazione carne fredda, prosciutto e uova.	Me gustaría un desayuno (*o* un almuerzo) de carne fiambre, de huevos con jamón.	Ik wens wat koud vlees, wat ham en eieren, voor het ontbijt.
◄Far colazione.	Desayunar.	Ontbijten.
La seconda colazione.	El almuerzo, El lunch.	De koffietafel, De lunch.

I am going on a motor coach tour to-day. Will you please give me a packed lunch?	Je fais aujourd'hui un circuit en autocar. Voulez-vous me donner un déjeuner empaqueté?	Ich mache heute eine Autobustour. Würden Sie mir bitte etwas zum Mittagessen einpacken?
Afternoon tea.	Le thé de l'après-midi.	Nachmittagstee.
Is it tea time?	Est-il l'heure du thé?	Ist es Zeit zum Tee?
Is there a tea dance to-day? (For Dancing terms, see pp. 234-237.)	Y a-t-il un thé dansant aujourd'hui?	Findet heute ein Tanztee statt?
At what time is the set meal? When do we dine?	À quelle heure est la table d'hôte? À quelle heure servez-vous le dîner?	Um wieviel Uhr ist die Table d'hôte? Um wieviel Uhr wird gespeist?
Keep a place, two places, for me at the table d'hôte. (See also pp. 134-135.)	Retenez-moi un couvert, deux couverts, à la table d'hôte.	Halten Sie bitte für mich einen Platz, zwei Plätze, an der Table d'hôte.
Can I dine in my room?	Puis-je dîner dans ma chambre?	Kann ich auf dem Zimmer essen?
Please have my supper brought up to my room. For fuller list of words and phrases, especially those concerning lunch and dinner, see EATING AND DRINKING, pp. 130-171.	Veuillez faire monter mon souper dans ma chambre.	Würden Sie bitte mein Abendbrot zu mir aufs Zimmer bringen lassen.

The charges, The bill	Les prix, La note	Die Preise, Die Rechnung
High-season charges.	Prix [de haute] saison.	Hochsaison-Preise.
Off-season charges.	Prix [de] hors saison.	Nachsaison-Preise.
Are the charges moderate or reasonable?	Le tarif est-il modique?	Sind die Preise mäßig?
Are your prices fixed officially or state controlled? Where in the hotel are they posted up?	Vos prix sont-ils homologués? Où dans l'hôtel sont-ils affichés?	Sind Ihre Preise amtlich festgesetzt? Wo im Hotel sind sie angeschlagen?
What do you charge for the room, for these rooms, per day, by the week, for a fortnight's stay?	Combien demandez-vous pour la chambre, pour cet appartement, par jour, par semaine, pour un séjour de quinze jours?	Was nehmen Sie für das Zimmer, für diese Zimmer, pro Tag, pro Woche, für einen vierzehntägigen Aufenthalt?
What extras are there?	Qu'y a-t-il comme suppléments?	Was für Aufschläge kommen noch dazu?
Does that include attendance?	Le service est-il compris?	Ist die Bedienung einbegriffen?
Is everything included? or Are your terms inclusive?	Tout est-il compris? Votre tarif s'entend-il tous frais compris?	Ist darin alles einbegriffen?
Have you anything better, cheaper, on the second, third, fourth, floor?	Avez-vous quelque chose de meilleur, de meilleur marché, au deuxième, troisième, quatrième, étage?	Haben Sie etwas Besseres, Billigeres, im zweiten, dritten, vierten, Stock?

Oggi andrò a fare un giro in autobus. Mi potreste mettere lo spuntino in un involto?	Voy a hacer hoy una excursión en autocar. Haga el favor de prepararme una fiambrera.	Ik ga vandaag een tocht maken per touringcar. Wilt U me als 't U belieft een lunchpakket geven?
Il tè del pomeriggio. È l'ora del tè? ◄C'è oggi un tè danzante?	El té de la tarde. ¿ Es la hora del té? ¿ Hay un té dansant hoy?	De namiddagthee. Is het theetijd? Is er vandaag een thé dansant?
A che ora è la tavola rotonda? A che ora è servito il pranzo? Riservatemi un posto, due posti, per me nella tavola rotonda.	¿ A qué hora sirven la comida? ¿ A qué hora se come? Resérveme un cubierto, dos cubiertos, para la comida.	Hoe laat is de table d'hôte? Hoe laat eten (of dineren) we? Reserveer een plaats, twee plaatsen, voor me aan de table d'hôte.
Posso avere il pranzo nella mia camera? Per favore, mandatemi la cena nella mia camera.	¿ Puedo comer en mi habitación? Haga el favor de pedir que me sirvan la cena en mi habitación.	Kan ik op mijn kamer eten? Laat mijn avondeten op mijn kamer serveren, als 't U belieft.

I prezzi, Il conto	Los precios, La cuenta	De prijzen, De berekening
◄I prezzi di stagione. I prezzi fuori stagione. Sono i prezzi moderati o ragionevoli? Sono i vostri prezzi fissati dall'ufficio competente? Dove sono esposti nell'albergo?	La tarifa de la gran sazón. La tarifa de fuera de sazón. ¿ Es moderada (o razonable) la tarifa? ¿ Son sus precios homologados o fijados oficialmente por el Estado? ¿ En qué lugar del hotel se exhiben?	Hoogseizoen prijzen. Buiten seizoen prijzen. Zijn Uw prijzen matig of redelijk? Zijn Uw prijzen officieel vastgesteld? Waar in het hotel zijn ze geafficheerd?
Che prezzo fate per la camera, per queste camere, al giorno, per settimana, per un soggiorno di quindici giorni?	¿ Cuánto carga usted por la habitación, por estas habitaciones, por día, por semana, por una estancia de quince días?	Wat vraagt U voor de kamer, voor deze kamers, per dag, per week, voor een veertiendaags verblijf?
◄Che cosa c'è di extra?	¿ Qué precios suplementarios hay?	Wat voor extra's zijn er?
Vi è compreso il servizio?	¿ Es incluso el servicio?	Is de bediening daarbij inbegrepen?
È tutto compreso? È tutto compreso nei vostri prezzi?	¿ Está todo incluso? ¿ Está todo comprendido en su tarifa?	Is alles inbegrepen? Is in Uw tarief alles inbegrepen?
Avete qualche cosa di meglio, più a buon mercato, nel secondo, nel terzo, nel quarto, piano?	¿ Tiene usted algo mejor, más barato, en el segundo, tercer, cuarto, piso?	Heeft U wat beters, goedkopers, op de tweede, derde, vierde, verdieping?

What are your en pension terms?	Quels sont vos prix en pension?	Wie sind Ihre Preise bei voller Pension?
That is rather too dear.	C'est un peu trop cher.	Das ist mir etwas zu teuer.
Waiter! Bring [me] my bill, Have my bill made out; I want to settle it.	Garçon! Apportez[-moi] ma note, Faites préparer ma note; je désire la régler.	Ober! Bringen Sie mir meine Rechnung, Lassen Sie mir bitte meine Rechnung ausstellen; ich möchte sie begleichen.
Let me have my bill this evening, as I am leaving to-morrow morning very early.	Donnez-moi ma note ce soir, car je pars demain matin de très bonne heure.	Geben Sie mir meine Rechnung bitte heute abend, da ich morgen sehr früh abreise.
Charge that to my account.	Portez cela à mon compte.	Setzen Sie das auf meine Rechnung.
What is this item?	Quel est cet article?	Was ist das für ein Posten?
I think there is a mistake. I have not had this.	Je crois qu'il y a une erreur. Je n'ai pas eu ceci.	Ich glaube, da ist ein Irrtum. Ich habe das nicht gehabt.
You have added it up wrongly.	Vous l'avez additionnée incorrectement.	Sie haben es falsch zusammengezählt.
Thank you, and good-bye.	Merci, et au revoir.	Besten Dank, und auf Wiedersehen.

EATING AND DRINKING	BOIRE ET MANGER	ESSEN UND TRINKEN
Generalities	**Généralités**	**Allgemeines**
A restaurant.	Un restaurant.	Ein Restaurant.
Can you tell me of a restaurant where the food is good, a restaurant which is to be recommended for its cooking?	Pouvez-vous m'indiquer un restaurant où l'on mange bien, un restaurant qui se recommande par sa cuisine?	Können Sie mir ein Restaurant nennen, wo man gut ißt, das wegen seiner guten Küche zu empfehlen ist?
Is it expensive, inexpensive? How much is the dinner?	Est-ce cher, économique? Combien compte-t-on le dîner?	Ist es teuer, billig? Was kostet das Abendessen?
Do they serve meals there at fixed prices?	Sert-on là des repas à prix fixe?	Werden dort Mahlzeiten zu festen Preisen serviert?
The table money or The cover charge.	Le [prix du] couvert.	Der Preis pro Gedeck.
Is wine included?	Le vin est-il compris?	Ist der Wein mit einbegriffen?
A Jewish (or kosher) restaurant.	Un restaurant israélite ou caucher ou kawcher ou kasher.	Ein jüdisches (oder Ein koscheres) Restaurant.
A café (on the Continent usually licensed to sell alcoholic drinks).	Un café.	Ein Café.
A [help your]self service café or A cafeteria.	Un restaurant où les clients se servent eux-mêmes, Une cafétérie.	Ein Restaurant mit Selbstbedienung.
The grill room.	La rôtisserie.	Der Grill Room.

Quali sono i vostri prezzi di pensione?	¿Cuáles son sus precios en pensión?	Hoeveel kost een kamer met pension?
◄Questo è un poco troppo caro.	Eso es un poco demasiado caro.	Dat is een beetje duur.
Cameriere! Portatemi il conto, Fate preparare il mio conto; io desidero saldare.	¡Camarero! Traiga mi cuenta, Haga preparar mi cuenta; quiero pagarla.	Ober! Breng [mij] mijn rekening, Laat mijn rekening klaarmaken; ik wens haar te betalen.
Fatemi avere il mio conto questa sera, perchè io partirò domani di buon'ora.	Prepáreme la cuenta para esta tarde, puesto que me marcho mañana por la mañana [muy] temprano.	Geef mij mijn rekening vanavond, daar ik morgenochtend zeer vroeg vertrek.
Mettete ciò sul mio conto.	Cárgueme eso en mi cuenta.	Schrijf dat op mijn rekening.
Cosa è questa partita?	¿Qué es este artículo o este asiento?	Wat is deze post?
◄Io credo che c'è un errore. Io non ho avuto questo.	Creo que hay un error. No he tenido esto.	Ik geloof, dat er een vergissing is. Ik heb dit niet gehad.
Voi l'avete sommato incorrettamente.	Se ha equivocado usted en la suma.	U heeft het verkeerd opgeteld.
Grazie, a rivederci.	Gracias, y adiós.	Dank U, en goedendag.

MANGIARE E BERE	COMIDAS Y BEBIDAS	ETEN EN DRINKEN
Generalità	**Generalidades**	**Algemeenheden**
Un ristorante.	Un restaurante.	Een restaurant.
Potete indicarmi un ristorante dove il cibo è buono, un ristorante raccomandato per la cucina?	¿Puede usted indicarme un restaurante en donde se come bien, un restaurante del que puede recomendarse la cocina?	Kunt U me een restaurant aanwijzen, waar het voedsel goed is, een restaurant, dat om zijn goede keuken bekend staat?
◄È caro, economico? Quanto si spende per il pranzo?	¿Es caro, económico? ¿Cuánto cargan por la comida?	Is het duur, goedkoop? Hoeveel kost het diner?
Si servono i pasti a prezzo fisso?	¿Sirven ahí comidas a precio fijo?	Serveren ze daar maaltijden voor vastgestelde prijzen?
Il prezzo del coperto.	El precio del cubierto.	Het couvert.
Il vino è compreso?	¿Es incluso el vino?	Is de wijn inbegrepen?
Un ristorante ebraico.	Un restaurante judío.	Een Joods (of kosjer) restaurant.
◄Un caffè.	Un café.	Een café.
Una caffetteria.	Una cafetería.	Een cafeteria.
La rosticceria.	El grill room.	De grillroom.

A snack bar.	Un casse-croûte.	Ein Imbißraum.
A wine shop or cellar.	Un cabaret.	Eine Weinstube, Ein Weinkeller.
A tavern.	Une taverne, Un cabaret.	Eine Taverne.
A tavern with gardens and dance hall.	Une guinguette.	Eine Trinkstube mit Garten und Tanzdiele.
A public house.	Un cabaret, Un estaminet, Une taverne, Une brasserie.	Ein Wirtshaus, Eine Bierstube.
A buffet (sideboard).	Un buffet.	Ein Buffet.
A buffet (at a ball).	Un souper debout.	Ein Buffet.
A bar (in a public house).	Un comptoir [de cabaret], Une buvette.	Eine Theke.
A bar (in a hotel).	Un bar.	Eine Bar.
A cocktail bar.	Un bar-comptoir.	Eine Cocktailbar.
A barman.	Un serveur, Un barman.	Ein Mixer.
A tea room or shop or Tea rooms.	Un salon de thé, Une pâtisserie.	Eine Teestube.
A waiter.	Un garçon [de café, etc.]	Ein Kellner.
The head waiter.	Le maître d'hôtel, Le premier garçon, Le chef de salle.	Der Oberkellner.
The wine waiter.	Le sommelier.	Der Weinkellner.
Waiter !	Garçon !	Ober ! oder Herr Ober !
A waitress.	Une fille de salle, Une servante, Une bonne.	Eine Kellnerin.
Waitress !	Mademoiselle !	Fräulein !
A cook.	Un cuisinier, Une cuisinière.	Ein Koch.
The head cook.	Le chef [de cuisine].	Der Küchenchef.
The bill [of fare] or The menu.	La carte [du restaurant] La carte du jour, Le menu.	Die Speisekarte, Das Menu.
[Give me] the bill of fare, please.	[Donnez-moi] la carte, s'il vous plaît.	[Geben Sie mir] die Speisekarte, bitte.
The wine list.	La carte des vins.	Die Weinkarte.
A course (of a meal).	Un service, Un plat.	Ein Gang.
A dish (of food). The special dish for the day.	Un plat. Le plat du jour.	Ein Gericht. Das Tagesgericht.
A portion, A half portion (of food).	Une portion, Une demi-portion.	Eine Portion, Eine halbe Portion.
For Breakfast see pp. 126-127.		
A lunch[eon] or A midday meal.	Un déjeuner [de midi], Un second déjeuner.	Das Mittagessen.
To lunch or To have (or To take) lunch. We will lunch at noon, at one o'clock.	Déjeuner. Nous déjeunerons à midi, à une heure.	[Zu] Mittag essen. Wir essen ums zwölf, um eins.
Tea. To have tea. I will take [some] tea.	Le thé. Prendre le thé. Je prendrai du thé.	Tee. Tee trinken. Für mich bitte Tee.
Tea time.	L'heure du thé.	Teezeit.
Dinner.	Le dîner.	Abendessen.
To dine or To have dinner.	Dîner.	Zu Abend essen.

Uno spuntino.	Un bar de fiambres.	Een cafetaria.
Un negozio di vino, Una cantina.	Una taberna, Una bodega.	Een wijnkelder.
◄ Una bettola, Un'osteria.	Una taberna.	Een herberg, een taverne.
Una bettola con giardino e sala da ballo.	Una taberna con jardín y salón de baile.	Een café met tuin en danszaal.
Una bettola.	Una taberna, Una cervecería.	Een café, Een kroeg.
Un buffet.	Un aparador de refrescos.	Een buffet.
Un buffet.	Un aparador.	Een staand buffet.
◄ Un bar, Un banco d'osteria.	Un bar.	Een buffet.
Un bar.	Un bar.	Een bar.
Un bar-cocktail.	Un bar coctél.	Een cocktail bar.
Un garzone di bar.	Un mozo de taberna.	Een barman.
Una sala da tè.	Un salón de té, Una confitería.	Een theesalon.
◄ Un cameriere.	Un camarero, Un mozo [de café, etc.]	Een kelner.
Il capo cameriere.	El maître d'hotel, El jefe de comedor.	De ober, De hoofdkelner.
Il coppiere.	El mayordomo de vinos.	De wijnkelder.
Cameriere !	¡ Camarero !	Ober!
Una cameriera.	Una camarera, Una sirvienta.	Een kelnerin, een serveuse.
◄ Cameriera !	¡ Camarera !	Juffrouw!
Un cuoco, Una cuoca.	Un cocinero, Una cocinera.	Een kok, Een kokkin.
Il capocuoco.	El chef, El primer cocinero.	De chef.
La lista (o La carta) dei piatti, Il menu.	La lista de platos.	Het menu, De spijskaart.
[Datemi] il menu, per favore.	Haga el favor de darme la lista de platos.	[Geef me] het menu, als 't U belieft.
◄ La lista dei vini.	La tarifa de los vinos.	De wijnkaart.
Una portata.	Un plato.	Een gerecht.
Un piatto. Il piatto speciale del giorno.	Un plato. El plato del día.	Een schotel. De speciale schotel van de dag.
Una porzione, Una mezza porzione.	Una porción, Una media porción.	Een portie. Een halve portie.
◄ La seconda colazione.	Un lunch, Un almuerzo.	Een lunch, Een koffiemaaltijd.
Prendere la seconda colazione. Noi prenderemo la seconda colazione a mezzogiorno, alle una.	Almorzar o Tomar el lunch. Almorzaremos (o Tomaremos el lunch) al mediodia, a la una.	Lunchen, Koffiedrinken. We zullen om twaalf uur, een uur, koffie drinken.
Il tè. Prendere il tè. Prendere del tè.	El té. Tomar el té. Tomaré té.	Thee. Theedrinken. Ik neem thee.
L'ora del tè.	La hora del té.	Theetijd, Het theeuurtje.
Il pranzo.	La comida.	Het diner, Het middageten.
◄ Pranzare.	Comer, Tomar la comida.	Dineren, Eten.

To dine out.	Dîner en ville.	Auswärts essen.
Supper.	Le souper.	Abendbrot.
To have supper.	Souper.	Abendbrot essen.
Supper time.	L'heure du souper.	Abendbrotzeit.
A cut off the joint.	Une tranche de rôti.	Ein Stück Braten.
A bottle of wine, of brandy, of beer.	Une bouteille de vin, d'eau-de-vie, de bière.	Eine Flasche Wein, Cognac, Bier.
A half-bottle of wine.	Une demi-bouteille de vin.	Eine halbe Flasche Wein.
A glass of wine.	Un verre de vin.	Ein Glas Wein.
A [small] glass of beer.	Un bock.	Ein [kleines] Glas Bier.
A large glass of beer.	Un demi (=demi-litre).	Ein großes Glas Bier.

The meal / Le repas / Die Mahlzeit

Waiter! Have you a table disengaged?	Garçon! Avez-vous une table libre?	Ober! Ist ein Tisch frei?
Where is my place or seat? Where may I sit? Where can we sit? Anywhere?	Où est mon couvert? Où puis-je m'asseoir? Où pouvons-nous nous placer? N'importe où?	Wo ist mein Platz? Wo kann ich mich hinsetzen? Wo können wir uns hinsetzen? Wo wir wollen?
Please keep a place for me at this table [here].	Veuillez me réserver un couvert à cette table [-ci].	Würden Sie mir bitte einen Platz an diesem Tisch reservieren?
I expect some friends. Can you give us a private room, a separate table, put us all together near the window?	J'attends des amis. Pourriez-vous nous donner un cabinet particulier, une petite table, nous placer tous ensemble près de la fenêtre?	Ich erwarte einige Freunde. Könnten Sie uns ein Privatzimmer zur Verfügung stellen, uns an einen Einzeltisch setzen, uns alle zusammen in die Nähe des Fensters setzen?
Are meals served on the terrace in fine weather?	Les repas sont-ils servis sur la terrasse pendant la belle saison?	Werden die Mahlzeiten bei gutem Wetter auf der Terrasse serviert?
Where is the lavatory?	Où est la toilette?	Wo ist die Toilette?
Have you a ladies' lavatory?	Avez-vous une toilette pour dames?	Gibt es hier eine Damentoilette?
Please put my coat, my hat, my stick, in the cloak room.	Veuillez déposer mon manteau, mon chapeau, ma canne, au vestiaire.	Würden Sie bitte meinen Mantel, meinen Hut, meinen Stock, in die Garderobe bringen?
I am hungry, thirsty, peckish. I want (or should like) something to eat or a bite of something, some [light] refreshments, to take something to drink.	J'ai faim, soif, la fringale. Je veux (ou Je voudrais) manger quelque chose, des rafraîchissements, prendre quelque chose à boire.	Ich habe Hunger, Durst, Appetit. Ich möchte etwas, eine Kleinigkeit, essen, etwas zu Trinken haben.
Have you anything ready? What have you ready?	Avez-vous quelque chose de prêt? Qu'avez-vous de prêt?	Haben Sie etwas, was schon fertig ist? Was haben Sie fertig da?
[At] what time (or o'clock) is dinner [served]?	À quelle heure le dîner est-il servi?	Um wieviel Uhr ist das Abendessen?

Mangiare fuori.	Comer fuera [de casa].	Buiten dineren.
La cena.	La cena.	Het souper, Het avond-eten.
Cenare.	Cenar.	Souperen.
L'ora della cena.	La hora de cenar.	Tijd voor het avondeten.
◀ Un pezzo d'arrosto.	Una tajada de carne.	Een plak vlees.
Una bottiglia di vino, di cognac, di birra.	Una botella de vino, de coñac, de cerveza.	Een fles wijn, cognac, bier.
Una mezza bottiglia di vino.	Media botella de vino.	Een halve fles wijn.
Un bicchiere di vino.	Una copa de vino.	Een glas wijn.
Un bicchiere [piccolo] di birra.	Una cerveza.	Een glas bier.
◀ Un bicchiere grande di birra.	Una cerveza grande.	Een groot glas bier.

I pasti	La alimentación	De maaltijd
Cameriere! Avete una tavola libera?	¡Camarero! ¿Hay una mesa libre?	Ober! Hebt U een tafel vrij?
Dov'è il mio posto o la mia tavola? Dove posso sedermi? Dove possiamo sederci? In qualunque posto?	¿Cuál es mi sitio? ¿Dónde puedo sentarme? ¿Dónde podemos sentarnos? ¿En cualquier sitio?	Waar is mijn plaats? Waar kan ik zitten? Waar kunnen wij zitten? Overal?
Per favore, riservatemi un posto a questa tavola.	Haga el favor de reservarme un sitio en esta mesa.	Wilt U een plaats voor me reserveren aan deze tafel.
Io aspetto degli amici. Ci potete dare una stanza privata, una tavola separata, metterci tutti insiemi vicino alla finestra?	Espero unos amigos. ¿Puede usted darnos un cuarto privado, una mesa aparte, colocarnos todos juntos cerca de la ventana?	Ik verwacht enkele vrienden, Kunt U ons een privé kamer geven, een tafel apart geven, ons allemaal te zamen bij het raam plaatsen?
◀ I pasti sono serviti nella terrazza, quando è buon tempo?	¿Se sirven comidas en la terraza cuando hace buen tiempo?	Worden maaltijden bij goed weer op het terras geserveerd?
Dov'è la sala per toeletta?	¿Dónde está el lavatorio?	Waar is het toilet?
Avete una sala da toeletta per signora?	¿Hay un lavatorio para señoras?	Heeft U een damestoilet?
Per favore, mettete il mio cappotto, il mio cappello, il mio bastone, nel vestiario.	Haga el favor de llevar mi sobretodo, mi sombrero, mi bastón, a la consigna.	Wilt U mijn jas, mijn hoed, mijn wandelstok, in de vestiaire afgeven.
Io ho fame, sete, voglia di uno spuntino. Vorrei qualche cosa da mangiare, fare uno spuntino, avere qualche cosa da bere.	Tengo hambre, Estoy hambriento, Tengo sed. Quisiera comer algo o un bocado, alguna cosa ligera, tomar algo de beber.	Ik heb honger, dorst, trek. Ik zou graag wat eten, wat lichte verversingen nuttigen, graag wat drinken.
◀ Avete qualche cosa pronto? [Que] cosa avete pronto?	¿Hay algo listo? ¿Qué hay ya preparado?	Heeft U iets klaar of gereed? Wat heeft U klaar?
A che ora si serve il pranzo?	¿A qué hora sirven la comida?	Hoe laat wordt het diner geserveerd?

What is there [to eat]? What have you to-day? What have we [got] for dinner? What is the main course or dish? What is the special dish for the day? What can you give me?	Qu'y a-t-il [à manger]? Qu'avez-vous [à m'offrir, à nous offrir] aujourd' hui? Qu'est-ce qu'il y a pour le dîner? Quelle est la pièce de résistance? Quel est le plat du jour? Que pouvez-vous me donner?	Was gibt es zu essen? Was haben Sie heute? Was gibt es heute zum Abendessen? Welches ist das Hauptgericht? Welches ist das Tagesgericht? Was können Sie mir geben?
Can you let me have something at once?	Auriez-vous quelque chose à me donner tout de suite?	Kann ich sofort etwas bekommen?
Can I have lunch, dinner, tea?	Puis-je déjeuner, dîner, prendre le thé?	Kann ich Mittagessen, Abendessen, Tee, bekommen?
Please prepare dinner for eight o'clock.	Veuillez préparer le dîner pour huit heures.	Würden Sie bitte das Abendessen für acht Uhr vorbereiten?
I, We, want something hot, cold, a substantial lunch, a snack, a few ham sandwiches.	Il me, nous, faut quelque chose de chaud, de froid, un déjeuner dînatoire, une collation ou un casse-croûte, quelques sandwich[e]s au jambon.	Ich möchte, Wir möchten, etwas Warmes, Kaltes, ein ausgiebiges Mittag, einen Imbiß, ein paar Schinkenschnitten.
What [roast] joints have you ready?	Qu'y a-t-il de prêt comme rôtis?	Was für einen Braten haben Sie da?
Have you any fruit?	Avez-vous des fruits?	Haben Sie irgendwelches Obst?
What ices have you?	Quelles glaces avez-vous?	Was für Eis haben Sie?
Is that dish off?	Ce plat est-il épuisé?	Ist dies Gericht gestrichen?
Make me an omelet[te].	Faites-moi une omelette.	Machen Sie mir bitte ein Omelette.
Please lay (or set) the table or the cloth.	Veuillez mettre (ou dresser) le couvert.	Wollen Sie bitte den Tisch decken.
I will take the set dinner.	Je dînerai à la table d'hôte.	Ich nehme das Menü.
I wish to dine from the bill of fare.	Je voudrais dîner à la carte.	Ich möchte nach der Karte (oder à la carte) essen.
I will take thick soup, clear soup.	Je prendrai du potage, du consommé.	Ich möchte Suppe, Bouillon.
Please give me a piece of fat, another piece of lean.	Donnez-moi, s'il vous plaît, un morceau de gras, encore un morceau de maigre.	Bitte geben Sie mir ein Stück mit Fett, noch ein Stück ohne Fett.
A small piece of cheese and some biscuits.	Un petit morceau de fromage et des biscuits.	Ein kleines Stück Käse und ein paar Kekse.
Is the camembert ripe?	Le camembert est-il fait?	Ist der Camembert durch?
Some more bread, please.	Encore du pain, s'il vous plaît.	Noch etwas Brot, bitte.
Please dress the salad.	Veuillez assaisonner la salade.	Würden Sie bitte den Salat anmachen.
For dessert, I'll have grapes.	Pour le dessert, je prendrai un raisin.	Zum Nachtisch möchte ich Trauben.
Thank you, I have enough.	Merci, j'en ai assez.	Danke, ich habe genug.

Cosa c'è da mangiare? Cosa avete oggi? Cosa possiamo avere per pranzo? Qual'è il piatto principale? Qual'è il piatto speciale del giorno? Cosa potete darmi?	¿Qué hay de comer? ¿Qué hay de comer hoy? ¿Qué hay para la comida? ¿Qué es el plato principal? ¿Qué es el plato del día? ¿Qué pueden darme?	Wat is er te eten? Wat heeft U vandaag? Wat hebben we voor het middageten? Wat is de hoofdschotel? Wat is de speciale schotel voor vandaag? Wat kunt U me geven?
Potete servirmi qualche cosa subito?	¿Pueden darme algo de comer en seguida?	Kunt U me meteen iets geven?
Posso avere la seconda colazione, il pranzo, il tè?	¿Puedo tomar el almuerzo, la comida, el té?	Kan ik lunchen, dineren, theedrinken?
◄ Per piacere preparate il pranzo per le otto.	Haga el favor de preparar la comida para las ocho.	Wilt U het diner voor acht uur bereiden.
Io desidero, Noi desideriamo, qualche cosa di caldo, di freddo, un pasto sostanzioso, uno spuntino, alcuni panini gravidi.	Quiero, Queremos, algo caliente, frío, un almuerzo sustancioso, un fiambre, unos emparedados de jamón.	Ik wens, wij wensen, iets warms, kouds, een stevige lunch, een hapje, een paar ham-sandwiches.
Che cosa avete pronto di arrosto?	¿Qué platos de carne [asada] hay listos?	Wat voor gebraad heeft U gereed?
Avete delle frutta?	¿Hay fruta?	Heeft U fruit?
Che gelati avete?	¿Qué mantecados (o helados) hay?	Wat voor soorten ijs heeft U?
◄ È esaurito quel piatto?	¿Se ha acabado ese plato?	Is deze schotel van het menu af?
Fatemi una frittata.	Prepáreme una tortilla.	Maak een omelet voor me.
Per favore, apparecchiate la tavola.	Haga el favor de poner la mesa.	Wilt U de tafel dekken.
Io mangerò alla tavola rotonda.	Comeré a la table d'hôte.	Ik eet aan de table d'hôte.
Io vorrei mangiare alla carta.	Deseo comer a la carta.	Ik wens à la carte te dineren.
◄ Io prenderei una zuppa crema, un brodo.	Tomaré la sopa, el consomé.	Ik neem dikke soep, dunne soep.
Per favore, datemi un pezzo di grasso, un altro pezzo di magro.	Haga el favor de darme un trozo de gordura, otro trozo de magro.	Wilt U me een stuk vet, nog een stuk mager, geven.
Un pezzettino di formaggio e qualche biscotto.	Un poco de queso con galletas.	Een klein stukje kaas en wat beschuitjes.
È il camembert a giusto punto?	¿Está [bien] maduro el camembert?	Is de Camembert rijp?
Un altro poco di pane, per piacere.	Haga el favor de darme más pan.	Nog wat brood, als 't U belieft.
◄ Per piacere condite l'insalata.	Haga el favor de aliñar la ensalada.	Maak de sla aan, als 't U belieft.
Per il dessert, io prenderò l'uva.	Para postre tomaré uvas.	Voor het dessert neem ik druiven.
Grazie, ne ho abbastanza.	Gracias, basta ya o con eso basta.	Dank U, ik heb genoeg.

Bring me another knife, please.	Apportez-moi un autre couteau, s'il vous plaît.	Bringen Sie bitte noch ein Messer.
I should like [to have] a drink. Give me something to drink.	Je voudrais prendre une consommation. Donnez-moi [quelque chose] à boire.	Ich möchte etwas zu Trinken haben. Bringen Sie mir bitte etwas zu Trinken.
I should like a long drink, a short drink.	Je voudrais boire un grand verre, un petit verre.	Ich möchte ein großes Glas, ein kleines Glas.
Give me a bottle, half a bottle, of Médoc (claret), a drop of brandy, a nip of whisky.	Donnez-moi une bouteille, une demi-bouteille, de médoc ou de vin de Médoc, une goutte de cognac, une goutte de whisky.	Geben Sie mir bitte eine Flasche, eine halbe Flasche, Médoc, einen Tropfen Cognac, einen Schluck Whisky.
Please open, uncork, this bottle.	Veuillez ouvrir, déboucher, cette bouteille.	Würden Sie bitte diese Flasche öffnen, entkorken.
Bring me another one (drink) or [Bring me] the same again.	Apportez-m'en encore un(e).	Bringen Sie mir noch Einen oder Dasselbe noch einmal.
Please bring the drinks outside (to the tables on the pavement in front of the café).	Veuillez apporter les consommations à la terrasse.	Würden Sie die Getränke bitte herausbringen.
I will take water.	Je prendrai de l'eau.	Ich werde Wasser trinken.
Bring a bottle of iced water, and two more glasses.	Apportez une carafe frappée, et deux verres de plus.	Bringen Sie mir bitte eine Karaffe eisgekühltes Wasser, und noch zwei Gläser.
Please ice a bottle of champagne.	Veuillez frapper [de glace] une bouteille de champagne.	Würden Sie bitte eine Flasche Champagner auf Eis legen.
Please take the chill off the wine.	Veuillez chambrer le vin.	Würden Sie den Wein bitte warm stellen.
Give me a light, please.	Donnez-moi du feu, s'il vous plaît.	Geben Sie mir bitte Feuer.
For cigarettes, etc., see pp. 208-209.		
A cup[ful].	Une tasse.	Eine Tasse.
A cup[ful] (small).	Une demi-tasse.	Eine kleine Tasse.
I would like a cup of tea, of coffee, of cocoa.	Je voudrais une tasse de thé, de café, de chocolat.	Ich möchte eine Tasse Tee, Kaffee, Kakao.
Waiter! Another (or One more) cup of coffee.	Garçon! Encore une tasse de café.	Ober! Noch eine Tasse Kaffee bitte.
A small coffee, please.	Une demi-tasse de café, s'il vous plaît.	Eine kleine Tasse Kaffee bitte.
A little more milk.	Un peu plus de lait.	Noch etwas Milch.
Yes, that will do nicely.	Oui, cela fera très bien mon, notre, affaire.	Ja danke, das ist genug.
May I trouble you for the salt?	Puis-je vous demander de vouloir bien me passer le sel?	Darf ich Sie um das Salz bitten.

Per favore, portatemi un altro coltello.	Haga el favor de traerme otro cuchillo.	Breng me een ander mes, als 't U belieft.
Io vorrei da bere. Portatemi qualche cosa da bere.	Quisiera (o Me gustaría) beber algo. Déme algo de beber.	Ik wil graag wat drinken. Geef me iets te drinken.
◄Io vorrei un bicchierone, un po' da bere.	Me gustaría una buena bebida, una pequeña bebida.	Ik wil graag een groot glas, een klein glas.
Portatemi una bottiglia, una mezza bottiglia, di Medoc, una goccia di cognac, un sorso di whisky.	Déme una botella, media botella, de Medoc, un sorbito de coñac, un traguito de whisky.	Geef me een fles, halve fles Médoc, een klein beetje cognac, een vinger whisky.
Per favore, aprite, sturate, questa bottiglia.	Haga el favor de destapar esta botella.	Wilt U deze fles openen, ontkurken.
Portatemene ancora un altro, un'altra.	Tráigame otra bebida o [Tráigame] otra como la anterior.	Breng me er nog een.
Per favore, portatemi la consumazione fuori o sulla terrazza.	Haga el favor de traer las bebidas a la terraza.	Wilt U de drank buiten brengen.
◄Io prenderei dell'acqua. Portatemi una bottiglia di acqua ghiacciata, e due altri bicchieri.	Tomaré agua. Tráiga una botella de agua enfriada con hielo, y dos vasos más.	Ik neem water. Breng een karaf ijswater en nog twee glazen.
Per favore, mettete sotto ghiaccio una bottiglia di sciampagna.	Haga el favor de poner una botella de champaña sobre hielo.	Wilt U een fles campagne op het ijs zetten.
Per favore, intiepidite il vino.	Haga el favor de templar el vino.	Wilt U de wijn op kamertemperatuur brengen.
Per favore, un fiammifero.	Haga el favor de darme alumbre.	Kunt U me een vuurtje geven als 't U belieft.
◄Una tazza [colma]. Una tazzina.	Una taza. Media taza.	Een kop. Een kopje.
Vorrei una tazza di tè, di caffè, di cioccolata.	Me gustaría una taza de té, de café, de chocolate.	Ik wil graag een kop thee, koffie, chocola, hebben.
Cameriere! Un'altra tazza di caffè.	¡Camarero! Otra taza (o Una taza más) de café.	Ober! Nog een kop koffie.
Per favore, una tazzina di caffè.	Haga el favor de media taza (o una tacita) de café.	Een kleintje koffie, als 't U belieft.
◄Un po' più di latte. Sì, ciò andrà molto bene.	Una poca más de leche. Sí, eso es; perfectamente.	Nog een scheutje melk. Ja, dat is uitstekend.
Per favore, mi potreste passare il sale?	Haga el favor de la sal.	Zoudt U me het zout willen aanreiken, als 't U belieft?

Please pass me the water, the mustard.	Veuillez me passer l'eau, la moutarde.	Würden Sie mir bitte das Wasser, den Senf, reichen.
What did you say? or I didn't catch that or I beg your pardon?	Plaît-il?	Wie bitte? oder Verzeihung?
Nothing more, thank you.	Rien de plus, merci.	Danke, ich möchte nichts mehr.
Please give the table a wipe.	Veuillez donner un coup de torchon ici.	Würden Sie bitte den Tisch abwischen.
Please clear the table or Please clear away.	Veuillez ôter le couvert, Veuillez desservir.	Wollen Sie bitte [den Tisch] abräumen.
A picnic.	Un pique-nique, Une partie de plaisir.	Ein Picknick.
To picnic.	Faire un pique-nique.	Ein Picknick veranstalten.
A picnic basket.	Un panier pique-nique.	Ein Picknickkorb.
A lunch[eon] basket (empty).	Un panier à provisions.	Ein Speisekorb.
A lunch[eon] basket (filled).	Un panier-repas.	Ein Speisekorb.

Complaints	**Réclamations**	**Beschwerden**
I'd like to have a word with the superintendent. Ask the head waiter to come here.	Je voudrais dire un mot au maître d'hôtel. Demandez au premier garçon de venir ici.	Ich möchte gern mit dem Direktor sprechen. Bitten Sie den Oberkellner her.
I don't care for this dish.	Ce plat ne me plaît pas.	Dieses Gericht schmeckt mir nicht.
I cannot eat this. Take it away.	Je ne peux [pas] manger ceci. Emportez-le.	Ich kann dies nicht essen. Würden Sie es bitte wegnehmen.
I do not like coffee, give me tea.	Je n'aime pas le café, donnez-moi du thé.	Ich trinke Kaffee nicht gern, bringen Sie mir bitte Tee.
I have no knife, fork.	Je n'ai pas de couteau, de fourchette.	Ich habe kein Messer, keine Gabel.
I ordered a chop a good while ago; and what about the beer?	Voilà longtemps que je vous ai commandé un chop; et la bière?	Ich habe vor einer ganzen Weile ein Kotelett bestellt; und wo bleibt das Bier?
I asked for half a bottle only, not a bottle.	C'est une demi-bouteille que j'ai demandée, et non pas une bouteille.	Ich habe eine halbe Flasche bestellt, nicht eine Flasche.
These plates are cold, please warm them.	Ces assiettes sont froides, veuillez les faire chauffer.	Diese Teller sind kalt, würden Sie sie bitte anwärmen.
This tea is too weak, is not strong enough, is too strong.	Ce thé est trop faible, n'est pas assez fort, est trop fort.	Der Tee ist zu schwach, ist nicht stark genug, ist zu stark.
Is this water drinkable, undrinkable? This food is uneatable. This fruit is unsound or is bad.	Cette eau est-elle buvable, imbuvable? Ce mets est immangeable. Ce fruit est gâté.	Ist dies Trinkwasser, kein Trinkwasser? Dies Essen ist ungenießbar. Dies Obst ist verdorben.

Per favore, passatemi l'acqua, la mostarda.	Haga el favor del agua, de la mostaza.	Wilt U me het water, de mosterd, aanreiken.
Cosa dite? *o* Come? *o* Scusi?	Dispense usted ¿qué fué lo que dijo?	Neem me niet kwalijk? *of* Wat zegt U?
Niente più, grazie.	Gracias, nada más.	Niets meer, dank U.
Per piacere date una pulita alla tavola.	Haga el favor de darle un repaso a la mesa.	Wilt U de tafel even schoonvegen.
Per favore, sparecchiate.	Haga el favor de quitar la mesa.	Wilt U de tafel afruimen.
Una scampagnata.	Una jira.	Een picknick.
Fare una scampagnata.	Ir de jira.	Picknicken.
Un cestino per scampagnata.	Una cesta de jira.	Een picknickmand.
Un cestino per provviste.	Una cesta para provisiones.	Een provisiemand.
Un cestino guarnito.	Una cesta de merienda *o* de lunch.	Een lunchpakket.

Reclami	**Quejas**	**Klachten**
Vorrei dire una parola al sorvegliante. Dite al primo cameriere di venire qui.	Desearía hablar un momento con el gerente. Pídale al jefe de comedor que venga.	Ik zou graag de directeur even willen spreken. Vraag de oberkelner hier te komen.
Questo piatto non mi piace.	No me gusta este plato.	Deze schotel staat me niet aan.
Io non posso mangiare ciò. Portatelo via.	No puedo comer esto. Lléveselo.	Ik kan dit niet eten. Haal het weg.
Non mi piace il caffè, portatemi il tè.	No me gusta el café, déme té.	Ik houd niet van koffie, geef me thee.
Io non ho il coltello, la forchetta.	No tengo cuchillo, tenedor.	Ik heb geen mes, vork.
Io ho ordinato da molto tempo una braciola; e la birra quando arriva?	Pedí una chuleta hace ya un rato; y ¿qué hay de la cerveza?	Ik heb een tijd geleden een cotelet besteld; en hoe zit het met het bier?
Io ho domandato una mezza bottiglia, non una bottiglia.	Pedí sólo media botella, no una botella.	Ik heb slechts om een halve fles gevraagd, geen hele.
Questi piatti sono freddi, per favore fateli riscaldare.	Estos platos están fríos, haga el favor de calentarlos.	De borden zijn koud, laat ze warm maken, als 't U belieft.
Questo tè è troppo debole, non è forte abbastanza, è troppo forte.	Este té está demasiado flojo, no está suficientemente fuerte, está demasiado fuerte.	Deze thee is te slap, is niet sterk genoeg, is te sterk.
È potabile, non potabile, quest'acqua? Questo cibo è immangiabile. Questa frutta è guasta *o* è cattiva.	¿Esta agua es bebible *o* potable, imbebible? Estos manjares están incomibles. Esta fruta no está buena *o* está podrida.	Is dit drinkwater, geen drinkwater? Dit voedsel is oneetbaar. Dit fruit is bedorven.

The bill	La note	Die Rechnung
Bring me the bill.	Apportez-moi la note *ou* l'addition.	Bringen Sie mir die Rechnung.
There is a mistake in the addition.	Il y a une erreur dans l'addition.	Da ist ein Additionsfehler.
To pay at the desk.	Payer à la caisse.	An der Kasse bezahlen. →
Keep the change for yourself (*as a tip*).	Gardez la monnaie pour vous (*comme pourboire*).	Behalten Sie das Kleingeld *oder* die Differenz (*als Trinkgeld*).
This (*tip*) is for you.	Ceci est pour vous.	Dies ist für Sie.

Tableware	Vaisselle de table et accessoires	Tischgeschirr
A bread knife.	Un couteau à pain.	Ein Brotmesser.
A bread saw.	Un couteau-scie a pain.	Ein gezahntes Brotmesser, Eine Brotsäge.
A breakfast cup.	Une tasse a dejeuner.	Eine Fruhstückstasse. →
A butter dish.	Un beurrier.	Eine Butterdose.
A carving knife.	Un couteau a découper.	Ein Tranchiermesser.
A castor *or* caster (*bottle*), see pepper castor, sugar castor.		
A champagne glass.	Une coupe à champagne.	Ein Champagnerglas, Ein Sektglas.
A cheese (*or* A little) knife.	Un couteau á dessert.	Ein kleines Messer.
A cheese (*or* A little) plate.	Une petite assiette plate.	Ein kleiner Teller. →
A cocktail shaker.	Un frappe-cocktail, Un shaker.	Ein Cocktail-Shaker, Ein Mischbecher.
A coffee cup.	Une tasse à café.	Eine Kaffeetasse.
A coffee pot.	Une cafétière, Une verseuse.	Eine Kaffeekanne.
A coffee spoon.	Une cuiller à café.	Ein Kaffeelöffel.
A cork.	Un bouchon.	Ein Korken. →
A corkscrew.	Un tire-bouchon.	Ein Korkenzieher.
A cream jug.	Un crémier.	Ein Sahnegießer, Ein Sahnekännchen.
A cruet.	Une ménagère, Un huilier.	Ein Essig- und Ölbehälter.
A decanter.	Une carafe [à vin, àliqueur].	Eine Karaffe, Eine Weinkaraffe.
A decanter (*small*).	Un carafon.	Eine kleine Karaffe. →
A dessert plate.	Une assiette à dessert.	Ein Dessertteller.
A dessert spoon.	Une cuiller à dessert, Une cuiller a entremets.	Ein Speiselöffel.
A dinner (*or* A meat) plate.	Une assiette plate.	Ein flacher Teller, Ein Eßteller.
A dish.	Un plat.	Eine Schüssel.
A drinking straw.	Un chalumeau paille pour boissons.	Ein Strohhalm. →
An egg cup.	Un coquetier.	Ein Eierbecher.
An egg spoon.	Une cuiller a œuf.	Ein Eierlöffel.
A finger bowl.	Un bol rince-doigts.	Eine Fingerschale.
A fish knife and fork.	Un couteau et une fourchette à poisson.	Ein Fischmesser und eine Fischgabel.
A fish slice.	Une truelle à poisson.	Ein Fischheber. →
A fork.	Une fourchette.	Eine Gabel.
A fruit knife.	Un couteau à fruit.	Ein Obstmesser.

Il conto	La cuenta	De rekening
Portatemi il conto.	Tráigame la cuenta.	Breng me de rekening.
C'è un errore nella somma.	Está equivocada la suma.	Er is een vergissing in de optelling.
◄Pagare alla cassa.	Páguese a la caja.	Aan de kassa betalen.
Tenete il resto per voi (come mancia).	Quédese con el cambio (como propina).	Laat het zo maar (als fooi).
Questo è per voi.	Para usted.	Dit is voor U.

Vasellame da tavola e accessori	La vajilla de mesa	Tafelgerei
Un coltello per pane.	Un cuchillo para pan.	Een broodmes.
Un coltello a sega per pane.	Un cuchillo de sierrecilla.	Een broodzaag.
◄Una tazza da caffè e latte.	Una taza grande.	Een ontbijtkopje.
Un piattino per burro.	Un mantequero.	Een botervlootje.
Un trinciante.	Un cuchillo de trinchar.	Een voorsnijmes.
Un bicchiere da sciampagna.	Una copa para champaña.	Een champagneglas.
Un coltellino.	Un cuchillo pequeño.	Een klein mes.
◄Un piattino.	Una platillo.	Een klein plat bord.
Un frappe-cocktail.	Un coctelero, Un frasco para mezclar cocteles.	Een cocktail shaker.
Una tazza da caffè.	Una taza para café.	Een koffiekop.
Una caffettiera.	Una cafetera.	Een koffiepot.
Un cucchiaino da caffè.	Una cuchara para café.	Een koffielepeltje.
◄Un tappo.	Un tapón, Un corcho.	Een kurk.
Un cavatappi.	Un tirabuzón.	Een kurketrekker.
Una brocchetta per crema.	Un jarro para crema.	Een roomkannetje.
Le ampolle, Un'oliera.	Una vinagrera.	Een olie en azijn stel.
Una caraffa [per vino, per liquori].	Una garrafa [para vino, para licores].	Een [wijn]karaf.
◄Una piccola caraffa.	Una garrafilla.	Een karafje.
Un piatto da frutta.	Un plato de postre.	Een dessertbord.
Un cucchiaio da dessert.	Una cuchara de postre.	Een dessertlepel.
Un piatto da tavola.	Un plato grande.	Een plat bord.
Un piatto.	Una fuente.	Een schotel.
◄Una cannuccia.	Una boquilla de paja.	Een rietje.
Un portovo.	Una huevera.	Een eierdop[je].
Un cucchiaino per uovo.	Una cucharita para hueveras.	Een eierlepeltje.
Un lavadita.	Un enjuagatorio.	Een vingerkom.
Un coltello ed una forchetta per pesce.	Un cuchillo y un tenedor para pescado.	Een vismes en vork.
◄Un tagliapesce.	Una tajadera para pescado.	Een visschep.
Una forchetta.	Un tenedor.	Een vork.
Un coltello da frutta.	Un cuchillo para fruta.	Een fruitmesje.

A glass.	Un verre.	Ein Glas.
A gravy boat.	Une saucière.	Eine Soßenschüssel, Ein Soßnapf.
A gravy spoon.	Une cuiller à ragoût.	Ein Soßenlöffel. ➤
An ice pail.	Un seau à glace.	Ein Eiskübel.
A jam pot.	Un pot à confitures.	Eine Marmeladendose.
A jug.	Un pot.	Ein Krug, Eine Kanne.
A knife.	Un couteau.	Ein Messer.
A liqueur glass.	Un verre à liqueur.	Ein Likörglas. ➤
A mustard pot.	Un moutardier.	Ein Senfglas.
A mustard spoon.	Une cuiller (ou Une pelle) à moutarde.	Ein Senflöffel.
A napkin.	Une serviette [de table].	Ein Mundtuch.
A napkin ring.	Un rond de serviette.	Ein Serviettenring.
Nutcrackers.	Des casse-noisettes.	Ein Nußknacker. ➤
A pepper box or castor.	Une poivrière.	Ein Pfefferstreuer.
A plate.	Une assiette.	Ein Teller.
A salad bowl.	Un saladier.	Eine Salatschüssel.
A salt cellar.	Une salière.	Ein Salzfaß.
A salt sifter.	Un poudrier, Une salière de table.	Ein Salzstreuer. ➤
A salt spoon.	Une pelle à sel.	Ein Salzlöffel.
A sauce boat.	Une saucière.	Eine Soßenschüssel, Ein Soßnapf.
A saucer.	Une soucoupe.	Eine Untertasse.
A serviette.	Une serviette [de table].	Ein Mundtuch.
A serviette ring.	Un rond de serviette.	Ein Serviettenring. ➤
A siphon.	Un siphon.	Ein Siphon.
A soup ladle.	Une cuiller à potage, Une louche.	Ein Aufschöpflöffel.
A soup plate.	Une assiette creuse.	Ein Suppenteller.
A soup tureen.	Une soupière.	Eine Suppenterrine.
A spoon.	Une cuiller.	Ein Löffel. ➤
A sugar basin.	Un bol à sucre.	Eine Zuckerdose.
A sugar sifter or dredger or castor.	Un saupoudroir à sucre.	Ein Zuckerstreuer.
The sugar tongs.	Les pinces à sucre.	Die Zuckerzange.
A table cloth.	Une nappe [de table].	Ein Tischtuch.
A table knife.	Un couteau de table.	Ein großes Messer. ➤
A tablespoon.	Une cuiller à bouche, Une cuiller à soupe.	Ein Eßlöffel.
A tea cloth (*table cloth*).	Une nappe à thé.	Eine Kaffeedecke.
A tea (or A glass) cloth (*wiper*).	Un torchon [de cuisine], Un essuie-verres.	Ein Küchenhandtuch Ein Gläsertuch.
A tea cosy.	Un couvre-théière.	Ein Teewärmer.
A teacup.	Une tasse à thé.	Eine Teetasse.
A teapot.	Une théière.	Eine Teekanne.
A teaspoon.	Une cuiller à thé.	Eiu Teelöffel.
A toast rack.	Un porte-rôties.	Eiu Toasthalter.
A tray.	Un plateau.	Ein Tablett.
A tumbler.	Un [verre] gobelet.	Ein Wasserglas. ➤
A water bottle.	Une carafe à eau.	Eine Wasserkaraffe.
A water jug.	Un pot à eau.	Eine Wasserkanne.
A wine glass.	Un verre à vin.	Ein Weinglas.

Un bicchiere.	Un vaso.	Een glas.
Una salsiera.	Una salsera.	Een juskom.
◄Un cucchiaio da salsiera.	Una cuchara de salsera.	Een juslepel.
Una secchia per ghiaccio.	Una cubeta para hielo.	Een ijsemmer.
Un vaso per conserva.	Un tarro para compota.	Een jampot.
Una brocca.	Un jarro.	Een kan.
Un coltello.	Un cuchillo.	Een mes.
◄Un bicchierino da liquori.	Una copita para licores.	Een likeurglas.
Una mostardiera.	Una mostacera.	Een mosterdpot.
Un cucchiaino da mostarda.	Una cucharita para mostaza.	Een mosterdlepeltje.
Un tovagliolo.	Una servilleta.	Een servet.
Un anello per tovagliolo.	Un servilletero.	Een servetring.
◄Uno schiaccianoci.	Un cascanueces.	Een notekraker.
Una pepaiola.	Un pimentero.	Een pepervaatje.
Un piatto.	Un plato.	Een bord.
Un'insalatiera.	Una ensaladera.	Een slakom.
Una saliera.	Un salero.	Een zoutvaatje.
◄Una saliera a spruzzo, Una saliera da tavola.	Un cernedor para sal.	Een zout strooibus.
Un cucchiaino da sale.	Una cucharita para sal.	Een zoutlepeltje.
Una salsiera.	Una salsera.	Een juskom.
Una sottocoppa.	Un platillo [de taza].	Een schotel.
Un tovagliolo.	Una servilleta.	Een servet.
◄Un anello per tovagliolo.	Un servilletero.	Een servetring.
Un sifone.	Un sifón.	Een sifon.
Un ramaiolo da brodo.	Un cucharón.	Een soeplepel.
Una scodella.	Un plato sopero.	Een soepbord.
Una zuppiera.	Una sopera.	Een soepterrine.
◄Un cucchiaio.	Una cuchara.	Een lepel.
Una zuccheriera.	Un azucarero.	Een suikerpot.
Una zuccheriera a spruzzo.	Un cernedor para azúcar.	Een suiker strooibus.
Le mollette per zucchero.	Las tenacillas del azúcar.	De suikertang.
Una tovaglia da tavola.	Un mantel.	Een tafellaken.
◄Un coltello da tavola.	Un cuchillo de mesa.	Een tafelmes.
Un cucchiaio da tavola.	Una cuchara de mesa.	Een eetlepel.
Una tovaglia da tè.	Un mantel para té.	Een theetafellaken.
Uno strofinaccio.	Un paño (de secar).	Een theedoek.
Un copri teiera.	Una cubierta para la tetera.	Een theemuts.
◄Una tazza da tè.	Una taza para té.	Een theekop.
Una teiera.	Una tetera.	Een theepot.
Un cucchiaino da tè.	Una cucharita.	Een theelepeltje.
Un portacrostini.	Una espetera [para tostadas].	Een toostrek.
Un vassoio.	Una bandeja.	Een dienblad.
◄Una coppa.	Un vaso.	Een bekerglas.
Una bottiglia da acqua.	Una garrafa para agua.	Een waterkaraf.
Una brocca da acqua.	Un jarro para agua.	Een waterkan.
Un bicchiere da vino.	Una copa.	Een wijnglas.

Foods and drinks, Cooking terms	Le boire et le manger, Termes de cuisine	Essen und Trinken, Küchenausdrücke
Aerated drinks.	Des boissons gazéifiées.	Kohlensäurehaltige Getränke.
Aerated lemonade. Aerated water.	De la limonade gazeuse. De l'eau gazeuse.	Brauselimonade. Brause→wasser.
Alcohol.	L'alcool.	Alkohol.
An almond.	Une amande.	Eine Mandel.
Anchovies.	Des anchois.	Anchovis.
Anchovy paste.	Du beurre d'anchois.	Anchovisbutter.
An appetizer (drink).	Un apéritif.	Ein Apéritif. →
An apple.	Une pomme.	Ein Apfel.
An apple charlotte.	Une charlotte [de pommes].	Ein Apfel Charlotte.
An apple fritter.	Un beignet aux pommes.	Ein Apfelbeignet.
An apple pie.	Une tourte aux pommes.	Eine Apfelspeise.
An apple tart.	Une tarte aux pommes.	Eine Apfeltorte. →
An apple turnover.	Un chausson aux pommes.	Eine Apfeltasche.
An apricot.	Un abricot.	Eine Aprikose.
An artichoke.	Un artichaut.	Eine Artischocke.
Asparagus.	Des asperges.	Spargel.
Asparagus tips.	Des pointes d'asperges.	Spargelspitzen. →
Bacon.	Du lard.	Speck.
Baked potatoes.	Des pommes de terre au four.	Gebackene Kartoffeln.
A banana.	Une banane.	Eine Banane.
Barley sugar.	Du sucre d'orge.	Gerstenzucker.
Barley water.	L'eau d'orge.	Gerstenwasser. →
A baton (bread).	Une flûte.	Ein Semmelbrot.
Beans. (See Broad, French, Haricot, Kidney, and Runner, Beans.)		
Beef.	Du bœuf.	Rindfleisch.
A beef steak.	Un bifteck.	Ein Beefsteak.
Beef tea.	Du bouillon de bœuf.	Fleischbrühe.
Beer.	De la bière.	Bier. →
Beetroot.	De la betterave.	Rote Rüben, Beete.
A beverage.	Un breuvage, Une boisson.	Ein Getränk.
A biscuit.	Un biscuit.	Ein Keks.
A bitter[s]. To have a bitter[s].	Un amer. Prendre un amer.	Ein Magenbitter. Einen Magenbitter trinken.
Blackberries.	Des mûres sauvages, Des mûres de ronce.	Brombeeren. →
Black coffee.	Du café noir, Du café nature.	Schwarzer Kaffee.
Black currants.	Du cassis.	Schwarze Johannisbeeren.
A bloater.	Un hareng bouffi.	Ein Bückling.
A boiled egg.	Un œuf à la coque.	Ein gekochtes Ei.
Boiled potatoes.	Des pommes de terre à l'eau, Des pommes de terre nature.	Gekochte Kartoffeln. →
A bomb (ice cream).	Une bombe [glacée].	Eine Eisbombe.
Bottled beer.	De la bière en bouteille.	Flaschenbier.
Brains (Cooking).	De la cervelle.	Bregen.
Braised.	Braisé, e.	Geschmort.
Brandy.	De l'eau-de-vie, Du cognac.	Kognak. →

Cibi e bibite, Termini di cucina	Comestibles y bebidas, Términos de cocina	Voedsel en drank, Kooktermen
Le bibite gasose.	Bebidas gaseosas.	Spuitdranken.
◄Una limonata gasosa. L'acqua gasosa.	Gaseosa de limón. Agua gaseosa.	Spuitlimonade. Spuitwater.
L'alcool.	Alcohol.	Alcohol.
Una mandorla.	Una almendra.	Een amandel.
Le acciughe.	Anchoas.	Ansjovis.
La pasta di acciughe.	Pasta de anchoas.	Ansjovisboter.
◄Un aperitivo.	Un aperitivo.	Een aperitief.
Una mela.	Una manzana.	Een appel.
Una mela Carlotta.	Una charlotte de manzanas.	Een appelcharlotte.
Una frittella di mela.	Una fritura de manzanas.	Een appelbeignet.
Una torta di mele	Un pastel de manzanas.	Appelgebak.
◄Una crostata di mele.	Una tarta de manzanas.	Een appeltaart.
Un dolce ripieno di mele.	Un pastelillo de manzanas con repulgo.	Een appelflap.
Un'albicocca.	Un albaricoque.	Een abrikoos.
Un carciofo.	Una alcachofa.	Een artisjok.
Gli asparagi.	Espárrago.	Asperges.
◄Le punte di asparagi.	Puntas de espárrago.	Aspergetoppen.
La ventresca, Il lardo.	Tocino.	Rookspek, of bacon.
Patate arrostite.	Patatas cocidas en horno.	Gesmoorde aardappelen.
Una banana.	Una banana.	Een banaan.
Lo zucchero d'orzo.	Alfeñique.	Gerstesuiker.
◄L'acqua d'orzo.	Hordiate.	Gerstewater.
Un filone.	Una rosca de pan francés.	Een stokbrood.
Del bue.	Carne de vaca.	Rundvlees.
Una bistecca.	Un biftec.	Een runderlapje.
Un brodo di bue.	Caldo de carne.	Bouillon.
◄La birra.	Cerveza.	Bier.
La bietola.	Remolacha.	Bieten.
Una bevanda.	Una bebida.	Een drank.
Un biscotto.	Una galleta.	Een bischuit[je].
Un amaro. Prendere un amaro.	Licor de raíces amargos. Tomar un aperitivo de licor de raíces amargos.	Een bitterje. Bitteren.
◄Le more.	Zarzamoras.	Bramen.
Un caffè nero.	Café [natural].	Zwarte koffie.
I ribes neri.	Grosellas negras.	Zwarte bessen.
Un'aringa affumicata.	Un arenque ahumado.	Een bokking.
Un uovo bollito.	Un huevo pasado por agua.	Een gekookt ei.
◄Le patate bollite.	Patatas cocidas.	Gekookte aardappelen.
Una bomba.	Un mantecado, Un bombe.	Een plombière.
Della birra in bottiglia.	Cerveza embotellada.	Gebotteld bier.
Il cervello.	Sesos.	Hersenen.
Stufato, a.	Cocido(a) en salsa.	Gesmoord.
◄Il cognac.	Brandy, Coñac.	Cognac.

A brandy and soda.	Une fine à l'eau de Seltz.	Kognak mit Sodawasser.
Brawn.	De la hure, Du fromage de porc.	Sülze.
Brazils *or* Brazil nuts.	Des noix d'Amérique *ou* du Brésil.	Paranüsse.
Bread.	Du pain.	Brot.
A bream (*fresh-water*).	Une brème.	Ein Brassen.
A bream (*sea*).	Un pagel.	Ein Seebrassen.
Breast of chicken.	Du blanc de volaille.	Hühnerbrust.
A brill.	Une barbue.	Ein Glattbutt.
The brisket.	La poitrine.	Das Bruststück.
Broad beans.	Des fèves de marais.	Saubohnen.
Broth.	Du bouillon.	Brühe, Bouillon.
Brown bread (*light*).	Du pain bis.	Braunbrot.
Brown bread (*dark*).	Du pain noir.	Schwarzbrot.
Brown sugar.	De la cassonade.	Brauner Zucker.
Brussels sprouts.	Des choux de Bruxelles.	Rosenkohl.
A bunch of grapes.	Une grappe de raisin.	Eine Weintraube.
Burgundy [wine].	Du bourgogne, Du vin de Bourgogne.	Burgunder.
Burnt almonds *or* Pralines.	Des amandes grillées, Des pralines.	Gebrannte Mandeln.
Butcher's meat.	De la viande de boucherie.	Fleisch.
Butter.	Du beurre.	Butter.
Buttered toast.	Des rôties au beurre, Du toast [beurré].	Toast mit Butter.
Cabbage.	Du chou.	Kohl.
A cabbage lettuce.	Une laitue pommée.	Ein Kopfsalat.
A cake.	Un gâteau.	Ein Kuchen.
Calf's head.	De la tête de veau.	Kalbskopf.
Calves-foot jelly.	De la gelée de pied de veau.	Kalbsfußgelée.
Camembert [cheese].	Du camembert, Du fromage de Camembert.	Camembert.
Canned goods. Canned salmon.	Des conserves [en boîtes]. Du saumon en boîte.	Konserven. Büchsenlachs.
Caper sauce.	De la sauce aux câpres.	Kapernsoße.
A capon.	Un chapon.	Ein Kapaun.
Carrots.	Des carottes.	Karotten, Mohrrüben.
Castor (*or* Caster) sugar.	Du sucre en poudre.	Feiner Zucker.
Cauliflower.	Des choux-fleurs.	Blumenkohl.
Cayenne pepper.	Du poivre de Cayenne.	Cayenne Pfeffer.
Celery.	Du céleri.	Sellerie.
Champagne.	Du champagne, Du vin de Champagne.	Champagner ; (*German variety*) Sekt.
Cheddar [cheese].	Du [fromage de] Cheddar.	Cheddarkäse.
Cheese.	Du fromage.	Käse.
Cherries.	Des cerises.	Kirschen.
Cheshire [cheese].	Du [fromage de] Chester.	Chesterkäse.
Chestnuts.	Des châtaignes. Des marrons.	Kastanien, Marronen.
Chewing gum.	De la gomme à mastiquer.	Kaugummi.
A chicken.	Un poulet.	Ein Hühnchen.
China tea.	Du thé de Chine.	Chinesischer Tee.
Chocolate (*as a confection or drink*).	Du chocolat.	Schokolade.

Un cognac con seltz.	Un coñac con sifón.	Een cognac met spuit-water.
La capaccia.	Carne mollar.	Hoofdkaas.
Le nocciole del Brasile.	Nueces del Brasil.	Braziliaanse noten.
Il pane.	Pan.	Brood.
Una scarda.	Un sargo.	Een brasem.
Un pagello.	Un pajel, Un besugo.	Een zeebrasem.
Il petto di pollo.	Pechuga de pollo.	Kippeborst.
Un rombo.	Un mero.	Een griet.
Il petto.	El pecho del animal	Borst, borststuk.
Le fave [di orto].	Habas.	Grote bonen.
Il brodo.	Caldo.	Bouillon.
Il pane bruno.	Pan bazo.	Bruin brood.
Il pane nero.	Pan moreno.	Zwart brood.
Lo zucchero greggio.	Azúcar terciada.	Bruine suiker, Cassonnade.
I broccoletti di Brusselles.	Coles de Bruselas.	Spruitjes.
Un grappolo d'uva.	Un racimo de uvas.	Een tros druiven.
Il vino di Borgondia.	Vino de Borgoña.	Bourgogne [wijn].
Le mandorle tostate.	Almendras tostadas.	Gebakken amandelen.
La carne del macellaio.	Carne de matanza.	Slagersvlees.
Il burro.	Manteca, Mantequilla.	Boter.
Il pane abbrustolito con burro.	Pan tostado con manteca.	Geboterde toost.
Il cavolo.	Coles, Berza.	Kool.
Una lattuga cappuccia.	Una lechuga repollada.	Kropsla.
Un dolce.	Un bizcocho, Un pastelillo.	Een koek, Een cake.
La testa di vitello.	Cabeza de ternera.	Kalfshoofd.
La gelatina di piede di vitello.	Jelatina de manos de ternera.	Kalfsvoet gelei.
Camembert.	Queso de camembert.	Camembert.
Le conserve in scatole.	Conservas alimenticias.	Conserven. Blikzalm, zalm uit blik.
Del salmone in scatola.	Salmón en lata.	
La salsa di capperi.	Salsa de alcaparras.	Kappertjessaus.
Un cappone.	Un capón.	Een kapoen.
Le carote.	Zanahorias.	Worteltjes.
Lo zucchero in polvere.	Azúcar fino.	Poedersuiker.
Il cavolfiore.	Coliflor.	Bloemkool.
Il pepe di Caienna.	Pimentón.	Cayenne peper.
Il sedano.	Apio.	Selderij.
Lo sciampagna, Il vino di Sciampagna.	Champaña, Vino de Champaña.	Champagne.
Il formaggio Cheddar.	Queso de Cheddar.	Cheddar kaas.
Il formaggio, Il cacio.	Queso.	Kaas.
Le ciliege.	Cerezas.	Kersen.
Il formaggio Chester.	Queso de Chester.	Cheshire kaas.
Le castagne.	Castañas.	Kastanjes.
La gomma da masticare.	Goma de mascar.	Kauwgom.
Un pollastro.	Un pollo.	Een kuiken.
Il tè di Cina.	Té de la China.	Chinese thee.
Cioccolata.	Chocolate.	Chocolade.

Chocolate creams.	Des chocolats fourrés à la crème.	Pralinen, Cremehütchen.
A chocolate éclair.	Un éclair au chocolat.	Ein Liebesknochen, Ein Schokoladenéclair.
Chocolates.	Des bonbons au chocolat.	Konfitüren.
A chop.	Un chop (*pronounce* shop).	Ein Kotelett.
Cider.	Du cidre.	Apfelwein. →
A clam.	Une palourde.	Eine Venusmuschel.
Claret.	Du bordeaux [rouge], Du vin de Bordeaux.	Rotwein, Bordeaux.
Clear soup.	Un consommé, Un bouillon.	Brühe, Bouillon.
Cobs or Cob nuts.	Des grosses noisettes, Des avelines.	Große Haselnüsse.
Cocoa (*as a drink*).	Du chocolat.	Kakao. →
Cockles.	Des clovisses, Des coques.	Herzmuscheln.
A cocktail.	Un cocktail.	Ein Cocktail.
A cod[fish].	Une morue, Un cabillaud.	Ein Dorsch, Ein Kabeljau.
Coffee.	Du café, Du moka.	Kaffee, Mokka.
Coffee, hot milk, rolls and butter.	Un café complet.	Kaffee mit heißer Milch, → Brötchen und Butter.
A cup of coffee with cream.	Une tasse de café crème, Un café crème.	Eine Tasse Kaffee mit Sahne.
Coffee with milk.	Du café au lait.	Milchkaffee.
Cold meat.	De la viande froide.	Kaltes Fleisch.
Condensed milk.	Du lait condensé *ou* concentré *ou* conservé.	Kondensierte Milch, Büchsenmilch.
Corned beef.	Du bœuf salé.	Pökelfleisch. →
A cos or A Cos lettuce.	Une laitue romaine.	[Ein] Römischer Salat.
A crab.	Un crabe.	Eine Krabbe.
Cranberries.	Des canneberges.	Kranichbeeren.
A crayfish or A crawfish (*fresh-water*).	Une écrevisse.	Ein Krebs.
A crayfish or A crawfish (*sea*).	Une langouste.	Eine Languste. →
Cream.	De la crème.	Sahne.
Cream cheese. *Compare* double-cream cheese.	Du fromage blanc.	Weißkäse.
A cream ice.	Une glace à la crème, Une crème glacée.	Ein Sahneneis.
Cress. (*See* Garden cress *and* Watercress.)		
The crust.	La croûte.	Die Kruste.
A crusty end or An end piece (*of French bread*).	Un croûton.	Ein Kanten. →
Crystallized fruits.	Des fruits candis.	Kandierte Früchte.
Cube sugar.	Du sucre en morceaux, Du sucre cassé.	Würfelzucker.
Cucumber.	Du concombre.	Gurke.
Currants (Red, White).	Des groseilles [à grappes], rouges, blanches.	Rote, Weiße, Johannisbeeren.
Currants (Black).	Du cassis.	Schwarze Johannisbeeren. →
Currants (*dried*).	Des raisins de Corinthe.	Korinthen.
Curry.	Du cari, Du kari.	Curry.
Custard.	De la crème [culinaire].	Eierrahm.

I cioccolatini alla crema.	Bombones de chocolate rellenos de crema.	Pralines.
Un eclair alla cioccolata.	Un eclair de chocolate.	Een chocolade éclair.
I cioccolatini.	Bombones de chocolate.	Chocolaadjes.
Una braciola.	Una costilla, Una chuleta.	Een karbonade, Een kotelet.
◄Un sidro.	Sidra.	Appelwijn, Cider.
Un'ostrica americana.	Una almeja, Una tellina.	Een Venusmossel.
Bordo, Il vino da Bordeaux.	Clarete, Vino tinto.	Bordeaux [wijn].
Un brodo, Un consommé.	Consomé, Caldo.	Heldere soep. Consommé.
Le avellane.	Avellanas [grandes].	Grote hazelnoten.
◄Una cioccolata.	Bebida de cacao.	Chocola[de].
Le telline.	Coquinas.	Hartmosselen.
Un cocktail.	Un cóctel.	Een cocktail.
Un merluzzo.	Un abadejo, Un bacalao.	Een kabeljauw.
Caffè.	Café.	Koffie.
◄Un caffè, latte caldo, panini e burro.	Un café completo.	Koffie, warme melk, broodjes en boter.
Una tazza di caffè con crema.	Una taza de café con crema.	Een kop koffie met room.
Caffè e latte.	Café con leche.	Koffie met melk; (½ and ⅓) Koffie verkeerd.
La carne fredda.	Carne fiambre.	Koud vlees.
Il latte condensato.	Leche condensada.	Gecondenseerde melk.
◄Il bue salato.	Cecina.	Corned beef, rundvlees in blik.
Una lattuga romana.	Una lechuga de oreja de mula.	Bindsalade, Bindsla.
Un granchio.	Un cangrejo.	Een krab.
La mortella di padule.	Arándanos.	Veenbessen.
Un gambero di fiume.	Un cabrajo [de rio].	Een rivierkreeft.
◄Un gambero di mare.	Un langostín.	Een zeekreeft.
La crema, La panna.	Nata, Crema.	Room.
Il formaggio di crema.	Queso de nata.	Roomkaas.
Un gelato alla panna.	Un helado de crema.	Roomijs.
La crosta.	La corteza (del pan).	De korst.
◄Una crosta tostata.	Un crouton, Un pico de pan francés.	Een korstje.
Le frutta candite.	Dulces de almíbar.	Gekonfijte vruchten.
Lo zucchero a quadretti o in chicchi.	Azúcar de terrón o en terrones.	Suikerklontjes.
Il cetriolo.	Pepino.	Komkommer.
Il ribes rosso, bianco.	Grosellas rojas, blancas.	Rode, Witte, bessen.
◄Il ribes nero.	Grosellas negras.	Zwarte bessen.
L'uva di Corinto.	Pasas de Corinto.	Krenten.
Il curry.	Curry, Salsa india.	Kerrie.
La crema dolce.	Natillas.	Vla.

A cutlet.	Une côtelette.	Ein Schnitzel, Ein Kotelett.
Dark lager.	De la bière brune.	Dunkles Bier.
Dates.	Des dattes.	Datteln.
Dessert.	Le dessert.	Der Nachtisch, Das Dessert.
Dessert grapes.	Du raisin de treille.	Weintrauben.
Dietary bread.	Du pain de régime.	Diätbrot.
Double-cream cheese.	Du fromage à la crème.	Vollrahmkäse.
Draught beer.	De la bière au tonneau ou à la pompe.	Bier vom Faß.
Dressed spinach.	Une purée d'épinards.	Spinat[puree].
A dry wine. Dry champagne.	Un vin sec. Du champagne sec.	Ein trockner Wein. Trockner Champagner.
A duck.	Un canard.	Eine Ente.
A duckling.	Un caneton.	Eine junge Ente.
Dutch cheese.	Du fromage de Hollande.	Edamer Käse.
Early fruits, Early vegetables.	Des primeurs.	Frühobst, Das erste Gemüse.
An éclair.	Un éclair.	Ein Éclair.
Eels.	Des anguilles.	Aale.
An eel pie.	Un pâté d'anguille.	Eine Aalpastete.
An egg.	Un œuf.	Ein Ei.
Endive.	De la chicorée.	Endivie.
An entrée.	Une entrée.	Eine Vorspeise, Der erste Gang.
Extra-dry champagne.	Du champagne brut.	Extra-trockner Champagner.
Fancy bread.	Du pain de fantaisie.	Feinbrot.
A fancy roll.	Un pain mollet.	Ein Wiener Brötchen, Ein Milchbrötchen.
Fat. Will you have fat or lean?	Du gras. Voulez-vous du gras ou du maigre?	Fett. Wollen Sie ein fettes Stück oder ein mageres Stück?
Fat meat.	De la viande grasse.	Fettes Fleisch.
Figs.	Des figues.	Feigen.
Filberts.	Des avelines.	Haselnüsse.
A fillet of beef.	Un filet de bœuf.	Ein Rinderfilet.
A fillet of sole or A filleted sole.	Des filets de sole.	Ein Seezungenfilet.
A fillet of veal.	Une rouelle de veau.	Ein Kalbsfilet.
Fish.	Du poisson.	Fisch.
A flounder (fish).	Un flet.	Eine Flunder.
A fowl.	Une volaille.	Ein Huhn.
French beans.	Des haricots.	Grüne Bohnen, Stangenbohnen.
French beans (unripe).	Des haricots verts.	Haricots verts.
Fresh butter.	Du beurre frais.	Frische Butter.
Fresh-water fish.	Des poissons d'eau douce.	Süßwasserfische.
Fried eggs.	Des œufs sur le plat.	Spiegeleier, Setzeier.
Fried fish.	Du poisson frit, De la friture.	Gebratener Fisch.
Fried potatoes.	Des pommes de terre frites, Des frites.	Bratkartoffeln.
A fried sole.	Une sole frite.	Eine gebratene Seezunge.
A fritter.	Un beignet.	Ein Puffer, Ein Beignet, Ein Krapfen.
Frozen meat.	De la viande frigorifiée.	Gefrierfleisch.

Una costoletta.	Una chuleta.	Een kotelet.
◄Una birra nera.	Cerveza obscura.	Donker [lager]bier.
I datteri.	Dátiles.	Dadels.
Il dessert.	Postres.	Het dessert.
L'uva da tavola.	Uvas finas.	Tafeldruiven.
Il pane da dieta.	Pan dietético.	Zoutloos brood.
◄Il formaggio di doppia crema.	Queso de doble nata.	Volvette kaas.
La birra di barile.	Cerveza en barril.	Bier uit het vat.
Un purè di spinaci.	Puré de espinaca.	Spinazie[puree].
Un vino secco. Dello sciampagna secco.	Un vino seco. Un champaña seco.	Een droge wijn. Droge champagne.
Un'anitra.	Un pato.	Een eend.
◄Un anitrotto.	Una anadeja, Un patito.	Een jonge eend.
Il formaggio d'Olanda.	Queso de bola.	Hollandse kaas.
Le frutta primaticce, I legumi primaticci.	Fruta temprana, Hortalizas tempranas.	Primeurs.
Un éclair.	Un eclair.	Een éclair.
Le anguille.	Anguilas.	Aal, Paling.
◄Un pasticcio di anguille.	Un pastel de anguilas.	Een palingpastei.
Un uovo.	Un huevo.	Een ei.
La indivia.	Escarola.	Andijvie.
Un primo piatto.	Una entrada.	Een voorgerecht.
Dello sciampagna asciutto.	Champaña extraseco.	Extra droge champagne.
◄Un pane di fantasia.	Pan de fantasía.	Luxe broodjes.
Un panino di lusso.	Un panecillo de fantasía.	Een kadetje.
Il grasso. Volete il grasso o il magro?	Gordura. ¿Quiere usted gordura o magro?	Vet. Wilt U vet of mager?
La carne grassa.	Carne grasienta.	Vet vlees.
I fichi.	Higos.	Vijgen.
◄Le avellane.	Avellanas.	Hazelnoten.
Un filetto di bue.	Un filete de carne de vaca.	Runderhaas.
Un filetto di sogliola.	Un filete de lenguado.	Tongfilet.
Un filetto di vitello.	Un filete de ternera.	Een kalfsschijf.
Il pesce.	Pescado.	Vis.
Il pesce passera.	Una acedía.	Een bot.
◄Un volatile.	Un gallo, Una gallina.	Een stuk gevogelte.
I fagiolini.	Judías.	Snijbonen.
I fagiolini verdi.	Judías verdes.	Sperciebonen.
Il burro fresco.	Manteca fresca.	Verse boter.
I pesci d'acqua dolce.	Pescado de agua dulce.	Zoetwatervis.
◄Le uova frittellate.	Huevos fritos.	Gebakken eieren.
Il pesce fritto.	Pescado frito.	Gebakken vis.
Le patate fritte.	Patatas fritas.	Gebakken aardappelen.
Una sogliola fritta.	Un lenguado frito.	Gebakken tong.
Una frittella.	Una fritura.	Een beignet, Een poffertje.
◄La carne congelata.	Carne de frigorífico.	Bevroren vlees.

Fruit.	Du fruit, Des fruits.	Obst, Früchte.
Fruit juice.	Du jus de fruit.	Fruchtsaft.
A fruit salad.	Une macédoine (ou Une salade) de fruits.	Ein Obstsalat.
A full-bodied wine	Un vin vineux ou corsé.	Ein voller Wein.
Game.	Du gibier.	Wild.
Game chips.	Des croustillons.	Gebratene Kartoffelscheiben.
A game pie.	Un pâté de gibier.	Eine Wildpastete.
Garden cress	Du cresson alénois.	Gartenkresse.
Garlic.	De l'ail.	Knoblauch.
Gherkins.	Des cornichons.	Pfeffergurken.
Gin.	Du gin.	Gin.
Ginger.	Du gingembre.	Ingwer.
Gingerbread.	Du pain d'épice.	Pfefferkuchen.
Golden syrup.	De la mélasse raffinée.	Reiner Sirup.
A goose.	Une oie.	Eine Gans.
Gooseberries.	Des groseilles vertes, Des groseilles à maquereau.	Stachelbeeren.
Gorgonzola [cheese].	Du gorgonzola, Du fromage de Gorgonzola.	Gorgonzola.
Granulated sugar.	Du sucre cristallisé.	Grober Zucker.
A grape fruit.	Une pamplemousse.	Eine Pampelmuse.
Grapes.	Du raisin.	Trauben, Weintrauben.
Grated breadcrumbs.	De la panure, De la chapelure.	Reibbrot.
Gravy.	Du jus.	Soße.
Greengages.	Des prunes de reine-claude, Des reines-claude.	Reineclauden.
Green peas.	Des petits pois, Des pois verts.	Grüne Erbsen, Schoten.
Greens.	Des herbages, Des légumes verts, De la verdure.	Grünes Gemüse.
A grey mullet.	Un mulet, Un muge.	Eine Meeräsche.
A grill or Grilled meat.	Une grillade, Une carbonnade.	Geröstetes Fleisch.
Grilled.	Grillé, e, À la carbonnade.	Geröstet oder Am Rost gebraten.
Ground rice.	De la farine de riz.	Reismehl.
A grouse.	Un petit coq de bruyère, Un tétras, Une grouse.	Ein Waldhuhn.
Gruyère [cheese].	Du gruyère, Du fromage de Gruyère.	Gruyère[käse].
A haddock.	Un aigrefin.	Ein Schellfisch.
A hake.	Un merlus.	Ein Hechtdorsch.
A halibut.	Un flétan.	Eine Heilbutte.
Ham.	Du jambon.	Schinken.
Ham and eggs.	Des œufs au jambon.	Setzeier mit Schinken.
A ham sandwich.	Un sandwich au jambon.	Eine Schinkenschnitte.
A hard-boiled egg.	Un œuf dur.	Ein hartes Ei.
Hard roe.	Des œufs [de poisson].	Rogen.
A hare.	Un lièvre.	Ein Hase.
Haricot beans (dried).	Des haricots secs.	Weiße Bohnen.
A haunch of venison.	Un quartier de chevreuil.	Eine Rehkeule.

Le frutta.	Fruta.	Fruit, Vruchten.
Il sugo di frutta.	Jugos de fruta, Almíbar.	Vruchtesap.
Un'insalata di frutta.	Una ensalada de frutas.	Een vruchtenslaatje.
Un **vino** sostanzioso.	Un vino de cuerpo.	Een volle wijn.
◀La cacciagione, La selvaggina.	Aves y/o Animales de caza.	Wild.
Patate a fettine fritte.	Croquetas de patatas.	Patates frites.
Un pasticcio di cacciagione.	Un pastel **de** ave de caza.	Een wildpastei.
Nasturzio d'orto.	Lepidio.	Sterrekers.
L'aglio.	Ajo.	Knoflook.
◀Il cetriolino marinato.	Pepinillos.	Augurken.
Il gin.	Gin.	Gin.
Lo zenzero.	Jengibre.	Gember.
Il panpepato.	Pan de jengibre.	Gemberkoek.
La melassa raffinata.	Melaza refinada.	Stroop.
◀Un'oca.	Un ganso.	Een gans.
L'uva spina.	Uvas espinas.	Kruisbessen.
Il gorgonzola.	Queso de Gorgonzola.	Gorgonzola kaas.
Lo zucchero cristallizzato.	Azúcar cristalizado.	Korrelsuiker.
Un grapefruit.	Una toronja.	Een pompelmoes.
◀L'uva.	Uvas.	Druiven.
Il pane grattugiato.	Pan rallado.	Paneermeel, Gestampte beschuit.
Il sugo di carne arrostita.	Salsa.	Jus.
Le susine verdi.	Ciruelas claudias.	Reine-claudes.
I piselli verdi.	Guisantes, Chícharos.	Erwten.
◀Gli erbaggi, I vegetali, Della verdura.	Verduras.	Groenten.
Un muggine cefalo.	Un mújol.	Een harder.
La carne alla gratella.	Carne asada a la parrilla.	Geroosterd vlees.
Cotto (*feminine* Cotta) sulla gratella.	A la parrilla.	Geroosterd.
La farina di riso.	Arroz molido.	Gemalen rijst.
◀Un gallo di montagna.	Un tetrao.	Een korhoen.
Il cacio Gruyère.	Queso de Gruyere.	Gruyère kaas.
Un merluzzo.	Un róbalo.	Een schelvis.
Un nasello.	Una pescada.	Een stokvis of andere schelvis.
Un rombo.	Un hipogloso.	Een heilbot.
◀Il prosciutto.	Jamón.	Ham.
Il prosciutto e le uova.	Huevos con jamón.	Gebakken eieren met ham.
Un panino imbottito di prosciutto.	Un emparedado de jamón.	Een ham sandwich.
Un uovo sodo.	Un huevo duro.	Een hard gekookt ei.
Le uova di pesce.	Hueva dura *o* recia.	Kuit, Viskuit.
◀Una lepre.	Una liebre.	Een haas.
I fagioli secchi.	Habichuelas.	Gedroogde bonen.
Un coscìotto di selvaggina.	Una anca de venado.	Een reeboutje.

Hazel nuts.	Des noisettes.	Haselnüsse.
A herring.	Un hareng.	Ein Hering.
High (of meat).	Avancé, e.	Angegangen.
High (of game).	Faisandé, e.	Hautgout.
A high-class wine.	Un vin de marque.	Ein erstklassiger Wein.
Hock.	Du vin blanc du Rhin.	Weißer Rheinwein.
Hollands [gin].	Du genièvre, Du schiedam.	Holländischer Genever.
Home-made wine.	De la liqueur de ménage.	Hausgemachter Wein.
Honey.	Du miel.	Honig.
Hors-d'œuvres.	Des hors-d'œuvre.	Hors d'œuvres.
Horse radish.	Du raifort.	Meerrettich.
A horseshoe roll.	Un croissant.	Ein Hörnchen.
Hothouse grapes.	Du raisin de serre.	Gewächshaustrauben.
Household bread.	Du pain de ménage.	Hausbackenbrot.
Ice.	De la glace.	Eis.
Ice cream.	De la crème glacée, De la glace à la crème.	Speiseeis, Sahneneis.
An iced cake.	Un gâteau glacé.	Ein Kuchen mit Zuckerguß.
Iced water. (See also pp. 138-139.)	De l'eau raffraichie de la glace.	Eisgekühltes Wasser.
Indian tea.	Du thé de Ceylan.	Indischer Tee.
Italian verm[o]uth.	Du vermouth de Turin.	Italienischer Wermut.
Jacket potatoes.	Des pommes de terre en robe [de chambre].	Pellkartoffeln.
Jam.	De la confiture, Des confitures.	Marmelade.
Jelly.	De la gelée.	Gelee.
A joint of meat.	Une pièce de viande.	Ein Braten.
Jugged hare.	Un civet de lièvre.	Hasenpfeffer.
Kale.	Du chou frisé.	Winterkohl.
A kidney (meat).	Un rognon.	Eine Niere.
Kidney beans.	Des haricots.	Grüne Bohnen, Stangenbohnen.
A kipper.	Un hareng salé et fumé.	Ein Räucherhering.
Lager [beer].	De la bière.	Bier.
Lamb.	De l'agneau.	Lammbraten.
A lamprey.	Une lamproie.	Eine Lamprete.
Leaf spinach.	Des épinards en branches.	Blattspinat.
Lean. Will you have fat or lean?	Du maigre. Voulez-vous du gras ou du maigre?	Mageres. Wollen Sie fettes oder mageres Fleisch?
Lean meat.	De la viande maigre.	Mageres Fleisch.
Leeks.	Des poireaux.	Lauch, Porree.
A leg of chicken.	Une cuisse de poulet.	Ein Hühnerbein.
A leg of mutton, A leg of lamb.	Un gigot.	Eine Hammelkeule.
A lemon.	Un citron.	Eine Zitrone.
A lemon sole or A lemon dab.	Une sole limande.	Eine Kliesche, Eine Scharbe.
Lemon squash.	Du citron pressé.	Echte Zitronenlimonade.
Lemonade, aerated, still.	De la limonade (ou De la citronnade) gazeuse, non gazeuse.	Brauselimonade, Zitronenwasser.
Lentils.	Des lentilles.	Linsen.
Lettuce.	De la laitue.	Salat.
Light lager.	De la bière blonde.	Helles Bier.

Le avellane.	Avellanas.	Hazelnoten.
Un'aringa.	Un arenque.	Een haring.
Passato, a.	Oliscado, a.	Goed bestorven.
Passato, a.	Oliscado, a.	Adellijk.
Un vino scelto.	Un vino de marca mayor.	Een prima wijn.
Il vino bianco del Reno.	Vino blanco del Rin.	Witte Rijnwijn.
Un ginepro olandese.	Ginebra holandesa.	Jenever, oude klare.
Un vino casalingo.	Vino fabricado en casa.	Eigengemaakte wijn.
Il miele.	Miel.	Honing.
Gli antipasti.	Ordubres.	Hors d'oeuvres.
Il ramolaccio.	Rábano picante.	Ramenas.
Un chifel.	Un croissant.	Een croissant.
L'uva di serra.	Uvas de invernadero.	Kasdruiven.
Il pane casereccio.	Pan casero.	Eigengebakken brood.
Il ghiaccio.	Hielo.	IJs.
Un gelato alla panna.	Crema helada, Helado de crema.	Roomijs.
Un dolce rivestito di zucchero.	Un bizcocho cubierto con alfeñique.	Een geglaceerde cake.
L'acqua ghiacciata.	Agua enfriada con hielo.	IJswater.
Il tè d'India.	Té de Ceilán.	Ceylon thee.
Il vermut[te] [italiano].	Vermut italiano.	Italiaanse vermouth.
Le patate in camicia.	Patatas asadas con la cáscara.	Aardappels in de schil.
La conserva dolce.	Compota, Conserva.	Jam.
La gelatina.	Jalea.	Gelei.
Un taglio di carne.	Un corte de carne.	Een stuk vlees.
Un intingolo di lepre.	Liebre a la inglesa.	Hazepeper.
Un carduccio.	Bretón.	Boerenkool.
Un rognone.	Un riñón.	Een nier.
I fagioli.	Frijoles ordinarios.	Snijbonen.
Un'aringa affumicata.	Un arenque ahumado.	Een gezouten en gerookte haring.
La birra.	Cerveza.	[Lager] bier.
L'agnello.	Cordero.	Lamsvlees.
La lampreda.	Una lamprea.	Een lamprei.
Gli spinaci in foglia.	Espinaca de hoja entera.	Bladspinazie.
Il magro. Lo volete grasso o magro?	Magro. ¿Quiere usted gordura o magro?	Mager. Neemt U vet of mager?
La carne magra.	Carne magra.	Mager vlees.
I porri.	Puerros.	Prei.
Una coscia di pollo.	Una pata de pollo.	Een kippepoot.
Una coscia di castrato, Una coscia di agnello.	Una pata de carnero, Una pata de cordero.	Een schapebout, Een lamsbout.
Un limone.	Un limón.	Een citroen.
Un passero.	Una limandela.	Een scharretong.
Una spremuta di limone.	Limonada [hecha de pulpa del limón].	Uitgeperste citroen, Kwast.
Una limonata gasosa, con acqua semplice.	Gaseosa de limón, Limonada no gaseosa.	Spuitlimonade of gazeuze, Waterlimonade.
Le lenticchie.	Lentejas.	Linzen.
La lattuga.	Lechuga.	Salade, Sla.
Una birra chiara.	Cerveza clara.	Licht [lager] bier.

Lime juice.	Du jus de citron [des Antilles].	Limonensaft.
A liqueur.	Une liqueur [de dessert].	Ein Likör.
A liqueur brandy.	Une fine [champagne].	Ein feiner Kognak. →
Lithia water.	De l'eau lithinée.	Lithium-Wasser.
Liver.	Du foie.	Leber.
A loaf [of bread].	Un pain, Une miche.	Ein Laib Brot.
Loaf sugar.	Du sucre en morceaux, Du sucre cassé.	Würfelzucker.
A lobster.	Un homard.	Ein Hummer.
A lobster salad.	Une salade de homard.	Ein Hummersalat.
A loin chop.	Un chop de filet.	Ein Filetstück.
Loin of mutton.	Du filet de mouton.	Hammelbraten mit Nierenstück.
Loin of veal.	De la longe de veau.	Kalbsfilet, Kalbsnierenbraten.
A lump of sugar.	Un morceau de sucre.	Ein Stück Zucker. →
Lump sugar.	Du sucre en morceaux, Du sucre cassé.	Würfelzucker.
Macaroni.	Le macaroni, Des macaronis.	Makkaroni.
A macaroon.	Un macaron.	Eine Makrone.
A mackerel.	Un maquereau.	Eine Makrele.
Marmalade.	De la confiture d'oranges.	Orangenmarmelade. →
Marrow (meat). (Compare Vegetable marrow.)	De la moelle.	Knochenmark.
Marzipan or Marchpane.	Du massepain.	Marzipan.
Mashed potatoes.	Une purée de pommes de terre.	Kartoffelbrei, Kartoffelpuree.
Mashed spinach.	Une purée d'épinards.	Spinat[puree].
Mashed turnips.	Une purée de navets.	Rübenpuree. →
A mayonnaise of salmon or A salmon mayonnaise.	Une mayonnaise de saumon.	Eine Lachsmayonnaise.
Mayonnaise [sauce].	De la [sauce] mayonnaise.	Mayonnaise[nsoße].
Meat.	De la viande.	Fleisch.
Meat soup.	Du potage [au] gras.	Fleischsuppe.
Medium champagne (between sweet and dry).	Du champagne demi-sec.	Mitteltrockner Champagner. →
A medlar.	Une nèfle.	Eine Mispel.
A melon.	Un melon.	Eine Melone.
Melted butter.	Du beurre fondu.	Geschmolzene Butter. →
A meringue.	Une meringue.	Ein Baiser.
Minced.	Haché, e.	Gemahlen.
Mincemeat.	De la chair à pâté.	Pastetenfüllung.
Milk.	Du lait.	Milch.
Milk chocolate.	Du chocolat lacté, Du chocolat au lait.	Milchschokolade.
Mineral water.	De l'eau minérale.	Mineralwasser.
Mint.	De la menthe.	Minze.
A mixed ice.	Une glace panachée.	Ein gemischtes Eis.
Mock turtle soup.	De la soupe à la fausse tortue.	Mock Turtle Suppe. →
Mulberries.	Des mûres.	Maulbeeren.
Mulled wine.	Du vin brûlé.	Glühwein.

Il succo di cedro.	Jugo de limón mejicano.	Limoensap.
Un liquore.	Un licor, Un cordial.	Een likeur.
Un cognac fino.	Un coñac fino.	Een fijne cognac.
L'acqua litina.	Agua de litina.	Lithine water.
Il fegato.	Hígado.	Lever.
Un pane, Una pagnotta.	Un pan, Una hogaza de pan.	Een brood.
Lo zucchero in chicchi o a quadretti.	Azúcar de terrón o en terrones.	Klontsuiker.
Un'arigusta.	Una langosta.	Een kreeft.
Un'arigusta con insalata.	Una ensalada de langosta.	Een kreeftenslaatje.
Una braciola di lombo.	Una costilla de filete.	Een lendestuk.
Una lombata di castrato.	Un filete de carnero.	Schaapslendestuk.
Una lombata di vitello.	Un filete de ternera.	Kalfslendestuk.
Un pezzetto (o Un chicco) di zucchero.	Un terrón de azúcar.	Een suikerklont.
Lo zucchero in chicchi o a quadretti.	Azúcar de terrón o en terrones.	Klontsuiker.
I maccheroni.	Macarrones.	Macaroni.
L'amaretto.	Un almendrado.	Een amandelkoekje.
Lo sgombro.	Un escombro.	Een makreel.
La marmellata di arancia.	Mermelada de naranjas.	Marmelade.
Il midollo.	Tuétano.	Merg.
Il marzapane.	Mazapán.	Marsepein.
Un purè di patate.	Patatas majadas, Puré de patatas.	Aardappelpuree.
Un purè di spinaci.	Puré de espinaca.	Spinazie.
Un purè di rape.	Puré de nabos.	Puree van rapen.
Il salmone con maionese.	Una mayonesa de salmón.	Een zalmmayonnaise.
La [salsa] maionese.	[Salsa] mayonesa.	Mayonnaise.
La carne.	Carne.	Vlees.
Il brodo di carne.	Sopa de carne.	Vleessoep.
Uno sciampagna semisecco.	Champaña seco mediano.	Half droge champagne.
Una nespola.	Un níspero.	Een mispel.
Un popone, Un melone.	Un melón.	Een meloen.
Il burro sciolto.	Manteca derretida.	Gesmolten boter.
Una meringa.	Un merengue.	Een meringue.
Tritato, a.	Picado, a.	Gehakt.
La carne tritata.	Confección de frutas picadas con especias.	Gehakt.
Il latte.	Leche.	Melk.
La cioccolata al latte.	Chocolate de leche.	Melkchocola[de].
L'acqua minerale.	Agua mineral.	Mineraal water.
La menta.	Menta.	Kruizemunt.
Una cassata siciliana.	Un helado mixto.	Een plombière.
La zuppa alla finta tartaruga.	Sopa hecha con cabeza de ternera a imitación de tortuga.	Nagemaakte schildpadsoep.
Le more di gelso.	Moras.	Moerbeien.
Il vino caldo o brulé.	Vino calentado con especias.	Bisschopswijn.

A mullet (*red*).	Un rouget.	Ein Röthling, Eine Seebarbe.
A mullet (*grey*).	Un mulet, Un muge.	Eine Meeräsche.
Mushrooms.	Des champignons.	Pilze, Champignons. →
Mushroom ketchup.	De la sauce aux champignons.	Pilzsoße.
Mussels.	Des moules.	Muscheln.
Mustard.	De la moutarde.	Mostrich, Senf.
Mustard sauce.	De la sauce moutarde.	Mostrichsoße, Senfsoße.
Mutton.	Du mouton.	Hammel.
A mutton cutlet.	Une côtelette de mouton.	Ein Hammelkotelett. →
Natives (*oysters*).	Des huîtres du pays.	Einheimische Austern.
A nectarine.	Un brugnon.	Eine Nektarine, Ein Nektarinenpfirsich.
New bread.	Du pain frais.	Frisches Brot.
New-laid eggs.	Des œufs frais.	Frische Eier. →
New potatoes.	Des pommes de terre nouvelles.	Junge Kartoffeln.
A non-alcoholic drink.	Une boisson sans alcool.	Ein alkoholfreies Getränk.
A non-vintage (*or* An undated) wine.	Un vin sans année, Un vin non-millésimé.	Ein Wein ohne besonderen Jahrgang.
Nougat.	Du nougat.	Nougat.
Nuts.	Des noix, Des noisettes.	Nüsse.
Olives.	Des olives.	Oliven. →
An omelet[te].	Une omelette.	Ein Omelette.
Onions.	Des oignons.	Zwiebeln.
An orange.	Une orange.	Eine Apfelsine, **Eine** Orange.
Orange marmalade.	De la confiture d'oranges.	Orangenmarmelade.
Orangeade.	De l'orangeade.	Orangeade. →
Ox tail soup.	De la soupe à la queue de bœuf.	Oxtail Suppe.
Ox tongue.	De la langue de bœuf.	Ochsenzunge.
Oysters.	Des huîtres.	Austern.
A pancake.	Une crêpe.	Ein Eierkuchen, Ein Pfannkuchen.
Parsley.	Du persil.	Petersilie. →
Parsnips.	Des panais.	Gelbe Rüben.
A partridge.	Une perdrix.	Ein Rebhuhn.
Pastry.	De la pâtisserie.	Gebäck, Kuchen, Teig.
A pasty.	Un pâté, Une bouchée.	Eine Pastete.
A pat of butter.	Un pain (*ou* Un rond) de beurre.	Ein Stück (*oder* Eine Scheibe) Butter.
A peach.	Une pêche.	Ein Pfirsich.
A pear.	Une poire.	Eine Birne.
Pearl barley.	De l'orge perlé.	Graupen.
Peas.	Des pois.	Erbsen, Schoten.
Pea soup.	De la soupe aux pois.	Erbsensuppe. →
Pease pudding.	Une purée de pois.	Erbsenpuree.
Pepper.	Du poivre.	Pfeffer.
A peppermint [lozenge].	Une pastille de menthe.	Ein Pfefferminzplätzchen.
A pheasant.	Un faisan.	Ein Fasan.
Pickles.	Des conserves au vinaigre.	In Essig eingemachte Gemüse. →
A piece of ice.	Un morceau de glace.	Ein Stück Eis.
A piece of toast.	Une tranche de pain grillé.	Eine Scheibe Toast.
A pie (*meat, fish*).	Un pâté.	Eine Pastete.

Una triglia minore.	Un salmonete.	Een harder.
Un muggine, Un cefalo.	Un mújol.	Een mul.
◄ I funghi.	Setas.	Paddestoelen.
Una salsa di funghi.	Salsa de setas.	Paddestoelensaus.
Le arselle.	Almejas.	Mosselen.
La mostarda.	Mostaza.	Mosterd.
Una salsa di mostarda.	Salsa de mostaza.	Mosterdsaus.
◄ Il castrato.	Carnero.	Schapevlees.
Una costoletta di castrato.	Una chuleta de carnero.	Een schaapskotelet.
Le ostriche del paese.	Ostras del país.	Inheemse oesters.
Una pesca noce.	Un nectáreo, Un nectarino.	Een gladde perzik, Een bloedperzik.
Il pane fresco.	Pan tierno.	Vers brood.
◄ Le uova fresche.	Huevos frescos.	Verse eieren.
Patatine tenere.	Patatas nuevas.	Nieuwe aardappelen.
Una bibita non alcoolica.	Una bebida sin alcohol.	Een alcoholvrije drank.
Un vino senza data.	Un vino sin añada.	Een landwijntje.
Un pasticcio di mandorle.	Turrón.	Noga.
Le nocciole.	Nueces.	Noten.
◄ Le olive.	Aceitunas.	Olijven.
Una frittata.	Una tortilla.	Een omelet, Eierstruif.
Le cipolle.	Cebollas.	Uien.
Un'arancia.	Una naranja.	Een sinaasappel.
La marmellata di arancia.	Mermelada de naranjas.	Sinaasappel marmelade.
◄ Un'aranciata.	Naranjada.	Sinaasappelsap.
Una zuppa di coda di bue o bove.	Sopa de cola de buey.	Ossestaartsoep.
La lingua di bue.	Lengua de buey.	Ossetong.
Le ostriche.	Ostras.	Oesters.
Una frittella.	Un panquec.	Een pannekoek.
◄ Il prezzemolo.	Perejil.	Peterselie.
Le pastinache.	Chirivía.	Pastinakken.
Una pernice.	Un perdiz.	Een patrijs.
La pasticceria.	Pastelería.	Gebak.
Un pasticcio.	Un pastel.	Een gebakje.
◄ Una pallina di burro.	Una bolilla de manteca.	Een klont[je] boter.
Una pesca.	Un melocotón.	Een perzik.
Una pera.	Una pera.	Een peer.
L'orzo perlato.	Cebada perlada.	Parelgort.
I piselli.	Guisantes, Chícharos.	Erwten.
◄ Una zuppa di piselli.	Potaje de guisantes.	Erwtensoep.
Un purè di piselli.	Un puré de guisantes.	Erwtenpuree.
Il pepe.	Pimienta.	Peper.
Una pasticca di menta.	Una pastilla de menta.	Een pepermunt.
Un fagiano.	Un faisán.	Een fazant.
◄ Gli acetini.	Salmuera.	Augurken (of Uitjes) uit het zuur.
Un pezzo di ghiaccio.	Un trozo de hielo.	Een stuk ijs.
Una fetta di pane arrostito.	Un pedazo de tostada.	Een sneetje toost.
Un pasticcio.	Un pastel.	Een pastei.

A pie (*fruit*).	Une tourte.	Eine gebackene Speise.
A pigeon.	Un pigeon.	Eine Taube.
Pigs' trotters.	Des pieds de porc.	Schweinefüße.
A pine[apple].	Un ananas.	Eine Ananas.
A plaice.	Une plie, Un carrelet.	Eine Scholle.
Plain biscuits.	Des biscuits secs.	Einfache Kekse.
Plain cakes.	Des biscuits secs.	Kaffeekuchen.
Plain cooking.	La cuisine bourgeoise.	Hausmacherskost.
A plain omelet[te].	Une omelette nature *ou* au naturel.	Ein einfaches Omelette.
A plover.	Un pluvier.	Ein Regenpfeifer.
Plovers' eggs (*for cooking*).	Des œufs de vanneau.	Kiebitzeier.
Plums.	Des prunes.	Pflaumen.
A poached egg.	Un œuf poché.	Ein verlorenes Ei, Ein poschiertes Ei.
A pomegranate.	Une grenade.	Ein Granatapfel.
Pork.	Du porc.	Schweinefleisch.
A pork chop.	Un chop de porc.	Ein Schweinskotelette, Ein Schweinerippchen.
Porridge (*oatmeal*).	De la bouillie [d'avoine].	Hafergrütze, Haferschleim, Haferbrei.
Port [wine].	Du porto, Du vin de Porto.	Portwein.
Potatoes.	Des pommes de terre.	Kartoffeln.
Potted meats.	Des conserves en vases, Des terrines.	Fleischkonserven.
Poultry.	De la volaille.	Geflügel.
Prawns.	Des crevettes roses, Des chevrettes, Des locustes, Des palémons, Des bouquets.	Steingarnelen, Sägegarnelen.
A preserve.	De la conserve, Des confitures, De la marmelade.	Eingemachtes, Eine Konserve.
Prunes.	Des pruneaux.	Backpflaumen.
A ptarmigan.	Une perdrix des neiges.	Ein Schneehuhn.
A pudding.	Un pudding, Un pouding.	Ein Pudding, Eine Mehlspeise.
A quail.	Une caille.	Eine Wachtel.
A quince.	Un coing.	Eine Quitte.
A rabbit.	Un lapin.	Ein Kaninchen.
Radishes.	Des radis.	Rettig ; Radieschen.
Raisins.	Des raisins secs.	Rosinen.
A rasher of bacon.	Une tranche de lard.	Eine Scheibe Speck.
Raspberries.	Des framboises.	Himbeeren.
Raw.	Cru, e.	Roh.
A red herring.	Un hareng saur.	Ein Pökelhering.
A red mullet.	Un rouget.	Ein Röthling, Eine Seebarbe.
Red pepper.	Du poivre rouge.	Paprika.
Red wine.	Du vin rouge.	Rotwein.
Rhubarb.	De la rhubarbe.	Rhabarber.
A rib steak.	Une entrecôte.	Ein Zwischenrippenstück.
Rice.	Du riz.	Reis.
Rice [milk] pudding.	Du riz au lait.	Reispudding.
A rissole.	Une rissole.	Eine Frikandelle.
Roast beef.	Du bœuf rôti, Du rosbif.	Roastbeef.

Una torta.	Un pastel, Una tarta.	Een taart.
Un piccione.	Un pichón.	Een duif.
Le zampe di maiale.	Manos de cerdo.	Varkenspoot.
Un ananasso.	Una piña, Una ananá.	Een ananas.
Un pesce passera.	Una platija.	Een schol.
I biscotti semplici.	Galletas secas.	Droge beschuitjes.
I dolci semplici.	Bizcocho.	Droge koek, Droge cake.
La cucina casalinga.	Cocina casera.	Eenvoudige keuken, De burgerpot.
Una frittata semplice.	Una tortilla [natural].	Een omelet nature.
Un piviere.	Una avefría.	Een pluvier.
Le uova di pavoncella.	Huevos de frailecito.	Kievitseieren.
Le susine.	Ciruelas.	Pruimen.
Un uovo affogato.	Un huevo escalfado.	Een gepocheerd ei.
Una melagrana.	Una granada.	Een granaatappel.
La carne di maiale.	Carne de puerco.	Varkensvlees.
Una braciola di maiale.	Una chuleta de puerco.	Een varkenskarbonade.
Una farinata di avena.	Potaje de avena.	Havermout.
Il porto, Il vino di Oporto.	Vino de Oporto.	Port[wijn].
Le patate.	Patatas.	Aardappels, Aardappelen.
La carne in scatola, La carne conservata.	Conservas de carne en tarros.	Zult.
Il pollame.	Aves de corral.	Pluimvee.
I palemoni.	Camarones grandes.	Steurgarnalen.
Una conserva.	Una conserva, Mermelada.	Confituren, Inmaak, Conserven.
Le prugne.	Ciruelas pasas.	Gedroogde pruimen.
Un francolino [di monte].	Una chocha.	Een sneeuwhoen.
Un budino.	Un budín.	Een pudding.
Una quaglia.	Un codorniz.	Een kwartel.
Una mela cotogna.	Un membrillo.	Een kwee[peer].
Un coniglio.	Un conejo.	Een konijn.
I ravanelli.	Rábanos.	Radijsjes.
L'uva secca.	Pasas.	Rozijnen.
Una fetta di ventresca.	Una lonja de tocino.	Een plak spek.
I lamponi.	Frambuesas.	Frambozen.
Crudo, a.	Crudo, a.	Rauw.
Un'aringa affumicata.	Un arenque ahumado.	Een bokking.
Una triglia minore.	Un salmonete.	Een nul.
Il pimento.	Pimentón.	Spaanse peper.
Un vino rosso.	Vino tinto.	Rode wijn.
Il rabarbaro.	Ruibarbo.	Rabarber.
Un'intracosta.	Un entrecote.	Een ribstuk.
Il riso.	Arroz.	Rijst.
Un budino di riso.	Arroz con leche.	Rijstebrij.
Una polpetta.	Una albóndiga.	Een rissole.
L'arrosto di bue Il rosbif[fe].	Carne asada, Rosbif.	Gebraden rundvlees.

Roast mutton, lamb.	Du rôti de mouton, d'agneau.	Hammelbraten, Lammbraten.
A roast sirloin [of beef].	Un aloyau rôti, Un rosbif.	Ein Lendenbraten, Ein Lendenstück [des Rindes].
A roll (of bread).	Un petit pain.	Ein Brötchen, Eine Semmel.
A round of toast.	Une rôtie.	Eine Scheibe Toast.
Rum.	Du rhum.	Rum.
A rumpsteak.	Un romsteck.	Ein Rumpsteak.
Runner beans.	Des haricots d'Espagne.	Feuerbohnen.
Saddle of mutton.	De la selle de mouton.	Hammelrücken.
Sago [milk] pudding.	Du sagou au lait.	Sago-Pudding.
A salad.	Une salade.	Ein Salat.
Salad oil.	De l'huile de table, De l'huile comestible.	Speiseöl.
A salmon.	Un saumon.	Ein Lachs, Ein Salm.
A salmon trout.	Une truite saumonée.	Eine Lachsforelle.
Salt.	Du sel.	Salz.
Salt butter.	Du beurre salé.	Gesalzene Butter.
Salt pork.	Du [porc] salé.	Gepökeltes Schweinefleisch.
Salt-water fish.	Des poissons de mer, De la marée.	Seefische.
A sandwich. A ham, A beef, sandwich.	Un sandwich. Un sandwich au jambon, au rosbif.	Eine Schnitte, Ein belegtes Brot. Eine Schinkenschnitte oder Ein Schinkenbrot, Eine Schnitte mit Roastbeef.
Sardines in oil.	Des sardines à l'huile.	Ölsardinen.
Sauce.	De la sauce.	Soße.
Sauerkraut.	De la choucroute.	Sauerkraut.
A sausage (fresh).	Une saucisse.	Ein Würstchen.
A sausage (smoked).	Un saucisson.	Eine Wurst.
Sauté potatoes.	Des pommes de terre sautées.	Bratkartoffeln.
A savoury omelet[te].	Une omelette aux fines herbes.	Ein pikantes (oder Ein gefülltes) Omelette.
A savoy [cabbage].	Un chou de Milan.	Ein Savoyenkohl.
Scallops.	Des pétoncles, Des peignes.	Kammuscheln.
Scarlet runners.	Des haricots d'Espagne.	Feuerbohnen.
Scrag of mutton.	Du collet de mouton.	Hammelhals.
Scrambled eggs.	Des œufs brouillés.	Rühreier.
Sea fish.	Des poissons de mer, De la marée.	Seefische.
Sea kale.	Du chou marin.	Seekohl.
Seasoning.	De l'assaisonnement.	Würzen.
Seltzer water.	De l'eau de Seltz.	Selterswasser.
Semolina [milk] pudding.	De la semoule au lait.	Griespudding.
Shallots.	Des échalotes.	Schalotten.
Shell fish.	Des coquillages.	Schalentiere.
Sherry: pale, golden, dark or brown, sweet, medium, dry.	Du xérès (pronounce kéréss) ou Du jerez, Du vin de Xérès ou de Jerez: pâle, doré, coloré, liquoreux, demi-sec, sec.	Sherry: heller, goldner, dunkler oder brauner, süßer, mittelsüßer, trockner.

L'arrosto di castrato, d'agnello.	Carnero, Cordero, asado.	Gebraden schapevlees, lamsvlees.
L'arrosto di lombo [di bue].	Solomillo de buey asado.	Een gebraden runderlendestuk.
◂Un panino.	Un panecillo.	Een broodje.
Una fetta di pane abbrustolito.	Una rebanada de tostada.	Een ronde toost.
Il rum.	Ron.	Rum.
Una fetta di culatta.	Un biftec.	Een biefstuk.
I fagiuoli rampicanti [a fiori rossi].	Judías verdes.	Klimbonen.
◂La schiena di castrato.	Lomo de carnero.	Een schapebout van lende.
Un budino di sago.	Sagú con leche.	Sagopudding, Sagopap.
Un'insalata.	Una ensalada.	Salade, Een slaatje.
L'olio da tavola.	Aceite de comer.	Slaolie.
Un salmone.	Un salmón.	Een zalm.
◂Una trota salmone.	Una trucha salmonada.	Een zalmforel.
Il sale.	Sal.	Zout.
Il burro salato.	Manteca salada.	Gezouten boter.
Il maiale salato.	Carne de puerco salada.	Gezouten varkensvlees, Pekelvlees.
Il pesce di mare.	Pescado de mar.	Zoutwatervis.
◂Un panino gravido. Un panino gravido di prosciutto, di rosbif.	Un emparedado, Un sandwich. Un emparedado de jamón, de carne de buey.	Een sandwich. Een ham, Een rosbief, sandwich.
Le sardine in olio.	Sardinas en lata.	Sardines in olie.
La salsa.	Salsa.	Saus.
Il salcrauti, Il sarcrauti.	Col ácida y fermentada.	Zuurkool.
Una salsiccia.	Una salchicha.	Een worst.
◂Il salame.	Un salchichón.	Een rookworst.
Le patate sautées.	Patatas sauté.	Gebakken aardappelen.
Una frittata di verdura.	Una tortilla con hierbas finas.	Een gekruide omelet.
Un cappuccio.	Una col común.	Een Savoye kool.
Gli smerli.	Pechinas.	Kammosselen.
◂I fagiolini rampicanti [a fiori rossi].	Judías verdes.	Klimbonen.
La collottola di castrato.	Cuello de carnero.	Halsstuk van schaap.
Le uova strapazzate.	Huevos revueltos.	Roereieren.
I pesci di mare.	Pescado de mar.	Zeevis.
Un cavolo marino.	Berza marina.	Zeekraal.
◂Il condimento.	Condimento.	Kruiderij.
L'acqua di seltz.	Agua de seltz.	Selz water.
Un budino di semolino.	Sémola con leche.	Griesmeelpap.
Gli scalogni.	Chalotes, Ascalonias.	Sjalotten.
Le conchiglie.	Mariscos.	Schaaldieren.
◂Il vino di Xeres: paglierino, dorato, oscuro, dolce, mezzo asciutto, asciutto.	[Vino de] Jerez: fino o amontillado, oloroso, generoso, vino de postre, vino de pasto, seco.	Sherry: licht, gouden, donker, zoet, halfdroog, droog.

A shoulder of mutton.	Une épaule de mouton, Une éclanche.	Hammelkeule, Schulterstück vom Hammel.
Shrimps.	Des crevettes grises, Des locustes, Des salicoques.	Garnelen.
A side dish.	Un entremets.	Ein Zwischengericht
A sirloin [of beef].	Un aloyau.	Ein Lendenstück (oder Ein Nierenstück) [vom Rind].
A skate.	Une raie.	Eine Glattroche. →
Skim[med] milk.	Du lait écrémé.	Abgerahmte Milch.
A slice of bread and butter.	Une beurrée, Une tartine de beurre.	Ein Butterbrot.
A slice of melon	Une tranche de melon.	Eine Melonenscheibe.
A smelt.	Un éperlan.	Ein Stint.
Smoked salmon.	Du saumon fumé.	Räucherlachs. →
A snipe.	Une bécassine.	Eine Sumpfschnepfe.
Soda [water].	Du soda, De l'eau de Seltz.	Sodawasser.
A soft-boiled egg.	Un œuf mollet, Un œuf à la mouillette.	Ein weiches Ei.
A soft drink.	Une boisson fraîche.	Ein alkoholfreies Getränk →
Soft roe.	De la laitance ou laite.	Milch (Fisch). →
A sole.	Une sole.	Eine Seezunge.
Soup, see Clear, Thick.		
Spaghetti.	Des spaghetti.	Spaghetti.
Spanish onions.	Des oignons doux d'Espagne.	Spanische Zwiebeln.
A sparkling wine.	Un vin mousseux.	Ein Schaumwein.
Spinach.	Des épinards.	Spinat. →
Spirits.	Des liqueurs [spiritueuses], Des spiritueux.	Spirituosen.
A sponge cake.	Un biscuit de Savoie.	Ein Biskuitkuchen.
A spring chicken.	Un poussin.	Ein Küken.
Spring greens.	Du chou de printemps.	Frühjahrskohl.
Spring onions.	Des petits oignons, Des ciboules.	Junge Zwiebeln. →
Stale bread.	Du pain rassis.	Altbackenes Brot.
A steak.	Une tranche.	Ein Steak.
A steak (beef).	Un bifteck.	Ein Beefsteak.
Steamed potatoes.	Des pommes de terre à la vapeur.	Dampfkartoffeln.
A stew.	Un ragoût.	Ein geschmortes Fleischgericht. →
Stewed mutton.	Un ragoût de mouton.	Ein Hammelragout.
Stewed plums, apples.	Une compote de prunes, de pommes.	Apfelkompott, Pflaumenkompott.
Still lemonade, see Lemonade.		
A still wine.	Un vin non mousseux.	Ein nicht schäumender Wein.
A stone fruit.	Un fruit à noyau.	Eine Kernfrucht.
Strawberries.	Des fraises.	Erdbeeren. →
A strawberry ice.	Une glace aux fraises.	Ein Erdbeereis.
Strawberry jam.	De la confiture de fraises.	Erdbeermarmelade.
Stuffed. Stuffing.	Farci, e. De la farce.	Gefüllt. Füllung.
A sucking pig.	Un cochon de lait.	Ein Ferkel.
Suet.	De la graisse de rognon.	Talg, Nierenfett. →
Sugar.	Du sucre.	Zucker.

Una spalla di castrato.	Un pernil brazuelo de carnero.	Een schaapsschouderstuk.
I gamberettini [di mare].	Camarones.	Garnalen.
Un entremets.	Un entremés.	Een tussengerecht.
Un lombo di bove.	Un solomo de carne [de vaca].	Een runderlendestuk.
◄Una razza.	Una liza.	Een vleet.
Il latte spannato.	Leche desnatada.	Afgeroomde melk.
Una fetta di pane col burro.	Una rebanada de pan con manteca.	Een boterham.
Una fetta di popone.	Una tajada de melón.	Een schijf meloen.
Un eperlano.	Un eperlano.	Een spiering.
◄Il salmone affumicato.	Salmón ahumado.	Gerookte zalm.
Un beccaccino.	Una agachadiza.	Een snip.
L'acqua gasosa, L'acqua di seltz.	Agua de soda, Agua de seltz.	Spuitwater, Sodawater.
Un uovo a bere.	Un huevo pasado por agua.	Een zacht gekookt ei.
Una bibita non alcoolica.	Una bebida sin alcohol.	Een alcoholvrije drank.
◄Il latte di pesce.	Hueva, Ovas de pescado.	Hom.
Una sogliola.	Un lenguado.	Een tong.
Gli spaghetti.	Spaghetti, Fideos largos.	Sphaghetti.
Le cipolle dolci di Spagna.	Cebollas dulces.	Spaanse uien.
Un vino spumante.	Un vino espumoso.	Een mousserende wijn.
◄Gli spinaci.	Espinaca.	Spinazie.
Le bevande spiritose.	Alcóholes.	Spiritualiën, Sterke drank.
Il pan di Spagna.	Un bizcochuelo.	Een moscovisch gebak.
Un pollastro.	Un polluelo.	Een kuiken.
Un cavolo di primavera.	Coles de primavera.	Voorjaarsgroenten.
◄Le cipolline.	Cebollitas de primavera.	Kleine uitjes.
Il pan raffermo.	Pan viejo.	Oud brood.
Una fetta.	Un tajada para asar.	Een lapje.
Una bistecca.	Un biftec.	Een biefstuk.
Le patate a bagnomaria.	Patatas cocidas en baño de María.	Gestoomde aardappelen.
◄La carne stufata, Lo stufato.	Un guisado.	Een ragoût.
Il castrato stufato.	Un guisado de carnero.	Een schaapsragoût.
Un composto di prugne, di mele.	Una compota de ciruelas, de manzanas.	Gestoofde pruimen, appels.
Un vino non spumante.	Un vino no espumoso.	Een niet-mousserende wijn.
Una frutta a nocciolo.	Una fruta de hueso.	Een steenvrucht.
◄Le fragole.	Fresas.	Aardbeien.
Un gelato alle fragole.	Un helado de fresa.	Aardbeienijs.
La conserva di fragole.	Mermelada de fresas.	Aardbeienjam.
Ripieno, a. Il ripieno.	Rellenado, a. Relleno.	Gevuld. Vulsel.
Un maialino da latte.	Un lechoncillo.	Een speenvarken.
◄Il grasso.	Sebo en rama, Grasa.	Niervet.
Lo zucchero.	Azúcar.	Suiker.

Sugar almonds.	Des dragées.	Gezuckerte Mandeln.
Sugar candy.	Du sucre candi.	Kandiszucker.
Sultanas.	Des raisins de Smyrne.	Sultaninen.
A sweet (*as dinner course*).	Un entremets [sucré], Un plat sucré.	Eine Süßspeise. →
A sweetbread.	Un ris de veau.	Ein Brøschen.
Sweet champagne.	Du champagne doux.	Süßer Champagner.
Sweet dessert wine.	Du vin de liqueur.	Süßer Dessertwein.
Sweet herbs.	Des herbes fines.	Küchengewächse.
Sweet [meats].	Des sucreries, Des bonbons.	Süßigkeiten. →
Sweet oil.	De l'huile douce.	Olivenöl, Speiseöl.
A sweet omelet[te].	Une omelette aux confitures.	Ein süßes Omelette, Ein Omelette aux confitures.
A sweet wine.	Un vin sucré *ou* doux *ou* liquoreux.	Ein Süßwein.
Swiss cheese.	Du fromage de Gruyère, Du gruyère.	Schweizer Käse.
Table water.	De l'eau minérale [naturelle].	Mineralwasser. →
A table wine.	Un vin de table.	Ein Tischwein.
Tangerines.	Des mandarines.	Mandarinen.
Tapioca [milk] pudding.	Du tapioca au lait.	Tapiokapudding.
A tart (*open*).	Une tarte.	Eine Torte.
A tart (*covered*).	Une tourte.	Eine Torte. →
Tea.	Du thé.	Tee.
Tea, rolls and butter.	Un thé complet.	Ein Teegedeck.
Tender (*said of meat*).	Tendre.	Weich.
Thick soup.	Un potage, Une soupe, Une purée.	Dicke Suppe.
A thin slice (*of bread, of meat*).	Une tranche mince, Une lèche.	Eine dünne Scheibe. →
A tin[ned] loaf.	Un pain platine.	Ein Kastenbrot.
Tinned goods. Tinned salmon.	Des conserves [en boîtes]. Du saumon en boîte.	Büchsenwaren *oder* Konserven. Büchsenlachs.
Toast. (*Compare* Buttered toast.)	Du pain grillé *ou* rôti.	Toast, Geröstetes Brot.
Tomatoes.	Des tomates.	Tomaten.
Tomato soup.	De la soupe aux tomates.	Tomatensuppe. →
Tongue.	De la langue.	Zunge.
Tough (*said of meat*).	Dur, e, Coriace.	Zäh.
A trifle *or* A tipsy cake.	Un gateau au madère.	Rumspeise.
Tripe.	Des tripes.	Kaldaunen, Fleck.
A trout.	Une truite.	Eine Forelle. →
Truffles.	Des truffes.	Trüffel.
A tunny.	Un thon.	Ein Thunfisch.
A turbot.	Un turbot.	Ein Steinbutt.
A turkey.	Une dinde, Un dindonneau.	Ein Truthahn.
Turnips.	Des navets.	Rüben. →
Turnip tops.	Des fanes de navets.	Rübenkraut.
A turtle.	Une tortue [de mer].	Eine Schildkröte.
Turtle soup.	De la soupe à la tortue.	Schildkrötensuppe.
An undercut of beef.	Un filet de bœuf.	Ein Rinderfilet.
Underdone.	Peu cuit, e.	Nicht gar, Halb gar. →
Underdone (*said of red meat*).	Saignant, e.	Roh, Halb roh.
Unleavened bread.	Du pain azyme.	Ungesäuertes Brot.
A vanilla ice.	Une glace à la vanille.	Ein Vanille-Eis.

Le mandorle inzuccherate.	Almendras garapiñadas.	Zoete amandelen.
Lo zucchero candito.	Azúcar cande.	Kandijsuiker.
L'uva sultana.	Pasas de Esmirna.	Sultanarozijnen.
Un dolce.	Un dulce.	Een nagerecht, Een toetje.
L'animella.	Lechecillas.	Zwezerik.
Uno sciampagna dolce.	Champaña dulce.	Zoete champagne.
Un vino dolce da dessert.	Vino dulce de postre.	Zoete dessertwijn.
Le erbucce.	Hierbas finas.	Kruiden.
Gli zuccherini, I dolci.	Dulces, Bombones.	Lekkers. Zoetigheden.
L'olio dolce.	Aceite de comer.	Zoete olie.
Una frittata inzuccherata.	Una tortilla de confitura.	Een zoete omelet.
Un vino dolce.	Un vino dulce.	Een zoete wijn.
Il cacio svizzero.	Queso suizo.	Zwitserse kaas.
L'acqua minerale [naturale].	Agua mineral natural.	Mineraalwater.
Un vino da tavola.	Un vino de mesa.	Een tafelwijn.
I mandarini.	Mandarinas.	Mandarijnen.
Un budino di tapioca.	Tapioca con leche.	Tapiocapudding.
Una torta.	Una tarta.	Een taart.
Una crostata.	Una torta, Un pastel.	Een taart.
Il tè.	Té.	Thee.
Un tè completo.	Un té completo.	Thee, broodjes en boter.
Tenero, a.	Tierno, a.	Mals.
Una zuppa.	Potaje, Puré.	Dikke soep.
Una fettina.	Una rebanada delgada.	Een dunne snee, Een dunne plak.
Un pane oblungo.	Un pan forma de lata.	Een casinobrood.
Le conserve in scatola. Il salmone in scatola.	Conservas alimenticias. Salmón en lata.	Conserven, Blikzalm.
Il pane abbrustolito.	Tostada, Pan tostado.	Toost.
I pomidoro, (singular Un pomodoro).	Tomates.	Tomaten.
Una zuppa al pomidoro.	Sopa de tomates.	Tomatensoep.
La lingua.	Lengua.	Tong.
Tiglioso, a.	Correoso, a.	Taai.
Una zuppa inglese.	Bizcocho borracho.	Een madeira cake.
La trippa.	Callos.	Pens, Darmen.
Una trota.	Una trucha.	Een forel.
I tartufi.	Trufas.	Truffels.
Un tonno.	Un atún.	Een tonijn.
Un rombo.	Un rodaballo.	Een tarbot.
Un tacchino.	Un pavo.	Een kalkoen.
Le rape.	Nabos.	Rapen.
Le foglie di rape.	Hojas de nabo.	Raapstelen.
Una tartaruga.	Una tortuga [de mar].	Een schildpad.
Una zuppa di tartaruga.	Sopa de tortuga.	Schildpadsoep.
Un filetto di bove.	Un filete de carne de vaca.	Ossehaas.
Poco cotto, a.	Soasado, a, A medio asar.	Niet gaar.
Al sangue.	Crudo, a.	Rood.
Pane non lievitato.	Pan ázimo.	Ongezuurd brood.
Un gelato alla vainiglia.	Un helado de vainilla.	Een vanille-ijs.

Veal.	Du veau.	Kalbfleisch.
A veal cutlet.	Une côtelette de veau.	Ein Kalbsschnitzel. →
Vegetable marrow.	De la courge à la moelle.	Länglicher Kürbis.
Vegetables.	Des légumes.	Gemüse.
Venison.	De la venaison, Du chevreuil.	Wildbret, Rehbraten.
Vermicelli soup.	Un potage au vermicelle.	Fadennudelsuppe.
Verm[o]uth, French	Du vermouth [français].	Französischer Wermut. →
Verm[o]uth, Italian	Du vermouth de Turin.	Italienischer Wermut.
Vinegar.	Du vinaigre.	Essig.
A vintage (or A dated) wine.	Un vin millésimé.	Ein Wein von einem guten Jahrgange, Ein Wachstum.
A wafer (*flat biscuit*).	Une gaufrette.	Eine Eiswaffel.
A wafer (*cornet*).	Une oublie, Un plaisir.	Eine Oblate.
A waffle.	Une gaufre.	Eine Waffel.
Walnuts.	Des noix.	Walnüsse.
Water.	De l'eau.	Wasser.
Watercress.	Du cresson [de fontaine].	Brunnenkresse.
A water ice.	Une glace à .l'eau, Un sorbet.	Ein Wassereis. →
A water melon.	Un melon d'eau.	Eine Wassermelone.
Well done.	Bien cuit, e.	Gar, Durch.
A Welsh rarebit.	Une rôtie à l'anglaise, Une rôtie au fromage.	Ein Welsh Rarebit.
Whisky.	Du whisky.	Whisky.
Whitebait.	De la blanchaille.	Kleiner Weißfisch. →
White bread.	Du pain blanc.	Weißbrot.
A white coffee.	Un café au lait.	Milchkaffee.
White sauce.	De la sauce blanche.	Weiße Soße.
White wine.	Du vin blanc.	Weißwein.
A whiting.	Un merlan.	Ein Weißfisch.
Wholemeal bread.	Du pain complet.	Vollkornbrot.
Wild strawberries.	Des fraises des bois.	Walderdbeeren.
Wine.	Du vin.	Wein.
Wine in the wood.	Du vin en cercles.	Wein vom Faß. →
Wine of the country.	Du vin du cru.	Landwein.
A wing of chicken.	Une aile de poulet.	Ein Hühnerflügel.
A woodcock.	Une bécasse.	Eine Waldschnepfe.
The yolk of an egg.	Le jaune d'un œuf.	Das Eigelb.

SHOPPING	EMPLETTES	EINKÄUFE
Making purchases	**Les achats**	**Besorgungen**
A shop.	Un magasin, Une boutique.	Ein Geschäft, Ein Laden.
A shop assistant.	Un commis, Une demoiselle, de magasin.	Ein(e) Verkäufer(in). →
A shop walker.	Un inspecteur.	Ein(e) Aufseher(in).
A [big] store*s* *or* A department[al] store[s].	Un grand magasin [de nouveautés].	Ein Kaufhaus, Ein Warenhaus.
A multiple shop.	Un magasin à succursales multiples.	Ein Geschäft mit vielen Zweigniederlassungen.
An arcade.	Un passage [à boutiques].	Eine Passage, Ein Bogengang.

Il vitello.	Ternera.	Kalfsvlees.
Una costoletta di vitello.	Una chuleta de ternera.	Een kalfskotelet.
Una zucca [di orto].	Médula vegetal.	Mergpompoen.
I legumi.	Hortalizas, Legumbres.	Groenten.
La cacciagione, La selvaggina.	Venado.	Wildbraad.
La minestra di vermicelli.	Sopa de fideos.	Vermicellisoep.
Un vermut[te] francese.	Vermut francés.	Franse vermouth.
Un vermut[te] [italiano].	Vermut italiano.	Italiaanse vermóuth.
L'aceto.	Vinagre.	Azijn.
Un vino con data.	Un vino de añada.	Een prima wijn.
Un brigidino.	Un barquillo plano.	Een wafeltje.
Un cialdone.	Un barquillo cónico.	Een oblie.
Una cialda.	Una oblea con fruta de sartén a la americana.	Een wafel.
Le noci.	Nueces.	Walnoten, Okkernoten.
L'acqua.	Agua.	Water.
Il crescione d'acqua.	Berro.	Waterkers.
Un sorbetto.	Un sorbete.	Een waterijs.
Un cocomero.	Una sandía.	Een watermeloen.
Ben cotto, a.	Bien cocido, a.	Gaar.
Un crostino di formaggio arrostito.	Queso con pan tostado a la inglesa.	Geroosterde (of Gesmolten) kaas.
Un whisky.	Whisky.	Whisky.
I pesciolini.	Boquerones pequeños.	Witvisch.
Il pane bianco.	Pan blanco.	Wit brood.
Un caffè e latte.	Un café con leche.	Koffie met melk; ($\frac{1}{2}$ and $\frac{1}{3}$) Koffie verkeerd.
Una salsa bianca.	Salsa blanca.	Witte saus.
Il vino bianco.	Vino blanco.	Witte wijn.
Un nasello, Un merlango.	Un merlán.	Een wijting.
Il pane integrale.	Pan íntegro.	Volkorenbrood.
Le fragole selvatiche.	Fresas silvestres.	Bosaardbeien.
Il vino.	Vino.	Wijn.
Il vino in botte.	Vino en barril.	Wijn in het vat.
Il vino paesano.	Vino del país.	Landwijn.
Un'ala di pollo.	Un alón de pollo.	Een kippevleugel.
Una beccaccia.	Una chocha.	Een houtsnip.
Il torlo di un uovo.	La yema de un huevo.	Een eierdooier.

LE SPESE	**LAS TIENDAS**	**BOODSCHAPPEN**
In giro per le spese	**Compras**	**Inkopen**
Un negozio, Una bottega.	Una tienda, Un almacén.	Een winkel.
Un commesso, Una commessa, di negozio.	Un tendero, Una muchacha, de tienda.	Een winkelbediende.
Un vigilante.	Un inspector.	Een winkelchef.
Un gran negozio, Un magazzino.	Grandes almacenes.	Een warenhuis.
Un negozio con succursali.	Un establecimiento con sucursales.	Een zaak met filialen.
Una galleria.	Un pasaje, Una galería.	Een winkelgalerij.

Where is there a baker, a pastrycook's shop?	Où y a-t-il un boulanger, une pâtisserie?	Wo gibt es hier einen→ Bäcker, eine Feinbäckerei?
Which is the best china shop?	Quel est le meilleur magasin de porcelaines?	Welches ist das beste Porzellangeschäft?
Where can I buy a hat, a Christmas present?	Où puis-je acheter un chapeau, un cadeau de Noël *ou* une étrenne?	Wo kann ich einen Hut, ein Weihnachtsgeschenk, kaufen?
Do you keep, sell, artistic novelties?	Est-ce que vous tenez, vendez, des articles de Paris?	Führen Sie, Verkaufen Sie, Geschenkartikel?
Where is the show room?	Où est le salon d'exposition?	Wo ist der Vorführungsraum?
Have you a price list, a catalogue, a special list concerning this article?	Est-ce que vous avez un prix courant, un catalogue, un prospectus de cet article?	Haben Sie eine Preisliste,→ einen Katalog, eine Sonderliste von diesem Artikel?
I should like to look at some picture postcards, some views, souvenirs, of Paris.	Je désire voir des cartes postales illustrées, des vues, souvenirs, de Paris.	Ich möchte mir ein paar Ansichtspostkarten, einige Ansichten, von Paris, Pariser Reiseandenken, ansehen.
Let me see it, them.	Faites voir.	Zeigen Sie es, sie, mir bitte.
That is not what I want.	Cela n'est pas ce qu'il me faut.	Das ist nicht, was ich suche.
This will do, will not do.	Ceci fait l'affaire, ne fait pas l'affaire.	Das ist das Richtige, ist nicht das Richtige.
Is that the only pattern, the only quality, you have in stock?	Est-ce là le seul modèle, la seule qualité, que vous ayez en magasin?	Ist das das einzige Muster,→ das Sie auf Lager haben? Ist das die einzige Qualität, die Sie auf Lager haben?
Have you something (a) better, (b) cheaper, (c) bigger, (d) smaller, (e) longer, (f) shorter, (g) wider, (h) narrower, (i) higher, (k) lower, (k) thicker, (l) thinner, (m) darker, (n) lighter?	Avez-vous quelque chose de (a) meilleur, (b) meilleur marché, (c) plus grand, (d) plus petit, (e) plus long, (f) plus court, (g) plus large, (h) plus étroit, (i) plus haut, (j) plus bas, (k) plus épais, (l) plus mince, (m) plus foncé, (n) plus clair?	Haben Sie etwas (a) Besseres, (b) Billigeres, (c) Größeres, (d) Kleineres, (e) Längeres, (f) Kürzeres, (g) Breiteres, (h) Schmäleres, (i) Höheres, (j) Niedrigeres, (k) Dickeres, (l) Dünneres, (m) Dunkleres, (n) Helleres?
I will take this one then.	Je prends celui-ci (celle-ci) donc.	Ich nehme also dies, diese.
How much is this, is this article?	Combien [vendez-vous] ceci, cet article?	Wieviel kostet dies, dieser Gegenstand?
How much are these apples a half-kilo? (*For various kinds of fruit see* **Foods and Drinks**, pp. 146-171, *and see* WEIGHTS AND MEASURES, *p.* 266.)	Combien le demi-kilo de ces pommes?	Wieviel kostet das Pfund Äpfel?
What are they a pair, a dozen?	Combien les vendez-vous la paire, la douzaine?	Was kostet das Paar, das→ Dutzend?
What is your lowest price?	Quel est votre dernier prix?	Ist das Ihr niedrigster Preis?

◄Dove si trova un fornaio, una pasticceria?	¿Dónde hay un panadero, una confitería?	Waar is een bakker, een banketbakkerij?
Qual'è il miglior negozio di porcellana?	¿Cuál es la mejor tienda para loza?	Wat is de beste porceleinwinkel?
Dove posso comprare un cappello, un regalo per Natale?	¿Dónde puedo comprar un sombrero, un regalo de pascuas?	Waar kan ik een hoed, een Kerstgeschenk, kopen?
Avete voi, Vendete voi, articoli di novità?	¿Tiene, Vende, usted novedades artísticas?	Verkoopt U Mode-artikelen.
Dov'è la sala di mostra?	¿Dónde está el cuarto de muestras?	Waar is de toonzaal of de toonkamer?
◄Avete una lista del prezzi, un catalogo, una lista speciale di questo articolo?	¿Tiene usted una lista de precios, un catálogo, una lista especial dedicada a este artículo?	Heeft U een prijslijst, een catalogus, een prospectus van dit artikel?
Io vorrei vedere delle cartoline postali illustrate, qualche veduta, ricordi, di Parigi.	Me gustaría ver algunas vistas postales, vistas, recuerdos, de París.	Ik wou graag wat prentbriefkaarten, wat stadsgezichten, souvenirs, van Parijs zien.
Fatemelo, Fatemeli, vedere.	Déjeme verlo, verlos.	Laat eens zien.
Questo non è quello che io desidero.	Esto no es lo que quiero.	Dat is niet wat ik hebben wil.
Questo può andare, Questo non va.	Esto servirá, no sirve.	Dit is goed, is niet goed.
◄È questo il solo modello, la sola qualità, che avete nel negozio?	¿Es este el único modelo, la única calidad, que hay en el establecimiento?	Is dat het enige model, de enige kwaliteit, die U in voorraad heeft?
Avete qualche cosa di (a) meglio, (b) più a buon mercato, (c) più grande, (d) più piccola, (e) più lunga, (f) più corta, (g) più larga, (h) più stretta, (i) più alta, (j) più bassa, (k) più grossa, (l) più leggera, (m) più oscura, (n) più chira?	¿Tiene usted algo (a) mejor, (b) más barato, (c) más grande, (d) más pequeño, (e) más largo, (f) más corto, (g) más ancho, (h) más angosto, (i) más alto, (j) más bajo, (k) más grueso, (l) más delgado, (m) más obscuro, (n) más claro?	Heeft U iets (a) beters, (b) goedkopers, (c) groters, (d) kleiners, (e) langers, (f) korters, (g) breders, (h) smallers, (i) hogers, (j) lagers, (k) dikkers, (l) dunners, (m) donkerders, (n) lichters?
Prenderò questo (feminine questa) allora.	Tomaré éste, ésta.	Dan neem ik (masculine, fem.) deze, (neuter) dit.
Questo quanto costa, Quanto costa questo articolo?	¿Cuánto vale esto, este artículo?	Hoeveel is dit, is dit artikel?
Quanto costa un mezzo chilo di queste mele?	¿Cuánto valen estas manzanas el medio kilo?	Hoeveel zijn deze appels per half kilo?
◄Quanto è al paio, alla dozzina?	¿Cuánto valen el par, la docena?	Hoeveel zijn ze per paar, per dozijn?
Qual'è l'ultimo prezzo?	¿Cuál es su último precio?	Wat is Uw laagste prijs?

It is rather dear. Can you not let me have it cheaper?	C'est assez cher. Ne pourriez-vous pas me le donner à meilleur marché?	Das ist mir etwas zu teuer. Können Sie mir nicht billiger lassen?
Can you change this article?	Pouvez-vous changer cet article?	Kann ich diesen Gegenstand umtauschen?
Nothing else. That is all, thank you.	Rien de plus. C'est tout, merci.	Sonst nichts. Das ist alles, danke sehr.

The bill
La note
Die Rechnung

Give me my bill.	Donnez-moi ma note.	Geben Sie mir bitte die Rechnung.
How much does it all come to? How much do you say? Please say it slowly.	Combien tout cela fait-il? Combien dites-vous? Dites-le lentement, s'il vous plaît.	Wieviel kostet das alles zusammen? Wieviel sagten Sie? Wollen Sie es bitte langsam sagen.
I think there is a mistake in the bill. Please correct it.	Il me semble qu'il y a une erreur dans la note. Veuillez la rectifier.	Ich glaube, an der Rechnung stimmt etwas nicht. Wollen Sie sie bitte richtig stellen.
You have not given me the right change.	Vous ne m'avez pas donné la monnaie juste.	Sie haben mir falsch herausgegeben.
Kindly receipt the bill.	Veuillez acquitter la note.	Wollen Sie bitte die Rechnung quittieren.
Where is the cash desk?	Où se trouve la caisse?	Wo ist die Kasse?

Delivery
La livraison
Lieferung

Can you send the goods on approval, cash on delivery?	Pouvez-vous envoyer les marchandises à condition, contre remboursement?	Können Sie mir die Waren auf Probe oder zur Auswahl, zahlbar bei Lieferung, schicken?
I will take this article [away] with me. Please wrap it up in brown paper, in tissue paper. Please pack it very carefully.	J'emporterai cet article avec moi. Veuillez l'envelopper dans du papier gris, dans du papier de soie. Veuillez l'empaqueter avec beaucoup de soin.	Ich nehme diesen Gegenstand gleich mit. Würden Sie ihn bitte in Packpapier, in Seidenpapier, einpacken. Verpacken Sie ihn bitte sehr sorgfältig.
Please send it, Please send the things, to Mr . ., to Mrs . ., to Miss . ., at the . . Hotel.	Veuillez l'envoyer, Veuillez envoyer les choses, à Monsieur . ., à Madame . ., à Mademoiselle . ., à l'Hôtel . . .	Schicken Sie es bitte, Schicken Sie die Sachen bitte, zu Herrn . ., zu Frau . ., zu Fräulein . ., ins . . Hotel.
Please send (or forward) this to me by post, by rail, to this address.	Veuillez m'expédier ceci par la poste, par fer, à cette adresse.	Senden Sie mir dies bitte per Post, per Bahn, an diese Adresse nach.
I am leaving on Friday evening. Can I rely on delivery by Friday afternoon?	Je pars vendredi soir. Puis-je compter sur la livraison pour vendredi après-midi?	Ich reise Freitag abend ab. Kann ich mich darauf verlassen, daß die Sachen bis Freitag nachmittag geliefert werden?
Can you get it for me by to-morrow for certain?	Pouvez-vous me le procurer pour demain pour sûr?	Können Sie es mir ganz bestimmt bis morgen besorgen?

È abbastanza caro. Non potete farmi una riduzione?

Es un poco caro. No me lo (la) puede dejar más barato?

Het is nogal duur. Kunt U het me niet voor minder geven?

Potete cambiarmi questo articolo?

¿Puede usted cambiarme este artículo?

Kunt U dit artikel ruilen?

Nient'altro. È tutto che desidero, grazie.

Nada más. Eso basta, gracias.

Niets anders. Dat is alles, dank U.

Il conto

La cuenta

De rekening

◄ Datemi il conto.

Déme la cuenta.

Geef me mijn rekening.

Qual'è l'importo totale? Quanto, dite? Per favore, parlatemi lentamente.

¿A cuánto viene todo junto? ¿Cuánto dice usted? Haga el favor de decirlo despacio.

Hoeveel is dat bij elkaar? Hoeveel zegt U? Wilt U het langzaam zeggen als 't U belieft.

Io credo che c'è uno sbaglio nel conto. Vogliate correggerlo.

Creo que hay un error en la cuenta. Haga el favor de rectificarlo.

Ik geloof, dat er een vergissing in de rekening gemaakt is. Wilt U die herstellen als 't U belieft.

Non mi avete dato il resto giusto. Vogliate quietanzare il conto.

Está equivocado el cambio. Haga el favor de poner el recibí.

U heeft me verkeerd teruggegeven. Wilt U de rekening kwiteren.

◄ Dov'è la cassa?

¿Dónde está la caja?

Waar is de kassa?

La consegna

La expedición

Aflevering

Potete mandarmi la merce in approvazione, pagamento alla consegna?

¿Puede usted enviar estos géneros a prueba, contra pago a la entrega?

Kunt U de goederen op zicht zenden onder rembours?

Porterò quest'articolo con me. Per favore, avvolgetelo in [una] cartascura, in carta velina. Favorite impaccarlo con cura.

Me llevaré este artículo conmigo. Haga el favor de envolverlo en papel de estraza, en papel de seda. Haga el favor de empaquetarlo muy esmeradamente.

Ik neem dit artikel mee. Pak het in pakpapier, als 't U belieft. Pak het zeer zorgvuldig in, als 't U belieft.

Prego mandarlo, Per favore mandate ogni cosa, al Signor . . , alla Signora . . , alla Signorina . . , all'Albergo . . .

Haga el favor de enviarlo, Haga el favor de enviar los artículos, al Señor . . , a la Señora . . , a la Señorita . . , en el Hotel de . . .

Zend het, Zend de voorwerpen naar de Heer .., naar Mevrouw .., naar Mejuffrouw .., in het . Hotel.

Per favore, speditemi questo a mezzo posta, per ferrovia, a questo indirizzo.

Haga el favor de enviarme esto por correo, por ferrocarril, a estas señas.

Zend mij dit per post, per spoor, naar dit adres.

◄ Io partirò venerdì sera. Posso contare per la consegna almeno per il pomeriggio per certo di venerdì?

Me marcho el viernes por la tarde. ¿Puede contar con recibir los géneros el viernes por la tarde temprano?

Ik vertrek Vrijdagavond. Kan ik erop vertrouwen dat het vrijdagmiddag bezorgd wordt?

Potete farmelo avere per domani?

¿Puede usted obtenérmelo para mañana sin falta?

Kunt U het beslist morgen voor me krijgen?

When can I have it ?	Quand pouvez-vous me le livrer ?	Wann kann ich es haben ?
How soon can you do it ? Don't disappoint me.	Pour quand pouvez-vous le faire ? Ne manquez pas à votre promesse.	Wie schnell können Sie es machen ? Lassen Sie mich bitte nicht im Stich.
Shall I wait or call again ?	Dois-je attendre ou repasser ?	Soll ich warten, oder lieber noch einmal vorbeikommen ?

A bookseller, Libraries	Un libraire, Les bibliothèques	Ein Buchhändler, Bibliotheken
A book[seller's] shop.	Une librairie.	Eine Buchhandlung, Ein Buchgeschäft.
A book.	Un livre.	Ein Buch.
A cheap edition.	Une édition à bon marché.	Eine billige Ausgabe.
A guide [book].	Un livret-guide, Un guide [de tourisme].	Ein Reiseführer.
A railway guide.	Un indicateur des chemins de fer.	Ein Kursbuch.
A magazine (*periodical*).	Une revue, Un magazine.	Eine Zeitschrift.
A pictorial.	Un journal illustré.	Eine illustrierte Zeitung.
Let me have some light reading, some fiction, a detective story, a novel with a sex interest, a book of short stories.	Donnez-moi quelques livres d'agrément, des romans, un roman policier, un roman intime, un livre de contes *ou* de nouvelles.	Geben Sie mir etwas Leichtes zum Lesen, ein paar Romane, einen Kriminalroman, einen erotischen Roman, ein Buch mit Novellen.
Is the edition out of print ?	L'édition est-elle épuisée ?	Ist die Ausgabe vergriffen ?
A circulating (*or* A lending) library.	Une bibliothèque circulante *ou* de prêt à domicile.	Eine Leihbibliothek.
How much is the subscription ?	Combien [est] l'abonnement ?	Was kostet das Abonnement ?
A public lending library.	Une bibliothèque municipale de prêt à domicile.	Eine öffentliche Leihbibliothek.
Can I have a look at the author catalogue, the subject catalogue ?	Puis-je consulter le catalogue des noms d'auteurs, le catalogue par ordre de matières ?	Kann ich mir den Autorenkatalog, den Inhaltskatalog, ansehen ?
Can I borrow a book ?	Puis-je emprunter un livre ?	Kann ich ein Buch ausborgen ?
How long can I keep it ?	Combien de temps puis-je le garder ?	Wie lange kann ich es behalten ?
A reference library.	Une bibliothèque où les livres se consultent sur place ; *Aussi:* Une bibliothèque d'ouvrages à consulter.	Eine Nachschlagebibliothek ; *Auch:* Eine Handbibliothek.

A bootmaker	Un bottier	Ein Schuhmacher, Ein Schuster
A shoemaker.	Un cordonnier.	Ein Schuhmacher, Ein Schuster.
A boot and shoe repairer.	Un cordonnier.	Ein Schuster.

Quando posso averlo?	¿Para cuándo puedo tenerlo?	Wanneer kunt U het me leveren?
Per quando lo potete fare? Non mancate di parola.	¿Cuándo es lo más pronto que puede usted hacerlo? No me falte.	Voor wanneer kunt U het doen? Laat me niet in de steek.
Devo aspettare o ritornare?	¿Me espero o vuelvo más tarde?	Zal ik wachten of weer langs komen?

Un libraio, Le biblioteche	**Un librero, Las bibliotecas**	**Een boekhandelaar, Bibliotheken**
◄Una libreria.	Una librería.	Een boekwinkel, Een boekhandel.
Un libro.	Un libro.	Een boek.
Un'edizione economica.	Una edición barata.	Een goedkope uitgave.
Una guida.	Un guía para viajeros o de turismo.	Een gids.
Una guida ferroviaria.	Un guía de ferrocarril.	Een spoorgids.
◄Una rivista.	Una revista.	Een tijdschrift.
Un giornale illustrato.	Una ilustración.	Een geïllustreerd blad.
Datemi qualche libro piacevole, qualche romanzo, un romanzo poliziesco, un romanzo passionale, un libro di novelle.	Déme alguna literatura ligera, alguna literatura novelesca, un cuento de detective, una novela de amorios, un libro de historietas.	Geef me wat lichte lectuur, wat romanliteratuur, een detectiveverhaal, een realistische roman, een boek met korte verhalen.
È esaurita questa edizione?	¿Está agotada esta edición?	Is de uitgave uitverkocht?
Una biblioteca circolante o di prestito.	Una biblioteca circulante o de préstamo.	Een uitleenbibliotheek.
◄Quanto è l'abbonamento?	¿Cuánto es la suscrición?	Hoeveel is de contributie?
Una biblioteca pubblica di prestito.	Una biblioteca municipal de préstamo.	Een openbare uitleenbibliotheek.
Posso consultare il catalogo per nomi d'autori, per soggetto?	¿Puedo ver la lista de autores, el catálogo de materia o de temas?	Kan ik de auteurscatalogus, de onderwerpencatalogus, even raadplegen?
Posso avere in prestito un libro?	¿Puedo tomar un libro prestado?	Kan ik een boek lenen?
Quanto tempo posso tenerlo?	¿Por cuánto tiempo puedo retenerlo?	Hoelang kan ik het houden?
◄Una biblioteca con libri da consultarsi sul posto; Anche: Una biblioteca per ricerche.	Una biblioteca de consulta.	Een bibliotheek, waar men boeken ter plaatse raadpleegt; Ook: Een referentie bibliotheek.

Uno stivalaio	**Un zapatero**	**Een schoenmaker**
Un calzolaio.	Un zapatero.	Een schoenmaker.
Un calzolaio per accomodature.	Un reparador de calzado.	Een schoenmaker.

Boots (high).	Des chaussures [montantes], Des bottes.	Stiefel.
Boots (half boots).	Des bottines.	Halbstiefel.
Shoes.	Des chaussures, Des souliers.	Schuhe.
For Sports shoes, see under Cycling, Walking, MOUNTAINEERING, BATHING.		
Bar shoes.	Des chaussures à barrette(s).	Spangenschuhe.
Brown shoes (yellowish).	Des chaussures jaunes.	Hellbraune Schuhe.
Brown shoes (tan).	Des chaussures havane.	Braune Schuhe.
Court shoes.	Des souliers décolletés.	Pumps.
Dress shoes (men's).	Des chaussures vernies (ou Des vernis) pour soirées.	Lackschuhe, Abendschuhe.
Galoshes or Overshoes.	Des caoutchoucs, Des couvre-chaussures.	Gummischuhe, Überschuhe.
Lace-up shoes.	Des souliers Richelieu.	Schnürschuhe.
Slippers.	Des pantoufles.	Pantoffeln.
Boot-laces.	Des lacets de chaussures.	Schubänder.
A buttonhook.	Un tire-bouton.	Ein Schuhknöpfer.
The size (in boots). I take eights, English size. A size larger, smaller.	La pointure. J'ai huit de pointure, pointure anglaise. Une pointure au-dessus, au-dessous.	Die Größe. Ich trage Größe acht, nach englischem Maß. Eine Nummer größer, kleiner.
Please mend, re-sole, re-heel, these shoes, rubber heels.	Veuillez raccommoder, ressemeler, remettre des talons à, ces souliers, talons en caoutchouc.	Würden Sie bitte diese Schuhe ausbessern, neu besohlen, an diese Schuhe neue Absätze machen, Gummiabsätze.
A chemist	**Un pharmacien**	**Ein Apotheker**
See also MEDICAL, pp. 258-265, and for Cosmetics, etc., see A hairdresser, pp. 188-193.)		
A chemist's shop.	Une pharmacie.	Eine Apotheke.
Give me, please, 30 grammes (=about an ounce) of carbonate of soda, 3 centilitres (= about an ounce) of tincture of iodine. (See WEIGHTS AND MEASURES, p. 266.)	Donnez-moi, s'il vous plaît, trente grammes de carbonate de soude, trois centilitres de teinture d'iode.	Geben Sie mir bitte dreißig Gramm kohlensaures Natron, drei Zentiliter Jodtinktur.
Please make up this prescription. When will it be ready?	Veuillez préparer cette ordonnance. Quand sera-t-elle prête?	Können Sie mir bitte dieses Rezept herstellen. Wann ist es fertig?
Absorbent (or Medicated) cotton wool.	Du coton hydrophile.	Medizinische Watte.
An antidote.	Un antidote, Un contre-poison.	Ein Gegengift.
An antiseptic.	Un antiseptique.	Ein antiseptisches Mittel.
An aperient.	Un laxatif, Un purgatif.	Ein Abführmittel.

Gli stivali.	Botas.	Laarzen.
◀Gli stivaletti.	Botines.	Bottines.
Le scarpe.	Zapatos.	Schoenen.
La scarpa con cinghia.	Zapatos de calle para mujer.	Riemschoenen.
Le scarpe gialle.	Zapatos de color claro.	Lichtbruine schoenen, Beige schoenen.
Le scarpe avana.	Zapatos de color.	Bruine schoenen.
◀Le scarpe scollate.	Zapatos bajos para mujer.	Pumps.
Le scarpe da società.	Zapatos de etiqueta.	Lakschoenen.
Le galosce.	Zapatos de goma.	Overschoenen.
Le scarpe con stringhe.	Zapatos de cordones.	Veterschoenen, Molières.
Le pantofole.	Zapatillas, Chancletas.	Pantoffels.
◀Le stringhe per scarpe.	Cordones para zapatos.	Schoenveters.
L'allacciabottoni.	Un abotonador.	Een knopehaak.
La grandezza o Il numero. Io porto otto, misura inglese. Un numero più grande, più piccolo.	La medida. Mi medida es la del número ocho, medida inglesa. Una medida más grande, más pequeña.	De maat. Ik neem maat acht, Engelse maat. Een grotere, kleinere, maat.
Prego raccomodarmi, risuolarmi, rimettere tacchi a, queste scarpe, tacchi di gomma.	Haga el favor de componer, poner nuevas suelas, nuevos tacones, a estos zapatos, tacones de caucho.	Kunt U deze schoenen repareren, verzolen, nieuwe hakken op deze schoenen zetten, rubber hakken.

Un farmacista	**Un farmacéutico**	**Een apotheker**
Una farmacia.	Una farmacia.	Een apotheek.
◀Per favore, datemi trenta grammi di carbonato di soda, tre centilitri di tintura di iodio.	Haga el favor de darme treinta gramos de carbonato de sosa, tres centilitros de tintura de yodo.	Geef me, als 't U belieft, dertig gram koolzure soda, drie centiliter jodiumtinctuur.
Per favore, preparatemi questa ricetta. Quando sarà pronta ?	Haga el favor de prepararme esta receta. ¿ Cuándo estará lista ?	Maak dit recept klaar, als 't U belieft. Wanneer is het klaar of gereed?
Il cotone idrofilo.	Algodón hidrófilo.	Hydrofiele watten.
Un antidoto, Un contravveleno.	Un antídoto.	Een tegengift.
Un antisettico.	Un antiséptico.	Een antiseptisch middel.
◀Un aperitivo, Un purgativo.	Un purgante, Un laxante.	Een laxeermiddel.

An aspirin [tablet].	Un comprimé d'aspirine.	Ein Aspirin.
A bandage. To bandage.	Un bandage. Bander.	Ein Verband. Verbinden.
Bath salts.	Du sel pour bain.	Badesalz.
Boracic acid.	De l'acide borique.	Borwasser.
Castor oil.	De l'huile de ricin.	Rhizinusöl.
A chemical. Chemicals.	Un produit chimique. Des produits chimiques.	Ein chemisches Mittel. Chemikalien.
Cod liver oil.	De l'huile de foie de morue.	Lebertran.
Cold cream.	De la crème de toilette.	Fettcreme.
A corn cure.	Un remède contre les cors.	Ein Hühneraugenmittel.
Cotton wool.	De l'ouate [de coton].	Watte.
Cough lozenges.	Des pastilles pour la toux.	Hustenbonbons.
A cough mixture.	Un sirop pour la toux.	Ein Hustenmittel, Ein Hustensirup.
Court plaster.	Du taffetas d'Angleterre.	Englischpflaster.
Embrocation.	De l'embrocation.	Eine Einreibung.
Epsom salt[s].	Du sel d'Epsom.	Epsom Salz.
Glycerin[e].	De la glycérine.	Glyzerin.
Insect powder.	De la poudre insecticide.	Insektenpulver.
Lint.	De la charpie.	Verbandmull.
A medicine or A physic.	Une médecine, Un médicament.	Eine Medizin, Eine Arzneimittel, Ein Medikament.
Menthol.	Du menthol.	Menthol.
Mouth wash.	De l'eau dentifrice.	Mundwasser.
An ointment.	Un onguent.	Eine Salbe.
A patent (or A proprietary) medicine.	Une spécialité pharmaceutique.	Ein gesetzlich geschütztes (ges. gesch.) Arzneimittel.
Peroxide of hydrogen.	De l'eau oxygénée.	Wasserstoffsuperoxyd.
Pills.	Des pilules.	Pillen.
A plaster.	Un emplâtre.	Ein Pflaster.
Quinine.	De la quinine.	Chinin.
A packet of sanitary towels.	Un paquet de serviettes hygiéniques.	Ein Paket Damenbinden.
Scent.	Du parfum.	Parfum.
A sedative.	Un sédatif, Un calmant.	Ein Beruhigungsmittel.
A Seidlitz powder.	Un sel de Sedlitz.	Seydlitzpulver.
Smelling salts.	Des sels [volatils] anglais, Des sels à respirer.	Riechsalze.
A cake of toilet soap.	Un pain de savon de toilette.	Ein Stück Toilettenseife.
A sponge.	Une éponge.	Ein Schwamm.
Sticking plaster.	De l'emplâtre adhésif.	Heftpflaster.
Toilet paper. A toilet roll.	Du papier hygiénique. Un rouleau hygiénique.	Toilettepapier, Klosettpapier. Eine Rolle Klosettpapier.
A tonic.	Un tonique, Un remontant.	Ein Stärkungsmittel.
A tooth brush.	Une brosse à dents.	Eine Zahnbürste.
Tooth paste, powder.	De la pâte, De la poudre, dentifrice.	Zahnpaste, Zahnpulver.

Una compressa di aspirina.	Una pastilla de aspirina.	Een aspirientje.
Una fascia. Fasciare.	Una venda. Vendar.	Een verband. Verbinden.
I sali per bagno.	Sales para el baño.	Badzout.
L'acido borico.	Ácido bórico.	Boorzuur.
◄ L'olio di ricino.	Aceite de castor.	Wonderolie.
Un prodotto chimico. I prodotti chimici.	Un producto químico. Productos químicos.	Een chemisch product. Chemische producten.
L'olio di fegato di merluzzo.	Aceite de hígado de bacalao.	Levertraan.
La crema per toeletta.	Crema de tocador.	Coldcream.
Un rimedio contro i calli, Un callifugo.	Un remedio para los callos.	Een middel tegen eksterogen.
◄ L'ovatta.	Algodón en rama.	Watten.
Le pastiglie per la tosse.	Pastillas para la tos.	Hoesttabletjes, Hoestpastilles.
Uno sciroppo per la tosse.	Una medicina (o Un jarabe) para la tos.	Een hoestdrank.
Il taffetà inglese.	Esparadrapo, Tafetán inglés.	Engelse pleister.
Una embrocazione.	Embrocación.	Een wrijfmiddel.
◄ Il sale d'Inghilterra, Il solfato di magnesia.	Sal de Higuera, Sales de Epsom.	Epsom zout.
La glicerina.	Glicerina.	Glycerine.
La polvere insetticida.	Polvos insecticidas.	Insektenpoeder.
La filaccia di cotone.	Hilas.	Pluksel.
Una medicina, Un medicamento.	Una medicina, Un medicamento.	Een geneesmiddel.
◄ Il mentolo.	Mentol.	Menthol.
L'acqua dentifricia.	Agua dentífrica.	Mondwater.
Un unguento.	Un ungüento.	Een zalf.
Una specialità farmaceutica.	Un remedio de patente.	Een patent-geneesmiddel.
L'acqua ossigenata.	Agua oxijenada.	Waterstof-peroxide.
◄ Le pillole.	Píldoras.	Pillen.
Un impiastro.	Un emplasto.	Een pleister.
Il chinino.	Quinina.	Kinine.
Un pacco di salviettine igieniche.	Un paquete de toallas higiénicas.	Een pak maandverband.
Il profumo.	Perfume.	Parfum, Odeur.
◄ Un sedativo, Un calmante.	Un calmante.	Een kalmerend middel.
Un sale di Seidlitz.	Un polvo de Seidlitz.	Een Seidlitzpoeder.
Il sale ammoniaco odoroso, I sali da aspirare.	Sales aromáticas.	Vlugzout.
Una saponetta da toeletta.	Una pastilla de jabón de tocador.	Een stuk toiletzeep.
Una spugna.	Una esponja.	Een spons.
◄ Il cerotto adesivo.	Emplasto adhesivo.	Hechtpleister.
La carta igienica. Un rotolo di carta igienica.	Papel para excusados. Un rollo de papel higiénico.	Closetpapier. Een rol closetpapier.
Un tonico.	Un tónico, Un reconstituyente.	Een versterkend middel.
Uno spazzolino per denti.	Un cepillo de dientes.	Een tandenborstel.
La pasta dentifricia, Il dentifricio in polvere.	Pasta dentífrica, Polvos para los dientes.	Tandpasta, Tandpoeder.

Clothes	L'habillement	Kleidung
(See also pp. 126-127.)		
A [general] draper.	Un marchand, Une marchande, de nouveautés.	Ein Tuchhändler, Ein Stoffgeschäft.
A fancy draper.	Un linger, Une lingère.	Ein Kurzwarenhändler.
A linen draper.	Une maison de blanc.	Ein Wäschegeschäft.
Drapery.	Des nouveautés.	Modeartikel.
Drapery (cloth).	La draperie.	Stoffe, Tuchwaren.
A dressmaker.	Une entrepreneuse de confection.	Ein Geschäft für Damenkleidung.
A dressmaker (tailoress).	Une couturière.	Eine Schneiderin.
A hatter. A hat shop.	Un chapelier. Une chapellerie.	Ein Hutmacher. Ein Hutgeschäft.
A hosier.	Un bonnetier.	Ein Strumpfwarenhändler, Eine Strumpfhandlung.
Hosiery.	De la bonneterie.	Strumpfwaren.
A milliner.	Une modiste, Un marchand, Une marchande, de modes.	Eine Putzmacherin, Ein Putzgeschäft, Ein Hutsalon.
Millinery.	Modes, Articles de modes.	Putzwaren, Modewaren.
A tailor.	Un tailleur.	Ein Schneider.
A sports outfitter.	Une maison pour fournitures de sports.	Ein Sportwarengeschäft.
Art needlework.	Des ouvrages de dames.	Feine Handarbeit.
A pattern or A model.	Un modèle.	Ein Muster.
A pattern or A sample.	Un échantillon.	Ein Muster.
The size (in gloves, hats, collars, etc.). My collar size is forty centimetres.	La pointure. Ma pointure de col est de quarante centimètres.	Die Größe. Meine Kragenweite ist vierzig Zentimeter.
Chest measurement.	La grosseur (ou Le tour) de poitrine.	Brustweite.
Hip measurement.	Le tour de hanches.	Hüftweite.
A tailor-made (or A tailored) costume.	Un costume [fait par] tailleur.	Ein Schneiderkostüm.
Show me (or Let me see) your patterns, the latest fashion (or style), the present-day fashions.	Montrez-moi (ou Faites-moi voir) vos échantillons, la dernière mode, les actualités de la mode.	Zeigen Sie mir Ihre Muster, die neusten Modelle, was man heute trägt.
I want (a) some sewing needles, (b) knitting needles, (c) pins, (d) safety pins, (e) cotton, (f) linen thread, (g) wool, (h) silk ribbon, (i) a thimble, (j) a pair of scissors, (k) buckles, (l) buttons, (m) hooks and eyes.	Je désire [avoir] (a) des aiguilles à coudre, (b) des aiguilles à tricoter, (c) des épingles, (d) des épingles de sûreté, (e) du coton, (f) du fil de lin, (g) de la laine, (h) du ruban de soie, (i) un dé [à coudre], (j) des ciseaux, (k) des boucles, (l) des boutons, (m) des agrafes et portes.	Ich möchte (a) Nähnadeln, (b) Stricknadeln, (c) Stecknadeln, (d) Sicherheitsnadeln, (e) Baumwollgarn, (f) Zwirn, (g) Wolle, (h) Seidenband, (i) Einen Fingerhut, (j) Eine Schere, (k) Schnallen, (l) Knöpfe, (m) Haken und Ösen.
Show me the stuff in the piece.	Faites-moi voir l'étoffe en pièce.	Zeigen Sie den Stoff bitte im Ganzen.

Vestiti	Ropas	Kleding
◄Un mercante di pannine.	Un mercero.	Een manufacturier.
Un mercante (*o* Un negoziante) d'articoli di fantasia.	Un mercero de novedades.	Een lingeriewinkel.
Un mercante di tela.	Un lencero, Una lencera.	Een linnenwinkel.
Delle novità.	Mercería.	Manufacturen.
La drapperia.	Pañería.	Laken.
◄Una sarta.	Una modista.	Een dameskleermaker, (*feminne*) Een modiste.
Una sarta.	Una modista de sastería.	Een naaister.
Un cappellaio. Una cappelleria.	Un sombrerero. Una sombrerería.	Een hoedenmaker. Een hoedenwinkel.
Un calzettaio.	Un calcetero.	Een handelaar in gebreid of geweven goed.
La calzetteria.	Calcetería.	Gebreid of geweven goed.
◄Una modista.	Una modista.	Een modiste.
Gli articoli di modista.	Artículos de moda.	Mode-artikelen.
Un sarto.	Un sastre.	Een kleermaker.
Un fornitore di indumenti sportivi.	Una casa de equipos para deportes.	Een sportwinkel.
I lavori d'ago fino.	Labores finos hechos con aguja.	Fijne handwerken.
◄Un modello.	Un modelo.	Een patroon, Een staal.
Un campione.	Una muestra.	Een monster.
La grandezza, Il numero. La grandezza del mio collo è di quaranta centimetri.	La medida. Mi medida para cuellos es de cuarenta centímetros.	De maat. Mijn maat in boorden is veertig centimeter.
La misura del petto.	Medida de pecho.	De borstmaat.
La misura delle anche.	Medida de cadera.	De heupmaat.
◄Un costume tailleur.	Un traje de señora hecho por sastre.	Een tailleur, Een mantelpak.
Mostratemi i vostri campioni, l'ultima moda, le mode del giorno.	Déjeme ver sus muestras, la última moda, las modas corrientes.	Laat me Uw stalen zien, de nieuwste mode, de hedendaagse mode.
Io desidero (*a*) degli aghi da cucire, (*b*) i ferri per maglia, (*c*) gli spilli, (*d*) le spille di sicurezza, (*e*) il cotone, (*f*) del filo di refe, (*g*) della lana, (*h*) un nastro di seta, (*i*) un ditale, (*j*) un paio di forbici, (*k*) delle fibbie, (*l*) dei bottoni, (*m*) dei ganci e delle magliette.	Necesito (*a*) unas agujas para coser, (*b*) unas agujas para medias, (*c*) unos alfileres, (*d*) unos imperdibles, (*e*) hilo de coser, (*f*) hilo de lino, (*g*) lana, (*h*) cinta de seda, (*i*) un dedal, (*j*) un par de tijeras, (*k*) hebillas, (*l*) botones, (*m*) corchetes y corchetas.	Ik wens (*a*) wat naainaalden, (*b*) breinaalden, (*c*) spelden, (*d*) veiligheidsspelden, (*e*) katoen, (*f*) linnen draad, (*g*) wol, (*h*) zijden lint, (*i*) een vingerhoed, (*j*) een schaar, (*k*) gespen, (*l*) knopen, (*m*) haken en ogen.
Fatemi vedere la stoffa in pezza.	Déjeme ver el género en la pieza entera.	Laat me de stof aan de rol zien.

Do you keep (*or* stock) outsizes?	Tenez-vous des tailles hors série?	Führen Sie Größen für die starke Figur?
I want a soft felt (*hat*) of the same shape as the one I am wearing.	Je voudrais un feutre souple (*ou* mou) de la même forme que celui-ci que je porte.	Ich möchte einen weichen Filzhut, dieselbe Form wie der, den ich aufhabe.
The brim is too wide, too narrow.	Le bord est trop large trop étroit.	Der Rand ist zu breit, zu schmal.
How does it suit me?	Comment me va-t-il?	Wie steht er mir?
Can this hat be altered?	Ce chapeau peut-il être transformé?	Kann dieser Hut geändert werden?
How long will it take to alter it *or* to put it right?	Combien de temps faut-il pour le rectifier?	Wie lange dauert die Änderung?
I want a lounge suit.	Il me faut un complet veston.	Ich möchte einen Straßenanzug.
Measure me for an overcoat, single-breasted, double-breasted.	Prenez-moi mesure pour un pardessus, droit, croisé.	Nehmen Sie bitte Maß für einen einreihigen, zweireihigen, Überzieher *oder* Mantel.
When shall I call to try it on?	Quand dois-je venir pour l'essayer?	Wann kann ich zur Anprobe kommen?
I will wear it now.	Je le mets tout de suite.	Ich ziehe ihn gleich an.
This garment does not fit, does not suit me. It is too tight, too loose.	Ce vêtement ne va pas, ne me sied pas. C'est trop serré, trop lâche.	Dieses Kleidungsstück sitzt nicht, steht mir nicht. Es ist zu eng, zu weit.
Please press these trousers.	Veuillez donner un coup de fer à ce pantalon.	Würden Sie bitte die Hosen bügeln.
How much is this cloth a metre?	Combien vendez-vous ce drap le mètre?	Wieviel kostet dieser Stoff pro Meter?
What do you charge for dry cleaning this suit?	Combien prenez-vous pour nettoyer à sec ce complet?	Was kostet es, diesen Anzug trocken reinigen zu lassen?
A belt.	Une ceinture.	Ein Gürtel.
A beret.	Un béret basque.	Eine Baskenmütze.
A blouse.	Une blouse.	Eine Bluse.
Braces (*men's*).	Des bretelles.	Hosenträger.
A cap.	Une casquette.	Eine Kappe, Eine Mütze.
A cape.	Une pèlerine.	Ein Umhang, Ein Cape.
Dress clothes (*men's*).	Des habits de soirée.	Abendkleidung.
A coat (*man's*).	Un manteau.	Ein Mantel.
A coat (*man's overcoat*).	Un pardessus.	Ein Überzieher.
A coat (*woman's*).	Une redingote.	Ein Mantel.
A coat (*woman's long*).	Un manteau.	Ein Mantel.
A coat (*woman's short*).	Une jaquette.	Eine Jacke.
A coat (*woman's woolly*).	Un gilet.	Eine Wolljacke.
A covert coat.	Un paletot.	Ein leichter Überzieher.
A dress coat.	Un habit de soirée.	Ein Frack.
A fur coat.	Un manteau de fourrure.	Ein Pelzmantel.
A rain coat.	Un manteau de pluie.	Ein Regenmantel.
A sports coat.	Un manteau [de] sport.	Ein Sportmantel.

Tenete dei tagli fuori misura?	¿Tiene usted tamaños desmesurados?	Heeft U zeer grote maten in voorraad?
→Io vorrei un feltro floscio della stessa forma di quello che porto.	Necesito un sombrero flexible de igual hechura al que llevo puesto.	Ik zou graag een slappe vilthoed willen hebben, dezelfde vorm als die ik op heb.
La tesa è troppo larga, troppo stretta.	El ala es demasiado ancha, demasiado angosta.	De rand is te breed, te smal.
Come mi sta o va?	¿Cómo me sienta?	Hoe staat hij me?
Questo cappello si può modificare?	¿Puede modificarse este sombrero?	Kan deze hoed vermaakt worden?
Quanto tempo prende per modificarlo?	¿Cuánto tiempo tardará en hacerse la modificación?	Hoe lang duurt het om hem te vermaken of in orde te laten brengen?
→Io desidero un vestito completo da mattina.	Necesito un traje de americana.	Ik wens een colbert-kostuum.
Prendetemi la misura per un pastrano, ad un petto, a doppio petto.	Tome mis medidas para un sobretodo, de pecho sencillo, de traslapo.	Neem mij de maat voor een overjas, één rij knopen, twee rijen knopen.
Quando posso venire per provarlo?	¿Cuándo puedo venir a probármelo?	Wanneer zal ik hem komen passen?
Lo metterò subito.	Me lo llevaré puesto.	Ik houd hem meteen aan.
Questo vestito non mi sta bene, non mi si confà. È troppo stretto, troppo largo.	Esta prenda no se me ajusta bien, no me sienta bien. Me está demasiado apretada, demasiado suelta.	Dit kledingstuk past niet, staat me niet. Het is te strak, te wijd.
→Per favore, pressatemi questi calzoni.	Haga el favor de plancharme este pantalón.	Wilt U deze pantalon persen.
Quanto costa questa stoffa al metro?	¿Cuánto vale este paño el metro?	Hoeveel kost dit laken per meter?
Che spesa porta il pulire a secco questo vestito completo?	¿Cuánto lleva usted por limpiar este traje?	Wat kost het om dit pak chemisch te laten reinigen?
Una cinta.	Un cinturón.	Een riem.
Un berretto basco.	Una boina.	Een muts.
→Una blusa, Una blusetta.	Una blusa.	Een blouse.
Le bretelle.	Tirantes.	Bretels.
Un berretto.	Una gorra.	Een pet.
Un mantello, Una pellegrina.	Una capa.	Een pelerine, Een cape.
Un abito da società.	Ropa de etiqueta.	Avondkleding.
→Una giubba.	Un gabán.	Een jas.
Un pastrano.	Un sobretodo.	Een overjas.
Un cappotto.	Un redingote.	Een mantel.
Una redingote.	Un redingote.	Een jas.
Una giacca.	Una chaqueta.	Een jasje.
→Un gilet.	Un abrigo de lana.	Een wollen jasje.
Un paletot.	Una gabardina.	Een korte overjas.
Un abito a coda di rondine.	Un frac.	Een rok[kostuum].
Una pelliccia.	Un abrigo de pieles.	Een bontjas, Een bontmantel.
Un impermeabile.	Un impermeable.	Een regenjas.
→Una giacca da sport.	Una chaqueta para deportes.	Een sportjas.

Colours: (a) black, (b) blue, (c) brown, (d) green, (e) grey, (f) pink, (g) red, (h) violet, (i) white, (j) yellow; (k) light, (l) dark.	Couleurs: (a) noir, (b) bleu, (c) brun, (d) vert, (e) gris, (f) rose, (g) rouge, (h) violet, (i) blanc, (j) jaune; (k) clair, (l) foncé.	Farben: (a) schwarz, (b) blau, (c) braun, (d) grün, (e) grau, (f) rosa, (g) rot, (h) lila, (i) weiß, (j) gelb; (k) hell, (l) dunkel.
A corset.	Un corset.	Ein Hüfthalter.
Evening dress (man's).	La tenue de soirée.	Abendanzug.
Evening dress (woman's).	La toilette de soirée.	Abenkleid.
A walking [out] dress.	Une robe de ville.	Ein Straßenkleid.
For Bathing dress, see pp. 252-253.		
A dance frock.	Une robe de bal.	Ein Tanzkleid.
Garters.	Des jarretières.	Strumpfbänder.
Kid gloves.	Des gants de [peau de] chevreau, Des gants de chevrotin.	Glacéhandhschuhe.
An evening gown.	Une robe du soir.	Ein Abendkleid.
A dressing gown.	Une robe de chambre, Un peignoir saut de lit.	Ein Morgenrock, Ein Schlafrock.
A coat (or A clothes) hanger.	Un porte-vêtements.	Ein Kleiderbügel.
A jacket.	Un veston.	Eine Jacke.
A bed jacket.	Une liseuse.	Eine Bettjacke.
A cardigan [jacket], A spencer [coat].	Un gilet, Une vareuse.	Eine Strickjacke.
A dinner jacket.	Un smoking.	Ein Smoking.
A dressing jacket.	Une matinée.	Eine Frisierjacke.
A jumper.	Une casaque.	Ein Jumper.
A dress protector.	Un dessous de bras.	Ein Armblatt.
A pull-over.	Un pull-over.	Ein Pullover.
Pyjamas or A sleeping suit.	Un pyjama.	Ein Pyjama, Ein Schlafanzug.
A scarf (man's).	Un cache-col.	Ein Schal, Ein Halstuch.
A scarf (woman's), A stole.	Une écharpe.	Ein Schal.
A two-piece suit or costume (coat and skirt).	Un ensemble deux pièces.	Ein Complet.
A shawl.	Un châle.	Ein Schal.
A skirt.	Une jupe.	Ein Rock.
Slacks (women's).	Un pantalon, Une culotte.	Lange Hosen.
Men's socks.	Des chaussettes pour hommes.	Herrensocken.
Ankle socks.	Des socquettes.	Söckchen.
Shoulder straps (women's).	Des bretelles.	Achselbänder.
Suspenders.	Des jarretelles.	Strumpfhalter.
A suspender belt.	Une ceinture porte-jarretelles.	Ein Strumpfbandgürtel.
Sock suspenders.	Des supports-chaussettes.	Sockenhalter.
A sweater.	Un chandail.	Ein Sweater.
A [neck]tie.	Une cravate.	Ein Schlips, Eine Kravatte.
An open-end tie.	Une [cravate] régate.	Ein langer Schlips.

Colori: (a) nero, (b) azzurro, (c) bruno, (d) verde, (e) grigio, (f) color rosa, (g) rosso, (h) violaceo, (i) bianco, (j) giallo; (k) chiaro, (l) scuro.	Colores: (a) negro, (b) azul, (c) moreno, (d) verde, (e) gris, (f) color de rosa, (g) rojo, (h) violeta, (i) blanco, (j) amarillo (k) claro, (l) obscuro.	Kleuren: (a) zwart, (b) blauw, (c) bruin, (d) groen, (e) grijs, (f) roze, (g) rood, (h) paars, (i) wit, (j) geel; (k) licht, (l) donker.
Un busto.	Un corsé.	Een korset.
Un abbigliamento da sera.	Un traje de frac.	Avondkleding, Avond-tenue.
Una toeletta da società.	Vestido de soirée.	Avondtoilet.
◄Un abito da passeggio.	Un traje de paseo.	Een middagjapon.
Un abito da ballo.	Un traje de baile.	Een baljapon.
Le giarrettiere.	Ligas.	Kousebanden.
I guanti di pelle di capretto.	Guantes de cabritilla.	Glacé handschoenen.
Una veste da sera.	Un traje de soirée.	Een avondjapon, Een avondtoilet.
◄Una vestaglia, Una veste da camera.	Una bata.	Een kamerjas, Een peig-noir.
Un attaccapanni.	Un colgadero.	Een klerenhanger, Een knaapje.
Una giacchetta.	Una chaqueta.	Een jasje.
Un matinée.	Una chaqueta de cama.	Een bedjasje.
Uno spenser[re], Una giacchetta.	Un cardigan, Una chaqueta de punto.	Een gebreid jasje.
◄Uno smoking.	Un smoking.	Een smoking.
Un matinée.	Un peinador.	Een ochtendjasje.
Un giubbettino, Un golf.	Un jumper.	Een trui.
I sottobraccia.	Una sobaquera.	Een sousbras.
Un pull-over.	Un pull-over.	Een pull-over.
◄Un [costume] pigiama.	Un pijama.	Een pyjama.
Una sciarpa.	Una bufanda.	Een das.
Una sciarpa.	Una palatina.	Een das, Een sjaal.
Un [costume] tailleur.	Un traje de falda y chaqueta.	Een deux-pièces.
Uno scialle.	Un pañolón.	Een sjaal.
◄Una sottana.	Una falda.	Een rok.
I calzoni, I pantaloni.	Un pantalón [de mujer], Bombachas.	Een lange broek, Een pantalon.
I calzini.	Calcetines de hombre.	Herensokken.
Le solette.	Calcetines de señora.	Anklets.
Le bretelle.	Tirantes de señora.	Schouderbandjes.
◄Le giarrettiere.	Suspendedores para medias.	Jarretels.
Una cinta porta bretelle.	Un cinturón de soporte.	Een jarretel-ceintuur.
Le cigne da calzini.	Ligas de hombre.	Sokophouders.
Una maglia a maniche lunghe.	Un jersey, Una chaqueta elástica de punto.	Een wollen sporttrui, Een sweater.
Una cravatta.	Una corbata.	Een das.
◄Una cravatta da regata.	Una corbata de cabo suelto.	Een das met open einde.

A bow [necktie].	Un nœud [-papillon].	Ein Querbinder.
A dress bow.	Une cravate de soirée.	Eine Frackkravatte, Eine Smokingkravatte.
A shirt stud.	Un bouton de chemise.	Ein Kragenknopf.
[A pair of] trousers.	Un pantalon.	Eine Hose.
Underclothing or Underwear or Foundation garments (women's).	Des [vêtements de] dessous.	Unterkleidung, Unterwäsche.
Underclothing or Underwear (men's).	Des sous-vêtements.	Unterkleidung, Unterwäsche.
(For specific articles of underclothing, see pp. 126-127.)		
A waistcoat.	Un gilet.	Eine Weste.
A waterproof.	Un imperméable, Un caoutchouc.	Ein Regenmantel, Ein Gummimantel.
A wrap (shawl).	Un tour de cou.	Ein Tuch, Ein Schal.
A wrap (evening).	Un manteau [du soir], Une sortie de bal ou de théâtre.	Ein Abendcape, Ein Abendumhang.
A wrap (bath or bathing).	Un peignoir de bain, Une sortie de bain.	Ein Bademantel, Ein Badecape.
A zip[p] (or A slide) fastener.	Une fermeture instantanée, Un fermoir à curseur.	Ein Reißverschluss.

A hairdresser	**Un coiffeur, Une coiffeuse**	**Ein Frisör, Eine Frisöse**
A barber.	Un barbier.	Ein Barbier.
A beard.	Une barbe.	Ein Bart.
A beauty parlour.	Un institut de beauté.	Ein Schönheitssalon.
Beauty preparations.	Des produits de beauté.	Schönheitsmittel.
Bobbed hair or A bob.	Des cheveux courts, genre Mistinguett.	Ein Bubikopf.
A French bob.	Une coiffure à la Jeanne d'Arc.	Ein Bubikopf mit Ponies.
The page-boy style, The dauphin style [of hairdressing].	La (ou Une) coiffure page, dauphin.	Der (oder Ein) Pagenkopf, Die Pagenfrisur.
A shingle, Shingled hair.	Une coupe à la garçonne, Les cheveux coupés à la garçonne.	Ein abgestufter Haarschnitt, Abgestufte Haare.
Brillantine.	De la brillantine.	Brillantine.
Chiropody.	Le soin des pieds.	Fußpflege.
A chiropodist.	Un(e) pédicure.	Ein(e) Pediküre.
A compact [powder].	Une [poudre] compacte, Un fard compact.	Kompakt-Puder.
A cosmetic.	Un cosmétique.	Ein kosmetisches Mittel.
A curl.	Une boucle, Un frison.	Eine Locke.
To curl the hair.	Friser les cheveux.	Das Haar locken.
Day (or Vanishing) cream.	De la crème de beauté.	Tagescreme, Mattcreme.
An eyebrow pencil.	Un crayon pour les yeux.	Ein Augenbrauenstift.
Eyebrow tweezers.	Des pinces à épiler.	Eine Augenbrauenpinzette.
Face massage.	Le massage facial.	Gesichtsmassage.

Una cravatta a fiocco.	Una corbata de lazo.	Een vlinderdas.
Una cravatta da società.	Una corbata de frac.	Een vlinderdas voor avondtenue.
Un bottoncino da camicia.	Un pasador de camisa.	Een overhemdsknoopje.
Un paio di calzoni.	Un pantalón.	Een pantalon, Een broek.
◄La biancheria di sotto.	Ropa interior.	Ondergoed.
Le sottovesti.	Ropa interior.	Ondergoed.
Un corpetto, Un panciotto.	Un chaleco.	Een vest.
Un impermeabile.	Un impermeable.	Een regenjas.
Uno scialle.	Un mantón, Un pañolón.	Een sjaal, Een halsdoek.
◄Un mantello di sera.	Un manto.	Een avondjas, Een avondcape.
Un accappatoio.	Un peinador (o Una bata) de baño.	Een badjas, Een kimono.
Una chiusura scorrevole.	Un prendedor instantáneo.	Een ritssluiting.

Un parrucchiere, Una pettinatrice	Un peluquero, Un(a) peinador(a)	Een kapper
Un barbiere.	Un barbero.	Een barbier.
Una barba.	Una barba.	Een baard.
◄Un istituto di bellezza.	Un salón de belleza.	Een schoonheidssalon.
I prodotti di bellezza.	Productos para belleza.	Schoonheidsmiddelen.
I capelli corti.	Cabello corto.	Kort recht afgeknipt haar.
I capelli corti alla Giovanna d'Arco.	Un peinado estilo Juana de Arco.	Pony.
La pettinatura alla paggio.	Un peinado estilo de paje.	Een pagekop.
◄Un taglio di capelli alla garçonne.	Cabello cortado a estilo muchacho.	Een jongenskop.
La brillantina.	Brillantina.	Brillantine.
La cura dei piedi.	Pedicura.	Pedicure.
Un(a) pedicure.	Un pedicuro, Un(a) callista.	Een pedicure.
Una cipria compatta.	Polvos de tocador comprimidos en forma de pastilla.	Een crème-puff.
◄Un cosmetico.	Un cosmético.	Een schoonheidsmiddel.
Un riccio.	Un rizo, Un bucle.	Een krul.
Arricciare i capelli.	Rizar el cabello.	Het haar krullen.
La crema di bellezza.	Crema volátil de belleza.	Vanishing cream.
Il lapis per sopracciglia.	Un pincel para las cejas.	Een wenkbrauwpotlood.
◄Le pinzette per sopracciglia.	Tenacillas depilatorias.	Een epileerpincet.
Il massaggio del viso.	Masaje facial.	Gezichtsmassage.

Face (or Toilet) powder.	De la poudre de riz.	Gesichtspuder.
A fringe.	Un devant de cheveux, Des cheveux à la chien.	Ponies.
The hair.	Les cheveux.	Das Haar.
A hair brush.	Une brosse à cheveux ou à tête.	Eine Haarbürste, Eine → Kopfbürste.
A [hair] comb.	Un peigne [coiffeur].	Ein Kamm.
A hair curler.	Une épingle à friser.	Ein Lockenwickler.
Hair cutting.	La coupe (ou La taille) de cheveux.	Haarschneiden.
A hairdressing saloon.	Un salon de coiffure.	Ein Frisiersalon.
A hair drier.	Un appareil à douche d'air.	Ein elektrischer Haartrock- → ner, Eine Trockenhaube.
A hair net.	Un filet à cheveux, Une résille.	Ein Haarnetz.
A hair slide.	Une barrette pour les cheveux.	Eine Haarspange.
Hair oil.	De l'huile à cheveux.	Haaröl.
A hairpin.	Une épingle à cheveux.	Eine Haarnadel.
A hair wash.	Une lotion pour les cheveux.	Ein Haarwasser. →
A hair waver.	Une épingle à onduler.	Eine Haarklammer.
Lipstick.	Un crayon (ou Un bâton de rouge) pour les lèvres.	Lippenstift.
Manicuring.	Le soin des mains.	Handpflege, Maniküre.
To manicure the hands.	Soigner les mains.	Die Hände maniküren.
A manicurist.	Un(e) manucure.	Ein(e) Maniküre. →
A moustache.	Une moustache.	Ein Schnurrbart.
A nail brush. A nail file. [A] nail scissors.	Une brosse à ongles. Une lime à ongles. Des ciseaux à ongles.	Eine Nagelbürste. Eine Nagelfeile. Eine Nagelschere.
Nail varnish.	Du vernis pour les ongles.	Nagellack.
Night (or Cold) cream.	De la crème de toilette.	Fettcreme, Nachtcreme.
An open razor.	Un rasoir à manche.	Ein Rasiermesser. →
A plait.	Une natte, Une tresse.	Ein Zopf.
To plait.	Natter, Tresser.	Einen Zopf flechten.
A powder box.	Une boîte à poudre.	Eine Puderdose.
A powder puff.	Une houppe à poudrer.	Eine Puderquaste.
Rouge.	Du rouge.	Rouge. →
Safety razor blades.	Des lames de rasoir de sûreté.	Rasierklingen für den Rasierapparat.
A shaving brush.	Un pinceau à barbe, Un blaireau.	Ein Rasierpinsel.
Shaving cream.	De la crème pour la barbe.	Rasiercreme.
A shaving stick.	Du savon à barbe en bâton.	Rasierseife.
A strop.	Un cuir [à rasoir], Un affiloir.	Ein Streichriemen. →
A strop (for safety blades).	Un repasseur.	Ein Klingenschärfer.

La cipria da toeletta.	Polvos de tocador.	[Gezichts]poeder.
Una frangia.	Un cerquillo.	Pony[haar].
I capelli.	El pelo (*usually = man's*); El cabello (*usually = woman's*).	Het haar.
◄Una spazzola per capelli.	Un cepillo de cabeza.	Een haarborstel.
Un pettine.	Un peine.	Een kam.
Un ferro da ricci.	Una horquilla para rizar.	Een krulpen.
Il taglio di capelli.	Cortadura de pelo, de cabello.	Het haarknippen.
Una sala da parrucchiere.	Una peluquería.	Een kapperswinkel.
◄Un apparecchio per asciugare i capelli.	Un aparato para secar el cabello.	Een föhn.
Una rete per capelli.	Una albanega *o* Una redecilla [para el cabello].	Een haarnet.
Un ferma capelli.	Un sostén para el cabello.	Een sierbaarspeld.
L'olio per capelli.	Aceite para la cabeza.	Haarolie.
Una forcella.	Una horquilla.	Een haarspeld.
◄Una lozione per capelli.	Una loción para la cabeza.	Een haarwater.
Il ferro per l'ondulazione.	Una horquilla para ondear.	Een golfpen.
Il rossetto per le labbra.	Una barrita para pintarse los labios.	Een lippenstift.
La manicura.	Manicura.	Manicure.
Curare le mani.	Cuidar y arreglar las manos y las uñas.	De handen manicuren.
◄Un(a) manicure.	Un manicuro, Una manicura.	Een manicure.
I baffi.	Un bigote.	Een snor.
Una spazzola per unghie.	Un cepillo para las uñas.	Een nagelborstel. Een
Una lima per unghie.	Una lima para las uñas. Unas tijeras para las uñas.	nagelvijl. Een nagelschaar.
Le forbici per unghie.		
La vernice per le unghie.	Barniz para las uñas.	Nagellak.
La crema per toeletta.	Crema de tocador.	Coldcream.
◄Un rasoio con manico mobile.	Una navaja de afeitar.	Een open scheermes.
Una treccia.	Una trenza.	Een vlecht.
Intrecciare.	Trenzar.	Vlechten.
Una scatola da cipria.	Una polvorera.	Een poederdoos.
Un piumino per cipria.	Una borla para polvos.	Een poederkwast.
◄Il rossetto.	Colorete.	Rouge.
Le lame per rasoio di sicurezza.	Cuchillas para maquinilla de afeitar.	Veiligheidsscheermesjes.
Un pennello per barba.	Una brocha de afeitar.	Een scheerkwast.
La crema per rasarsi.	Crema de afeitar.	Scheercrème.
Un bastoncello di sapone per barba.	Jabón de afeitar en barrita.	Een staaf scheerzeep.
◄Una striscia per affilare il rasoio.	Un asentador de navajas [de afeitar].	Een aanzetriem.
Una stecca per affilare il rasoio.	Un asentador para cuchillas de maquinilla de afeitar.	Een scheermesslijper.

A style of hairdressing.	Une coiffure.	Eine Frisur.
Sunburn cream, lotion.	De la crème, De la lotion, contre le hâle.	Sonnenbrandcreme, Flüssigkeit gegen Sonnenbrand.
Sun-tan cream.	De la crème pour brunir la peau.	Creme für die Hautbräunung.
Shave or hair-cut? (*barber's question*).	Pour la barbe **ou** les cheveux ?	Rasieren oder Haarschneiden?
To shave. Shaving.	Raser. La barbe.	Rasieren. Rasieren.
I want a shave. Shave me.	Je veux me faire raser *ou* Je veux me faire faire la barbe. Rasez-moi *ou* Faites-moi la barbe.	Ich möchte mich rasieren lassen. Würden Sie mich bitte rasieren.
No spray or powder, please.	Pas de pulvérisateur ni de poudre, s'il vous plaît.	Nicht scharf nachwaschen, keinen Puder, bitte.
I want my hair cut.	Je veux me faire couper (*ou* tailler) les cheveux.	Ich möchte mir die Haare schneiden lassen.
Short behind. Not too short. Long in front. Without a parting.	Courts par derrière. Pas trop courts. Longs sur le devant. Pas de raie.	Hinten kurz, bitte. Nicht zu kurz. Vorne bitte länger. Ohne Scheitel.
Part in the middle, on the side.	Faites-moi la raie au milieu, sur le côté.	Ziehen Sie mir den Scheitel in der Mitte, an der Seite.
Just trim it.	Rafraîchissez seulement.	Schneiden Sie es nur ein wenig kürzer.
I want my hair singed.	Je désire me faire flamber les cheveux.	Würden Sie bitte die Spitzen absengen.
Please give me a wet shampoo, a dry shampoo *or* a scalp massage.	Veuillez me faire un shampooing, une friction.	Waschen Sie mir bitte den Kopf, Geben Sie mir ein Trocken-Shampoo *oder* eine Kopfmassage.
I don't want the clippers.	Je ne veux pas de la tondeuse.	Nicht mit der Haarschneidemaschine.
Nothing on [the hair].	Rien sur les cheveux.	Nichts ins Haar, bitte.
Please give me a brush.	Veuillez me donner un coup de brosse.	Bürsten Sie mich bitte ab.
Please **set** this razor for me.	Veuillez me repasser ce rasoir.	Würden Sie mir bitte dies Rasiermesser schleifen.
I wish to have my hair dressed *or* done.	Je voudrais me faire coiffer.	Ich möchte mich frisieren lassen.
I want my hair washed.	Je désire me faire laver la tête.	Ich möchte mir die Haare (*oder* den Kopf) waschen lassen.
I want my hair waved. Please give me a perm[anent wave].	Je veux me faire onduler [les cheveux]. Veuillez me faire une [ondulation] permanente.	Ich möchte mir die Haare wellen lassen. Machen Sie mir bitte eine Dauerwelle.

A jeweller, A watchmaker, An optician	**Un bijoutier** *ou* **Un joailler, Un horloger, Un opticien**	**Ein Juwelier, Ein Uhrmacher, Ein Optiker**
A brooch.	Une broche.	Eine Brosche.
A brooch (*bar shaped*).	Une barrette.	Eine Nadel.

Una foggia di pettinatura.	Un estilo (o Una moda) de peinado.	Een haarstijl.
La crema, La lozione, contro l'abbruciatura.	Crema, Loción, para evitar la quemadura del cutis por el sol.	Een crème, Een lotion, tegen zonnebrand.
La crema per l'abbronzatura della pelle.	Crema para broncear el cutis.	Een crème voor het bruinbranden van de huid.
◄La barba o il taglio dei capelli?	¿ Afeitar o cortar el pelo ?	Scheren of knippen?
Rasare. Il farsi la barba.	Afeitar. Afeitado.	Scheren. Het scheren.
Voglio farmi la barba. Rasatemi.	Necesito afeitarme. Aféiteme.	Ik wil me laten scheren. Scheer me.
Nè polverizzatore, nè cipria, per favore.	No me dé rocío ni me ponga polvos.	Geen lotion of poeder als 't U belieft.
Desidero farmi tagliare i capelli.	Necesito cortarme el pelo.	Ik wil mijn haar laten knippen.
◄Corti dietro. Non troppo corti. Lunghi davanti. Senza la scriminatura.	Corto por detrás. No demasiado corto. Largo por delante. Sin raya.	Kort van achteren. Niet te kort. Lang van voren. Zonder scheiding.
Con la scriminatura in mezzo, da un lato.	Hágame la raya en medio, al lado.	Maak de scheiding in het midden, opzij.
Giusto una spuntatina.	Un repaso nada más.	Knip het alleen wat bij.
Desidero passare la fiamma sui capelli.	Quiero que me quemen los cabos del pelo.	Ik wil mijn haar laten onduleren.
Vorrei mi faceste uno shampoo, una frizione.	Haga el favor de darme un champú, una frotación.	Geef me een shampoo, een hoofdmassage.
◄Non voglio la macchinetta.	No quiero la trasquiladora.	Ik wil geen tondeuse.
Nulla sui capelli.	No me ponga nada en la cabeza.	Niets op het haar.
Per favore, datemi un colpo di spazzola.	Haga al favor de darme un cepillado.	Borstel me even als 't U belieft.
Per favore, affilatemi questo rasoio.	Haga el favor de afilarme esta navaja.	Wilt U dit scheermes voor me slijpen.
Vorrei pettinarmi.	Necesito que me arreglen el cabello o el pelo.	Ik wil me laten kappen.
◄Desidero farmi lavare la testa.	Necesito lavarme el cabello o la cabeza.	Ik wil mijn haar laten wassen.
Desidero farmi ondulare i capelli. Per favore, fatemi una ondulazione permanente.	Necesito ondearme el cabello. Haga el favor de hacerme una onda permanente.	Ik wil mijn haar laten watergolven. Geef me een permanent.

Un gioielliere, Un orologiaio, Un ottico	**Un joyero, Un relojero, Un óptico**	**Een juwelier, Een horlogemaker, Een opticien**
Uno spillone, Un fermaglio. Un fermaglio oblungo.	Un broche. Un prendedor.	Een broche. Een langwerpige broche.

A diamond ring.	Une bague garnie de diamants.	Ein Brillantring.
Earrings.	Des boucles d'oreilles.	Ohrringe.
A gold chain.	Une chaîne d'or.	Eine goldene Kette.
A jewel.	Un bijou, Un joyau.	Ein Schmuckstück.
A jewel case.	Un écrin [à bijoux].	Ein Schmuckkasten.
A pearl necklace.	Un collier de perles.	Eine Perlenkette.
Is this [of] real gold or [of] imitation gold? Is it [a] silver gilt?	Ceci est-il en or véritable ou en similor? Est-ce en vermeil *ou* en argent doré?	Ist dies echtes Gold oder eine Imitation? Ist es Silber vergoldet?
Is this ring [of] eighteen carat gold? Is it hall-marked? Where is the hall-mark?	Cet anneau est-il en or à dix-huit carats [de fin]? Est-il contrôlé *ou* poinçonné? Où est le [poinçon de] contrôle?	Ist dieser Ring aus achtzehn karatigem Gold? Hat er einen Stempel? Wo ist der Stempel?
Please reset the stone in this ring, this emerald, this opal, this ruby, this sapphire, this turquoise.	Veuillez remonter la pierre dans cet anneau, cette émeraude, cette opale, ce rubis, ce saphir, cette turquoise.	Würden Sie bitte den Stein in diesem Ring, diesen Smaragd, diesen Opal, diesen Rubin, diesen Saphir, diesen Türkis, neu fassen.
A silver watch.	Une montre d'argent.	Eine silberne Uhr.
A lever watch.	Une montre à ancre.	Eine Ankeruhr.
A wrist[let] watch.	Une montre de poignet.	Eine Armbanduhr.
A strap watch (*man's*), A watch on bracelet (*woman's*).	Une montre [sur] bracelet.	Eine Armbanduhr mit Lederarmband. Eine Armbanduhr mit Metallarmband.
My watch has stopped *or* is out of order; I cannot get it to go. Perhaps the main spring is broken.	Ma montre ne marche plus; je ne peux pas la faire marcher. Peut-être que le grand ressort est cassé.	Meine Uhr ist stehen geblieben *oder* ist kaputt; ich kann sie nicht zum Gehen bringen. Vielleicht ist die Hauptfeder gesprungen.
My watch does not keep [good] time, is always fast, is always slow. Will you regulate it for me?	Ma montre n'est pas juste *ou* bien réglée, avance toujours, retarde toujours. Voulez-vous me la régler?	Meine Uhr geht nicht gut, geht immer zu schnell, geht immer zu langsam. Könnten Sie sie mir bitte regulieren?
Can you repair this watch? I can only leave it for .. days.	Pouvez-vous réparer cette montre? Je peux vous la laisser .. jours seulement.	Können Sie diese Uhr reparieren *oder* zurecht machen? Ich kann sie nur .. Tage hier lassen.
Is my watch done yet? When will it be ready?	Ma montre est-elle enfin finie? Quand sera-t-elle prête?	Ist meine Uhr jetzt fertig? Wann ist sie fertig?
A spectacle maker.	Un lunetier.	Ein Brillenmacher.
Horn-rimmed spectacles. I am short-sighted, long-sighted.	Des lunettes en écaille. Je suis myope, presbyte.	Eine Hornbrille. Ich bin kurzsichtig, weitsichtig.
Eyeglasses, rimless.	Des binocles, Des lorgnons, Des pince-nez, sans monture.	Randlose Augengläser, Eine randlose Brille.
Dark, Coloured, glasses (*spectacles*).	Des lunettes noires, teintées.	Eine dunkle, Eine farbige, Brille.
Sun glasses.	Des lunettes contre le soleil.	Eine Sonnenbrille.

Un anello di diamanti.	Una sortija de diamantes o de brillantes.	Een diamanten ring.
Un paio di orecchini.	Zarcillos.	Oorbellen.
Una catena d'oro.	Una cadena de oro.	Een gouden ketting.
Un gioiello.	Una joya.	Een juweel.
Un astuccio per gioielli.	Un escriño, Un estuche.	Een juwelenkistje.
Una collana di perle.	Un collar de perlas.	Een parelcollier.
È questo vero oro o imitazione? È di argento dorato?	¿Es esto de oro legítimo o de imitación? ¿Es de plata dorada?	Is dit echt goud of namaak goud? Is het verguld zilver?
È quest'anello oro a diciotto carati? È marcato? Dov'è la marca?	¿Es esta sortija de dieciocho quilates? ¿Tiene la marca de contraste? ¿Dónde está la marca de contraste?	Is deze ring achttien karaats goud? Is hij gewaarmerkt? Waar is het waarmerk?
Per favore, rimontate la pietra in quest'anello, questo smeraldo, questo opale, questo rubino, questo zaffiro, questa turchese.	Haga el favor de montar de nuevo la piedra en esta sortija, esta esmeralda, este ópalo, este rubí, este zafiro, esta turquesa.	Wilt U de steen, deze smaragd, deze opaal, deze robijn, deze saffier, deze turkoois, weer in deze ring zetten.
Un orologio d'argento.	Un reloj de plata.	Een zilveren horloge.
Un orologio ad áncora.	Un reloj de escape.	Een ankerhorloge.
Un orologio da polso.	Un reloj de muñeca.	Een polshorloge.
Un orologio braccialetto.	Un reloj de muñeca [con correa], Un reloj de pulsera [de señora].	Een armbandhorloge.
Il mio orologio si è fermato o Il mio orologio non va più; non posso farlo andare. Forse è rotta la grande molla.	Se ha parado, está descompuesto, mi reloj; no puedo hacerlo andar. Puede ser que se haya roto el muelle real.	Mijn horloge staat stil; ik kan het niet aan de gang krijgen. Misschien is de grote veer gebroken.
Il mio orologio ha bisogno di essere regolato, va sempre avanti, va sempre indietro. Volete regolarmelo?	Mi reloj no marca [bien] la hora, está siempre adelantado, está siempre atrasado. ¿Quiere hacer el favor de ajustármelo?	Mijn horloge loopt niet gelijk, loopt altijd voor, loopt altijd achter. Wilt U het voor me regelen?
Potete accomodare questo orologio? Ve lo posso lasciare solo per .. giorni.	¿Puede usted componer este reloj? Solo puedo dejárselo por .. días.	Kunt U dit horloge repareren? Ik kan het slechts .. dagen bij U laten.
Il mio orologio è pronto? Quando sarà fatto?	¿Está ya mi reloj? ¿Para cuándo estará listo?	Is mijn horloge al klaar? Wanneer is het gereed?
Un ottico.	Un anteojero.	Een brillenmaker.
Gli occhiali cerchiati in corno. Io sono miope, presbite.	Gafas con montadura de cuerno. Soy corto de vista o miope, Soy présbite.	Een bril met hoornen montuur. Ik ben bijziende, verziende.
Gli occhialini, senza montatura.	Lentes (o Quevedos) sin montadura.	Een lorgnet zonder montuur.
Occhiali oscuri, colorati.	Gafas negras u obscuras, coloridas.	Een bril met donkere, gekleurde glazen.
Gli occhiali da sole.	Gafas contra el sol.	Een zonnebril.

Field glass[es].	Une jumelle de campagne.	Ein Fernglas.
Opera glass[es].	Des jumelles de théâtre, Des lorgnettes de spectacle.	Ein Opernglas.

Money. Exchange	**Argent. Opérations de change**	**Geld. Geldwechsel**
I have no .. money on me ; do you take English money ?	Je n'ai pas d'argent français sur moi ; acceptez-vous la monnaie anglaise ?	Ich habe kein deutsches Geld bei mir ; nehmen Sie englisches Geld ?
Can you cash this cheque for me ?	Pouvez-vous me payer ce chèque ?	Können Sie mir diesen Scheck einlösen ?
Have you [got] any change ?	Avez-vous de la monnaie ?	Haben Sie Kleingeld *oder* Haben Sie Geld zum Herausgeben ?
Can you give me change for a .. (*value*) piece, change me an English pound (*or* £1) note ?	Pouvez-vous me donner la monnaie d'une pièce de .., me changer un billet anglais d'une livre ?	Können Sie mir auf ein .. Stück herausgeben, mir einen englischen Pfund-schein wechseln ?
Can you oblige me with some silver, copper or nickel, for this .. (*value*) note ?	Auriez-vous la bonté de me donner de la monnaie d'argent, du billon, contre ce billet de .. ?	Könnten Sie so freundlich sein, mir für diesen .. Schein etwas Silbergeld, Kupfergeld oder Nickelgeld, zu geben ?
I have no change, no coppers.	Je n'ai pas de monnaie, de sous.	Ich habe kein Kleingeld, kein Kupfergeld.
Have you not given me too much, too little ?	Ne m'avez-vous pas donné trop, trop peu ?	Haben Sie mir nicht zu viel, zu wenig, gegeben ?
Is this coin good (*or* current) here, is it bad, is it legal tender ?	Cette pièce a-t-elle cours ici, est-elle fausse, est-elle monnaie légale ?	Ist dieses Geldstück gültig, ist es falsch, ist es gesetzliches Zahlungsmittel ?
Is there a bank, an exchange [office], in this place, near here ?	Y a-t-il une banque, un bureau de change, dans cette localité, près d'ici ?	Gibt es in diesem Ort, hier in der Nähe, eine Bank, eine Wechselstube ?
I want to change some English money into .. money.	Je voudrais changer de l'argent anglais contre de l'argent français.	Ich möchte etwas englisches Geld in Deutsches umtauschen oder umwechseln.
What is the [rate of] exchange on London to-day ?	Quel est le cours (*ou* le taux) du change sur Londres aujourd'hui ?	Wie steht der Kurs für Auszahlung London heute ?
French francs, Belgian francs, Swiss francs, German marks, Italian liras *or* lire, Spanish pesetas, Dutch guilders, American dollars.	Des francs français, des francs belges, des francs suisses, des marks allemands, des lires italiennes, des pesetas espagnoles, des florins hollandais, des dollars américains.	Französische Francs, Belgische Francs, Schweizer Francs *oder* Schweizer Franken, Deutsche Mark, Italienische Lire, Spanische Peseten, Holländische Gulden, Amerikanische Dollars.
I want to cash this traveller's cheque.	Je désire encaisser ce chèque de voyage.	Ich möchte diesen traveller's cheque (*oder* diesen Reisescheck) einlösen.

Un binocolo da campagna.	Anteojos de campaña.	Een veldkijker.
Un binocolo da teatro.	Gemelos de teatro.	Een toneelkijker.

Moneta. Operazioni di cambio	**Moneda. Operaciones de cambio**	**Geld. Geld wisselen**
Non ho con me moneta italiana; accettate moneta inglese ?	No traigo moneda española. ¿ Acepta usted moneda inglesa ?	Ik heb geen Hollands geld bij me; neemt U Engels geld aan?
Potete pagarmi questo cheque o questo assegno [bancario] ?	¿ Puede usted pagarme este cheque ?	Kunt U deze cheque aan me uitbetalen?
◀ Avete danaro spicciolo ?	¿ Tiene usted cambio ?	Heeft U wisselgeld?
Potete voi cambiarmi un pezzo di .., cambiarmi un biglietto (o una banconota) inglese di una [lira] sterlina ?	¿ Puede usted cambiarme una moneda de .., un billete inglés de una libra [esterlina] ?	Kunt U me wisselgeld geven voor een stuk van .., een Engels biljet van een pond voor me wisselen?
Potete darmi argento, rame, nichel, per questo biglietto da .. ?	¿ Quiere usted hacer el favor de cambiarme este billete de .. en plata, en calderilla o niquel ?	Kunt U me van dienst zijn met wat zilvergeld, kopergeld, voor dit biljet van ..?
Non ho spiccioli, niente rame.	No tengo cambio, calderilla.	Ik heb geen wisselgeld, geen kopergeld.
Non mi avete dato troppo, troppo poco ?	¿ No me ha dado usted demasiado, demasiado poco ?	Heeft U me niet te veel, te weinig, teruggegeven?
◀ È valevole questa moneta, è falsa, ha corso legale ?	¿ Vale aquí esta pieza, es falsa, es moneda corriente ?	Is dit muntstuk hier geldig, is het vals, is het wettig betaalmiddel?
C'è una banca, un ufficio di cambio, in questa località, qui vicino ?	¿ Hay aquí, por aquí cerca, un banco, una agencia de cambios ?	Is er een bank, een wisselkantoor, in deze plaats, hier in de buurt?
Desidero cambiare della moneta inglese in moneta italiana.	Deseo cambiar moneda inglesa en moneda española.	Ik wens wat Engels geld voor Hollands geld in te wisselen.
Qual'è il cambio su Londra oggi ?	¿ Cuál es el tipo de cambio de hoy sobre Londres ?	Wat is de wisselkoers met Londen vandaag?
I franchi francesi, I franchi belgi, I franchi svizzeri, I marchi tedeschi, Le lire italiane, Las pesetas spagnola, I fiorini olandesi, I dollari americani.	Francos franceses, Francos belgas, Francos suizos, Marcos alemanes, Liras italianas, Pesetas españolas, Florines holandeses, Dolares norteamericanos.	Franse franken, Belgische franken, Zwitserse franken, Duitse marken, Italiaanse lires, Spaanse pesetas, Hollandse guldens, Amerikaanse dollars.
◀ Desidero incassare questo traveller's cheque.	Deseo cobrar este traveller's cheque.	Ik wens deze travellers's cheque (of deze reischeque) te incasseren.

I want to draw ten pounds on this letter of credit.	Je veux prendre dix livres sur cette lettre de crédit.	Ich möchte zehn Pfund auf diesen Kreditbrief abheben.
Give me .. in notes and the remainder in silver.	Donnez-moi .. en billets et le reste en argent.	Geben Sie mir .. in Banknoten *oder* in Scheinen, und den Rest in Silber.
Give me large, small, notes *or* large, small, denominations, and some small money *or* coin *or* change.	Donnez-moi de gros, de petits, billets *ou* de grosses, de petites, coupures, et de la petite (*ou* menue) monnaie *ou* de l'appoint.	Geben Sie mir große, kleine, Banknoten, und etwas Kleingeld *oder* Wechselgeld.

A photographer, Photography
Un, Une, photographe, La photographie
Ein Fotograf, Die Fotografie

Colour photography.	La photographie en couleurs.	Farbenfotografie.
A photo[graph].	Une photo[graphie].	Ein Foto, Eine Fotografie,➤ Eine Aufnahme.
I want my photograph taken. Can you take me now ?	Je désire me faire photographier. Pouvez-vous me tirer maintenant ?	Ich möchte mich fotografieren lassen. Können Sie mich sofort aufnehmen ?
When can I sit for my portrait ?	Quand puis-je poser pour mon portrait ?	Wann kann ich mein Portrait machen lassen ?
Can I go into the studio ?	Puis-je entrer dans le salon de pose ?	Kann ich ins Atelier gehen ?
When can I have a proof ?	Quand puis-je avoir une épreuve ?	Wann kann ich einen Rohabzug haben ?
Please give me one dozen rapid plates, some roll films, a six, an eight, a twelve, exposure spool, [size:] .. by .. centimetres.	Donnez-moi, s'il vous plaît, une douzaine de plaques rapides, des pellicules en bobines *ou* en rouleaux, une bobine de six, de huit, de douze, poses, [dimensions :] .. sur .. centimètres.	Bitte geben Sie mir ein Dutzend hochempfindliche Platten, einige Rollfilme, eine Spule mit sechs, mit acht, mit zwölf, Aufnahmen, [Größe :] .. mal .. Zentimeter.
Have you a dark room ?	Est-ce que vous avez une chambre noire ?	Haben Sie eine Dunkelkammer ?
Will you please develop and print these negatives ? I want one print from each, on glossy paper, on matt smooth paper, on carbon paper. When will they be done ?	Voulez-vous développer et tirer ces clichés ? Je désire avoir une épreuve de chacun, sur du papier brillant, sur du papier mat lisse, sur du papier au carbone. Quand seront-elles prêtes ?	Würden Sie bitte diese Negative entwickeln und abziehen ? Ich brauche je einen Abzug, auf Glanzpapier, auf glattem Mattpapier, auf Kohlepapier. Wann sind sie fertig ?
This negative is weak. Can you intensify it ?	Ce cliché est faible. Pouvez-vous le renforcer ?	Dieses Negativ ist zu schwach. Können Sie es verstärken ?
I want an enlargement made from this negative. The image is very sharp, a little fuzzy, fogged.	Je désire faire faire un agrandissement de ce cliché. L'image est très nette, un peu floue, voilée.	Ich brauche eine Vergrößerung von diesem Negativ. Das Bild ist sehr scharf, etwas unscharf, verschwommen.

Vorrei ritirare dieci sterline su questa lettera di credito.	Deseo girar diez libras esterlinas a cuenta de esta carta de crédito.	Ik wil tien pond opnemen. op deze kredietbrief.
Datemi . . in biglietti ed il resto in argento.	Déme . . en billetes y el resto en plata.	Geef me . . in biljetten en de rest in zilvergeld.
Datemi dei biglietti di grosso, di piccolo, taglio, e moneta spicciola.	Déme billetes de gran, de pequeña, denomina-ción, y alguna moneda pequeña o cambio suelto.	Geef me grote, kleine, biljetten of grote, kleine, coupures, wat klein geld.

Un fotografo, La fotografia
Un fotógrafo, Una fotógrafa, Fotografía
Een fotograaf Fotografie

La fotografia a colori.	Fotografía en colores.	Kleurenfotografie.
◄Una fotografia.	Una foto[grafía].	Een foto[grafie].
Desidero farmi una foto-grafia. Potete farmela ora ?	Deseo hacerme un retrato. ¿ Puede usted hacérmelo ahora mismo ?	Ik wil me laten foto-graferen. Kunt U me nu nemen ?
Quando posso posare per il ritratto ?	¿ Cuándo puedo venir a retratarme ?	Wanneer kan ik voor mijn portret zitten ?
Posso entrare nello studio ?	¿ Puedo pasar al taller ?	Kan ik het atelier binnengaan ?
Quando posso avere una prova ?	¿ Cuándo puedo tener la prueba ?	Wanneer kan ik een proef hebben ?
◄Per favore, datemi una dozzina di lastre rapide, delle pellicole su rocchetti, un rocchetto da sei, da otto, da dodici, esposizioni, [grandezza:] . . per . . centimetri.	Haga el favor de una docena de placas rápidas, unas películas en carretes, un carrete de seis, de ocho, de doce, ex-posiciones, [dimen-siones:] de . . por . . centímetros.	Geef me een dozijn snelle platen, wat rol-films, een film voor zes, acht, twaalf, op-namen, [maat:] . . bij . . centimeter.
Avete una camera oscura ?	¿ Tiene usted una cámara obscura ?	Heeft U een donkere kamer ?
Volete sviluppare e stam-pare queste negative ? Desidero una prova per ciascuna, su carta lucida, su carta opaca liscia, su carta carbone. Quando saranno pronte ?	¿ Quiere usted hacer el favor de revelar e im-primir estos negativos ? Deseo un ejemplar de cada uno, sobre papel lustroso,sobre papel mate de grano alisado, sobre papel carbono. ¿ Cuándo estarán listos ?	Wilt U deze negatieven ontwikkelen en afdruk-ken als 't U belieft ? Ik wens één afdruk van ieder, op glanzend papier, op glad mat papier, op carbon-papier. Wanneer zijn ze klaar ?
Questa negativa è debole. Potete rafforzarla ?	Este negativo está algo débil. ¿ Puede usted reforzarlo ?	Dit negatief is zwak. Kunt U het verster-ken ?
Desidero un ingrandimento di questa negativa. L'im-magine è molto netta, non chiara, velata.	Deseo una ampliación de este negativo. La imagen está muy aguda, un tanto vellosa, velada.	Ik wil een vergroting laten maken van dit negatief. Het beeld is zeer scherp, een beetje vaag, wazig.

I am afraid the camera moved a little.	Je crains que l'appareil n'ait bougé un peu.	Ich muß den Apparat leider etwas bewegt haben
Please mount these photos. I want them unmounted. Give me some mounts, a paste-on mount, a slip-in mount, a paste-on album, a slip-in album.	Veuillez faire monter ces photos. Je veux les avoir non montées. Donnez-moi des cartons [pour montages photographiques], un carton pour coller les épreuves, un carton passe-partout, un album à coller, un album à passe-partout.	Bitte ziehen Sie diese Foto auf. Ich möchte sie unaufgezogen haben. Geben Sie mir einige Bogen Karton, einen Karton zum Aufziehen, ein Passe-Partout, ein Fotoalbum zum Aufkleben, ein Fotoalbum zum Einschieben.
Will you retouch this photograph?	Voulez-vous retoucher cette photographie?	Würden Sie dieses Foto bitte retouchieren?
Is it allowed to take photographs on board the aeroplanes, to film this scene?	Est-il permis de prendre des photographies à bord des avions, de filmer cette scène?	Darf man an Bord eines Flugzeugs fotografieren, diesen Vorgang filmen?
What [time of] exposure do you recommend under these conditions, without risking over-exposure, under-exposure?	Quel temps de pose (ou Quelle pose) recommandez-vous dans ces conditions, sans risquer un excès de pose, un manque de pose?	Welche Belichtungszeit raten Sie mir unter diesen Umständen, ohne Gefahr der Überbelichtung, Unterbelichtung?
What stop should I use for this light?	Quel diaphragme doit-on employer pour cette lumière?	Was für eine Blende soll ich bei diesem Licht benutzen?
Stand still. I am going to focus, I am going to snap[-shot] you.	Restez immobile. Je vais mettre au point, je vais prendre un instantané de vous.	Bleiben Sie stehen, ich will den Apparat auf sie einstellen, ich will Sie aufnehmen.
A photographic camera.	Un appareil (ou Une chambre) photographique.	Ein Fotoapparat, Eine Kamera.
A daylight-loading roll-film camera.	Un appareil pour pellicules en bobine se chargeant en plein jour.	Eine Kamera für Rollfilme, die bei Tageslicht eingesetzt werden können.
A vest-pocket camera.	Un appareil se mettant dans la poche du gilet.	Ein Westentaschenapparat.
A cinematographic camera.	Un appareil cinématographique.	Eine Filmkamera.
A collapsible view-finder.	Un viseur redresseur.	Ein zusammenklappbarer Sucher.
A dark slide.	Un châssis négatif, Un châssis porte-plaques.	Eine Kassette.
An extension tripod.	Un trépied extensible.	Ein ausziehbares Stativ.
An exposure meter.	Un pose-mètre.	Ein Belichtungsmesser.
A lens.	Un objectif.	Eine Linse, Ein Objektiv.
A light filter or An ortho (or A colour) screen.	Un écran orthochromatique.	Eine Gelbscheibe.
A photo[graph] frame.	Un porte-photo[graphie].	Ein Fotorahmen.

Temo che la macchina is sia mossa un poco.	Me temo que se movió un poco el aparato.	Ik ben bang, dat het toestel een beetje bewogen heeft.
Per favore, montatemi queste fotografie. Io le voglio senza montatura. Datemi delle montature, un cartone per incollare le prove, una montatura passe-partout, un album da incollare, un album a passe-partout.	Haga el favor de montar estas fotografías. Las quiero sin montar. Déme unos cartones [para montar], un cartón para pegar con goma, uno de passepartout, un album para engomar, un album de passepartout.	Plak deze foto's als 't U belieft op. Ik wil ze niet opgeplakt. Geef mij een paar vellen karton, opzetkarton, karton met gleuven, een inplakalbum, een insteekalbum.
Volete ritoccarmi questa fotografia?	¿Quiere usted hacer el favor de retocar esta fotografía?	Wilt U deze foto retoucheren?
È permesso di prendere qualche fotografia a bordo dell'aeroplano, di prendere una film di questa scena?	¿Es permitido tomar fotografías a bordo de los aviones, hacer una vista cinematográfica de esta escena?	Is het veroorlofd foto's te nemen aan boord van de vliegtuigen, dit taf[e]reel te filmen?
Quanto tempo di posa consigliate voi in queste condizioni, senza arrischiare una esposizione eccessiva, una esposizione deficiente?	¿Cuánto tiempo de exposición recomienda usted bajo estas condiciones para evitar el riesgo de exposición excesiva, de insuficiente exposición?	Wat voor belichtingstijd raadt U aan onder deze omstandigheden, zonder overbelichting, onderbelichting, te riskeren?
Che diaframma devo usare con questa luce?	¿Qué diafragma (o abertura) debo emplear para esta luz?	Wat voor stop (of diafragma) moet ik voor dit licht gebruiken?
State fermo. Ora metto a foco, vi farò un'istantanea.	No se mueva. Voy a enfocarle, voy a hacerle un instantáneo.	Sta stil. Ik ga instellen. ik ga een kiekje van U nemen.
Una macchina fotografica, Un apparecchio fotografico.	Un aparato fotográfico, Una cámara fotográfica.	Een fototoestel, Een kiektoestel.
Una macchina fotografica per pellicole su rocchetti da cambiarsi in pieno giorno.	Un aparato para películas en carrete a colocar en plena luz.	Een toestel voor rolfilms, dat in het daglicht geladen kan worden.
Una macchina fotografica tascabile.	Un aparato para ir en el bolsillo del chaleco.	Een vestjeszak toestel.
Un apparecchio cinematografico.	Un aparato cinematográfico.	Een filmtoestel, Een filmapparaat.
Un mirino pieghevole.	Una visera plegadiza.	Een opvouwbare zoeker.
Un telaio portalastre.	Un chasis de negativos, Un portaplacas.	Een negatieve plaat.
Un [trep]piede estensibile.	Un trípode telescópico o de corredera.	Een uittrekbare driepoot.
Un posa-metro, Un misuratore dell'esposizione.	Un medidor de exposición.	Een belichtingsmeter.
Un obbiettivo.	Un lente.	Een lens.
Un filtro ortocromatico.	Un filtrador de luz, Un filtro ortocromático.	Een geelfilter.
Una cornice per fotografia.	Un marco portafotografías.	Een fotolijst.

A shutter (*camera*).	Un obturateur.	Ein Verschluß.
The post [office]	**Le bureau de poste, La poste**	**Das Postamt, Die Post**
An air [mail] fee.	Une surtaxe aérienne.	Eine Luftpostgebühr.
An air [mail] letter.	Une lettre-avion.	Ein Luftpostbrief. →
An air [mail] parcel.	Un colis-avion.	Ein Luftpostpaket.
A book of stamps.	Un carnet de timbres.	Ein Briefmarkenheft
A cable. To cable.	Un câble. Câbler.	Ein Kabel. Kabeln.
Care of *or* c/o.	Aux [bons] soins de, Chez.	Per Adresse *oder* p.A., Bei *oder* b/.
The general post office.	L'hôtel des postes.	Das Hauptpostamt. →
An insured parcel.	Un colis avec valeur déclarée, Un colis chargé.	Ein versichertes Paket.
An international money order.	Un mandat-poste international.	Eine internationale Postanweisung.
A letter card.	Une carte-lettre.	Eine Briefkarte.
Please forward (*notice on letter*).	Veuillez faire suivre.	Bitte nachsenden.
The postmaster. The postmistress.	Le maître de poste, Le receveur des postes. La maîtresse de poste, La receveuse des postes.	Der Postmeister, Die Post→ meisterin, Der Postdirektor, Die Postdirektorin.
A postcard.	Une carte postale.	Eine Postkarte.
The postman, The postwoman.	Le facteur [des postes], La factrice [des postes].	Der Briefträger, Die Briefträgerin, Der Postbote, Die Postbotin.
A postmark. (*See 24-HOUR CLOCK SYSTEM, p. 267.*)	Un timbre [de la poste].	Eine Briefmarke.
The post office guide.	L'indicateur universel des P.T.T. (= Postes, Télégraphes et Téléphones).	Das Postbuch.
Printed matter (*post*).	Imprimés.	Drucksache. →
The parcel post. By parcel post.	Le service des colis postaux. Par colis postal.	Die Paketpost. Per Paketpost.
The parcel[s] office.	Le bureau de messageries.	Das Paketamt.
A registered envelope.	Une enveloppe de lettre chargée ou recommandée.	Ein eingeschriebener Briefumschlag.
A reply-paid telegram.	Un télégramme avec réponse payée, Un télégramme-réponse.	Ein Telegramm mit bezahlter Antwort.
The sender (*of a letter, a parcel*).	L'expéditeur, L'expéditrice.	Der Absender. →
The sender (*of a money order*).	L'envoyeur, L'envoyeuse.	Der Absender.

Un otturatore.	Un obturador.	Een sluiter.

L'ufficio postale, La posta | La administración de correos, El correo | Het postkantoor, De post

Una sopratassa per posta aerea.	Un recargo de correo aéreo.	Een luchttarief.
◄Una lettera per via aerea.	Una carta por correo aéreo.	Een luchtpostbrief.
Un pacco per via aerea.	Un envío por avión.	Een luchtpostpakket.
Un libretto di francobolli.	Un libretín de sellos [de correo]	Een postzegelboekje.
Un cablogramma. Cablografare, Spedire un cablogramma.	Un cable[grama]. Cablegrafiar.	Een [kabel]telegram. Telegraferen.
Presso.	S/a (= Suplicado a).	Per adres of p/a.
◄L'ufficio postale centrale, La posta centrale.	La administración central de correos.	Het hoofdpostkantoor.
Un pacco con valore dichiarato.	Un envío asegurado.	Een verzekerd pakket.
Un vaglia (o Un mandato) postale internazionale.	Una libranza postal internacional.	Een internationale postwissel.
Una carta-lettera.	Una carta-tarjeta [postal].	Een kaartbrief.
Da far seguire o Da recapitare.	Sírvase reexpedir.	Gelieve door te zenden.
◄Il direttore, La direttrice, delle poste.	El administrador (o El jefe) de correos. La administradora (o La jefa) de correos.	De directeur, De directrice, van het postkantoor.
Una cartolina postale.	Una tarjeta postal.	Een briefkaart.
Il postino, La postina.	El cartero, La cartera.	De postbode (*man or woman*).
Un bollo postale.	El timbre de la administración de correos.	Een postmerk.
L'indicatore postale.	El guía general de correos, telégrafos y teléfonos.	De gids van post en telegraafkantoren.
◄Stampa.	Impresos.	Drukwerk.
Il pacco postale. Per pacco postale.	El servicio de paquetes postales. Por paquete postal.	De pakketpost. Per pakketpost.
L'ufficio pacchi postale.	El despacho de paquetes postales.	Het pakket en ijlgoederen bureau.
Una busta raccomandata.	Un sobre certificado.	Een aangetekende enveloppe.
Un telegramma con risposta pagata.	Un telegrama con contestación franqueada.	Een telegram met betaald antwoord.
◄Il mittente, La mittente.	El expedidor, La expedidora.	De afzender, (*feminine*) De afzendster.
Il mittente, La mittente.	El remitente, La remitenta.	De zender, (*feminine*) De zendster.

A telegraph boy, A telegraph messenger.	Un petit télégraphiste, Un facteur des télégraphes.	Ein Telegrafenbote.
A telegraph office.	Un bureau télégraphique.	Ein Telegrafenamt.
To be called for (at post office).	Poste restante, Bureau restant.	Postlagernd, Poste Restante.
A wireless telegram or A radiogram.	Un télégramme sans fil, Un sans-fil, Un radiogramme.	Ein drahtloses Telegramm.→
Wireless telegraphy.	La télégraphie sans fil, La T.S.F.	Drahtlose Telegrafie.
What are the inland, foreign, postage rates? What is the postage on this letter?	Quels sont les tarifs postaux du régime intérieur, pour l'étranger? Quel est l'affranchissement pour cette lettre?	Welches sind die Postgebühren (oder Wie ist der Posttarif) für das Inland, für das Ausland? Wie hoch ist die Gebühr für diesen Brief?
A . . (value) [postage] stamp, please.	Un timbre[-poste] de . ., s'il vous plaît.	Eine . . Briefmarke, bitte.
Can one send a letter by air mail to . .? Is there an air mail to . .?	Peut-on expédier une lettre par avion à . .? Y a-t-il une poste aérienne (ou une poste-avion) pour . .?	Kann man einen Brief per Luftpost nach . . senden? Gibt es eine Luftpost nach . .?
(For posting, collection and delivery of letters, see pp. 112-115.)		
Are there any letters for Mr . ., Mrs . ., Miss . .?	Y a-t-il des lettres pour Monsieur . ., Madame . ., Mademoiselle . .?	Sind Briefe für Herrn . .,→ Frau . ., Fräulein . ., da?
I want to send this parcel. How much is it?	Je veux envoyer ce colis. Combien y a-t-il à payer?	Ich möchte dies Paket absenden. Was kostet das?
I want this letter registered, this packet insured.	Je veux faire recommander cette lettre, faire charger ce paquet.	Ich möchte diesen Brief einschreiben lassen, dieses Paket versichern lassen.
Is this letter overweight? Kindly weigh this letter [for me]. How many kilos does the parcel weigh?	Cette lettre pèse-t-elle trop? Veuillez [me] peser cette lettre. Combien de kilos le colis pèse-t-il?	Hat dieser Brief Übergewicht? Würden Sie bitte diesen Brief wiegen? Wieviel Kilo wiegt dies Paket?
I am the addressee of this parcel, of this remittance.	Je suis le, la, destinataire de ce colis, de cet envoi.	Ich bin der Empfänger dieses Pakets, dieser Sendung.
Here is my full name and [my full] address.	Voici mes nom et prénom(s) et mon adresse complète.	Hier ist mein voller Name→ und meine [volle] Adresse.
Must I fill up a printed form? Please give me a money order form, a telegram form.	Dois-je remplir une formule imprimée? Veuillez me donner une formule de mandat-poste [ordinaire], une formule de télégramme.	Muß ich ein gedrucktes Formular ausfüllen? Bitte geben Sie mir ein Formular für eine Postanweisung, ein Telegrammformular.
What is the registration fee, the fee for an express letter, the poste restante fee?	Quel est le droit de recommandation, la taxe d'une lettre par exprès, la surtaxe de poste restante?	Was beträgt die Einschreibegebühr, die Gebühr für einen Expreßbrief, die Gebühr für postlagernde Briefe?

Un fattorino del telegrafo.	Un mensajero de telégrafos.	Een telegrambesteller.
Un ufficio telegrafico. Ferma in posta.	Un despacho de telégrafos. Poste restante.	Een telegraafkantoor. Poste restante.
◄Un radiotelegramma, Un telegramma senza fili.	Un radiotelegrama.	Een draadloze telegram.
Il telegrafo senza fili.	La radiotelegrafía, La telegrafía sin hilos.	Draadloze telegrafie.
Quant'è la tariffa postale interna, per l'estero? Quant'è l'affrancatura per questa lettera?	¿Cuáles son los tipos de franqueo para el interior, para el extranjero? ¿Cuánto es el franqueo para esta carta?	Wat zijn de binnenlandse, buitenlandse, posttarieven? Hoeveel moet er op deze brief?
Un francobollo di . . , per piacere.	Haga el favor de un sello de a . . .	Een postzegel van .., als 't U belieft.
Si può spedire una lettera per via aerea a . .? C'è un corriere postale aereo per . .?	¿Se puede enviar una carta por correo aéreo (o por avión) a . .? ¿Hay correo aéreo para . .?	Kan men een brief per luchtpost naar .. zenden? Gaat er luchtpost naar ..?
◄Ci sono lettere per il Signor . ., la Signora . ., la Signorina . .?	Hay cartas para el Señor . ., la Señora . . , la Señorita . .?	Zijn er brieven voor de Heer .., Mevrouw .., Juffrouw ..?
Io desidero spedire questo pacco. Quanto è il costo?	Deseo enviar este paquete. ¿Cuánto es [el franqueo]?	Ik wil dit pakket versturen. Hoeveel is het?
Vorrei raccomandare questa lettera, assicurare questo pacchetto.	Deseo certificar esta carta, asegurar este paquete.	Ik wil deze brief laten aantekenen, dit pakket laten verzekeren.
Questa lettera passa di peso? Per favore, pesate questa lettera. Quanti chilogrammi pesa questo pacco?	¿Excede esta carta el peso normal? Haga el favor de pesarme esta carta. ¿Cuántos kilos pesa el paquete?	Is deze brief te zwaar? Wilt U deze brief voor me wegen. Hoeveel kilo weegt het pakket?
Io sono il destinatario, la destinatrice, di questo pacco, di questa rimessa.	Soy el destinatario de este paquete, de esta remesa.	Ik ben de geadresseerde van dit pakket, van deze overmaking of remise.
◄Ecco il mio nome e cognome ed indirizzo completo.	Aquí tiene usted mi nombre completo y mis señas completas.	Hier is mijn volledige naam en adres.
Devo riempire un modulo [a stampa]? Per favore, datemi un modulo per vaglia postale, un modulo per telegramma.	¿Debo llenar un formulario impreso? Haga el favor de [darme] un formulario para una libranza postal, un formulario para telegrama.	Moet ik een gedrukt formulier invullen? Geef mee een postwisselformulier, een telegramformulier als 't U belieft.
Qual'è la tassa per le raccomandate, la tassa per una lettera espresso, la soprattassa per ferma in posta?	¿Cuánto vale el sello del certificado, el franqueo para una carta por correo expreso, el recargo para poste restante?	Wat is het tarief voor aantekenen, het tarief voor een expres brief, voor poste restante?

What is the rate per word? *(telegram.)* (*For* telephoning, *see pp.* 114-117.)	Quel est le tarif par mot?	Was bezahlt man pro Wort?

A stationer	**Un papetier, Une papetière**	**Ein Papierhändler**
A stationer's shop.	Une papeterie.	Ein Papiergeschäft, Eine Schreibwarenhandlung.
Stationery.	De la papeterie, Des articles de papeterie.	Schreibwaren. →
A newsagent.	Un marchand de journaux.	Ein Zeitungshändler, Ein Zeitungsverkäufer.
An artists' colourman.	Un marchand de couleurs pour artistes peintres.	Ein Geschäft für Zeichenartikel und Malartikel.
Blotting paper.	Du papier buvard.	Löschpapier.
Colours in tubes for oil and water-colour painting.	Des couleurs en tubes pour la peinture à l'huile et l'aquarelle.	Farben in Tuben für Ölmalerei und Aquarelle.
A crayon.	Un [crayon] pastel.	Ein Zeichenstift. →
An envelope.	Une enveloppe.	Ein Briefumschlag.
Foreign note paper.	Du papier pelure.	Das Überseepapier.
A fountain pen.	Un stylographe, Un porteplume [à] réservoir.	Eine Füllfeder, Ein Füllfederhalter.
Indiarubber.	De la gomme [à effacer].	Radiergummi.
Ink.	De l'encre.	Tinte. →
A lead pencil; soft, medium, hard.	Un crayon de mine de plomb; tendre, moyen, dur.	Ein Bleistift; weich, mittel weich, hart.
Letter paper.	Du papier à lettres [in-quarto].	Briefpapier [Oktavformat].
A [news]paper. A daily [paper].	Un journal. Un [journal] quotidien.	Eine Zeitung. Eine Tageszeitung.
Note paper.	Du papier à lettres [in-octavo].	Briefpapier [Quartformat].
A picture postcard. A view.	Une carte postale illustrée. Une vue.	Eine Ansichtskarte. Eine→ Ansicht.
Have you a good plan of the town, of the environs of . .?	Avez-vous un bon plan de la ville, des environs de Paris?	Haben Sie einen guten Stadtplan, einen Plan der Umgebung von Berlin.
A quire (*of paper*).	Une main.	Vierundzwanzig Bogen.
How many sheets does this packet contain?	Combien ce paquet contient-il de feuilles?	Wieviel Blatt sind in dieser Packung?
A sketch book.	Un album (*ou* Un cahier) de dessin.	Ein Skizzenheft, Ein Zeichenheft.
Steel pens *or* nibs, broad pointed, medium pointed, fine pointed, turned up points, ball pointed.	Des plumes [à écrire] en acier, à pointes larges, à pointes moyennes, à pointes fines, à pointes arrondies, à pointes boules.	Stahlfedern mit breiter→ Spitze, Stahlfedern mit mittelbreiter Spitze, Spitze Stahlfedern, Stahlfedern mit nach oben gebogener Spitze, Stahlfedern mit Kugelspitze

Qual'è la tariffa per ogni parola ?	¿ Qué es la tarifa por palabra ?	Wat is het tarief per woord?

Un cartolaio	**Un papelero**	**Een kantoorboek- handelaar**
Un negozio di cartolaio.	Una papelería.	Een kantoorboekhandel.
◄La cartoleria, Gli articoli di cartoleria.	Papelería.	Schrijfbehoeften.
Un venditore di giornali.	Un vendedor de periódicos.	Een krantenverkoper.
Un negoziante di colori per artisti.	Un vendedor de pinturas para artistas pintores.	Een verfhandelaar voor kunstschilders.
La carta suga.	Papel secante.	Vloeipapier.
I colori in tubetti per pittura ad olio ed ad acquarello.	Colores en tubos para pintar al óleo y a la acuarela.	Kleuren in tubes voor olieverf en waterverf schilderijen.
◄Un lapis, Un pastello.	Un creyón, Un lápiz de tiza de color.	Een tekenkrijt.
Una busta.	Un sobre.	Een enveloppe.
La carta da lettere per l'estero.	Papel de escribir para el extranjero.	Lompenpapier.
Una penna stilografica.	Una pluma estilográfica, Una pluma fuente.	Een vulpen.
La gomma.	Goma de borrar.	Vlakgom.
◄L'inchiostro.	Tinta.	Inkt.
Una matita ; morbida, media, dura.	Un lápiz de mina ; suave, mediana, dura.	Een potlood; zacht, middelsoort, hard.
La carta da lettere.	Papel de escribir [en cuarto].	Briefpapier.
Un giornale. Un giornale quotidiano.	Un periódico. Un diario.	Een krant of Een cou- rant. Een dagblad.
La carta per biglietti.	Papel de escribir [en octavo].	Schrijfpapier.
◄Una cartolina [postale] illustrata. Una veduta.	Una vista postal. Una vista.	Een prentbriefkaart. Een ansicht.
Avete una buona pianta della città, dei dintorni di Roma ?	¿ Tiene usted un buen plano de la población, de los abrededores de Madrid ?	Heeft U een goede platte- grond van de stad, van de omstreken van Amsterdam?
Ventiquattro fogli.	Una mano.	Een boek.
Quanti fogli contiene questo pacchetto ?	¿ Cuántas hojas contiene este paquete ?	Hoeveel vellen bevat dit pak?
Un album (o Un libretto) da disegnare.	Una libreta para dibujar.	Een schetsboek.
◄I pennini d'acciaio, con punta larga, con punta media, con punta sottile, con punta rovesciata, con punta tonda.	Plumas de acero [para escribir], de puntagruesa, de punta mediana, de punta fina, de punta torcida hacia arriba, de punta de bola o de punta esférica.	Stalen pennen, met brede punten, met middelsoort punten, met fijne punten, met ronde punten, met balpunten.

A gummed wrapper.	Une bande gommée.	Ein gummiertes Kreuzband.
A writing pad.	Un bloc de correspondance.	Ein Schreibblock.
A tobacconist	**Un débitant de tabac**	**Ein Tabakhändler, Ein Zigarrenhändler**
A tobacconist's shop.	Un débit (*ou* Un bureau) de tabac (*in France, also sells postage stamps*).	Ein Zigarrengeschäft.
Give me a packet of tobacco, strong, medium, mild, coarse cut, fine cut.	Donnez-moi un paquet de tabac, fort, moyen, doux, grosse coupe, fine coupe.	Geben Sie mir ein Päckchen Tabak, starken, mittelstarken, milden, Grobschnitt, Feinschnitt.
Do you keep English cigarettes, loose tobacco?	Tenez-vous des cigarettes anglaises, du tabac non empaqueté?	Haben Sie englische Zigaretten, losen Tabak?
How much are these the twenty-five, the fifty, the hundred, the box, the packet of ten, twenty?	Combien coûtent ceux-ci les vingt-cinq, les cinquante, le cent, la boîte, le paquet de dix, de vingt?	Was kosten fünfundzwanzig Stück, fünfzig Stück, Was kostet das Hundert, die Schachtel, ein Zehnerpaket, ein Zwanzigerpaket?
An ash tray.	Un cendrier [de fumeur].	Ein Asch[en]becher.
Book matches.	Des allumettes en carnet.	Taschenzündhölzer, Flache Streichhölzer.
A box of safety matches.	Une boîte d'allumettes de sûreté.	Eine Schachtel Sicherheitszündhölzer.
A briar (*or* brier) pipe, straight, bent, vulcanite mouthpiece.	Une pipe en bruyère, droite, courbe, tuyau ébonite.	Eine Bruyerepfeife *oder* Eine Briarpfeife, gerade, gebogen, Mundstück aus Galalith.
A cigarette case.	Un étui à cigarettes.	Ein Zigarettenetui.
Cigarette papers.	Des papiers à cigarettes.	Zigarettenpapier.
Cork-tipped cigarettes.	Des cigarettes à bouts de liège.	Zigaretten mit Korkmundstück.
Flints for lighter.	Des pierres à briquet.	Feuersteine für das Feuerzeug.
A Havana cigar.	Un cigare de la Havane.	Eine Havannazigarre.
A petrol lighter.	Un briquet à essence.	Ein Benzinfeuerzeug.
Plain cigarettes	Des cigarettes ordinaires.	Zigaretten ohne Mundstück.
Snuff.	Du tabac à priser.	Schnupftabak.
A tobacco pouch.	Une blague à tabac.	Ein Tabaksbeutel.
Virginia [tobacco].	Du virginie.	Virginiatabak.
SIGHTSEEING	**CURIOSITÉS**	**SEHENSWÜRDIG-KEITEN**
Generalities	**Généralités**	**Allgemeines**
What is there to see here?	Qu'y a-t-il à voir ici?	Was gibt es hier zu sehen?
Are there any spots at . . worth seeing?	Y a-t-il à . . des sites dignes d'intérêt?	Gibt es irgendwelche sehenswerten Punkte in . .?

Una carta ingommata da involto.	Una faja engomada.	Een gegomde adresband.
Carta da lettere in blocco.	Un bloc de papel de escribir.	Een schrijfblok, Een bloc-note.

Un tabaccaio	**Un tabaquero o Un estanquero**	**Een tabakshandelaar, Een sigarenwinkelier**
Un negozio di tabacchi.	Un estanco, Una tabaquería.	Een tabakswinkel. Een sigarenzaak.

Datemi un pacchetto di tabacco, forte, medio, dolce, tagliato grosso, tagliato fine.	Déme un paquetillo de tabaco, fuerte, mediano, suave, de hebra gruesa, de hebra fina.	Geef me een pak sterke, middelsoort, milde, grofgesneden fijngesneden tabak.
◄Avete sigarette inglesi, tabacco sciolto?	¿Tiene usted cigarrillos (o pitillos) ingleses, tabaco suelto?	Heeft U Engelse sigaretten, losse tabak?
Quanto costano ogni venticinque, cinquanta, cento, Quanto costa per scatola, il pacchetto di dieci, venti?	¿Cuánto valen estos los veinticinco, los cincuenta, el ciento, la caja, la cajetilla de diez, de veinte?	Hoeveel kosten deze per vijf en twintig, per vijftig, per honderd, per doos, per pakje van tien, twintig?
Un portacenere.	Un cenicero.	Een asbak[je].
I fiammiferi staccabili.	Fósforos en librillo.	Lucifers in een boekje.
Una scatola di fiammiferi di sicurezza.	Una caja de fósforos amorfos.	Een doos veiligheids-lucifers.
◄Una pipa di radica di scopa, dritta, curva, con bocchino d'ebonite.	Una pipa fabricada de madera de brezo, recta, encorvada, con boquilla de vulcanita.	Een bruyèrepijp, recht, gebogen met ebonieten mondstuk.
Un portasigarette.	Una pitillera, Una cigarrillera.	Een sigarettenkoker.
Le carte da sigarette.	Papeles de fumar.	Vloeitjes.
Le sigarette con bocchino di sughero.	Cigarrillos emboquillados con corcho.	Sigaretten met kurk-filter.
Le pietre focaie per l'accendi-sigaro.	Piedra de chispa para encendedor.	Vuursteentjes voor een aansteker.
◄Un sigaro avana.	Un puro (o Un cigarro) habano.	Een havana sigaar.
Un accendi-sigaro a benzina.	Un encendedor de bencina.	Een benzineaansteker.
Le sigarette ordinarie.	Cigarrillos corrientes.	Sigaretten zonder mond-stuk.
Il tabacco da naso.	Rapé.	Snuiftabak.
Una borsa per tabacco.	Una bolsa para tabaco.	Een tabakszak.
◄Il tabacco Virginia.	Tabaco de Virginia.	Virginia[tabak].

LE CURIOSITA	**OBJETOS Y PUNTOS DE INTERÉS**	**BEZIENSWAAR-DIGHEDEN**
Generalità	**Generalidades**	**Algemeenheden**
Che cosa c'è da vedere qui?	¿Qué hay que ver aquí?	Wat valt er hier te bezichtigen?
Ci sono cose a . . che val la pena di vedere?	¿Hay algunos lugares en . . que merecen la pena ver?	Zijn er te . . bezienswaardige plekjes.

Is it a sight worth seeing ?	Cela vaut-il la peine d'être vu ?	Ist es sehenswert ?
Is the mountain scenery fine ?	Les paysages de montagnes sont-ils beaux ?	Ist die Gebirgslandschaft schön ?
I want to see the sights of the town.	Je désire voir les curiosités de la ville.	Ich möchte mir die Sehens- würdigkeiten der Stadt ansehen.
Will you show me round the law courts ?	Voulez-vous me piloter (ou me guider) dans le palais de justice ?	Können Sir mir das Justiz- gebäude zeigen ?
Are there any museums worthy of a visit ?	Y a-t-il des musées qui méritent une visite ?	Gibt es hier irgendwelche sehenswerten Museen ?
Is the castle open to the public ? Can it be visited every day, cer- tain days only, only in the absence of the owners ?	Le château est-il ouvert au public ? Peut-il être visité tous les jours, certains jours seulement, seulement en l'absence des propriétaires ?	Ist das Schloß für Besucher geöffnet ? Kann man es täglich, nur an bestimm- ten Tagen, nur in Abwe- senheit des Eigentümers, besichtigen ?
Where should one apply for an order, the neces- sary permit, to visit the château ?	Où faut-il s'adresser pour un billet d'entrée, l'auto- risation nécessaire, pour visiter le château ?	Wo erhält man eine Ein- trittskarte, die nötige Eintrittserlaubnis, für das Schloß ?
Is there an admission (or entrance) fee ?	Y a-t-il un droit d'entrée ?	Kostet der Eintritt etwas ?
What is the price of admis- sion, the charge for visiting this monument, the armoury ?	Combien l'entrée, la visite de ce monument, de la salle d'armes ?	Was kostet der Eintritt, der Besuch dieses Denk- mals, der Rüstkammer ?
Where is the entrance, the exit ?	Où est l'entrée, la sortie ?	Wo ist der Eingang, der Ausgang ?
What is the charge for a guide ?	Combien faut-il payer pour un guide ?	Was kostet die Führung ?
No, thank you, I don't want a guide. I just want to wander round.	Non, merci, je n'ai pas besoin de guide. Je veux seulement aller çà et là.	Nein, danke, ich brauche keinen Führer. Ich möchte nur so herum- wandern.
Is there an interpreter for the English language in the establishment ?	Y a-t-il un interprète pour la langue anglaise dans l'établissement ?	Gibt es im Hause einen englischen Dolmetscher ?
Is there an extensive view, a fine vista, an imposing panorama, from the top of the tower ?	Y a-t-il une vue étendue, une belle échappée [de vue], un imposant pano- rama, du haut de la tour ?	Hat man von der Turm- spitze einen weiten Aus- blick, eine schöne Aus- sicht, einen eindrucks- vollen Rundblick ?
Is it advisable to devote an extra day to visiting the grottoes ? The stalactites and stalag- mites are rather interest- ing, are they not ?	Est-il à conseiller de con- sacrer un jour supplé- mentaire à la visite des grottes ? Les stalactites et stalagmites sont assez intéressantes, n'est-ce pas ?	Sollte man noch einen Tag zugeben, um die Grotten zu besichtigen ? Die Stalakmiten und Stalak- titen sind recht interes- sant, nicht wahr ?
Show me the palace, the orchards, the rose gar- den, the private chapel, the tombs of the kings, X.'s house, the house in	Faites-moi voir le palais, les vergers, la roseraie, la chapelle particulière, les tombeaux des rois, la maison de X., la maison	Zeigen Sie mir den Palast, den Obstgärten, den Rosengarten, die private Kapelle, die Königs- graber, X.'s Haus, Y.'s

Merita ciò di essere visitato?	¿ Es cosa que vale la pena ver ?	Is het bezienswaardig?
Sono belli i paesaggi delle montagne?	¿ Es hermoso el paisaje montañés ?	Is het berglandschap mooi?
◄ Desidero vedere le curiosità della città.	Deseo ver los puntos de interés de la población.	Ik wil de bezienswaardigheden van de stad zien.
Volete farmi visitare il palazzo di giustizia ?	¿ Quiere usted conducirme a ver los tribunales (o la sala) de justicia ?	Wilt U me door het gerechtshof leiden?
Vi sono dei musei degni di esser visitati ?	¿ Hay museos que son dignos de visitarse ?	Zijn er musea die een bezoek waard zijn?
È il castello aperto al pubblico ? Si può visitarlo ogni giorno, certi giorni solamente, solo nell'assenza dei proprietari ?	¿ Está abierto al público el castillo ? ¿ Puede visitarse todos los días, sólo en ciertos días, sólo durante ausencia de los dueños ?	Is het kasteel open voor het publiek? Kan het iedere dag, slechts op bepaalde dagen, slechts gedurende de afwezigheid van de bezitters, bezocht worden?
Dove bisogna rivolgersi per avere il biglietto d'ingresso, il permesso necessario, per visitare il castello ?	¿ Dónde se debe ir para solicitar una orden, el permiso necesario, para visitar el chateau ?	Waar moet men een toegangskaart, de benodigde vergunning, aanvragen, om het kasteel te bezoeken?
◄ Si paga per entrare ?	¿ Hay que pagar derecho de entrada ?	Wordt er entree geheven?
Qual'è il prezzo di ingresso, quanto costa per visitare questo monumento, l'armeria ?	¿ Cuánto es el precio de entrada, el precio para visitar este monumento, la armería ?	Wat is de toegangsprijs, de prijs voor het bezoeken van dit monument, de wapenzaal?
Dov'è l'ingresso, l'uscita ?	¿ Por dónde es la entrada, la salida ?	Waar is de ingang, de uitgang?
Che tariffa si paga per una guida ?	¿ Cuánto es el honorario de un cicerone ?	Hoeveel kost het als ik een gids neem?
No, grazie, io non ho bisogno di una guida. Io voglio giusto fare un giro.	No, gracias, no necesito cicerone. Sólo quiero dar una vuelta.	Nee, dank U, ik wil geen gids. Ik wil alleen maar wat ronddwalen.
◄ Vi è un interprete della lingua inglese sul posto ?	¿ Hay un intérprete de inglés en el establecimiento ?	Is er een Engelse tolk in het gebouw?
C'è una veduta estesa, una bella vista, un panorama imponente, dall'alto della torre ?	¿ Hay una vista extensiva, una bella vista, un grandioso panorama, desde lo alto de la torre ?	Is er een weids uitzicht? een mooi vergezicht, een indrukwekkend panorama, vanaf de torenspits?
È consigliabile di dedicare una giornata extra per visitare le grotte ? Gli stalattiti e gli stalagmite sono abbastanza interessanti, non è vero ?	¿ Se aconseja dedicar un día extra para visitar las grutas ? Las estalactitas y las estalagmitas son bastante interesantes ¿ no es cierto ?	Is het raadzaam een extra dag te wijden aan het bezoeken van de grotten? De stalactieten en stalagmieten zijn interessant, nietwaar?
Mostratemi il palazzo, gli orti, il roseto, la cappella privata, le tombe dei re, la casa di X., la casa nella quale nacque Y.,	Enséñeme el palacio, los huertos, los rosales, la capilla particular, las tumbas de los reyes, la casa de X., la casa en	Laat mij het paleis, de boomgaarden, de rozentuin, de privé kapel, de koningsgraven, het huis van

which Y. was born, the Z. memorial, some old mansions.	dans laquelle Y., est né, le monument[commemoratif] Z., quelques vieux hôtels [particuliers].	Geburtshaus, das Z. Denkmal, einige alte Herrenhäuser.
I am interested in curio[sitie]s, in the Norman variety of the Romanesque, in Gothic, medieval, architecture, in the Renaissance style.	Je m'intéresse aux curiosités ou aux raretés, à l'architecture romane, gothique, du moyen âge, au style [de la] Renaissance.	Ich interessiere mich für Raritäten, für romanische, gotische, mittelalterliche, Architektur, für den Renaissancestil.
Has this building been restored?	Cet édifice a-t-il été restauré?	Ist dieses Gebäude restauriert?
Are there any Roman, Egyptian, antiquities in this museum?	Y a-t-il des antiquités romaines, égyptiennes, dans ce musée?	Gibt es in diesem Museum römische, ägyptische, Altertümer?
Is this vase, this large Chinese, Japanese, vase, an original or a replica?	Ce vase, Cette grande potiche chinoise, japonaise, est-il (-elle) un original ou une réplique?	Ist diese Vase, diese große chinesische, japanische, Vase, ein Original oder eine Kopie?
To what school does this picture, that painting, belong, French, German, English, Dutch, Flemish, Italian, Spanish?	À quelle école appartient ce tableau[-ci], cette peinture[-là], française, allemande, anglaise, hollandaise, flamande, italienne, espagnole?	Aus welcher Schule stammt dieses Bild, das Gemälde, aus der Französischen, Deutschen, Englischen, Holländischen, Flämischen, Italienischen, Spanischen?
Who is the painter of this portrait, this landscape, this sea scape, this miniature, this oil painting, this water colour, this ceiling painting?	Qui est l'auteur de ce portrait, ce paysage, cette marine, cette miniature, cette peinture à l'huile, cette aquarelle, cette peinture de plafond?	Von welchem Maler ist dieses Porträt, diese Landschaft, dieses Seestück, diese Miniatur, dieses Ölgemälde, dieses Aquarell, dieses Deckengemälde?
To which century did this painter, this paintress. belong?	À quel siècle ce peintre appartient-il, cette femme peintre appartient-elle?	In welchem Jahrhundert hat dieser Maler, diese Malerin, gelebt?
B.C. (*before Christ*).	av. J.-C. (*say* avant Jésus-Christ.)	a. C. (*say* ante Christum).
A.D. (*Anno Domini*).	ap[r]. J.-C. (*say* après Jésus-Christ.)	p. C. (*say* post Christum),
Do the galleries contain any Greek sculptures? Who is the sculptor, the sculptress, of this bust, this equestrian statue, this marble group, this bronze statuette, this terra cotta figurine? By whom is it?	Les galeries renferment-elles des sculptures grecques? Qui est le sculpteur, la femme sculpteur, de ce buste, cette statue équestre, ce groupe de marbre, cette statuette de bronze, cette figurine de terre cuite? C'est de qui?	Enthalten die Galerien griechische Skulpturen? Von welchem Bildhauer, welcher Bildhauerin, ist diese Büste, dieses Reiterstandbild, diese Marmorgruppe, diese kleine Bronzefigur, dieses Terracottafigürchen? Von wem ist dies?

il monumento commemorativo di Z., qualche palazzo antico.	que nació Y., el monumento conmemorativo de Z., algunas mansiones antiguas o casas señoriales.	X., het huis waar Y. geboren is, het Z. gedenkteken, vat oude herenhuizen, zien.
Sono interessato nelle curiosità, nell'architettura romanica, gotica, medievale, nello stile del Rinascimento.	Me interesan las curiosidades o las rarezas, la arquitectura románica, gótica, medioeval, al estilo del renacimiento.	Ik stel belang in curiositeiten, in Romaanse, Gothische, middeleeuwse, architectuur, in de Renaissance stijl.
◄Questo edificio ha subito dei restauri ?	¿ Ha sido restaurado este edificio ?	Is dit gebouw gerestaureerd ?
C'è in questo museo qualche antichità romana, egiziana ?	¿ Hay antigüedades romanas, egipcias, en este museo ?	Zijn er Romeinse, Egyptische, antiquiteiten in dit museum ?
È questo vaso, questo grande vaso cinese, giapponese, originale o una copia ?	¿ Es este jarrón, este gran jarrón chino, japonés, un ejemplar original o auténtico, o es una reproducción ?	Is deze vaas, deze grote Chinese, Japanse, vaas een origineel of een kopie ?
A quale scuola appartiene questo quadro, quel dipinto, francese, tedesco, inglese, olandese, fiammingo, italiano, spagnolo ?	¿ A qué escuela pertenece este cuadro, aquella pintura, la francesa, la alemana, la inglesa, la holandesa, la flamenca, la italiana, la española ?	Tot welke school behoort dit schilderij, dat schilderij, Franse, Duitse, Engelse, Hollandse, Vlaamse, Italiaanse, Spaanse?
Chi è l'autore di questo ritratto, questo paesaggio, questa marina, questa miniatura, questo quadro ad olio, questo acquarello, quell'affresco nella volta ?	¿ Quién es el pintor de este retrato, este paisaje, esta marina, esta miniatura, esta pintura al óleo, esta acuarela, este [decorado de] techo ?	Wie is de schilder van dit portret, dit landschap, dit zeegezicht, dit miniatuur, dit olieverf schilderij, dit waterverf schilderij, deze plafondschildering?
◄Di che secolo è questo pittore, questa pittrice ?	¿ A qué siglo pertenece este pintor, esta pintora ?	Tot welke eeuw behoorde deze schilder, deze schilderes ?
a.C. (*say* avanti Cristo).	a. de J.C. (*say* antes de Jesucristo).	v.C. (*say* voor Christus).
d.C. (*say* dopo Cristo).	A.C. (*say* Año de Cristo).	A.D. (*say* Anno Domini).
Contengono le gallerie sculture greche ? Chi è lo scultore, la scultrice, di questo busto, questa statua equestre, questo gruppo in marmo, questa statuetta di bronzo, questa figurina di terracotta ? Chi è l'autore o l'artista ? o Di chi è ?	¿ Hay esculturas griegas en las galerías ? ¿ Quién es el escultor, la escultora, de este busto, esta estatua ecuestre, este grupo en mármol, esta figurilla de bronce, esta figurilla de terracota ? ¿ Por quién es ?	Bevat het museum beeldhouwwerken? Wie is de beeldhouwer, (*sculptress*) de beeldhouwster, van dit borstbeeld, dit ruiterstandbeeld dit marmerbeeldje, dit terra cotta beeldje? Door wie is het gemaakt?

Where is the collection of ancient marbles, the collection of modern sculptures?	Où se trouve le musée des marbres antiques, le musée des sculptures modernes?	Wo ist die Sammlung antiker Marmorskulpturen, die Sammlung moderner Skulpturen?
In which room are the drawings, the tapestries, the ceramics?	Dans quel salon se trouvent les dessins, les tapisseries, les céramiques?	In welchem Raum sind die Zeichnungen, die Wandteppiche, die Keramiken?
Can photographs, souvenirs, be had in the vestibule?	Peut-on se procurer des photographies, des souvenirs, dans le vestibule?	Gibt es in der Eingangshalle Fotografien, Andenken, zu kaufen?
I want to visit the battlefields, the war graves, the war memorial, the tomb of the Unknown warrior. Where is the roll of honour?	Je désire visiter les champs de bataille, les tombes de la guerre, le monument aux morts de la guerre, le tombeau du Soldat inconnu. Où est la liste de ceux qui sont morts pour la patrie?	Ich möchte die Schlachtfelder, die Soldatengräber, das Gefallenendenkmal, das Grab des Unbekannten Soldaten, besichtigen. Wo ist die Ehrentafel für die Gefallenen?
A curator.	Un conservateur.	Ein Kustos.
A caretaker.	Un gardien, Une gardienne.	Ein Museumsdiener.
An attendant (at a museum).	Un gardien.	Ein Wärter.
A chair attendant.	Un chaisier, Une chaisière, Un loueur, Une loueuse, de chaises.	Ein Stühlevermieter.

Sights of nature / Les spectacles de la nature / Naturschönheiten

(See also under **Generalities**, above.)		
An arbour.	Une tonnelle, Un berceau, Un cabinet de verdure.	Eine Laube.
An avenue bordered with ancient trees, with stately oaks. A magnificent forest with various kinds of trees.	Une avenue bordée d'arbres centenaires, de chênes majestueux. Une magnifique forêt aux essences diverses.	Eine von alten Bäumen, von prächtigen Eichen, eingefaßte Allee. Ein herrlicher Mischwald.
A beauty spot.	Un site pittoresque.	Ein malerischer Punkt.
The botanical garden[s].	Le jardin des plantes.	Der botanische Garten.
A cascade. A cataract. A rapid.	Une cascade. Une cataracte. Un rapide.	Eine Kaskade oder Ein kleiner Wasserfall. Ein Katarakt oder Ein großer Wasserfall. Eine Stromschnelle.
A cave or A cavern.	Une caverne, Un antre, Un souterrain.	Eine Höhle.
A chasm.	Un abîme, Un gouffre.	Eine Kluft, Eine Schlucht.
A cliff (coast).	Une falaise.	Eine Klippe.
A cliff (inland).	Un rocher [en escarpement].	Ein Felsen.
A covered walk.	Une allée en berceau.	Ein Laubengang.
A flower bed.	Un parterre fleuri.	Ein Blumenbeet.
A flower garden.	Un jardin fleuriste.	Ein Blumengarten.

Dov'è la raccolta di antichi marmi, la raccolta di sculture moderne ?	¿ Dónde está la colección de mármoles antiguos, la colección de esculturas modernas ?	Waar is de verzameling antiek marmer, de verzameling modern beeldhouwwerk ?
In quale aula sono i disegni, gli arazzi, le ceramiche ?	¿ En cuál de las salas están los dibujos, los tapices, la cerámica ?	In welke kamer bevinden zich de tekeningen de gobelins, de keramiek ?
Si possono comprare fotografie, ricordi, nel vestibolo ?	¿ Pueden obtenerse fotografías, recuerdos, en el vestíbulo ?	Kan men in de vestibule foto's, souvenirs, verkrijgen ?
Io voglio visitare i campi di battaglia, le tombe dei caduti in guerra, il monumento ai morti della guerra, la tomba al Milite ignoto. Dov'è la lista di quelli che son morti per la patria ?	Deseo visitar los campos de batalla, las sepulturas de la guerra, el monumento conmemorativo de la guerra, la tumba del Guerrero incógnito. ¿Dónde está la lista de los muertos por la patria ?	Ik wens de slagvelden, de oorlogsgraven, het oorlogsgedenkteken, het graf van de Onbekende Soldaat, te bezoeken. Waar is de lijst der gesneuvelden ?
Un conservatore.	Un conservador.	Een curator.
Un guardiano, Una guardiana.	Un conserje.	Een huisbewaarder.
Un custode.		
Un locatore, Una locatrice, di sedie.	Un guardián.	Een suppoost.
	Un alquilador de sillas.	Een stoelverhuurder, (feminine) stoelverhuurster.

Gli spettacoli della natura	**Espectáculos de la naturaleza**	**Natuurschoon**
Una pergola, Un frascato.	Una enramada, Una glorieta.	Een prieel.
Un viale fiancheggiato da antichi alberi, da maestose querci. Una magnifica foresta con specie d'alberi diversi.	Una alameda de viejos árboles, una avenida lindada de majestuosos robles. Un hermoso bosque poblado de diversas espécies de árboles.	Een laan omzoomd met oeroude bomen, met statige eiken. Een prachtig woud, met verscheidene boomsoorten.
Un punto pittoresco.	Un lugar pintoresco.	Een schilderachtige plek.
Il giardino botanico.	Los jardines botánicos.	De plantentuin.
Una cascata. Una cateratta.	Una cascada. Una catarata. Un rabión o Un recial.	Een watervalletje. Een waterval. Een stroomversnelling.
Una grotta, Una caverna, Una spelonca.	Una cueva, Un antro.	Een grot.
Un baratro.	Un abismo.	Een afgrond.
Una costa dirupata.	Un farallón.	Een klip.
Una balza, Una rupe.	Una escarpa.	Een steile rots.
Un viale pergolato.	Un pasaje cubierto.	Een berceau.
Un aiuola.	Un macizo [de jardín].	Een bloemperk.
Un giardino di fiori.	Un jardín [de flores].	Een bloementuin.

A fountain (*as in public gardens, squares*). The fountains of Versailles.	Une fontaine. Les grandes eaux de Versailles.	Ein Springbrunnen. Die Wasserkünste von Versailles.
A grove.	Un bocage, Un bosquet.	Ein Gehölz.
A landscape garden.	Un jardin à l'anglaise, Un jardin paysager.	Ein englischer Garten, Ein Landschaftsgarten.
An ornamental lake.	Un bassin, Un miroir d'eau, Une pièce d'eau.	Ein künstlicher See.
A shady park sheltered from the winds.	Un parc ombragé à l'abri du vent.	Ein schattiger windgeschützter Park.
A marble quarry.	Une carrière de marbre.	Ein Marmorbruch.
A rock (*or* An Alpine) garden.	Un jardin de rocaille, Un jardin alpestre.	Ein Steingarten.
A rocking (*or* A logan) stone.	Un rocher branlant.	Ein Wagstein.
A shrubbery.	Une plantation d'arbrisseaux, Un bosquet.	Ein Buschwerk, Ein Strauchwerk.
A [water]fall. I should very much like to go and see the falls of the Rhine at Schaffhausen.	Une chute [d'eau]. Je voudrais bien aller voir les chutes du Rhin à Schaffhouse.	Ein Wasserfall, Ein Fall. Ich würde mir gern den Rheinfall bei Schaffhausen ansehen.
An active, An extinct, volcano.	Un volcan en activité, éteint.	Ein tätiger, Ein erloschener, Vulkan.
The zoological garden[s] *or* The zoo.	Le jardin zoologique, Le zoo.	Der zoologische Garten, Der Zoo.
For mountain scenery, *see under* MOUNTAINEERING (*pp.* 242-247.)		

Art terms	**Termes des beaux-arts**	**Ausdrücke aus der Kunst**
(*See also under* **Generalities,** *above.*)		
An art gallery.	Une galerie (*ou* Un musée) des beaux-arts.	Eine Kunstausstellung.
A picture gallery.	Une galerie de tableaux, Un musée de peintures.	Eine Bildergalerie, Eine Gemäldegalerie.
The armour (*ancient*).	L'armure.	Die Rüstung, Der Panzer.
A cameo.	Un camée.	Eine Gemme.
A coin (*ancient*).	Une médaille.	Eine Münze.
A collection of coins *or* medals.	Une collection de médailles, Un médaillier.	Eine Münzensammlung, Eine Medaillensammlung.
Enamels.	Des émails.	Schmelzarbeiten.
Engravings.	Des gravures, Des estampes.	Stiche.
Etchings.	Des gravures à l'eau-forte, Des eaux-fortes.	Radierungen.
A fresco.	Une fresque.	Ein Fresko.
An intaglio.	Une intaille.	Ein Intaglio.
A mosaic.	Une mosaïque.	Ein Mosaik.
A plaster cast.	Un [moulage au] plâtre.	Ein Gipsabguß.
A sarcophagus.	Un sarcophage.	Ein Sarkophag.

Una fontana. Le fontane di Versaglia.	Una fuente. Las grandes fuentes de Versalles.	Een fontein. De waterwerken van Versailles.
Un boschetto.	Una arboleda, Un boscaje.	Een bosje.
◄Un giardino all'inglese.	Un jardín proyectado por un paisajista, Un jardín a la inglesa.	Een Engelse tuin.
Un lago ornamentale.	Un lago ornamental o pintoresco.	Een vijver.
Un parco ombreggiato protetto contro il vento.	Un parque frondoso guarecido de los vientos.	Een schaduwrijk park tegen de wind beschut.
Una cava di marmo.	Una cantera de mármol.	Een marmergroeve.
Un giardino alpestre.	Un jardín formado de peñas, Un jardín alpestre.	Een rotstuin.
◄Un sasso barcollante.	Un peñón mecedor.	Een schommelsteen.
Un fruticeto, Un boschetto all'inglese.	Un boscaje de arbustos.	Een heesterplantsoen, Een bosje.
Una cascata [d'acqua]. Mi piacerebbe molto di andare a vedere le cascate del Reno a Sciaffusa.	Una caida [de agua]. Me gustaría mucho ir a ver las caidas del Rin en Escafusa.	Een waterval. Ik zou erg graag de watervallen van de Rijn in Schaffhausen willen zien.
Un vulcano attivo, estinto.	Un volcán vivo. Un volcán extinto o apagado.	Een nog werkende, Een uitgedoofde vulkaan.
Il giardino zoologico.	Los jardines zoológicos.	De dierentuin.

Termini per le belle arti	**Términos de las bellas artes**	**Kunsttermen**
◄Una galleria di belle arti.	Un museo de bellas artes.	Een museum.
Una galleria di quadri o di pitture, Una pinacoteca.	Un museo de pinturas.	Een schilderijenmuseum.
L'armatura.	La armadura, El arnés.	De wapenrusting.
Un cammeo.	Un camafeo.	De camee.
Una moneta.	Una moneda.	Een muntstuk.
◄Una collezione di monete, di medaglie.	Una colección numismática.	Een muntverzameling.
Gli smalti.	Esmaltes.	Emaille.
Le incisioni.	Grabados.	Gravures.
Le acque forti.	Grabados al aguafuerte.	Etsen.
Un affresco.	Una pintura al fresco.	Een fresco.
◄Un intaglio.	Una obra de talla ; (gem) Un entalle.	Een intaglio.
Un mosaico.	Un mosáico.	Een mozaïek.
Un gesso.	Un yeso.	Een gipsen beeld.
Un sarcofago.	Un sarcófago.	Een sarcofaag.

A triptych.	Un triptyque.	Ein Triptychon.
A woodcut.	Une gravure sur bois.	Ein Holzschnitt.

Architectural terms · Termes d'architecture · Ausdrücke aus der Architektur

(For Ecclesiastical architecture, see below.)		
An amphitheatre.	Un amphithéâtre.	Ein Amphitheater.
An aqueduct.	Un aqueduc.	Ein Aquadukt.
An arcade.	Une arcade, Des arcades.	Eine Arkade.
An arch.	Une voûte.	Ein Bogen.
A triumphal arch.	Un arc de triomphe.	Ein Triumphbogen.
An archway.	Un passage voûté.	Ein Bogengang.
An archway *(gateway)*.	Un portail.	Ein Torweg.
A balcony.	Un balcon.	Ein Balkon.
The banqueting hall.	La salle des festins ou des fêtes.	Der Festsaal, Der Bankettsaal.
A bas-relief.	Un bas-relief.	Ein Flachrelief.
A bay *(Architecture)*.	Une travée.	Ein Joch.
A building.	Une construction, Un bâtiment, Un édifice ; Un monument.	Ein Gebäude.
A buttress.	Un contrefort.	Ein Strebepfeiler.
A flying buttress.	Un arc-boutant.	Ein Strebebogen.
A cairn.	Une mont-joie.	Ein Steingrabhügel.
A campanile.	Un campanile.	Ein Kampanile.
Castellated *or* Battlemented.	Crénelé, e.	Mit Türmchen und Zinnen versehen.
A feudal castle surrounded by moats.	Un château féodal entouré de douves ou de fossés.	Eine von Wallgräben umgebene Burg.
The clock tower.	La tour de l'horloge.	Der Uhrenturm.
A fluted column *or* pillar.	Une colonne cannelée.	Eine kannelierte Säule.
A country seat	Un château, Un manoir.	Ein Landsitz.
A courtyard.	Une cour.	Ein Hof.
A cromlech *or* dolmen. A menhir. A monolith.	Un dolmen. Un menhir. Un monolithe.	Ein Kromlech, Ein Dolmen. Ein Menhir. Ein Monolith.
A donjon.	Un donjon.	Ein Bergfried, Ein Hauptturm.
A drawbridge *(over a castle moat)*.	Un pont-levis.	Eine Zugbrücke.
A dungeon *(in castle, etc.)*.	Un cachot.	Ein Burgverlies, Ein Kerker.
A façade.	Une façade.	Eine Fassade.
A forecourt.	Une avant-cour.	Ein Vorhof.
A fortification.	Une fortification.	Eine Befestigung.
A fortified place.	Une place forte, Une place de guerre.	Ein befestigter Ort.
A fortress.	Une forteresse.	Eine Festung.
A foundation stone.	Une première pierre.	Ein Grundstein.
A Greek fret.	Une grecque.	Ein gebrochener Stab.

Un trittico.	Un tríptico.	Een triptiek.
◄Un incisione in legno, Una xilografia.	Un grabado en madera.	Een houtsnede.

Termini di architettura / Términos de arquitectura / Bouwkundigetermen

Un anfiteatro.	Un anfiteatro.	Een amfitheater.
Un acquedotto.	Un acueducto.	Een aquaduct.
Un'arcata.	Una arcada.	Een booggang.
Un arco, Una volta.	Un arco.	Een boog, Een gewelf.
◄Un arco trionfale.	Un arco triunfal.	Een zegeboog.
Un passaggio arcato, Un passaggio a volta.	Un pase bajo un **arco**, Un pasaje abovedado.	Een gewelfde gang.
Un portone.	Un portal.	Een booghek.
Un balcone.	Un balcón.	Een balkon.
Una sala per banchetti.	La sala de festines.	De feestzaal.
◄Un basso rilievo.	Un bajorelieve.	Een bas-reliëf.
Un intercolonnio.	Un intercolumnio.	Een nis.
Un edificio, Un fabbricato.	Un edificio, Una construcción.	Een gebouw.
Un contrafforte.	Un contrafuerte.	Een beer, Een contrefort.
Un arco a sprone, Un arco d'appoggio.	Un arbotante.	Een draagboog.
◄Un monticello di pietre, Un tumulo.	Un montón de piedras para señal.	Een stenen grafheuvel.
Un campanile.	Un campanario.	Een klokketoren.
Merlato, a, Con bastioni e torri.	Encastillado, a.	Van torens en kantelen voorzien.
Un castello feudale circondato da fosse.	Un castillo feudal cercado por fosos.	Een feudaal kasteel omringd door grachten.
La torre dell'orologio.	La torre gnomónica.	De klokketoren.
◄Una colonna scanalata.	Una columna acanalada.	Een begroefde pilaar.
Un maniero, Una villa di campagna.	Una casa de campo, Una torre.	Een landgoed.
Un cortile.	Un patio.	Een hof.
Un dolmen. Un menhir. Un monolito.	Un dolmen. Un menhir. Un monolito.	Een hunnebed. Een menhir. Een monoliet.
Un mastio, Un torrione.	La torre más elevada (de un antiguo castillo).	Een slottoren.
◄Un pontelevatoio.	Un puente levadizo.	Een ophaalbrug.
Una prigione sotterranea, Una [prigione] segreta.	Una mazmorra, Un calabozo.	Een kerker.
Una facciata.	Una fachada.	Een gevel.
Un'anticorte.	Un atrio.	Een voorplein.
Una fortificazione.	Una fortificación.	Een versterking.
◄Una piazzaforte.	Una plaza fuerte.	Een versterkte plaats.
Una fortezza.	Un fuerte.	Een vesting.
Una prima pietra.	Una piedra fundamental.	Een eerste steen.
Una greca.	Una greca.	Griekse rand.

A frieze.	Une frise.	Ein Fries.
A garden city. Town planning.	Une cité-jardin, L'urbanisme.	Eine Gartenstadt. Der Städtebau.
A gargoyle.	Une gargouille.	Ein Wasserspeier.
A gate[way].	Une porte, Une entrée.	Ein Eingangstor.
An intrados.	Un intrados.	Ein Bogenanfang.
A lintel.	Un linteau.	Ein Oberbalken.
A mausoleum.	Un mausolée.	Ein Mausoleum.
A historical monument.	Un monument historique.	Ein historisches Denkmal.
A mullion.	Un meneau.	Ein Fensterstab.
An oriel [window].	Une fenêtre en encorbellement.	Ein Erker.
A pier (*masonry pillar*).	Un trumeau.	Ein Pfeiler.
A porch (*palace*).	Un porche.	Eine Vorhalle.
A portal.	Un portail.	Ein Portal.
The ramparts.	Les remparts.	Die Wallanlagen.
A royal, A baronial, residence.	Une résidence royale, seigneuriale.	Eine königliche, Eine herrschaftliche, Residenz.
Ruins. Roman ruins.	Des ruines. Des ruines romaines.	Ruinen. Römische Ruinen.
A spandrel.	Un tympan.	Ein Zwickel.
The grand staircase.	Le grand escalier, L'escalier d'honneur.	Das Treppenhaus.
State rooms *or* appartments (*palace*).	De grands appartements [d'apparat].	Prunkräume.
A tesselated pavement.	Un pavé de mosaïque.	Ein Mosaikfußboden, Ein Mosaikpflaster.
A tower.	Une tour.	Ein Turm.
A town hall *or* A guildhall.	Un hôtel de ville, Une maison de ville, Une mairie.	Ein Rathaus.
A tumulus.	Un tumulus.	Ein Tumulus, Ein Hügelgrab.
A turret.	Une tourelle.	Ein kleiner Turm, Ein Türmchen.
A groined vault.	Une voûte d'arête.	Ein Kreuzgewölbe.
A wing (*of a building*).	Une aile.	Ein Flügel, Ein Seitenbau.

Ecclesiastical architecture	**L'architecture ecclésiastique**	**Kirchenarchitektur**
An abbey founded in eleven forty-five, built in the twelfth (*or* 12th) century.	Une abbaye fondée en onze cent quarante-cinq, construite au douzième (*ou* XIIᵉ) siècle.	Eine elfhundertfünfundvierzig gegründete, im zwölften (*oder* 12.) Jahrhundert gebaute, Abtei.
The north, The south, aisle.	Le collatéral (*ou* Le bas-côté) nord, sud.	Das nördliche, Das südliche, Seitenschiff.
The high altar.	Le maître-autel, Le grand autel.	Der Hochaltar.
An altar piece.	Un retable, Un tableau d'autel.	Ein Altargemälde.
The ambulatory	Le déambulatoire.	Der Wandelgang.
An apse.	Une abside.	Eine Apsis.

Un fregio.	Un friso.	Een fries.
Una città giardino. Il piano regolatore della città.	Una ciudad jardín. Urbanización.	Een tuindorp. Stadsuitbreidingsplannen.
Una doccia sporgente scolpita.	Una gárgola.	Een waterspuwer.
Un portone.	Una entrada, Un portal.	Een poort, Een hek.
Un intradosso.	Un intradós.	Een binnenwelving.
Un architrave.	Un dintel.	Een bovendorpel.
Un mausoleo.	Un mausoleo.	Een mausoleum.
Un monumento storico.	Un monumento histórico.	Een historisch monument.
Un regolo.	Un montante.	Een middenstijl.
Una finestra **gotica** in accollo.	Un mirador.	Een erker [raam].
Un pilastro.	Una pila.	Een pijler.
Un portico.	Un pórtico.	Een voorportaal.
Un portale.	Un portal.	Het portaal.
I baluardi.	El terraplén, El pretil.	Het bolwerk.
Una residenza reale, baroniale.	Un palacio (o Una casa) real, Una casa señorial.	Een koninklijke, Een adellijke, residentie.
Le rovine. Le rovine romane.	Ruinas. Ruinas romanas.	Ruïnes. Romeinse ruïnes.
Il timpano.	Un tímpano.	Een timpaan.
La scala grande, Lo scalone, La scala regia.	La gran escalera.	De hoofdtrap.
Le sale regie.	Los salones de recepción, Las cámaras reales.	Staatsiekamers.
Un pavimento a mosaico.	Un pavimento de mosaico.	Een mozaïekvloer.
Una torre.	Una torre.	Een toren.
Un palazzo municipale, Un municipio.	Un ayuntamiento, Una casa consistorial.	Een stadhuis, Een raadhuis.
Un tumulo.	Un túmulo.	Een grafheuvel.
Una torretta.	Una torrecilla.	Een torentje.
Una volta a spigolo.	Una bóveda de arista.	Een kruisgewelf.
Un'ala.	Un ala.	Een vleugel.

L'architettura di chiesa	**Arquitectura eclesiastica**	**Kerkelijke architectuur**
Un'abbazia fondata nel millecentoquarantacinque, costruita nel dodicesimo (o XII°) secolo.	Una abadía fundada en mil ciento cuarenta y cinco, edificada en el siglo doce o XII.	Een abbij gegrondvest in elf honderd vijf en veertig, in de twaalfde (of 12de) eeuw.
La navata nord, sud.	La nave del norte, del sur.	De noord, De zuid zijbeuk.
L'altar maggiore.	El altar mayor.	Het hoogaltaar.
Una pala d'altare, Un ancona.	Un retablo.	Een altaarbeeld.
L'ambulatorio.	La galería, El paseo.	De wandelgang.
Un'abside.	Un'abside.	Een absis.

A baptist[e]ry.	Un baptistère.	Eine Taufkapelle.
A basilica.	Une basilique.	Eine Basilika.
A belfry.	Un beffroi, Un clocher.	Ein Glockenturm.
The bells.	Les cloches.	Die Glocken, Das Läutwerk.
A great bell.	Une grosse cloche, Un bourdon.	Eine große Glocke. →
A calvary.	Un calvaire.	Ein Kreuzberg.
A catacomb.	Une catacombe.	Eine Katakombe.
A cathedral.	Une cathédrale.	Ein Dom, Eine Kathedrale.
A chancel or A choir.	Un chœur.	Ein Chor.
The Lady Chapel.	La chapelle absidale, La chapelle de la Vierge.	Die Marienkapelle. →
The chimes.	Le[s] carillon[s].	Das Glockenspiel.
A church.	Une église ; (of French protestants) Un temple.	Eine Kirche.
A parish church.	Une église paroissiale.	Eine Pfarrkirche.
A Roman Catholic church.	Une église catholique.	Eine römisch-katholische Kirche.
Is this the collegiate church where the queen was buried ?	Est-ce ici l'église collégiale où fut ensevelie la reine ?	Ist dies die Kollegienkirche, → wo die Königin begraben ist ?
The churchyard.	L'enclos (ou La cour) (ou Le jardin) de l'église.	Der Kirchhof.
The churchyard (graveyard).	Le cimetière, Le champ du repos.	Der Kirchhof, Der Friedhof.
The churchyard (public square).	La place.	Der Platz [vor der Kirche], Der Domplatz.
Here lies . ., Here lie . . (on grave).	Ci-gît . ., Ci-gisent . ., Ici repose(nt) . . .	Hier liegt . ., Hier liegen...
The clerestory.	La claire-voie, La fenêtre haute.	Das lichte Geschoß, Das Fensterschoß des Hauptschiffes.
A cloister.	Un cloître.	Ein Kloster.
A convent or A nunnery.	Un couvent.	Ein Nonnenkloster.
A crypt.	Une crypte.	Eine Krypta.
The font.	Les fonts.	Das Taufbecken.
The gallery (in cathedral, etc.).	La tribune.	Die Empore, Die Empor- → kirche.
A hermitage.	Un ermitage.	Eine Einsiedelei.
A monastery.	Un monastère.	Ein Kloster, Ein Mönchskloster.
The nave.	La nef.	Das Hauptschiff.
An organ.	Un orgue.	Eine Orgel.
An organ loft.	Une tribune d'orgues.	Ein Orgelchor. →
An organ pipe.	Un tuyau d'orgue.	Eine Orgelpfeife.
An ossuary or A charnel house.	Un ossuaire.	Ein Beinhaus.
A pier (masonry pillar).	Un trumeau.	Ein Pfeiler.
A porch.	Un porche.	Eine Säulenhalle.
A portal.	Un portail.	Ein Portal. →
A priory.	Un prieuré.	Eine Priorei.
The pulpit.	La chaire [du prédicateur].	Die Kanzel.
A reliquary.	Un reliquaire, Une châsse.	Ein Reliquienschrein.
A reredos.	Un retable.	Ein Altarblatt.

Un battistero.	Un bautisterio.	Een doopkapel.
Una basilica.	Una basílica.	Een basiliek.
Una cella (o Una torre) campanaria.	Un campanario.	Een klokketoren.
Le campane.	Las campanas.	De klokken.
◄Un campanone.	Una gran campana.	De grote klok.
Un calvario.	Un calvario.	Een kruisberg.
Una catacomba.	Una catacumba.	Een catacombe.
Un duomo, Una cattedrale.	Una catedral.	Een kathedraal, Een dom.
Un coro.	Un coro.	Een koor.
◄La cappella della Madonna.	La capilla de la Virgen, La capilla de Nuestra Señora.	De Mariakapel.
Il cariglione.	El campaneo.	Het klokkenspel.
Una chiesa.	Una iglesia.	Een kerk.
Una chiesa parrocchiale.	Una [iglesia] parroquial.	Een parochiekerk.
Una chiesa cattolica romana.	Una iglesia católica apostólica.	Een katholieke kerk.
◄È questa la chiesa collegiale dove fu sepolta la regina ?	¿ Es esta la iglesia colegial donde fué sepultada la reina ?	Is dit de collegiale kapel waar de koningin is begraven?
Il recinto della chiesa.	El jardín de la iglesia.	Het kerkhof.
Il camposanto.	El cementerio.	Het kerkhof, De begraafplaats.
La piazza.	La plaza [de la iglesia].	Het kerkplein.
Qui giace .. , Qui giacciono ...	Aquí yacen los restos [mortales] de . . .	Hier rust .. , Hier rusten ...
◄La navata superiore.	La claraboya.	Het hoograam.
Un chiostro.	Un claustro.	Een klooster.
Un convento.	Un convento [de monjas].	Een nonnenklooster.
Una cripta.	Una cripta.	Een grafkelder.
La fonte battesimale.	La fuente de bautismo.	De doopvont.
◄La tribuna.	La tribuna.	De galerij.
Un eremo.	Una ermita.	Een kluis.
Un monastero.	Un monasterio.	Een monnikenklooster.
La navata.	La nave.	Het schip.
Un organo.	Un órgano.	Een orgel.
◄Una tribuna dell'organo.	Una tribuna de órgano.	Een orgelkoor.
Una canna d'organo.	Un cañón de órgano.	Een orgelpijp.
Un ossario	Un osario.	Een knekelhuis[je].
Un pilastro.	Una pila, Un machón.	Een pijler.
Un portico.	Un pórtico.	Een portaal.
◄Un portale.	Un portal.	Een poort.
Un priorato.	Un priorato.	Een priorij.
Il pulpito.	El púlpito.	De kansel.
Un reliquario.	Un relicario.	Een reliekschrijn.
Un dossale.	Un retablo.	Een altaarscherm.

A rood screen.	Un jubé.	Ein Heiligengitter.
A shrine (sanctuary).	Un sanctuaire.	Ein Heiligenschrein.
A shrine (reliquary).	Une châsse, Un reliquaire.	Ein Reliquienschrein.
A spandrel.	Un tympan.	Ein Zwickel.
Stained glass (in church, etc.) A stained glass window. A rose window.	Des vitraux peints. Une verrière. Une rose ou Une rosace.	Glasmalerei. Ein buntes Kirchenfenster. Eine Fensterrose.
A steeple.	Un clocher [pointu].	Ein Spitzturm.
A synagogue.	Une synagogue.	Eine Synagoge.
A tomb.	Un tombeau.	Ein Grab.
A tower.	Un tour.	Ein Turm.
The north transept. The south transept.	Le transept nord. Le transept sud.	Der Nordtransept. Der Südtransept.
The triforium.	Le triforium.	Das Triforium.
A tympanum.	Un tympan [d'arcade].	Ein Tympanon, Ein Bogenfeld.
A vestry.	Une sacristie.	Eine Sakristei.

Public Worship	Le culte public	Öffentlicher Gottesdienst
Is there an English church in the place?	Y a-t-il une église anglaise (ou anglicane) dans la localité?	Gibt es in dem Ort eine englische (oder anglikanische) Kirche?
At what time is the church service or divine service? When is high mass, low mass, celebrated?	À quelle heure est le service de l'église ou l'office divin? Quand la grand-messe, la messe basse, est-elle célébrée?	Um wieviel Uhr ist der Gottesdienst? Wann wird das Hochamt, die Stillmesse, zelebriert?
The communion service.	La célébration de la communion.	Die Austeilung des heiligen Abendmahls.

ENTERTAINMENTS, SHOWS, ETC. (= et cetera)	DIVERTISSEMENTS, SPECTACLES, ETC. (= et cœtera)	VERGNÜGUNGEN, AUFFÜHRUNGEN, USW. (= und so weiter)

The theatre	Le théâtre	Das Theater
An opera house.	Un opéra.	Ein Opernhaus.
An open-air theatre.	Un théâtre en plein air.	Ein Freilichttheater.
Shall we go to the theatre?	Est-ce que nous allons au théâtre?	Wollen wir ins Theater gehen?
What are they playing (or What is on) at present?	Que joue-t-on (ou Qu'est-ce qui se joue) actuellement?	Was für ein Stück läuft jetzt? Was gibt es augenblicklich?
What is the plot of the play?	Quelle est l'intrigue de la pièce?	Was für eine Handlung hat das Stück?
Who plays the leading part?	Qui joue le premier rôle?	Wer spielt die Hauptrolle?
Which is the star turn? When does the star (actor or actress) come on [the stage]?	Quel est le clou de la représentation? L'étoile (ou La vedette) quand entre-t-elle en scène?	Welches ist die Hauptnummer? Wann tritt der Hauptdarsteller, die Hauptdarstellerin, auf?

◄Un tramezzo tra navata e coro.	Una reja veladora.	Een koorhek.
Un tabernacolo.	Un santuario.	Een heiligdom.
Un reliquario.	Un relicario.	Een reliekschrijn.
Un timpano.	Un tímpano.	Een timpaan.
I vetri colorati.　Una vetrata depinta.　Un finestrone a rosa.	Vidrio de color.　Una ventana de vidrio de color.　Un rosetón.	Gebrandschilderd.　Een gebrandschilderd raam.　Een rozetvenster.
◄Una guglia.	Una espira.	Een spitse toren.
Una sinagoga.	Una sinagoga.	Een Jodenkerk,　Een synagoog.
Una tomba.	Una tumba.	Een graf.
Una torre.	Una torre.	Een toren.
Il transetto nord.　Il transetto sud.	El crucero del norte. El crucero del sur.	Het noorder dwarsschip.　Het zuiderdwarsschip.
◄Il triforio.	El triforium.	Het triforium.
Un timpano.	Un faldón.	Een timpaan.
Una sagrestia.	Un vestuario, Una sacristía.	Een sacristie, een consistoriekamer.

Il culto publico	**El culto divino**	**Openbare godsdienstoefening**
C'è una chiesa inglese in questa località?	¿Hay una iglesia anglicana en la localidad?	Is er een Engelse kerk in de gemeente?
A che ora ci sono le funzioni (o c'è il servizio divino) in chiesa?　A che ora c'è la messa cantata, la messa bassa?	¿A qué hora es el oficio religioso?　¿A qué hora se canta la misa mayor, se dice misa?	Hoe laat is de kerkdienst?　Wanneer is er hoogmis, laagmis?
◄La celebrazione della comunione.	La sagrada comunión.	De communie dienst.

DIVERTIMENTI, SPETTACOLI,　ECC. (= eccetera)	**DIVERSIONES, ESPECTÁCULOS, ETC.** (= et cetera)	**VERMAKELIJK-HEDEN VOORSTELLINGEN ENZ.** (= enzovoort)
Il teatro	**El teatro**	**Het theater, Des schouwburg**
Un teatro dell'opera.	Un teatro de ópera.	Een opera.
Un teatro all'aperto.	Un teatro a la intemperie.	Een openluchttheater.
Vogliamo andare al teatro?	¿Vamos al teatro?	Zullen we naar de schouwburg gaan?
Cosa si recita in questo momento?	¿Qué están dando (o Qué presentan) actualmente?	Wat geven ze (of Wat wordt er gegeven) op het ogenblik?
◄Qual'è l'intreccio della recita?	¿Qué es el argumento de la función?	Wat is de intrige van het stuk?
Chi fa la prima parte?	¿Quién desempeña el papel principal?	Wie speelt de hoofdrol?
Quale parte è affidata al primo attore?　Quando entra in scena il primo attore, la prima attrice?	¿Cuál es el número de gala?　¿Cuándo sale [a escena] el, la, estrella?	Wat is het hoofdnummer?　Wanneer komt de ster op het toneel?

Is there a matinée, an evening performance?	Y a-t-il une [représentation en] matinée, une [représentation de] soirée?	Gibt es eine Matinee, eine Abendvorstellung?
When is the first performance, the last performance (or night), of the play?	Quand donne-t-on la première [représentation], la dernière représentation, de la pièce?	Wann ist die Erstaufführung oder die Premiere, die letzte Aufführung, des Stückes?
Is there no performance (or Is it closed) this evening?	Y a-t-il relâche ce soir?	Findet heute abend keine Aufführung statt oder Ist das Theater heute abend geschlossen?
When do they open the doors?	Quand ouvre-t-on les portes?	Wann werden die Türen geöffnet?
Do we have to line up or queue up?	Faut-il faire [la] queue?	Müssen wir uns anstellen?
When does the performance begin, end?	Quand la séance commence-t-elle, finit-elle?	Wann beginnt die Aufführung? Wann ist die Aufführung zu Ende?
At what time does the curtain go up or rise?	À quelle heure lève-t-on le rideau?	Wann geht der Vorhang auf?
Are there any seats or is there standing room only?	Y a-t-il de places ou y a-t-il des places debout seulement?	Gibt es Sitzplätze oder nur Stehplätze?
House full.	Complet.	Ausverkauft.
An attendant (theatre).	Une placeuse, Une ouvreuse.	Eine Platzanweiserin.
I want to leave my coat in the cloak room.	Je désire déposer mon manteau au vestiaire.	Ich möchte meinen Mantel in der Garderobe abgeben.
The auditorium.	La salle.	Der Zuschauerraum.
The crush room.	Le foyer [public].	Das Foyer.
The footlights.	La rampe.	Die Rampenlichter.
The stage or The boards.	La scène, Les planches.	Die Bühne, Die Bretter.
The box office.	Le bureau [de location], Le [bureau de] contrôle, La location, La caisse, Le guichet.	Die Theaterkasse.
A box.	Une loge.	Eine Loge.
A stage box.	Une [loge d']avant-scène.	Eine Proszeniumsloge.
A pit box.	Une baignoire.	Eine Parkettloge.
The dress circle. A dress-circle seat.	Le [premier] balcon, La corbeille. Un fauteuil de [premier] balcon.	Der erste Rang. Ein Platz im ersten Rang.
The upper circle.	La seconde galerie.	Der zweite Rang.
The gallery.	La troisième (ou La dernière) galerie, L'amphithéâtre.	Die Galerie, Der dritte Rang.
The pit.	Le parterre.	Das Parkett.
A stall.	Un fauteuil.	Ein Sperrsitz.
An orchestra stall.	Un fauteuil d'orchestre.	Ein Orchestersitz.
Where can one get tickets?	Où trouve-t-on des billets?	Wo ist der Kartenverkauf?
Are there still seats to be had for to-night's performance? How much are the seats? What is the price of admission	Y a-t-il encore des places libres pour la représentation de ce soir? Combien les places? Combien le prix des fauteuils? Je	Gibt es noch Karten für die heutige Abendvorstellung? Was kosten die Plätze? Was kosten die Parkettplätze? Ich

C'è una rappresentazione di giorno, di sera ?	¿ Hay representación por la tarde, por la noche ?	Is er een middagvoorstelling, een avondvoorstelling?
Quando c'è la prima rappresentazione, l'ultima rappresentazione, della recita ?	¿Cuándo es el estreno (o la primera representación), la última representación, de la función ?	Wanneer is de eerste voorstelling, de laatste voorstelling, van het stuk?
Non c'è rappresentazione (o C'è riposo) questo sera ?	¿ No hay función (o representación) esta tarde ?	Is er geen voorstelling vanavond?
A che ora si aprono le porte ?	¿Cuándo abren las puertas ?	Wanneer gaan de deuren open?
Bisogna far la coda ?	¿ Hay que hacer cola ?	Moeten wij in de rij staan?
Quando comincia, finisce, la recita ?	¿Cuándo empieza, termina, la función ?	Wanneer begint, eindigt, de voorstelling?
A che ora si leva il sipario ?	¿ A qué hora sube el telón ?	Hoe laat gaat het scherm op?
Ci sono posti a sedere o soltanto posti in piedi ?	¿ Hay asientos o hay que estar de pie ?	Zijn er zitplaatsen of zijn er enkel staanplaatsen?
Completo.	Completo.	Uitverkocht.
Una inserviente, Una maschera.	Una acomodadora.	Een ouvreuse.
Io voglio lasciare il cappotto nel vestiario.	Deseo depositar mi sobretodo en el vestuario.	Ik wens mijn jas in de vestiaire af te geven.
La sala.	La sala.	De zaal.
Il foyer.	El salón de descanso, El foyer.	De foyer.
I lumi della ribalta.	Las candilejas.	Het voetlicht.
Il palcoscenico.	El escenario, Las tablas.	Het toneel. De planken.
L'ufficio vendita biglietti.	La taquilla.	Het plaatsbureau.
Un palco.	Un palco.	Een loge.
Un palco di proscenio.	Un palco escénico.	Een toneelloge.
Un palco di platea.	Un palco de platea.	Een parterre loge.
La prima galleria. Una poltrona della prima galleria.	Sillones entresuelo. Un sillón entresuelo.	Het eerste balkon. Een plaats op het eerste balkon.
La seconda galleria.	El segundo entresuelo.	Het tweede balkon.
L'ultima galleria.	El paraíso, El gallinero.	Het schellinkje.
La platea.	La platea.	Het parterre.
Una poltrona.	Una butaca.	Een fauteuil.
Una poltrona d'orchestra.	Una butaca de platea.	Een orkestfauteuil.
Dove si possono prendere i biglietti ?	¿Dónde se toman los billetes ?	Waar kan men plaatsen krijgen?
Ci sono ancora posti disponibili per la recita di questa sera ? Quanto costano i posti ? Qual'è il prezzo della poltrona ?	¿Quedan localidades para la representación de esta tarde ? ¿ A cuánto son [las localidades] ? ¿ Cuánto es la entrada	Zijn er nog plaatsen te krijgen voor de voorstelling van vanavond? Hoeveel kosten de plaatsen? Wat is de

to the stalls? I want two tickets for the stalls, in or about the eighth row, near the end, in the centre.	désire deux billets pour les fauteuils, au huitième rang ou environ, près du bout, au milieu.	möchte zwei Sperrsitze, ungefähr in der achten Reihe, an der Ecke, in der Mitte.
Are these seats numbered?	Ces places sont-elles numérotées?	Sind diese Plätze numeriert?
Entertainment tax.	La taxe sur les spectacles.	Vergnügungssteuer.
A [theatrical] play. A three-act play. The third scene of act two.	Une pièce [de théâtre]. Une pièce en trois actes. La troisième scène du second acte.	Ein Theaterstück. Ein Stück in drei Akten. Die dritte Szene im zweiten Akt.
A ballet.	Un ballet.	Ein Ballett.
A comic opera.	Un opéra bouffe.	Eine komische Oper.
A costume piece or play.	Une pièce historique.	Ein historisches Drama.
A curtain raiser.	Un lever de rideau.	Ein Einakter vor dem Hauptstück.
A drama.	Un drame.	Ein Drama.
A gala. A gala performance.	Un gala. Une représentation de gala.	Eine Gala. Eine Galavorstellung.
A light opera or An operetta.	Une opérette [légère].	Eine Operette.
A musical comedy.	Une comédie musicale.	Ein Singspiel.
A mystery [play].	Un mystère, Un miracle.	Ein Mysterium, Ein Passionsspiel.
An opera.	Un opéra.	Eine Oper.
A revue.	Une revue.	Eine Revue.
A sketch (*playlet*).	Une saynète, Une esquisse dramatique.	Ein Sketch.
A spectacular play (*of the pantomime type*).	Une féerie.	Ein Festspiel.
A tragedy.	Une tragédie.	Eine Tragödie, Ein Trauerspiel.
An interlude or An entr'acte.	Un entracte.	Ein Zwischenspiel.
The interval or The interlude.	L'intermède.	Die Pause.
Please give me a programme, a book of the words, an opera glass, a pass-out check.	Veuillez me donner un programme, un livret [d'opéra], d'opéra-comique, d'opérette], une jumelle [de théâtre], une contremarque.	Geben Sie mir bitte ein Programm, ein Textbuch, ein Opernglas, eine Kontrollmarke.
The cast.	La distribution [des rôles].	Die Besetzung.
An actor.	Un acteur, Un comédien.	Ein Schauspieler.
An actress.	Une actrice, Une comédienne.	Eine Schauspielerin.
A ballet dancer.	Un danseur, Une danseuse, Un figurant, Une figurante, Une ballerine.	Ein Ballettänzer, Eine Ballettänzerin.

Io desidero due biglietti per le poltrone, verso la ottava fila, verso l'estremità, nel centro.	y el precio de la butaca? Quiero dos butacas de la fila ocho o en su proximidad, cerca de la extremidad, en el centro.	toegangsprijs, voor de fauteuils? Ik wil twee fauteuil (of twee stalles), op de of in de buurt van de achtste rij, vrij achteraan, in het midden.
◄Sono numerati questi posti?	¿ Son numerados estos asientos ?	Zijn deze plaatsen genummerd?
La tassa sullo spettacolo.	Impuesto sobre espectáculos.	De vermakelijkheidsbelasting.
Una recita. Una recita in tre atti. La terza scena del secondo atto.	Una función de teatro. Una función de tres actos. La escena tercera del segundo acto.	Een toneelstuk. Een stuk in drie bedrijven. De derde scène van het tweede bedrijf.
Un balletto.	Un baile [de teatro], Un balé.	Een ballet.
Un'opera buffa.	Una zarzuela.	Een komische opera.
◄Una rappresentazione storica.	Una comedia de capa y espada, Un drama histórico.	Een historisch stuk.
Una commediola preludiante, Un ante-recita.	Una pieza preliminar.	Een voorstukje.
Un dramma.	Un drama.	Een drama.
Di gala. Una rappresentazione di gala.	Una gala. Una función de gala.	Een gala-avond. Een galavoorstelling.
Un'operetta.	Una opereta.	Een operette.
◄Una commedia in musica.	Una zarzuela.	Een muzikale komedie.
Un mistero, Un miracolo.	Un auto sacramental.	Een passiespel.
Un'opera.	Una ópera.	Een opera.
Una rivista.	Una revista.	Een revue.
Una macchietta.	Un sainete.	Een schets.
◄Una rappresentazione spettacolosa.	Una representación aparatosa.	Een kijkstuk.
Una tragedia.	Una tragedia.	Een tragedie.
Un intermezzo.	Un entreacto.	Een tussenbedrijf. Een intermezzo.
L'intervallo.	El intermedio.	De pauze.
Per favore, datemi un programma, un libretto, i binocoli, una contromarca.	Haga el favor de darme un programa, un folleto de la letra, un par de gemelos [de teatro], un billete de readmisión.	Geef me een programma, een libretto, een toneelkijker, een sortie als 't U belieft.
◄La distribuzione delle parti.	El reparto de papeles.	De rolverdeling.
Un attore.	Un actor, Un cómico.	Een toneelspeler, Een acteur.
Un'attrice.	Una actriz, Una cómica.	Een toneelspeelster, Een actrice.
Un ballerino, Una ballerina.	Un bailarín, Una bailarina.	Een balletdanser, (feminine) Een balletdanseres.

Encore ! To encore.	Bis ! Bisser.	Da capo ! Da capo rufen.

The cinema *or* **The picture palace** *or* **The pictures**	**Le cinéma[tographe] *ou* Le ciné**	**Das Kino**
A news theatre.	Un ciné-actualités.	Ein Wochenschaukino. →
A silent film. A sound film.	Un film muet. Un film sonore.	Ein stummer Film. Ein Tonfilm.
A talking picture *or* film.	Un film parlant.	Ein Sprechfilm.
A colour film.	Un film en couleurs.	Ein Farbenfilm.
A comedy film.	Une ciné-comédie.	Ein Lustspielfilm.
A comic film.	Un film comique.	Ein Groteskfilm. →
An instructional film.	Un film documentaire.	Ein Kulturfilm.
A musical film.	Un film musical.	Ein musikalischer Spielfilm.
A news film *or* reel.	Un film d'actualité	Eine Wochenschau.
A topical film.	Un film de reportage.	Ein Reportagefilm.
A slow-motion picture.	Un film [tourné] au ralenti.	Ein Zeitlupenfilm. →
A close-up.	Un premier plan, Un gros plan.	Eine Grossaufnahme.
Is there a continuous performance ?	Y a-t-il spectacle permanent ?	Ist die Vorstellung fortlaufend ?

Music, The music hall	**La musique, Le music-hall**	**Musik, Das Varieté**
A band *or* An orchestra.	Une musique, Un orchestre, Une harmonie.	Eine Kapelle, Ein Orchester.
A brass band.	Une fanfare.	Eine Kapelle mit Blasinstrumenten.
A dance band.	Un orchestre de danse.	Eine Tanzkapelle. →
A military band.	Une musique militaire.	Eine Militärkapelle.
A string band.	Un orchestre à cordes.	Ein Streichorchester.
The bandmaster.	Le chef de musique.	Der Kapellmeister.
A bandsman.	Un musicien.	Ein Musiker.
A bandstand.	Un kiosque à musique.	Ein Musikpavillon. →
A full orchestra.	Un grand orchestre.	Ein großes Orchester.
The conductor (*band*).	Le chef d'orchestre.	Der Dirigent.
A vocal and instrumental concert.	Un concert vocal et instrumental.	Ein Konzert mit Gesang und Orchester.
An open-air concert.	Un concert en plein air.	Ein Konzert im Freien.
A sacred concert.	Un concert spirituel.	Ein Kirchenkonzert.
Chamber music.	La musique de chambre.	Kammermusik.
The overture.	L'ouverture.	Die Ouverture.
A singer.	Un chanteur, Une chanteuse ; Une cantatrice.	Ein(e) Sänger(in).
A solo. Instrumental solos.	Un solo. Des soli d'instruments.	Ein Solo. Instrumentensolos.
A soloist.	Un(e) soliste.	Ein(e) Solist(in). →

Bis ! Bissare.	¡ Bis ! ¡ Bis !, ¡ Venga más ! Pedir la repetición.	Bis! Bisseren.

Il cinema[tografo]	**El cine**	**Debioscoop**
◄Un cinema di attualità.	Un cine de actualidades.	Een nieuwsbioscoop.
Una film muta. Una film sonora.	Una película muda. Una película de sonido.	Een stomme film. Een geluidsfilm.
Una film parlante.	Una película hablada.	Een sprekende film.
Una film a colori.	Una película en colores.	Een kleurenfilm.
Una film-commedia.	Una comedia cinematográfica.	Een vrolijke film.
◄Una film buffa.	Un sainete cinematográfico.	Een komische film.
Una film educativa.	Una película instructiva.	Een documentaire.
Una film musicale.	Una película musical.	Een operettefilm.
Una film di attualità.	Una película de actualidades.	Een nieuwsfilm.
Una film su soggetti del giorno.	Una película de asuntos tópicos.	Een reportagefilm.
◄Una film rallentata.	Una película proyectada a paso lento.	Een vertraagd opgenomen film.
Una visuale ravvicinata, Un grosso piano.	Una fotografía cinematográfica a quema ropa.	Een close-up.
C'è uno spettacolo continuo ?	¿ Hay representación contínua ?	Is er een doorlopende voorstelling?

La musica, Caffè concerto	**Música, El salón de conciertos**	**Muziek Het varététheater**
Una banda musicale, Un' orchestra.	Una orquesta, Una música.	Een muziekkoprs, Een orkest.
Una fanfara.	Una música de instrumentos de metal.	Een fanfarekorps.
◄Un'orchestrina per ballo.	Una orquesta de baile.	Een dansorkest.
Una banda militare.	Una charanga.	Een militair muziekkorps.
Un'orchestra a corde.	Una orquesta de instrumentos de cuerda.	Een strijkorkest, Een strijkje.
Il capo musico.	El músico mayor.	De kapelmeester.
Un bandista, Un suonatore.	Un músico de orquesta.	Een muzikant.
◄Un chiosco per musica.	Una tribuna de orquesta.	Een muziektent.
Un'orchestra completa.	Una gran orquesta.	Een groot orkest.
Il direttore.	El director.	De dirigent.
Un concerto vocale ed istrumentale.	Un concierto vocal e instrumental.	Een vocaal en instrumentaal concert.
Un concerto all'aperto.	Un concierto a la intemperie.	Een openluchtconcert.
◄Un concerto sacro.	Un concierto de música sagrada.	Een concert van gewijde muziek.
La musica di camera.	Música de salón.	Kamermuziek.
Il preludio.	La obertura.	De ouverture.
Un(a) cantante.	Un cantante, Una cantatriz.	Een zanger, (feminine) Een zangeres.
Un [as]solo. [As]soli per istrumenti.	Un solo. Solos de música instrumental.	Een solo. Instrumentale soli.
◄Un(a) soloista.	Un(a) solista.	Een solist, (feminine) Een soliste.

A tenor. A barytone. A bass. A soprano. A mezzo-soprano. A contralto.	Un ténor. Un baryton. Une basse. Un soprano. Un mezzo-soprano. Un contralto.	Ein Tenor. Ein Bariton Ein Baß. Ein Sopran Ein Mezzosopran. Ein Kontralto.
A prima donna or A diva.	Une prima donna, Une diva.	Eine Primadonna, Eine Diva.
An artiste.	Un(e) artiste.	Ein Artist.
A quick-change artiste.	Un acteur à transformations.	Ein Verkleidungskünstler.
A comic actor.	Un comique.	Ein Komiker. →
A comic song	Une chanson burlesque, Une chansonnette.	Ein Kouplet.
A comic turn.	Un numéro comique.	Eine komische Nummer.
A humorist (entertainer).	Un diseur, Une diseuse, de chansonnettes.	Ein(e) Chansonsänger(in).
A radiogramophone.	Un radiophonographe.	Ein Radio-Grammophon.
Gramophone records, needles.	Des disques, Des aiguilles, de phonographe.	Grammophonplatten, → Grammophonnadeln.
A dance record with vocal refrain.	Un disque de danse chantée.	Eine Tanzplatte mit Refraingesang.
Broadcasting or The radio or The wireless	**La radio[diffusion] ou La télégraphie sans fil ou La sans-fil ou La T.S.F.**	**Der Rundfunk oder Das Radio**
A broadcasting station.	Un poste de radiodiffusion ou d'émission.	Eine Rundfunkstation, Eine Sendestation.
This is Radio-Paris.	Ici [poste de] Radio-Paris.	Hier ist Radio-Paris.
The announcer.	Le, La, microphoniste, Le speaker.	Der Ansager, Die Ansagerin.
A commentator.	Un radio-reporter.	Ein Rundfunksprecher. →
What is to-day's broadcasting?	Quelles sont les auditions du jour?	Was gibt es heute im Radio?
Have you [got] the wireless (or broadcasting) programme? What does it consist of: concerts, light music, gramophone records, talks, dance music, jazz, relays?	Est-ce que vous avez le programme de la T.S.F.? En quoi consiste-t-il: concerts, musique légère, disques de phonographe, causeries, danses, jazz, relais?	Haben Sie das heutige Rundfunkprogramm? Woraus besteht es: aus Konzerten, leichter Musik, Grammophonplatten, Vorträgen, Tanzmusik, Jazzmusik, Übertragungen?
May I listen in to your wireless set, to the children's hour, to-night's news [bulletin], to-night's weather report, for the time signal?	Puis-je écouter votre poste de T.S.F., l'heure de la jeunesse, les informations (ou le bulletin des informations ou le journal parlé) de ce soir, le bulletin météorologique de ce soir, le signal horaire?	Darf ich mir etwas in Ihrem Radio anhören, Darf ich mir in Ihrem Radio die Kinderstunde, heute abend die Nachrichtensendung, heute abend den Wetterbericht, die Zeitangabe, anhören?
The reception is much troubled by atmospherics.	La réception est très troublée par des perturbations atmosphériques.	Der Empfang leidet sehr unter atmosphärischen Störungen.

Un tenore. Un baritono. Un basso. Un soprano. Un mezzo-soprano. Un contralto.	Un tenor. Un baritono. Un bajo. Una soprano o Una tiple. Una mezzo soprano. Una contralto.	Een tenor, Een bariton. Een bas, Een sopraan. Een mezzo-sopraan. Een alt.
Una prima donna, Una diva.	Una primadonna, Una primera cantatriz, Una diva.	Een primadonna.
Un artista, Un'artista. Un trasformista.	Un(a) artista. Un transformista.	Een artieste. Een transformatie artieste.
◄Un attore comico. Una canzonetta.	Un cómico. Una canción burlesca.	Een komiek. Een komisch liedje.
Un numero comico. Un umorista, (feminine) Un'umorista.	Un número cómico. Un(a) humorista.	Een komisch nummer. Een humorist.
Un radiogrammofono.	Un radiogramófono.	Radiogramofoon.
◄I dischi, Gli aghi, di grammofono.	Discos, Agujas, de gramófono.	Gramofoonplaten. Gramofoonnaalden.
Un disco di ballabile cantato.	Un disco de música para bailar con canto.	Een dansplaat met vocaal refrein.
La radiodiffusione o **La telegrafia senza fili**	**La radio[difusion]** o **La telegrafia sin hilos**	**De radio[omroep]**
Una stazione radio-trasmittente.	Una estación de radio, Una estación radiofónica.	Een omroepstation.
Parla Radio-Paris.	Esta es Radio-Paris.	Hier Radio-Parijs.
L'annunziatore, L'annunziatrice.	El locutor, El anunciador, La anunciadora.	De omroeper, (feminine) De omroepster.
◄Un commentatore.	Un comentarista.	Een commentator.
Quali sono le audizioni di oggi?	¿Cuáles son los programas de la radio de hoy?	Wat zijn de programma's vandaag?
Avete il programma delle radio-trasmissioni? In che consiste: in concerti, musica leggera, dischi, discorsi, musica da ballo o musica ballabile, jazz, collegamenti?	¿Tiene usted los programas de la radio? ¿De qué consisten: conciertos, música ligera, discos de gramófono, charlas, música de baile, jazz, retransmisiones?	Heeft U het radioprogram? Waaruit bestaat het: concerten, lichte muziek, gramofoonplaten, praatjes, dansmuziek, heruitzendingen?
Posso ascoltare al vostro apparecchio, il programma dei bambini, il bollettino di notizie di questa notte, le notizie meteorologiche di questa notte, il segnale orario?	¿Me permite usted escuchar a su radio? ¿Se puede sintonizar su aparato de radio para la hora juvenil, el boletín de noticias, de esta tarde, el pronóstico meteorológico de esta tarde, la señal de la hora?	Mag ik naar Uw radiotoestel naar het kinderuurtje, het nieuwsbericht van vanavond, het weerbericht van vanavond, het tijdsein, luisteren?
La recezione è disturbata da elementi atmosferici.	La recepción está muy interrumpida por interferencias atmosféricas.	De ontvangst wordt zeer belemmerd door atmosferische storingen.

Dancing	La danse	Der Tanz
A dance, A ball.	Une danse, Un bal.	Ein Tanz, Ein Ball. →
Is there a dance hall in this town? Are there [any] dance partners there?	Y a-t-il une salle de bal (ou un bal) (ou un dancing) dans cette ville? Y a-t-il des danseurs et danseuses [de l'établissement]?	Gibt es in dieser Stadt ein Tanzlokal? Gibt es dort Eintänzer und Eintänzerinnen?
A ballroom.	Un salon de bal.	Ein Ballsaal.
The dance floor.	La piste de danse.	Der Tanzboden.
A gala night (at dance hall).	Une redoute.	Ein Gala-Abend.
A night club.	Un établissement (ou Une boîte) de nuit.	Ein Nachtklub. →
A cabaret [show] or A floor show.	Des attractions.	Ein Kabaret.
A clog dance.	Une sabotière.	Ein Holzschuhtanz.
A cocktail dance.	Un apéritif dansant.	Ein Cocktail-Danse.
A country dance.	Une danse rustique	Ein Dorftanz.
A dinner dance.	Un dîner dansant.	Ein Abendessen mit→ anschließendem Tanz.
An evening dance.	Une soirée dansante.	Ein Tanzabend.
A subscription dance.	Un bal par souscription.	Ein Subskriptions-Ball.
A supper dance.	Un souper dansant.	Ein Tanz, mit anschließendem Abendessen.
A tap (or A step) dance.	Une danse à claquettes.	Ein Stepptanz.
A tea dance, every day from four p.m.	Un thé dansant, chaque jour à partir de seize heures.	Ein Tanztee, täglich von→ vier Uhr an.
Is evening dress essential, optional?	La tenue de soirée est-elle de rigueur, facultative?	Ist Abendanzug erwünscht, nicht notwendig?
Is it advisable to provide oneself with fancy dress for fancy dress balls?	Est-il bon de se munir de déguisements pour les bals travestis ou de travestis pour les bals costumés?	Glauben Sie, man sollte sich ein Kostüm für Kostümfeste besorgen?
Is there a running buffet, a sit-down supper?	Y a-t-il un buffet, un souper assis?	Gibt es ein Fliegendes Buffet, ein gedecktes Abendessen?
A partner (at a dance).	Un, Une, partenaire, Un danseur, Une danseuse, Un cavalier, Une dame.	Ein(e) Tanzpartner(in).
Will you dance this waltz with me?	Voulez-vous danser cette valse avec moi?	Darf ich Sie um diesen→ Walzer bitten?
The modern waltz., The old-fashioned waltz. The tango. The fox trot. The quick step.	La valse anglaise. La valse pivotée. Le tango. Le fox-trot. Le quickstep.	Der Englische Walzer. Der Wiener Walzer. Der Tango. Der Foxtrott. Der Quickstep.

Il ballo	El baile	Het dansen
◄Una danza, Un ballo.	Un baile, Un baile de etiqueta.	Een dans, Een bal.
C'è una sala da ballo in questa città? Ci sono ballerini e ballerine?	¿Hay una sala de baile en esta población? ¿Tienen allí bailadores y bailadoras (o (either gender) parejas) del establecimiento?	Is er een dansgelegenheid in deze plaats? Zijn daar danspartners?
Una sala da ballo.	Un salón de baile.	Een danszaal, Een balzaal.
Il pavimento della sala da ballo.	La pista de bailar.	De dansvloer.
Una serata di gala.	Una gala, Una fiesta.	Een gala avond.
◄Un casino notturno.	Un círculo (o Un club) nocturno.	Een nachtclub.
Un trattenimento.	Diversiones.	Attracties.
Un ballo con zoccoli.	Un zapateado [con chanclos].	Een klompendans.
Un cocktail danzante.	Una reunión de baile con cocteles.	Een cocktail-dansant.
Una contraddanza all'inglese.	Un baile rústico.	Een boerendans.
◄Un diner danzante.	Una comida con baile.	Een diner-dansant.
Una serata danzante.	Un sarao.	Een dansavondje.
Un ballo per sottoscrizione.	Un baile por subscripción.	Een inschrijfbal.
Un souper danzante.	Una cena con baile.	Een souper-dansant.
Un tap dance.	Un zapateado.	Een tap dance.
◄Un tè danzante, ogni giorno dalle quattro pomeridiane.	Un té dansant, todos los días a partir desde las dieciseis horas.	Een thé-dansant, iedere dag (of dagelijks) vanaf vier uur 's middags.
È essenziale, facoltativo, il vestito di sera?	¿Es de rigor vestir de etiqueta, o es discrecional?	Is avondkostuum verplicht, naar keuze?
È consigliabile di premunirsi di un abito da maschera per il ballo mascherato?	¿Conviene ir provisto de disfraz para baile[s] de traje?	Is het raadzaam zich van een kostuum te voorzien voor gekostumeerde bals?
C'è un servizio di buffet, una cena servita a tavola?	¿Hay aparador, cena completa?	Is er een buffet, een souper waarbij men aan tafel zit?
Un cavaliere, Una dama.	Una pareja (man or woman), Un(a) consorte.	Een partner.
◄Posso fare questo valzer con Lei?	¿Quiere usted bailar este vals conmigo?	Wilt U deze wals met mij dansen?
Il valzer inglese. Il valzer viennese. Il tango. Il fox-trot. Il quick-step.	El vals inglés. El vals vienés. El tango. El fox-trot. El quick-step.	De Engelse wals. De Weense wals. De tango. De foxtrot. De quickstep.

Shall we sit out this dance?	Voulez-vous que nous causions pendant cette danse?	Wollen wir diesen Tanz auslassen?
A paper hat (*at a dance*).	Une coiffure de cotillon.	Eine Papiermütze.
A paper streamer.	Un serpentin.	Eine Papierschlange.
An air (*or* A toy) balloon.	Un ballon à air.	Ein Luftballon.

The races / Les courses / Rennen

Shall we go to the races?	Est-ce que nous allons aux courses?	Wollen wir zum Rennen gehen?
A horse race.	Une course de chevaux.	Ein Pferderennen.
A flat race.	Une course plate.	Ein Flachrennen.
A steeplechase.	Une course d'obstacles.	Ein Hindernisrennen.
Greyhound racing *or* Dog racing *or* The dogs.	Les courses de lévriers.	Hunderennen.
A greyhound racing track.	Un cynodrome.	Eine Hunderennbahn, Ein Hundestadion.
The [race] card.	Le programme [des courses].	Die Rennkarte, Die Karte.
Is there a race course in this neighbourhood?	Y a-t-il un champ de courses dans ces parages?	Ist hier eine Rennbahn in der Nähe?
A race horse.	Un cheval de course.	Ein Rennpferd.
A race meeting.	Une réunion de courses.	Ein Rennen.
How many times will this jockey ride to-day?	Combien de montes ce jockey aura-t-il aujourd'hui?	Wieviele Rennen wird der Jockey heute reiten?
The judge.	Le juge.	Der Schiedsrichter.
The paddock.	L'enceinte du pesage, Le pesage.	Der Sattelplatz.
Weighing-in.	Le pesage.	Wiegen.
The weighing-in room.	Le pesage.	Der Wiegeraum.
The stakes.	Le prix.	Der Preis.
The stands.	Les tribunes.	Die Tribünen.
The grand stand.	La grande tribune.	Die Haupttribüne.
[The] probable starters and jockeys.	Les partants et montes probables.	Die voraussichtlichen Renner und Jockeys.
The starter (*person*).	Le starter.	Der Starter.
The starting post.	Le poteau de départ, La barrière.	Der Startplatz.
To lead, To win, by a length, by a head.	Mener, Gagner, d'une longueur, d'une tête.	Um eine Pferdelänge, Um einen Kopf, führen, gewinnen.
The winning post.	Le poteau d'arrivée.	Das Ziel.
Which horse won [the race]?	Quel cheval a gagné [la course]?	Welches Pferd hat gewonnen?
A dead heat.	Une course nulle, Une course à égalité.	Ein totes Rennen.
The horse was beaten on the post.	Le cheval a été battu au poteau.	Das Pferd wurde am Ziel geschlagen.
To back a horse.	Parier sur (*ou* pour) un cheval.	Auf ein Pferd setzen.
To back a horse for a place.	Parier sur un cheval placé.	Auf Platz setzen.
A backer.	Un parieur.	Ein Wetter.

Vogliamo conversare durante questo ballo?	¿Vamos a sentarnos a charlar un rato en vez de bailar está pieza?	Zullen wij deze dans uitzitten?
Una acconciatura.	Una gorra de fantasía.	Een papieren muts.
Una stella filante.	Una serpentina.	Een serpentine.
◄Un palloncino.	Un globo de niño o de juguete.	Een luchtballon.

Le corse / Las carreras / De wedrennen

Vogliamo andare alle corse?	¿Vamos a las carreras?	Zullen we naar de wedrennen gaan?
Una corsa ippica.	Una carrera de caballos.	De paardenrennen.
Una corsa senza ostacoli.	Una carrera llana.	Een ren.
Una corsa ad ostacoli.	Una carrera de vallas.	Een wedren met hindernissen.
◄La corsa di levrieri.	Carreras de galgos.	De windhondenrennen.
Un cinodromo.	Una pista para carreras de galgos.	Een draverij.
Il programma [delle corse].	El programa [de las carreras].	Het programma [van de wedrennen].
C'è un campo di corse da queste parti?	¿Hay un hipódromo en este vecindario?	Is er een renbaan in deze buurt?
Un cavallo da corsa.	Un caballo de carrera.	Een renpaard.
◄Una riunione di corse.	Una reunión de carreras.	Een draverij.
Quante volte correrà questo fantino oggi?	¿En cuántas carreras tomará parte hoy este jockey?	Hoeveel keren rijdt deze jockey vandaag?
Il giudice.	El juez.	De rechter.
Il recinto.	El corral.	De paddock.
Il pesaggio.	Pasar el pesaje.	De pesage.
◄Il pesaggio.	El pesaje.	De pesage.
Le poste.	Los premios.	De prijs.
Le tribune.	Las tribunas.	De tribunes.
La tribuna centrale.	La tribuna principal.	De overdekte [tribune].
I cavalli e i fantini probabili.	Probables competidores y jockeys.	De vermoedelijke deelnemers en jockeys.
◄Lo starter.	El largador, El starter.	De starter.
Il punto di partenza.	La partida.	De startpaal.
Essere avanti, Vincere, di una lunghezza, d'una testa.	Tomar la delantera, Ganar, por un cuerpo (o un largo), por una cabeza.	Leiden, Winnen, met een lengte, met een hoofdlengte.
Il punto d'arrivo, La metà, Il traguardo.	La meta.	De eindpaal.
Quale cavallo ha vinto [la corsa]?	¿Qué caballo ha ganado [la carrera]?	Welk paard heeft gewonnen [de wedren]?
◄Una corsa morta o indecisa o nulla.	Un empate.	Een dead heat.
Il cavallo fu vinto al traguardo.	El caballo fué batido sobre la meta.	Het paard werd op de eindstreep verslagen.
Puntare su un cavallo.	Jugar a un caballo.	Op een paard wedden.
Puntare su un cavallo per una posta.	Jugar a un caballo a placé.	Wedden dat een paard tot de eerste drie zal horen.
Uno scommettitore.	Un apostador.	Een wedder.

A bet. To bet (or To lay) a hundred to one, two to one, on a horse.	Un pari. Parier (ou Mettre) cent contre un, le double contre le simple, sur un cheval.	Eine Wette. Hundert zu eins, zwei zu eins, auf ein Pferd wetten.
A bookmaker. Betting with bookmakers.	Un bookmaker. Le pari à la cote.	Ein Buchmacher. Wetten beim Buchmacher.
Betting on the totalizator.	Le pari mutuel.	Wetten am Totalisator.
What is the betting (or What are the odds) on this horse?	Quelle cote fait ce cheval?	Wie stehen die Wetten bei diesem Pferd?
Sundry entertainments	Divertissements divers	Vergnügungen verschiedener Art
Shall we take the children to the circus?	Est-ce que nous menons les enfants au cirque?	Wollen wir mit den Kindern in den Zirkus gehen?
Do we want tickets or do we go through a turnstile?	Nous faut-il des billets ou passons-nous un tourniquet[-compteur]?	Brauchen wir Eintrittskarten, oder geht man durch ein Kontrollgitter?
What is the price of admission?	Combien l'entrée?	Was kostet der Eintritt?
An aquarium.	Un aquarium.	Ein Aquarium.
An exhibition.	Une exposition, Un salon.	Eine Ausstellung.
An agricultural (or A cattle) show.	Un concours (ou Un comice) agricole.	Eine landwirtschaftliche Ausstellung.
An aircraft exhibition or An aero[nautical] show.	Un salon de l'aviation.	Eine Flugzeugausstellung.
A cycle show.	Un salon du cycle.	Eine Fahrradausstellung.
A dog show.	Une exposition canine.	Eine Hundeausstellung.
A flower show.	Une exposition florale ou de fleurs.	Eine Blumenausstellung.
A freak show (at a fair).	Une galerie de phénomènes.	Eine Abnormitätenschau
A horse show.	Un concours hippique.	Eine Pferdeausstellung, Ein Schaureiten.
A motor show.	Un salon de l'automobile.	Eine Automobilausstellung.
A fish market.	Une halle aux poissons, Une poissonnerie.	Ein Fischmarkt.
A flower market.	Un marché aux fleurs.	Ein Blumenmarkt.
An ice skating rink.	Une piste de patinage sur glace.	Eine künstliche Eisbahn.
A roller skating rink.	Une piste de patinage à roulettes.	Eine Rollschuhbahn.
A carnival.	Un carnaval.	Ein Karneval.
A casino.	Un casino.	Ein Kasino.
A gaming room.	Une salle de jeu.	Ein Spielsaal.
The croupier.	Le croupier.	Der Croupier.
Roulette (game and apparatus).	La roulette.	Roulette.
Put down your stakes.	Faites votre jeu, Faites vos jeux.	Einsätze bitte.

◄Una scommessa. Scommettere (o Puntare) cento ad uno, due a uno, su un cavallo.	Una apuesta. Apostar (o Jugar) a ciento a uno, a dos a uno, sobre un caballo.	Een weddenschap. Honderd tegen één, Twee tegen één, op een paard wedden.
Un bookmaker.	Un tomador de apuestas.	Een bookmaker.
Scommettere col bookmakers.	Apostar con tomadores de apuestas.	Het wedden met bookmakers.
Scommettere sul totalizzatore.	Apostar en las apuestas mútuas.	Het wedden op de totalisator.
Quali sono le poste su questo cavallo.	¿Cuánto pagan contra este caballo?	Hoe is de notering op dit paard?

Divertimenti vari   Diversiones diversas   Diverse vermakelijkheden

◄Vogliamo portare i ragazzi al circo?	¿Vamos a llevar los niños (o los chicos) al circo?	Zullen we met de kinderen naar het circus gaan?
Occorre prendere i biglietti o si passa attraverso l'arganello?	¿Hay que tomar billetes o se pasa por un torniquete?	Moeten wij kaartjes hebben of gaan we door een tourniquet?
Qual'è il prezzo d'ingresso?	¿Cuánto es la entrada?	Wat is de toegangsprijs?
Un aquario.	Un acuario.	Een aquarium.
Un'esposizione.	Una exposición.	Een tentoonstelling.
◄Una mostra agricola, Un concorso di bestiame.	Una exposición agrícola, Una exposición de ganado.	Een landbouwtentoonstelling.
Una mostra di aviazione.	Una exposición aeronáutica.	Een luchtvaarttentoonstelling.
Una mostra di biciclette.	Una exposición de bicicletas.	Een rijwieltentoonstelling.
Una mostra di cani.	Una exposición canina.	Een hondententoonstelling.
Una mostra floreale.	Una exposición botánica.	Een bloemententoonstelling.
◄Un'esibizione di fenomeni.	Una galería de monstruosidades.	Een monstrositeitentent.
Un concorso ippico.	Un concurso hípico.	Een paardententoonstelling.
Una mostra automobilistica.	Una exposición de automóviles.	Een autotentoonstelling.
Un mercato di pesci.	Un mercado de pescadería, Una pescadería.	Een vismarkt.
Un mercato di fiori.	Un mercado de flores.	Een bloemenmarkt.
◄Una pista di pattinaggio sul ghiaccio.	Un patinadero de hielo.	Een ijsbaan.
Una pista di pattinaggio a rotelline.	Un patinadero para patines de ruedas.	Een rolschaatsbaan.
Un carnevale.	Un carnaval.	Een carnaval.
Un casino.	Un casino.	Een casino.
Una sala di giuoco.	Un salón de juego.	Een speelzaal.
◄Il croupier.	El crupista.	De croupier.
La roulette.	La ruleta.	Roulette.
Fate il vostro giuoco.	Hagan sus apuntes.	Faites vos jeux.

To play for high stakes.	Jouer gros jeu.	Hoch spielen.
To break the bank.	Faire sauter la banque.	Die Bank sprengen.
A race meeting or A rally (*motor cars or aeroplanes*).	Un rallye.	Ein Rally. →
A cycle-racing track.	Un vélodrome.	Eine Radrennbahn.
An air race.	Une course d'avions.	Ein Luftrennen.
A road race.	Une course sur route.	Ein Straßenrennen.
A beauty parade (*cars*).	Un concours d'élégance.	Eine Autoparade. →
A stadium.	Un stade.	Ein Stadion. →
The arena.	L'arène.	Die Arena.
The grand stand.	La grande tribune.	Die Haupttribüne.
The pleasure grounds.	Le parc d'agrément.	Der Vergnügungspark.
Fireworks.	Des feux d'artifice.	Feuerwerk.
Flood lighting.	L'éclairage (*ou* L'illumination) par projection.	Scheinwerferbeleuchtung. →
A clown (*circus*).	Un clown.	Ein Clown.
A coin machine.	Un appareil à sous.	Ein Spielautomat.
A conjurer, -or.	Un escamoteur, Un prestidigitateur.	Ein Zauberer.
A conjuring trick.	Un tour de-passe-passe.	Ein Zauberkunststück.
A contortionist.	Un(e) contorsionniste.	Ein Schlangenmensch. →
A fair. A horse fair. I want to see all the fun of the fair.	Une foire. Une foire aux chevaux. Je veux voir toutes les curiosités de la foire.	Ein Jahrmarkt. Ein Pferdemarkt. Ich möchte mir gern den ganzen Jahrmarktsbetrieb ansehen.
A fête (*at a fair*).	Une fête foraine.	Ein Jahrmarktsfest.
A fortune teller.	Un diseur, Une diseuse, de bonne aventure.	Ein(e) Wahrsager(in).
A fun fair.	Une foire aux plaisirs.	Ein Rummel.
A funny man (*circus*).	Un auguste.	Ein dummer August. →
A juggler.	Un jongleur, Un escamoteur.	Ein Jongleur.
A pin table.	Un billard américain.	Ein Glücksautomat.
A Punch and Judy show.	Une représentation de guignol, Un guignol.	Ein Kasperletheater.
A roundabout or A merry-go-round.	Un manège [de chevaux de bois].	Ein Karussel.
A side show (*at an exhibition*).	Un spectacle payant.	Eine Nebenvorstellung. →
A side show (*at a fair*).	Un spectacle forain.	Eine Schaubude.
A scenic railway or A switchback.	Des montagnes russes.	Eine Berg- und Talbahn, Eine Achterbahn.
A shooting gallery.	Un stand de tir.	Ein Schießstand.
An itinerant strong man.	Un hercule forain.	Ein Jahrmarktsathlet.
A swing.	Une balançoire.	Eine Schaukel.
A torchlight procession, tattoo.	Une procession, Une retraite, aux flambeaux.	Ein Fackelzug, Ein Zapfenstreich mit Fackelzug.

Puntare forte.	Jugar fuerte.	Grof spelen.
Far saltare il banco.	Desbancar.	De bank laten springen.
◄Una reunione di corse.	Una reunión de carreras.	Een rally.
Un velodromo.	Un velódromo.	Een wielerbaan.
Una gara d'aviazione.	Una carrera aérea.	Een vliegwedstrijd.
Una corsa su strada.	Una carrera de carretera.	Een wegren.
Un concorso di eleganza.	Un concurso de elegancia.	Een auto concours.
◄Uno stadio.	Un estadio.	Een station.
L'arena.	La arena, La pista ; (*Bullring*) La plaza de toros.	De arena.
La tribuna centrale.	La tribuna principal.	De overdekte [tribune].
Il parco di piacere.	El parque de recreo.	Het amusementspark.
I fuochi artificiali.	Fuegos artificiales.	Vuurwerk.
◄L'illuminazione [concentrata] per proiezione.	Alumbrado por proyección.	Het vloedlicht.
Un pagliaccio.	Un payaso de circo.	Een clown.
Una macchina automatica a soldi.	Un aparato automático de monedas.	Een speelautomaat, Een flipperkast.
Un prestigiatore.	Un prestidigitador, Un escamoteador.	Een goochelaar.
Un giuoco di bussolotti.	Un juego de manos.	Een goocheltoer.
◄Un(a) contorsionista.	Un(a) contorsionista.	Een slangemens.
Una fiera. Una fiera di cavalli. Desidero vedere tutti i divertimenti della fiera.	Una feria. Una feria de caballos. Quiero ver todas las diversiones de la feria.	Een jaarmarkt. Een paardenmarkt. Ik wil de hele markt zien.
Una festa.	Una fiesta de feria, Una verbena.	Een kermisfeest.
Un sortilego, Una sortilega.	Un sortflego, Una sortflega. Una gitana [que dice la buenaventura].	Een waarzegger, (*feminine*) Een waarzegster.
Una giostra di divertimento.	Un feria de holgorio.	Een kermis.
◄Un buffone.	Un bufón, Un Gedeón, Un Marcelino.	Een domme august.
Un giocoliere.	Un escamoteador.	Een jongleur.
Un biliardo americano.	Un billar americano.	Een Russisch biljart.
Il teatrino di Pulcinella.	Una representación de guiñol.	Een poppenkastvertoning.
Una giostra. Un carosello.	Los caballitos.	Een draaimolen.
◄Una mostra secondaria.	Una función (o Una exhibición) secundaria.	Een bij-attractie, Een nevenvoorstelling.
Una mostra estranea.	Un espectáculo de feria.	Een kermisvertoning.
Una montagna russa.	Una montaña rusa.	Een roetsjbaan.
Un tiro [a segno].	Un puesto de tiro al blanco.	Een schiettent.
Un ercole ambulante.	Un gimnasta de feria.	Een rondreizende sterke man.
◄Un'altalena.	Un columpio.	Een schommel.
Una processione, Una ritirata, con torce.	Una procesión, Una retreta, con antorchas.	Een fakkeloptocht, Een fakkeltaptoe.

MOUNTAINEERING	ALPINISME	BERGSTEIGEN
Climbing; Mountaineering.	L'escalade *ou* L'ascension; Les ascensions *ou* L'alpinisme.	Klettern; Bergsteigen.
I want to see the sunrise, the sunset. At what hour does it occur?	Je veux voir le lever, le coucher, du soleil. À quelle heure a-t-il lieu?	Ich möchte mir den Sonnenaufgang, den Sonnenuntergang, ansehen. Um wieviel Uhr ist er?
A climber, A mountaineer.	Un(e) ascensionniste, Un(e) alpiniste.	Ein(e) Bergsteiger(in).
I want to climb that mountain, Mont Blanc, Monte Rosa, the Matterhorn.	Je veux escalader (*ou* faire l'ascension de) cette montagne[-là], faire l'ascension du mont Blanc, du mont Rose, du mont Cervin.	Ich möchte diesen Berg, den Mont Blanc, den Monte Rosa, das Matterhorn, besteigen.
Can this slope be climbed? Is it difficult, steep *or* precipitous, easy *or* gentle?	Peut-on gravir cette pente? Est-elle ardue, raide *ou* escarpée, douce?	Läßt sich dieser Abhang besteigen? Ist er schwierig, steil *oder* abschüssig, flach?
What is the height (*or* the altitude) of the mountain, of the snow line, of the timber (*or* tree) line [above sea level]?	Quelle est la hauteur (*ou* l'altitude) de la montagne, de la limite des neiges éternelles, de la limite forestière [au-dessus du niveau de la mer]?	Wie hoch ist der Berg, die Schneegrenze, die Baumgrenze [über dem Meeresspiegel]?
Should one provide oneself with a guide, with a porter, with ropes, for this ascent?	Doit-on se munir d'un guide, d'un porteur, de cordes, pour cette ascension?	Sollte man sich einen Bergführer, einen Träger, Seile, für diesen Aufstieg verschaffen?
Which is the way up the mountain? Does this path lead to the hut?	Quel est le chemin pour gravir la montagne? Ce sentier conduit-il à la cabane *ou* à la hutte?	Welches ist der Weg auf diesen Berg? Führt dieser Pfad zur Hütte?
Must we go up to the top of this hill, pass along this ridge, this precipice, pass under this hanging glacier?	Faut-il monter jusqu'au haut de cette colline, passer le long de cette croupe, ce précipice, passer par-dessous ce glacier suspendu?	Müssen wir auf diesen Hügel herauf, auf diesem Bergrücken, an diesem Abgrund, entlanggehen, unter diesem hängenden Gletscher durchgehen?
Can we pass safely underneath this overhanging rock?	Pouvons-nous passer en sécurité en dessous de ce rocher qui surplombe?	Können wir ungefährdet unter diesem überhängenden Felsen hindurch?
Should we cut steps here, set a piton in the ice, in the rock, in the ground?	Devons-nous tailler des marches ici, planter un piton dans la glace, dans le roc, dans le sol?	Wollen wir hier Stufen einhauen, einen Kletterhaken (*oder* ein Eishaken) in das Eis, in den Felsen, in den Boden, schlagen?
What is the name of this range of hills, this gorge, this ravine, this torrent, those rocks, that	Comment s'appelle cette chaîne de collines, cette gorge[-ci], ce ravin *ou* cette ravine, ce torrent,	Wie heißt diese Hügelkette, diese Schlucht, dieser Hohlweg, dieser Gebirgsstrom, Wie heißen diese

ALPINISMO	ALPINISMO	BERGBEKLIMMEN
La scalata, L'ascensione; L'alpinismo.	La escalada, La ascensión; Alpinismo.	Het klimmen: Bergbeklimmen.
Desidero vedere la levata, il tramonto, del sole. A che ora avviene?	Deseo ver la salida, la puesta, del sol. ¿A qué hora tendrá lugar?	Ik wil de zonsopgang, de zonsondergang, zien. Hoe laat is die?
Un alpinista, (feminine) Un'alpinista.	Un escalador, Una escaladora, Un(a) alpinista.	Een bergbeklimmer, Een alpinist, (feminine) Een bergbeklimster, Een alpiniste.
◄ Voglio fare la scalata di questa montagna, Monte Bianco, Monte Rosa, Monte Cervino.	Deseo ascender aquella montaña, Monte Blanco, Monte Rosa, Monte Cervino.	Ik wil die berg, de Mont Blanc, de Monte Rosa, beklimmen.
Si può far la scalata da questo versante? È difficile, ripido o a precipizio, facile o comodo?	¿Es posible la subida de este declive? ¿Es dificultoso, empinado o escarpado, suave?	Kan deze helling beklommen worden? Is zij moeilijk, steil, gemakkelijk of geleidelijk?
Qual'è l'altitudine della montagna, Dove cominciano il limite delle nevi perpetue, il limite forestale [dal livello del mare]?	¿Qué es la altitud de la montaña, del límite de las nieves, de la vegetación selvática [sobre el nivel del mar]?	Hoe hoog is de berg, de sneeuwgrens, de boomgrens (boven de zeespiegel).
È necessario munirsi di una guida, d'un facchino, di corde, per questa ascensione?	¿Debe uno proveerse de un guía, de un portero, de cuerdas, para esta ascensión?	Moet men zich van een gids voorzien, van een drager, van touwen, voor deze bestijging?
Qual'è la via per salire sulla montagna? Questo sentiero conduce alla capanna?	¿Cuál es el camino para subir la montaña? ¿Conduce este sendero a la cabaña?	Welke weg voert naar omhoog? Leidt dit pad naar de hut?
◄ Occorre salire fino alla sommità di questa collina, passare lungo questa groppa, questo precipizio, passare sotto questo ghiacciaio sospeso?	¿Tenemos que subir hasta la cumbre de esta colina, caminar por este cerro, este precipicio, pasar por debajo de este helero colgante?	Moeten wij tot de top van deze heuvel gaan, langs deze bergrug, deze afgrond, gaan, onder deze hangende gletsjer doorgaan?
Possiamo passare con sicurezza sotto questa roccia strapiombante o minacciante?	¿Podemos pasar sin peligro por debajo de este peñón que sobresale?	Kunnen wij veilig onder deze overhangende rots doorgaan?
Dobbiamo tagliare dei gradini qui, piantare un piton nel ghiaccio, nella roccia, nel terreno?	¿Debemos tajar escalones aquí, clavar un pitón en el hielo, en la roca, en la tierra?	Moeten wij hier treden uithakken, een pikkel in het ijs, in de rots, in de grond, zetten?
Come si chiama questa catena di colline, questo burrone, questo borro, questo torrente, quelle	¿Cómo se llama esta cordillera, este desfiladero, esta cañada, este torrente, estos peñones,	Wat is de naam van deze heuvelrij, deze kloof, dit ravijn, deze bergstroom, die rotsen,

snow-capped peak up there, that spur across there, that valley, that village down there ?	ces rochers[-là], cette cime chenue là-haut, ce contrefort là en travers, cette vallée, ce village là-bas ?	Felsen, Wie heißt der schneebedeckte Gipfel dort drüben, der Gebirgsvorsprung auf der anderen Seite, das Tal, das Dorf dort unten ?
Where do we cross the glacier ?	Où traversons-nous le glacier ?	Wo überqueren wir den Gletscher ?
Can we jump this crevasse, pass over this snow bridge or lid ?	Pouvons-nous franchir cette crevasse [glaciaire], traverser ce pont de neige ?	Können wir über diese Gletscherspalte springen, über diese Schneebrücke gehen ?
Is this a lateral or a medial moraine ?	Ceci est-il une moraine latérale ou médiane ?	Ist dies eine Seitenmoräne oder eine Mittelmoräne ?
Should we not rope here ?	Ne devons-nous pas encorder ici ?	Wollen wir uns hier nicht anseilen ?
Do we have to pass a night in a chalet, in a [mountain] shelter ?	Faut-il passer une nuit dans un chalet, dans un [chalet-]refuge ?	Werden wir eine Nacht in einer Sennhütte, in einer Berghütte, verbringen müssen ?
Shall we reach the hut before nightfall ?	Allons-nous atteindre la hutte avant la tombée de la nuit ?	Werden wir die Hütte erreichen, bevor es dunkel wird ?
How long will it take to reach the summit or to get to the top, to get over the pass ?	Combien de temps faudra-t-il pour atteindre le sommet, pour franchir le col ?	Wie lange braucht man bisherauf zum Gipfel, um über den Pass, zu kommen ?
Do you think [that] it will snow, rain, [that] there will be a snow storm or a blizzard, a snow squall, a thunderstorm ?	Croyez-vous qu'il neigera, pleuvra, qu'il s'élèvera une tempête de neige, une bourrasque de neige, un orage ?	Glauben Sie, es wird schneien, regnen, es gibt einen Schneesturm, einen kurzen Schneesturm, ein Gewitter ?
Mind that snowdrift !	Attention à cet amoncellement de neige !	Achtung ! Da ist eine Schneewehe.
Are avalanches to be feared ?	Les avalanches sont-elles à craindre ?	Ist mit Lawinen zu rechnen ?
How far are we from the end of our journey ? I am very tired, footsore. I must rest awhile. I can go no farther.	À quelle distance sommes-nous de la fin de notre voyage ? Je suis très fatigué, éclopé. Il faut que je me repose un peu. Je ne peux pas aller plus loin.	Wie weit haben wir es noch ? Ich bin sehr müde, Meine Füße sind wundgelaufen. Ich muß mich etwas ausruhen. Ich kann nicht weiter.
I fear snow blindness, mountain sickness. Would it not be better to go down at once ?	Je crains la cécité des neiges, le mal des montagnes. Ne vaudrait-il pas mieux descendre tout de suite ?	Ich habe Angst vor Schneeblindheit, Bergkrankheit. Wäre es nicht besser, sofort abzusteigen ?
The Alps.	Les Alpes, Les monts.	Die Alpen.
An Alpine club.	Un club alpin.	Ein Alpenverein, Ein Alpenklub.
A ladies' Alpine club.	Un club des femmes alpinistes.	Ein Alpenklub für Damen.
The alpenglow.	L'alpenglühen.	Das Alpenglühen.
A crag.	Un rocher [anfractueux].	Eine Felsspitze, Ein spitzer Felsen.

rocce, quella cima coperta di neve lassù, quello sperone attraverso, quella valle, quel villaggio laggiù?	ese picacho allá arriba coronado de nieve, aquel estribo que atraviesa por allá, esa valle, esa aldea allá abajo?	die met sneeuw bedekte top daarboven, die overdwarse uitloper daar, dat dal, dat dorp daar beneden?
Dove attraversiamo il ghiacciaio?	¿Por dónde atravesamos el helero?	Waar steken wij de gletsjer over?
◄Possiamo saltare quel crepaccio, attraversare questo ponte di neve?	¿Podemos saltar al través de esta hendedura, pasar por encima de este pontón de nieve?	Kunnen wij over deze gletsjerspleet springen, deze sneeuwbrug oversteken?
Questa è una morena laterale o mediana?	¿Es esta una morena lateral o del centro?	Is dit een laterale of een mediaire moraine?
Non dobbiamo qui legarci con le corde?	¿No deberemos enlazarnos (o amarrarnos) aquí?	Moeten wij ons hier niet aan elkaar vastbinden?
Dobbiamo pernottare in una capanna, in un rifugio?	¿Tendremos que pasar una noche en una cabaña, en un refugio [de montaña]?	Moeten wij een nacht in een chalet, in een berghut, doorbrengen?
Raggiungeremo la capanna prima che faccia notte?	¿Llegaremos a la cabaña antes del anochecer?	Zullen we de hut voor het vallen van de avond bereiken?
◄Quanto tempo prende per arrivare alla sommità o alla cima, per attraversare il passo?	¿Cuánto tiempo se tardará en llegar hasta la cumbre, atravesar el paso?	Hoe lang hebben we nodig om de top te bereiken, over de pas te gaan?
Credete che nevicherà, pioverà, che ci sarà una bufera di neve, una tormenta, un temporale?	¿Cree usted que nevará, que lloverá, que habrá una tormenta de nieve, una nevasca, una tronada?	Denkt U, dat het gaat sneeuwen, regenen, dat er een sneeuwstorm, een sneeuwbui, onweer, op komst is?
Attenzione a quell'ammasso di neve!	¡Tenga cuidado con esa ventisca!	Pas op die sneeuwbank!
C'è da temere le valanghe?	¿Hay que temer aludes?	Zijn er lawines te vrezen?
Quanto manca per arrivare alla fine della nostra gita? Io sono molto stanco (*feminine* stanca), Mi dolgono i piedi. Ho bisogno di riposare un poco. Non posso proseguire.	¿A qué distancia estamos del fin de nuestro viaje? Estoy muy cansado, Tengo los pies doloridos. Tengo que descansar un rato. No puedo más.	Moeten we nog veel verder? Ik ben erg moe, Ik moet een poosje rusten. Ik kan niet verder gaan.
◄Io temo la cecità della neve, il mal di montagna. Non sarebbe meglio scendere subito?	Temo la ceguera causada por el reflejo de la nieve, el mal de montañas. ¿No valdría más descender en seguida?	Ik ben bang voor sneeuwblindheid, bergziekte. Zou het niet beter zijn meteen te dalen?
Le Alpi, I monti.	Los Alpes.	De Alpen.
Un club alpino.	Un club alpino.	Een Alpenclub.
Un club alpino femminile.	Un club alpino de señoras.	Een Alpenclub voor dames.
Il rosso splendore delle Alpi.	El resplandor rojo de los Alpes.	Het alpengloeien.
◄Una roccia.	Un despeñadero.	Een klip, Een rots.

A cragsman, A crags-woman.	Un(e) ascensionniste de rochers.	Ein(e) Felsenkletter(in).
Glacial snow or Névé or Firn.	Du névé.	Firn.
Can we glissade down this snow slope, this stone slide?	Pouvons-nous descendre en glissade cette pente de neige, cette traînée d'éboulis?	Können wir diesen Schnee-hang, diesen Felsabhang, herunterrutschen?
A snow cornice. A ridge or An arête. A serac.	Une corniche de neige. Une arête ou Une croupe. Un sérac.	Ein Schnee-Überhang. Ein Kamm oder Ein Grat. Ein Serac.
A snow field. An Alpine stick. An alpenstock.	Un champ de neige. Une canne alpine. Une grande canne alpine, Un alpenstock.	Ein Schneefeld. ➤ Ein Bergstock. Ein Alpenstock.
The spike (of an alpen-stock).	La pique.	Die Spitze.
An aneroid [barometer]. Climbing boots.	Un baromètre anéroïde. Des bottines d'escalade, Des chaussures de mon-tagne.	Ein Aneroidbarometer. Bergschuhe, Nagelschuhe. ➤
Please put [some] nails, crampons, on these boots.	Veuillez mettre des clous, des crampons, à ces chaussures.	Würden Sie bitte Nägel, Steigeisen, in diese Schuhe schlagen.
A climbing rope.	Une corde d'ascension ou d'escalade.	Ein Kletterseil.
An ice axe. Ice crampons [with] .. points. A rucksack.	Un piolet. Des crampons à glace à .. pointes. Un sac de montagne, Un sac d'alpiniste, Un sac de touriste.	Ein Eispickel. Steigeisen, mit .. Spitzen.➤ Ein Rucksack.
Skis. Snow boots, with zip fastener.	Des skis. Des chaussures pour la neige, avec fermeture instantanée.	Skier. Schneestiefel mit Reißver-schluß.
Snow goggles.	Des lunettes à neige, Des lunettes d'alpiniste.	Eine Schneebrille.
Snow shoes.	Des raquettes à neige.	Schneeschuhe. ➤

BATHING, SWIM-MING, THE SEASIDE, SPAS	**BAINS, NATATION, PLAGES, EAUX**	**BADEN, SCHWIMMEN, STRAND, BADEORTE**
I am going to the seaside.	Je vais au bord de la mer.	Ich fahre an die See.
Which is the nicest seaside resort, bathing resort, in the North, in the South, of France?	Quelle est la plus jolie plage, station balnéaire, dans le nord, dans le midi, de la France?	Welches ist der hübscheste Seebadeort, Badeort, in Nordfrankreich, in Süd-frankreich?

Un ascensionista di rocce, (*feminine*) Un'ascensionista di rocce.	Un(a) escalador(a) de rocas.	Een rotsbeklimmer, (*feminine*) Een rotsbeklimster.
Nevaio.	Nieve glacial.	Névé.
Possiamo noi slittare giù per questo declivio nevoso, questa strisciata di pietre ?	¿ Podemos bajar deslizándonos por este declive de nieve, de piedra ?	Kunnen wij deze sneeuwhelling, deze steenverschuiving, afglijden?
Una cornice di neve. Una groppa. Un seracco.	Una cornisa de nieve. Un cerro. Un seraco.	Een overhangende sneeuwrand. Een rug. Een serac.
◄ Un campo di neve.	Un campo de nieve.	Een sneeuwveld.
Un bastone alpino.	Una estaca alpestre.	Een bergstok.
Un alpenstock.	Una estaca alpestre larga, Un alpenstock.	Een alpenstok.
Il puntone.	La espiga.	De ijzeren punt.
Un barometro aneroide.	Un barómetro aneroide.	Een aneroïde barometer.
◄ Gli stivali da alpinista.	Botas de montaña.	Berglaarzen, Bergschoenen.
Per favore, mettetemi dei chiodi, i chiodi da ghiaccio, in questi stivali.	Haga el favor de ponerme unos clavos, unas púas para trepar, en estas botas.	Wilt U wat spijkers, sporen, op deze laarzen zetten, als 't U belieft.
Una corda da scalata.	Una cuerda para escalar.	Een klimtouw.
Una picozza per ghiaccio.	Un pico para el hielo.	Een ijsbijl.
◄ I chiodi da ghiaccio a . . punta.	Puas para andar sobre el hielo, de . . picos.	IJssporen met . . punten.
Un sacco da montagna.	Un saco alpestre.	Een rugzak.
Le schie.	Skis.	Skis.
Gli stivali per la neve, con chiusura scorrevole.	Botas para la nieve, con prendedores instantáneos.	Sneeuwschoenen, met ritssluiting.
Gli occhiali per la neve.	Anteojeras para la nieve.	Een sneeuwbril.
◄ Le scarpe per la neve.	Raquetas para andar sobre la nieve.	Sneeuwschoenen.

BAGNI, NUOTO, SPIAGGE, STAZIONI BALNEARIE	**BAÑOS, NATACIÓN, LAS PLAYAS, BALNEARIOS**	**HET BADEN, HET ZWEMMEN, DE ZEEKANT, BADPLAATSEN**
Io vado al mare.	Voy a la playa.	Ik ga naar een badplaats [aan zee].
Qual'è la più graziosa spiaggia, stazione balnearia, nel nord, nel sud, della Francia ?	¿ Cuál es la más atractiva orilla del mar, el más atractivo lugar de balneario, en el norte, en el sur, de Francia ?	Wat is de aardigste zeebadplaats, de aardigste badplaats, in het noorden, in het zuiden, van Frankrijk?

Is the beach (or Are the sands) good?	La plage est-elle bonne?	Ist der Strand gut?
Is the beach fashionable, quiet? Is the air bracing, relaxing?	La plage est-elle mondaine, discrète? L'air est-il tonique, amollissant?	Herrscht am Strand viel Betrieb?, Ist der Strand leer? Ist die Luft kräftig, weich?
Shall we go for a walk along the [sea]shore or the foreshore?	Est-ce que nous allons faire une promenade le long du rivage [de la mer]?	Wollen wir einen Strand-→ spaziergang machen?
A shingle (or A pebble) beach.	Une grève (ou Une plage) de galets.	Ein steiniger Strand.
A private beach or Private sands (belonging to hotel, etc.).	Une plage de sable réservée.	Ein Privatstrand.
A breakwater or A groyne.	Un brise-lames, Un brisant, Un môle.	Eine Buhne, Ein Wellenbrecher.
A coastguard.	Un agent de police des côtes à terre.	Eine Strandwache.
The parade or The esplanade (at seaside).	L'esplanade, La digue-promenade.	Die Uferpromenade. →
A pier. The pier (at seaside).	Une jetée. La jetée-promenade.	Ein Landungssteg. Der Seesteg.
The [sea] front.	La promenade [de la mer].	Die Uferpromenade.
A sea wall.	Une digue.	Ein Deich.
The shores of the lake.	Les bords (ou Les rives) du lac.	Die Ufer des Sees.
The surf.	La barre de plage ou Le ressac.	Die Brandung. →
A surf board.	Un aquaplane.	Ein Wellengleitbrett.
Surf riding.	Le sport de l'aquaplane.	Wellenreiten.
A water tournament.	Une joute sur l'eau.	Ein Wasserturnier.
Aquatic sports.	Des sports nautiques.	Wassersport.
A bather.	Un baigneur, Une baigneuse.	Ein Badender, Eine Ba-→ dende.
When does the bathing season begin, end?	Quand la saison balnéaire commence-t-elle, finit-elle?	Wann beginnt, endet, die Badesaison?
Is the bathing mixed there?	Le bain est-il mixte en cet endroit-là?	Baden Herren und Damen dort zusammen?
I should like to have a bathe or a dip. Is there any sea bathing, river bathing, a bathing establishment, a swimming bath or pool, here?	Je voudrais me baigner ou faire trempette. Y a-t-il ici des bains de mer, des bains de rivière, un établissement de bains, un bassin (ou une école) de natation ou une piscine?	Ich möchte gern baden. Kann man hier Seebäder, Flußbäder, nehmen? Gibt es hier eine Badeanstalt, ein Schwimmbad?
Is there a bathing place on this river?	Y a-t-il une baignade sur cette rivière?	Gibt es in diesem Fluß eine Stelle zum Baden?
Is the bathing good, safe, here, at this time of day, at this time of the year?	Le bain est-il bon, sans danger, dans cet endroit, à l'heure actuelle, à cette époque de l'année?	Ist das Baden hier, zu-→ gesetzt, zu dieser Jahreszeit, angenehm, ungefährlich?

È buona la spiaggia?	¿Es buena la playa?	Is het strand goed?
È la spiaggia di moda, tranquilla? È l'aria tonica, snervante?	¿Es de alta moda, informal, la playa? ¿Son tónicos, relajadores, los aires?	Is het een mondain, een rustig strand? Is de lucht verkwikkend, verzachtend?
◄Vogliamo andare a fare una passeggiata lungo la riva del mare?	¿Vamos a dar un paseo por la playa o por la orilla?	Zullen wij een strandwandeling maken?
Una splaggia ghiaiosa.	Una playa de chinas o de arenas chinosas.	Een kiezelstrand.
Una spiaggia riservata o privata.	Una playa privada o reservada.	Een privé strand.
Un riparo.	Un rompeolas, Una escollera.	Een golfbreker.
Un guardacoste.	Un guarda de costas.	Een kustwachter.
◄La passeggiata lungo il mare.	El paseo, La ribera.	De boulevard.
Una gettata. La gettata.	Un muelle. El espolón.	Een pier. De wandelpier.
La marina, Il lido.	El paseo [de la orilla].	De boulevard.
Una diga. Le rive del lago.	Un dique. Las orillas del lago.	Een dijk. De oevers van het meer.
◄La risacca.	La resaca, La marejada.	De branding.
Un aquaplane. Lo sport dell'aquaplane.	Un acuaplano. El deporte de acuaplano, Acuaplaneo.	Een waterski. Waterskiën.
Una gara aquatica. Gli sports nautici.	Un torneo acuático. Deportes acuáticos.	Een watertoernooi. Watersporten.
◄Un(a) bagnante.	Un(a) bañador(a).	Een bader, (feminine) Een baadster.
Quando ha inizio, Quando finisce, la stagione dei bagni?	¿Cuándo comienza, termina, la temporada de los baños?	Wanneer begint, eindigt, het badseizoen?
Sono misti i bagni colà?	¿Son mixtos los baños en ese punto?	Is het baden daar gemengd?
Vorrei fare un bagno o una tuffata. Vi sono dei bagni di mare, dei bagni di fiume, V'è uno stabilimento di bagni, una piscina, qui?	Me gustaría bañarme. ¿Hay aquí baños de mar, baños en el río, un establecimiento (o una escuela) de natación, una piscina?	Ik zou graag baden of een duikje nemen. Zijn er hier zeebaden, rivierbaden, Is er hier een badinrichting, een zwembad?
C'è un posto adatto per fare un bagno nel fiume?	¿Hay un lugar para bañarse en este río?	Is er in deze rivier een plaats waar men kan baden?
◄Il bagno è buono, senza pericolo, qui, in questo momento del giorno, a quest'epoca dell'anno?	¿Es este un buen lugar, un lugar sin peligro, para bañarse a esta hora del día, en esta época del año?	Kan men hier goed, veilig, baden, op deze tijd van de dag, op deze tijd van het jaar?

Is the beach, the bay, the cove, safe? or Is the bathing from the beach, in the bay, the cove, safe?	La plage, La baie, L'anse, est-elle sûre?	Ist das Baden an diesem Strand, in der Bucht, in der kleinen Bucht, ungefährlich?
Is there a strong tide (or current) running between the island and the shore?	Y a-t-il un fort courant entre l'île et le rivage?	Ist zwischen der Insel und dem Ufer eine starke Strömung?
When is high tide or high water, low tide or low water? Is the tide rising, falling? Is the tide turning or on the turn?	Quand la marée est-elle haute, basse? La marée monte-t-elle, descend-elle? La marée change-t-elle?	Wann ist Flut, Ebbe? Steigt, Fällt, das Wasser? Ist jetzt Flutwechsel?
Is the sea too rough for bathing this morning? I know how to swim. I am a good, a strong, swimmer.	La mer est-elle trop agitée pour le bain ce matin? Je sais nager. Je suis bon nageur, bonne nageuse, grand nageur, grande nageuse.	Ist das Meer heute früh zu stürmisch zum Baden? Ich kann schwimmen. Ich bin ein guter, ein tüchtiger, Schwimmer, eine gute, eine tüchtige, Schwimmerin.
Is the water very cold?	L'eau est-elle très froide?	Ist das Wasser sehr kalt?
Swimming.	La natation.	Das Schwimmen.
An open-air swimming bath or pool.	Une piscine en plein air.	Ein Schwimmbad im Freien.
A sea-water swimming bath.	Une piscine d'eau de mer.	Ein Schwimmbad mit Seewasser.
When do the baths open, close?	Quand ouvre-t-on, ferme-t-on, les bains?	Wann werden die Bäder geöffnet, geschlossen?
What is the depth of water in the bath, at the deep end, at the shallow end?	Quelle est la profondeur de l'eau de la piscine, au bout le plus profond, au bout peu profond?	Wie tief ist das Wasser, in der Badeanstalt, an der tiefsten Stelle, an der flachsten Stelle?
Will you teach me the breast stroke, the side stroke, the overarm stroke, the back stroke, how to swim under water, how to tread water, how to float, how to dive?	Voulez-vous m'enseigner la brasse ou la nage en grenouille, la nage de côté, la coupe (ou la nage) à l'indienne, la nage (ou la brasse) sur le dos, comment nager entre deux eaux, comment nager debout, comment faire la planche, comment plonger?	Können Sie mir Brustschwimmen, Seitenschwimmen, Hand-über-Hand - Schwimmen, Rückenschwimmen, Unterwasserschwimmen, Wassertreten, auf dem Wasser Treiben, Tauchen, beibringen.
To take a dive or a plunge, a running dive.	Faire le plongeon sans élan, le plongeon avec élan.	Kopfsprung, Kopfsprung mit Anlauf, machen.
Can you do the high dive?	Pouvez-vous faire le plongeon d'une grande hauteur?	Können Sie vom höchsten Sprungbrett springen?
A diving (or A spring) board.	Un plongeoir, Un tremplin.	Ein Sprungbrett.
A diving raft.	Un radeau-plongeoir.	Ein Floß.

La spiaggia, La baia, L'ansa, è sicura ?	¿ Puede uno bañarse sin peligro desde esta playa, esta bahía, esta ensenada ?	Is het strand, de baai, de kleine baai, veilig ? of Kan men aan het strand, in de baai, de kleine baai, veilig baden ?
C'è una forte corrente tra l'isola e la spiaggia ?	¿ Hay corriente fuerte entre la isla y la orilla ?	Is er een sterke stroom tussen het eiland en de oever ?
Quando la marea è alta, bassa ? Sale, Si ritira, la marea ? Sta per cambiare la marea ?	¿ Cuándo está la marea alta, baja ? ¿ Esta la marea subiendo, bajando ? ¿ Está la marea a punto de subir o de bajar ?	Wanneer is het vloed, eb ? Is het nu vloed, eb ? Is het tij aan het keren ?
Il mare è troppo mosso per fare il bagno questa mattina ? Io so nuotare. Io sono un buono, un resistente, nuotatore, una buona, resistente nuotatrice.	¿ Está el mar demasiado borrascoso para poderse bañar esta mañana ? Sé nadar. Soy buen nadador, buena nadadora, Soy nadador(a) fuerte.	Is de zee te woelig om vanochtend te baden ? Ik kan zwemmen. Ik ben een goede zwemmer, (feminine) een goede zwemster, een flinke zwemmer, (feminine) een flinke zwemster.
L'acqua è molto fredda ? Il nuoto. Una piscina all'aperto.	¿ Está muy fría el agua ? Natación. Una piscina a la intemperie o al aire libre.	Is het water erg koud ? Het zwemmen. Een open zwembad.
Una piscina d'acqua di mare.	Una piscina de agua de mar.	Een zwembad voorzien van zeewater.
Quando si aprono, si chiudono, i bagni ?	¿ Cuándo se abren, se cierran, los baños ?	Wanneer worden de baden geopend, gesloten ?
Qual'è la profondità dell'acqua nella piscina, nella parte più profonda, nella parte meno profonda ?	¿ Que profundidad tiene el agua en la piscina, a la extremidad más profunda, a la extremidad menos profunda ?	Wat is de diepte van het water in het zwembad ? aan het diepe einde, aan het ondiepe einde ?
Volete insegnarmi il nuoto a ranocchio, il nuoto alla marinara, il nuoto a taglio, il nuoto a pancia in aria, come nuotare sott'acqua, come nuotare in piedi, come fare il morto, come fare il tuffo ?	¿ Quiere usted enseñarme a nadar de pecho, de lado, a brazo elevado, de espalda, nadar por debajo del agua, pisar agua, flotar, zambullir ?	Wilt U mij de schoolslag, de zijslag, de borstcrawl, de rugslag, leren (=teach), mij onder water zwemmen, watertrappen, drijven, duiken, leren ?
Fare un tuffo, un tuffo con slancio.	Dar una zambullida, una zambullida a la carrera.	Duiken, Duiken met aanloop.
Potete fare il tuffo da una grande altezza ?	¿ Sabe usted tirarse desde lo alto ?	Kunt U van de hoge springplank duiken ?
Un trampolino.	Un trampolín.	Een springplank.
Una zattera per tuffo.	Una plataforma (o Una balsa) flotante.	Een duikvlot.

Has anyone ever swum across the mouth of this river?	Est-il jamais arrivé que quelqu'un ait traversé l'embouchure de ce fleuve à la nage?	Hat jemand schon einmal die Mündung des Flußes durchschwommen?
Do you go in for sun bathing? I have a good mind to have a sun bath.	Est-ce que vous vous adonnez aux bains de soleil? J'ai grande envie de prendre un bain de soleil.	Nehmen Sie gern Sonnenbäder? Ich habe große Lust auf ein Sonnenbad.
I should like to hire a beach tent or a bathing tent, a tent umbrella. How much is it?	Je voudrais louer une tente de plage, un parasol. C'est combien?	Ich möchte gern ein Strandzelt, einen Strandschirm, mieten. Was kostet das?
Do you sell (a) men's bathing caps, (b) women's bathing caps, (c) bath robes or bathing wraps, (d) towelling beach coats, (e) canvas shoes with hemp soles, (f) sun bonnets, (g) swimming belts, (h) pneumatic floats, (i) pneumatic boats, (j) rubber floating toys, (k) balls for beach games?	Est-ce que vous vendez (a) des bonnets de bain pour hommes, (b) des bonnets de bain pour femmes, (c) des peignoirs de bain, (d) des peignoirs éponge, (e) des espadrilles, (f) des bavolets, (g) des ceintures de natation, (h) des flotteurs pneumatiques, (i) des bateaux pneumatiques, (j) des animaux flottants ou en caoutchouc, (k) des ballons pour jeux de plage?	Verkaufen Sie (a) Badekappen für Herren, (b) Badekappen für Damen, (c) Badecapes, (d) Bademäntel, (e) Leinenschuhe mit Strohsohlen, (f) Strandhüte, (g) Schwimmgürtel, (h) Schwimmkissen, (i) Gummiboote, (j) Gummitiere, (k) Bälle für Strandspiele?
Have you any swimming shoes, beach (or sand) shoes, bathing sandals?	Est-ce que vous avez des souliers de natation, des souliers de plage ou des souliers "bains de mer" [pour marcher dans le sable], des sandales de bain?	Haben Sie Badeschuhe, Strandschuhe, Badesandalen?
A bathing (or A swimming) costume or suit or dress.	Un maillot (ou Un costume) de bain.	Ein Badeanzug.
A bathing dress competition.	Un concours de maillots.	Eine Badeanzug-Schönheitskonkurrenz.
Bathing drawers.	Un caleçon de bain.	Badehosen.
A bathing slip.	Un petit caleçon, Un caleçon forme slip.	Ein Badeanzug mit Überwurf.
Beach wear.	Des costumes de plage.	Strandkleidung.
A bathing box.	Une cabine de bain.	Eine Badezelle.
A bathing machine.	Une cabine de bain [sur roues].	Ein Badekarren.
Are the dressing rooms tended?	Les cabines de déshabillage sont-elles surveillées? Les déshabilloirs sont-ils surveillés?	Werden die Badezellen bewacht?
A bath attendant or A bathman.	Un garçon de bain, Un baigneur.	Ein Badediener.
A bath attendant or A bathwoman.	Une fille de bains, Une baigneuse.	Eine Badefrau.
Please give me a towel.	Donnez-moi, s'il vous plaît, une serviette [de toilette].	Geben Sir mir bitte ein Handtuch.

È stato mai attraversata da qualcuno a nuoto la bocca del fiume?	¿Ha habido en alguna ocasión alguno que haya nadado a través de la desembocadura de este río?	Heeft iemand ooit deze riviermond overzwommen?
Vi piace fare la cura dei bagni di sole? Io ho un grande desiderio di fare i bagni di sole.	¿Se dedica usted al baño de sol? De buena gana tomaría yo un baño de sol.	Doet U aan zonnebaden? Ik heb zin om een zonnebad te nemen.
←Io vorrei prendere in affitto (od a nolo) una tenda da spiaggia, un ombrello a tenda. Quanto costa?	Me gustaría alquilar una tiendesilla de playa, una sombrilla [de playa]. ¿Cuánto es?	Ik zou graag een tent op het strand of een badtent, een zonnetent, huren. Hoeveel is het?
Vendete (a) berretti da bagno per uomini, (b) berretti da bagno per donne, (c) accappatoi da bagno, (d) accappatoi a spugna, (e) scarpe di canavaccio con suole di canapa, (f) cappelli da sole,(g) cinture da nuoto, (h) galleggianti pneumatici, (i) barche pneumatiche, (j) giocattoli di gomma galleggianti, (k) palle per giuochi di spiaggia?	¿Vende usted (a) capuchos de baño para hombre, (b) capuchos de baño para mujer, (c) trajes de baño, (d) batas toallas, (e) alpargatas, (f) sombreros para el sol, (g) cinturones de natación, (h) balsas neumáticas, (i) botes neumáticos, (j) juguetes flotantes de goma, (k) pelotas para juegos en la playa?	Verkoopt U (a) herenbadmutsen, (b) damesbadmutsen, (c) badjassen of badcapes, (d) strandcapes van handdoekstof, (e) linnen schoenen, (f) zonnehoeden, (g) zwemvesten, (h) luchtbanden, (i) rubber boten, (j) drijvend speelgoed van rubber, (k) strandballen?
Avete scarpe da nuoto, scarpe da spiaggia, sandali da bagno?	¿Tiene usted zapatos de natación, zapatos para la playa, sandalias de baño?	Heeft U zwemschoenen, strandschoenen, badsandalen?
Un costume da bagno.	Una malla (o Un traje) de baño.	Een badpak, Een zwempak.
Un concorso per costumi da bagno.	Un concurso de trajes de baño.	Een badpakken concours.
←Le mutandine da bagno.	Calzoncillos de baño.	Een zwembroek.
I calzoncini.	Un calzoncillo de forma slip, Un slip.	Een zwembroekje.
Gli indumenti da spiaggia.	Ropa para la playa.	Strandkleding.
Una cabina da bagno.	Una caseta de baños.	Een badhokje.
Una cabina da bagno [su ruote].	Una caseta de baños [sobre ruedas].	Een badkoets.
←Sono sorvegliati i gabinetti da toeletta?	¿Están cuidadas (o atendidas) las casetas [de baño]?	Worden de kleedhokjes bewaakt?
Un bagnino.	Un bañero.	Een badmeester.
Una bagnina.	Una bañera.	Een badvrouw.
Per piacere datemi un asciugamano.	Haga el favor de darme una toalla.	Geef me een handdoek, als 't U belieft.

A child has fallen into the water. A man is drowning. Is there a life buoy, a rope, a grapnel, at hand?	Un enfant est tombé dans l'eau. Il y a un homme qui se noie. Y a-t-il tout proche une bouée de sauvetage, une corde, un grappin?	Ein Kind ist ins Wasser gefallen. Ein Mann ist am Ertrinken. Ist eine Rettungsboje, ein Strick, ein Dregganker, zur Hand?
To go to a watering place or a spa.	Aller à une ville d'eaux ou eaux eaux.	In einen Badeort gehen. →
A hydropathic establishment or A hydro.	Un établissement hydro-thérapique.	Eine Kaltwasserheilanstalt.
To take a water cure. To take the water in the pump room (at a spa).	Prendre une cure d'eau. Prendre les eaux dans la buvette.	Eine Kaltwasserkur machen. In der Trinkhalle Brunnen trinken.
A sulphur spring. An alkaline spring. A hot spring. Thermal baths.	Une source sulfureuse. Une source alcaline. Une source thermale. Des thermes.	Eine Schwefelquelle. Eine alkalische Quelle. Eine heiße Quelle. Thermal-bäder.
I want [to take] a hip bath, a hot sea-water bath, a steam (or vapour) (or Russian) bath, a Turkish bath, a sulphur bath, a mud bath, sunlight treatment.	Je voudrais [prendre] un bain de siège, un bain chaud d'eau de mer, un bain de vapeur, un bain turc, un bain sulfureux, un bain de boue[s minérales], le traitement solaire.	Ich möchte ein Sitzbad, ein heißes Seewasserbad, ein Dampfbad, ein tür-kisches Bad oder ein Schwitzbad, ein Schwe-felbad, ein Schlammbad, [eine] Höhensonnen-bestrahlung, nehmen.
The hot (or sweating) room (bath).	L'étuve sèche.	Der Heißluftraum. →
The steam room (bath).	L'étuve humide.	Der Dampfraum.

BOATING	COURSES EN BATEAU	BOOTFAHREN
A boat. To boat. Boating. Shall we go boating?	Un bateau ou Un canot. Canoter. Le canotage. Allons-nous faire une partie de canot?	Ein Boot. Bootfahren, Rudern. Das Bootfah-ren. Wollen wir Bootfahren (oder Rudern) gehen?
A boat hook.	Une gaffe pour l'amarrage des bateaux], Un croc [de batelier].	Ein Bootshaken.
A boat house.	Un garage [pour bateaux].	Ein Bootshaus.
A boatman	Un marin, Un canotier.	Ein Bootsmann. →
A boat race.	Une course de bateaux, Une course à l'aviron.	Ein Bootsrennen.
A canoe.	Un canoë.	Ein Kanu.
Canoeing.	Le canoëisme.	Der Kanusport.
A fishing boat.	Un bateau de pêche.	Ein Fischerboot.
A house boat.	Un bateau d'habitation.	Ein Hausboot.
A moonlight trip on the lake.	Une sortie sur le lac au clair de lune.	Eine Mondscheinpartie auf dem See.
A motor boat (private).	Un canot automobile.	Ein Motorboot.

Un ragazzo è cascato nell'acqua. Un uomo si è annegato. C'è vicino un boa da salvataggio, una corda, un grappino?	Se ha caido al agua un niño. Se está ahogando un hombre. ¿Hay a mano una boya salvavidas, una cuerda, un arpeo?	Er is een kind in het water gevallen. Er verdrinkt een man. Is er een reddingsboei, een touw, een dreg, bij de hand?
◄ Andare ad una stazione balneária.	Ir a un balneario.	Naar een badplaats gaan.
Uno stabilimento idroterapico.	Un establecimiento hidropático.	Een inrichting voor een waterkuur.
Fare una cura d'acqua. Prendere le acque nella sala delle sorgenti.	Tomar una cura de aguas de manantial o de aguas minerales. Tomar las aguas en [la sala de] la fuente.	Een waterkuur volgen. De wateren in de kuurzaal (of de drinkhal) gebruiken.
Una sorgente sufurea. Una sorgente alcalina. Una sorgente d'acqua calda od Una sorgente termale. I bagni termali.	Un manantial sulfúrico. Un manantial alcalino. Un manantial termal. Baños termales.	Een zwavelbron. Een alkalische bron. Een warme bron. Warme baden.
Desidero un semicupio, un bagno caldo di acqua di mare, un bagno a vapore, un bagno turco, un bagno sulfureo, un bagno di fango, un trattamento solare.	Quiero tomar un baño de cadera o de lebrillo, un baño caliente de agua de mar, un baño de vapor, un baño turco, un baño de azufre, un baño de lodo, un tratamiento de sol o solar.	Ik wens een heupbad [te nemen], een warm zeewaterbad, een stoombad, een Turks bad, een zwavelbad, een modderbad, zonbehandeling.
◄ La stanza da sudare.	La estufa seca.	De zweetkamer.
La stanza a vapore.	La estufa húmeda.	De stoomkamer.

GITE IN BARCA   PASEOS EN BOTE   BOOTTOCHTEN

Una barca. Andare in barca. Una gita in barca. Vogliamo andare a fare una gita in barca?	Un bote. Pasear en bote. Un paseo en bote. ¿Vamos a dar un paseo en bote?	Een boot. Boottochtjes maken. Een boottochtje. Zullen wij een boottochtje maken?
Una gaffa [per ammarrare].	Un bichero.	Een bootshaak.
Una rimessa per barca.	Un garaje para botes.	Een botenhuis.
◄ Un barcaiolo.	Un botero, Un barquero.	Een bootsman.
Una corsa di barche.	Una regata a remos.	Een roeiwedstrijd.
Un canotto. Un sandolino. Il canottaggio.	Una canoa. Ir en canoa.	Een kano. Kanoën.
Una barca da pesca.	Un barco de pesca.	Een vissersboot.
◄ Una barca per abitazione.	Una casa-embarcación.	Een woonark.
Una gita sul lago al chiaro di luna.	Un paseo en el lago a la luz de la luna.	Een tochtje op het meer in het maanlicht.
Un canotto automobile.	Un autobote, Un bote de gasolina.	Een motorboot.

A motor boat (*public service*).	Une vedette.	Ein Motorboot.
A regular motor boat service.	Un service régulier de vedettes.	Ein regelmäßiger Motorbootverkehr.
An oar.	Un aviron.	Ein Ruder.
An outboard motor.	Un moteur hors bord, Un propulseur amovible.	Ein Außenbordmotor.
A paddle (*for canoe*).	Une pagaie.	Ein Paddel.
The painter.	La bosse.	Die Fangleine.
A pleasure boat, yacht, steamer.	Un bateau, Un yacht, Un vapeur, de plaisance.	Ein Vergnügungsboot, Eine Jacht, Ein Vergnügungsdampfer.
A punt. A punt pole. To punt. To punt a boat.	Un bachot *ou* Une plate. Une perche. Pousser du fond. Conduire un bateau à la perche.	Ein Prahm, Eine Schauke. Staaken. Ein Boot staaken.
Push off *or* Shove off (*the boat*)!	Poussez au large	Stoßen Sie ab!
Rowing.	Le canotage, La nage [d'aviron], L'aviron.	Rudern.
I should like to go for a row.	Je voudrais faire une promenade en bateau.	Ich möchte rudern gehen.
A row[ing] boat.	Un bateau à rames.	Ein Ruderboot.
A row[ing] boat (*for pleasure*).	Un bateau de promenade.	Ein Ruderboot.
A rowing club.	Un cercle de l'aviron, Un club nautique.	Ein Ruderverein.
The rowlocks.	Les dames de nage, Les demoiselles, Les toletières, Le système.	Die Ruderklampen.
A sailing regatta.	Une régatte à voile.	Eine Segelregatta.
A sailing trip with boatman.	Une course en bateau à voile avec batelier.	Eine Segelfahrt mit dem Bootsmann.
A sea trip.	Une promenade en mer.	Eine Seefahrt.
A skiff.	Une yole, Un skiff.	Ein Skiff.
A sliding seat (*boat*).	Un banc à coulisse.	Ein Rollsitz.
A speed (*or* A racing) boat.	Un [canot] glisseur, Un glisseur de course.	Ein Rennboot.
A thwart.	Un banc [de nage].	Eine Bootsducht.
To wade in the sea.	Patauger dans la mer.	Im Meer waten.
Yachting.	Le yachting.	Das Jachtsegeln.

FISHING	**LA PÊCHE**	**FISCHEN**
Shall we go fishing, shrimping, prawning?	Est-ce que nous allons à la pêche, à la pêche à la crevette, à la pêche à la crevette rose?	Wollen wir fischen gehen, Garnelen, Steingarnelen, fangen?
Can you tell me where the fishing grounds are *or* where to fish?	Pouvez-vous m'indiquer les lieux de pêche?	Können Sie mir sagen, wo man fischen gehen kann?

Un autoscafo.	Una lancha a motor.	Een motorboot.
Un servizio regolare di autoscafi.	Un servicio regular de lanchas a motor.	Een geregelde motorbootdienst.
◄ Un remo.	Un remo.	Een roeiriem.
Un motore fuori bordo.	Un motor montado al exterior del bote.	Een buitenboordmotor.
Una pagaia.	Un canalete, Una paleta.	Een pagaai.
La barbetta.	El atadero.	Een vanglijn.
Un battello, Uno yacht, Un piroscafo, di piacere.	Un bote, Un yate, Un vapor, de recreo.	Een plezierboot, Een plezierjacht, Een plezierstoomboot.
◄ Una barchetta a fondo piatto, Un barchino. Una pertica da barchino. Spingersi con la pertica. Condurre una barca con la pertica.	Una batea, Un barquichuelo de fondo plano. Una percha, Una vara. Ir en batea. Impeler un bote apoyando una vara en el fondo del río.	Een punter. Een boom. Bomen. Een schuit bomen.
Spingete al largo!	¡Empuje hacia afuera!	Alles los!
Un'imbarcazione a remi.	Remar, Bogar.	Het roeien.
Io vorrei andare a remare.	Me gustaría dar un paseo en bote, Me gustaría remar un rato.	Ik zou graag een roeitochtje maken.
Una barca a remi.	Un bote de remos.	Een roeiboot.
◄ Una barca da gita.	Un bote de remos de recreo.	Een roeiboot.
Un circolo canottieri.	Un club náutico.	Een roeiclub.
Gli scalmi.	Las escalameras.	De dollen.
Una regata a vela.	Una regata de veleros.	Een zeilwedstrijd.
Una gita in barca a vela con batteliere.	Un paseo en velero con barquero.	Een zeiltochtje met een bootsman.
◄ Una gita in mare.	Un paseo en el mar.	Een zeetocht.
Uno schifo	Un esquife.	Een skiff.
Un banco scorrevole.	Un asiento corredizo.	Een glijbankje.
Una barca da corsa.	Un esquife de carrera.	Een raceboot.
Un banco.	Un banco de remeros.	Een roeibank.
◄ Squazzare nel mare.	Vadear en el mar.	Pootje baden in de zee.
Il yachting.	El yachting, El deporte de los yates.	Het jachtzeilen, De jachtzeilsport.

PESCA	**LA PESCA**	**VISSERIJ**
Vogliamo andare a pescare, alla pesca dei gamberettini, dei palemoni?	¿Vamos de pesca, pesca de camarones, de camarones grandes?	Zullen we gaan vissen, garnalen gaan vissen, steurgarnalen gaan vissen?
Potete indicarmi dove poter pescare?	¿Puede usted indicarme en dónde están los lugares en los que se puede pescar?	Kunt U me zeggen waar de visgronden zijn?

Can I fish at this spot?	Est-ce que je peux pêcher en cet endroit?	Kann ich an dieser Stelle fischen?
Is there a fisherman here who can accompany me?	Y a-t-il ici un pêcheur pouvant m'accompagner?	Ist hier ein Fischer, der mich begleiten kann?
Will the fish take this bait?	Le poisson mordra-t-il à cet appât?	Kann man den Fisch mit diesem Köder anfüttern?
Is this fish edible?	Ce poisson est-il comestible?	Ist dieser Fisch eßbar?
Is there in this place a supplier of fishing tackle, a dealer in fishing requisites?	Y a-t-il dans cette localité un fournisseur d'engins de pêche, un marchand d'articles de pêche?	Gibt es in diesem Ort einen Lieferanten für Angelgerät, ein Geschäft für Angelutensilien?

MEDICAL CARE

SOINS MÉDICAUX

ÄRZTLICHE BEHANDLUNG

(*See also* A chemist, *pp.* 178-181.)

Generalities

Généralités

Allgemeines

A doctor *or* A physician.	Un médecin, Un docteur.	Ein Arzt, Ein Doktor.
A surgeon.	Un chirurgien.	Ein Chirurg.
An eye doctor.	Un médecin oculiste.	Ein Augenarzt.
A hospital receiving paying patients. A nursing home.	Un hôpital qui reçoit des malades payants. Une maison de santé *ou* Une clinique.	Ein Krankenhaus für zahlende Patienten. Eine Klinik.
A hydropathic [establishment] *or* A hydro. (*For* Spa bathing, *see pp.* 254-255.)	Un établissement hydrothérapique.	Eine Kaltwasserheilanstalt.
A sanatorium.	Un sanatorium.	Ein Sanatorium.
A cure resort.	Un centre (*ou* Une station) de cure.	Ein Kurort.
The water cure.	La cure d'eau.	Die Wasserkur.
A rest cure.	Une cure de repos.	Eine Liegekur.
A Bath chair.	Un fauteuil roulant.	Ein Rollstuhl, Ein Rollsessel.
A [sick] nurse.	Un(e) garde-malades.	Ein Krankenwärter, Eine Krankenschwester.
A nurse (*in a hospital*).	Un infirmier, Une infirmière.	Ein Krankenwärter, Eine Krankenschwester.
The matron.	L'infirmière en chef.	Die Oberin.
Should I take medical advice?	Dois-je consulter un médecin?	Sollte ich einen Arzt konsultieren?
I must see a doctor. Can you tell me of a good doctor, preferably one who speaks English? Send for a doctor at once.	Il faut que je voie un médecin. Pouvez-vous m'indiquer un bon médecin, de préférence quelqu'un qui parle anglais? Faites venir un médecin immédiatement.	Ich muß zum Arzt gehen. Können Sie mir einen guten Arzt empfehlen, möglichst einen, der Englisch kann. Lassen Sie sofort einen Arzt holen.

Posso pescare in questo luogo?	¿Puedo uno pescar en este lugar?	Kan ik op deze plek vissen?
◀C'è un pescatore che potrebbe accompagnarmi?	¿Hay por aquí un pescador que puede acompañarme?	Is er een visser hier, di me kan vergezellen?
Abboccherà il pesce all'esca?	¿Morderán los peces a este cebo?	Wil de vis in dit aas happen?
È questo pesce buono a mangiare?	¿Es comible este pescado?	Is deze vis eetbaar?
Vi è in questo posto un fornitore di attrezzi per la pesca, un mercante di articoli di pesca?	¿Hay en esta localidad un surtidor de aparejos de pesca, un comerciante de requisitos para la pesca?	Is er in deze plaats een leverancier van visgerei, een handelaar in hengelaars benodigdheden?

CURE MEDICHE	TRATAMIENTO MÉDICO	GENEESKUNDIGE HULP
Generalità	**Generalidades**	**Algemeenheden**
Un dottore, Un medico.	Un médico, Un doctor.	Een dokter, Een arts.
◀Un chirurgo.	Un cirujano.	Een chirurg.
Un oculista.	Un oculista.	Een oogarts.
Un ospedale che riceve malati paganti. Una clinica od Una casa di salute.	Un hospital que recibe pacientes a base de pago. Una clínica [de curación].	Een ziekenhuis, dat betalende patienten opneemt. Een verpleeginrichting.
Uno stabilimento idroterapico.	Un establecimiento hidropático.	Een inrichting voor een waterkuur.
Un sanatorio.	Un sanatorio.	Een sanatorium.
◀Una stazione di cura.	Un centro de curación.	Een kuuroord.
La cura di acque.	La cura de agua.	De waterkuur.
Una cura di riposo.	Una cura de descanso.	Een rustkuur.
Una carrozzella da malato.	Una silla sobre ruedas.	Een rolstoel.
Un infermiere, Un'infermiera.	Un enfermero, Una enfermera.	Een ziekenverzorger, (feminine) Een ziekenverzorgster.
◀Un infermiere, Un'infermiera.	Un enfermero, Una enfermera.	Een verpleger, Een broeder, (fem.) Een verpleegster, Een zuster.
L'infermiera capo.	La directora de institución.	De directrice.
Debbo consultare un medico?	¿Debo consultar un médico?	Moet ik een arts raadplegen?
Io debbo vedere un dottore.	Necesito ver un médico.	Ik moet naar de dokter.
Potete voi indicarmi un buon dottore, preferibilmente uno che parli inglese? Fate venire un dottore subito.	¿Sabe usted de un buen médico, preferiblemente uno que habla inglés? Mande en seguida a llamar un médico.	Kunt U me een goede dokter aanraden, bij voorkeur één die Engels spreekt? Haal meteen een dokter.

There has been a bad accident. Help! Call an ambulance. Bring a stretcher, first aid. Go and fetch a doctor quickly.

Il a eu un accident grave. Au secours! Faites venir une ambulance. Apportez un brancard, les secours d'urgence. Allez vite chercher un médecin.

Ein schwerer Unfall hat sich ereignet. Hilfe! Lassen Sie ein Kranken-auto holen. Bringen Sie eine Tragbahre, erste Hilfe. Holen Sie bitte rasch einen Doktor.

I have met with an accident. I am in a sorry plight. Can you dress a wound, tend an injured man, an injured woman?

Je suis victime d'un accident. Je suis mal-en-point. Pouvez-vous panser une blessure, panser un blessé, une blessée?

Mir ist ein Unfall zuge-→ stoßen. Ich bin in einem schlimmen Zustand. Können Sie eine Wunde verbinden, nach einem verletzten Mann, nach einer verletzten Frau, sehen?

To be seriously injured, fatally injured, knocked down by a motor cycle, run over by a motor car.

Être gravement blessé, blessé à mort, renversé par une motocyclette, écrasé par une auto-mobile.

Schwer verwundet, Tötlich verwundet, Von einem Motorrad umgefahren, Von einem Auto über-fahren, sein.

Is the patient out of danger?
Is the doctor at home? When will he return?

Le malade est-il, La malade est-elle, hors d'affaire?
Le docteur est-il chez lui? Quand rentrera-t-il?

Ist der Kranke, die Kranke, außer Gefahr?
Ist der Doktor zu Hause? Wann kommt er nach Hause?

Where is the surgery or the consulting room? What are the doctor's consulting hours?

Où est le cabinet (ou le salon) de consultation? Quelles sont les heures de consultation du doc-teur?

Wo ist das Sprechzimmer? Wann hat der Doktor Sprechstunden?

Should I do better to ask for an appointment?
I have come to ask for a consultation by appoint-ment.

Ferais-je mieux de de-mander un rendez-vous?
Je suis venu pour de-mander une consulta-tion sur rendez-vous.

Soll ich mich lieber vorher-→ anmelden?
Ich komme, um mich zu einer Konsultation anzu-melden.

Can you give me an appointment for next Monday about two o'clock? What time will suit you?
What is your fee?
I feel unwell, ill.

Pouvez-vous prendre ren-dez-vous pour lundi pro-chain vers deux heures? Quelle heure vous con-viendra?
Quels sont vos honoraires?
Je me sens indisposé, malade.

Können Sie mich für näch-sten Montag, etwa zwei Uhr, annehmen? Welche Zeit paßt Ihnen?
Wie hoch ist Ihr Honorar?
Ich fühle mich nicht gut, krank.

What is my compaint? or What is wrong (or the matter) with me?

Qu'est-ce que j'ai?

Was fehlt mir? Was habe→ ich? Was ist mit mir los?

Can anything be done [for it]? What must I do?

Y a-t-il moyen d'y remé-dier? Que dois-je faire?

Kann man etwas dagegen tun? Was soll ich tun?

A diet. I am on a diet. My doctor in London put me on a diet. What should I eat, drink?

Un régime. Je suis au régime. Mon docteur à Londres m'a mis au régime. Que dois-je manger, boire?

Eine Diät. Ich habe eine Diät. Mein Arzt in Lon-don hat mich auf Diät gesetzt. Was soll ich essen, trinken?

A meat diet.

Une alimentation carnée, Un régime gras.

Eine Fleischdiät.

Vi è stata una grave disgrazia. Aiuto! Fate venire un'ambulanza. Portate una barella, un pronto soccorso. Andate presto a cercare un dottore.	Ha ocurrido un grave accidente. ¡Socorro! Llame una ambulancia. Traigan una camilla, primeros auxilios. Vaya pronto a buscar un médico.	Er heeft een ernstig ongeluk plaats gehad. Help! Roep een ambulance. Breng een draagbaar, eerste hulp. Ga gauw een dokter halen.
◄Io sono vittima di una disgrazia. Mi trovo in un triste caso. Potete voi medicare una ferita, curare un ferito, una donna ferita?	He sido víctima de un accidente. Estoy en un gran apuro. ¿Sabe usted curar una herida o una lesión, socorrer un herido, una herida?	Ik heb een ongeluk gehad. Ik ben er slecht aan toe. Kunt U een wond verbinden, een gewonde man, een gewonde vrouw, verbinden?
Essere gravemente ferito, mortalmente ferito, abbattuto da una motocicletta, investito da un'automobile.	Estar gravemente herido, mortalmente herido o herido a muerte, derribado por una motocicleta, atropellado por un automóvil.	Ernstig gewond. Dodelijk gewond. Omvergereden door een motorfiets, Overreden door een auto.
Il malato, La malata, è fuori di pericolo?	¿Está ya fuera de peligro el (la) paciente?	Is de patient buiten gevaar?
È in casa il dottore? Quando ritorna?	¿Está el doctor? ¿Cuándo regresará?	Is de dokter thuis? Wanneer komt hij thuis?
Dov'è il gabinetto del chirurgo, la sala delle consultazioni? Quali sono le ore di consultazioni del dottore?	¿Dónde está la cirujía o el gabinete de consulta? ¿Cuáles son las horas de consulta del doctor?	Waar is de spreekkamer? Wanneer heeft de dokter spreekuur?
◄È meglio fare un appuntamento?	¿Sería preferible pedir una cita?	Kan ik beter een afspraak maken?
Sono venuto per fissare un appuntamento per un consulto.	Vengo a pedir cita para una consulta.	Ik kom een afspraak maken voor een consult.
Potete fissare un appuntamento per lunedì prossimo verso le due pomeridiane? Qual'è l'ora che più Le conviene?	¿Puede usted darme cita para el lunes próximo a eso de las dos? ¿Qué hora le convendría a usted?	Kunt U een afspraak maken voor aanstaande maandag om ongeveer twee uur? Welk uur schikt U?
Quali sono i suoi onorari?	¿Cuánto es su honorario?	Wat is Uw honorarium?
Mi sento indisposto, malato.	Me siento mal, Estoy enfermo.	Ik voel me onwel, ziek.
◄Qual'è la mia malattia? Cosa ho di male?	¿Qué tengo? ¿De qué padezco?	Wat is mijn kwaal? Wat is er niet met mij in orde?
Si può fare qualche cosa? Che debbo fare?	¿Tiene remedio? ¿Qué es lo que debo hacer?	Kan er iets aan gedaan worden? Wat moet ik doen?
Una dieta od Un regime. Io sono in dieta. Il mio dottore di Londra mi ha sottoposto a dieta. Cosa debbo mangiare, bere?	Un régimen. Estoy bajo régimen. Mi médico en Londres me ha sometido a régimen. ¿Qué debo comer, beber?	Een dieet. Ik ben op een dieet. Mijn dokter in Londen heeft me op een dieet gezet. Wat moet ik eten, drinken?
Una dieta di carne.	Un régimen de carne.	Een vleesdieet.

Must I stay in bed? When may I get up?	Dois-je garder le lit? Quand pourrai-je me lever?	Muß ich im Bett bleiben? Wann darf ich aufstehen?
Will you give me a prescription, a tonic?	Voulez-vous me donner une ordonnance, un tonique?	Geben Sie mir ein Rezept, ein Kräftigungsmittel.
What are the directions for use? What is the dose? One tablespoonful, two teaspoonfuls, a wineglassful, three times a day.	Quel est le mode d'emploi? Quelle est la dose? Une cuillerée à bouche, deux cuillerées à thé, un verre à Bordeaux, trois fois par jour.	Wie nimmt man dieses Mittel ein? Welche Dosis nimmt man? Einen Eßlöffel, zwei Teelöffel, ein Weinglasvoll, dreimal täglich.
I feel a little, much, better.	Je me sens un peu, beaucoup, mieux.	Mir ist etwas, viel, besser.
When should I come again? When will you come again?	Quand dois-je repasser? Quand reviendrez-vous?	Wann soll ich wiederkommen? Wann kommen Sie wieder?
Massage. A masseur. A masseuse.	Le massage. Un masseur. Une masseuse.	Massage. Ein Masseur. Eine Masseuse.
Please massage this stiff joint, this bad limb.	Veuillez masser cette articulation raide, ce membre malade.	Würden Sie bitte dieses steife Gelenk, dieses kranke Glied, massieren.

Ailments	**Maladies**	**Krankheiten**
I have lost my appetite.	J'ai perdu l'appétit.	Ich habe den Appetit verloren.
I am bilious, constipated.	Je suis bilieux, constipé.	Ich bin gallenleidend, verstopft.
I have caught a chill.	J'ai pris [un coup de] froid.	Ich habe mich erkältet.
I have caught [a] (or have taken) cold. I have a bad cold, nasal catarrh, bronchitis. I have a cold in the head, in the chest.	Je me suis enrhumé ou J'ai pris un rhume. Je suis très enrhumé, J'ai un catarrhe nasal, la bronchite. Je me suis enrhumé du cerveau, de la poitrine.	Ich habe mir eine Erkältung zugezogen. Ich habe eine starke Erkältung, Schnupfen, Bronchitis. Ich habe Kopfschnupfen, eine Erkältung auf der Brust.
I have a cough.	J'ai une toux.	Ich habe Husten.
I have dysentery, diarrhoea.	J'ai la dysenterie, la diarrhée.	Ich habe Ruhr, Durchfall.
I have an (or the) earache, a (or the) face ache.	J'ai une douleur d'oreille, une névralgie faciale.	Ich habe Ohrenschmerzen, Neuralgie im Gesicht.
I am feverish. I have a temperature.	J'ai la fièvre. J'ai de la température.	Mir ist fiebrig, Ich habe Fieber oder Temperatur.
I have a headache.	J'ai mal à la tête.	Ich habe Kopfschmerzen.
Can you give me something for [an attack of] indigestion, for dyspepsia?	Pouvez-vous me prescrire un remède pour une indigestion, pour la dyspepsie?	Können Sie mir etwas gegen Verdauungsstörungen, gegen Schwerverdaulichkeit, geben?
I have an attack of influenza, the shivers.	J'ai un accès de grippe, le frisson.	Ich habe einen Grippeanfall, Schüttelfrost.
It is .. days since I had a motion [of the bowels].	Il y a .. jours que je ne suis pas allé à la selle.	Seit .. Tagen habe ich keinen Stuhl gehabt.

Debbo rimanere a letto? Quando potrò alzarmi?	¿Tengo que quedarme en cama? ¿Cuándo podré levantarme?	Moet ik in bed blijven? Wanneer mag ik opstaan?
◄Volete darmi una prescrizione *od* una ricetta, un tonico?	¿Quiere usted recetarme algo, darme un tónico?	Wilt U me een recept, een versterkend middel geven?
Qual'è la direzione per l'uso? Qual'è la dose? Un cucchiaio da tavola, due cucchiaini da caffè, un bicchiere da vino, tre volte al giorno.	¿Cómo debe tomarse? ¿Qué es la dosis? Una cucharada grande, dos cucharadas pequeñas, una copita, tres veces al día.	Wat zijn de gebruiksaanwijzingen? Wat is de dosis? Een eetlepel, twee theelepels, een wijnglas, drie keer per dag.
Io mi sento un poco, molto, meglio.	Me siento un poco, mucho, mejor.	Ik voel mij wat, veel, beter.
Quando debbo ripassare? Quando ritornerà Lei?	¿Cuándo deberé venir de nuevo? ¿Cuándo volverá usted a venir?	Wanneer moet ik terugkomen? Wanneer komt U terug?
Il massaggio. Un uomo, Una donna, che fa il massaggio.	Masaje. Un(a) masajista.	Massage. Een masseur. Een masseuse.
◄Per favore, fatemi il massaggio in questa articolazione irrigidita, in questo membro malato.	Hágame el favor de sobar esta articulación rígida, este miembro dolorido *o* lisiado.	Masseer dit stijve gewricht, dit zieke lid, als 't U belieft.
Malattie	**Enfermedades**	**Ziekten**
Io ho perduto l'appetito.	He perdido el apetito.	Ik ben mijn eetlust kwijt.
Io sono bilioso, **stitico**.	Estoy bilioso, estreñido.	Ik heb last van gal, van verstopping.
Ho preso un fresco.	He agarrado un enfriamiento.	Ik heb kou gevat.
Mi sono raffreddato *o* Mi sono buscato un raffreddore. Sono molto raffreddato. Ho un catarro nasale, la bronchite. Ho preso un raffreddore di testa, di petto.	He cogido un constipado *o* un resfriado. Tengo un fuerte constipado, un catarro de la nariz, bronquitis. Tengo un catarro de cabeza, de pecho.	Ik heb een verkoudheid opgedaan. Ik ben erg verkouden, Ik heb neuscatarrh, bronchitis. Ik ben neusverkouden, borstverkouden.
◄Ho la tosse.	Tengo tos.	Ik hoest.
Ho la dissenteria, la diarrea.	Tengo disentería, diarrea.	Ik heb dysentrie, diarree.
Ho un dolore all'orecchio, un dolore facciale.	Tengo dolor en la oreja, un dolor neurálgico en la cara.	Ik heb oorpijn, pijn in mijn gezicht.
Sono febbricitante.	Tengo calentura.	Ik ben koortsig *of* Ik heb koorts.
Ho il dolor di testa.	Tengo dolor de cabeza.	Ik heb hoofdpijn.
◄Potete darmi qualche cosa contro l'indigestione, contro la dispepsia?	¿Puede usted recetarme un remedio para una indigestión, para la dispepsia?	Kunt U me iets geven tegen indigestie *of* slechte spijsvertering?
Ho un attacco di influenza, i brividi.	Tengo un ataque de influenza *o* de gripe, de escalofrío.	Ik heb een griepaanval, rillingen.
Sono .. giorni dacchè non ho avuto funzioni corporali.	Hace ya .. días desde que he podido evacuar el vientre.	Het is .. dagen geleden dat ik voor het laatst ontlasting heb gehad.

I am suffering from neuralgia in the jaw, in the face.	Je souffre d'une névralgie de la mâchoire, de la face.	Ich leide an Neuralgie in der Backe, im Gesicht.
I have a pain. My eyes pain me.	J'ai une douleur. Mes yeux me font souffrir.	Ich habe Schmerzen. Meine Augen tun mir weh.
I have a touch of rheumatism,	J'ai un peu de rhumatisme.	Ich habe einen Anflug von Rheumatismus.
I am suffering from sickness or nausea.	J'ai mal au cœur ou J'ai des nausées.	Ich leide an Übelkeit.
I did not sleep well last night.	Je n'ai pas bien dormi cette nuit.	Ich habe letzte Nacht schlecht geschlafen.
I have a sore throat, a relaxed throat. I am suffering from hoarseness.	J'ai mal à la gorge, la pharyngite. J'ai de l'enrouement.	Ich habe Halsschmerzen, einen rauhen Hals. Ich leide an Heiserkeit.
Have you a remedy to relieve mosquito bites?	Est-ce que vous avez un remède pour soulager les piqûres de moustiques?	Haben Sie ein Mittel gegen Moskitostiche?

At the dentist	Chez le dentiste	Beim Zahnarzt
A dental surgeon.	Un chirurgien dentiste.	Ein Zahnarzt.
I have [the] toothache, a raging toothache.	J'ai mal aux dents, une rage de dents.	Ich habe Zahnschmerzen, unerträgliche Zahnschmerzen.
I want a tooth out or drawn.	Je désire me faire arracher une dent.	Ich möchte mir einen Zahn ziehen lassen.
It is this lower tooth, upper tooth, front tooth, back tooth, molar[tooth], canine [tooth], wisdom tooth, which aches or hurts me.	C'est cette dent de dessous, dent de dessus, dent de devant, dent du fond, [dent] molaire, [dent] canine, dent de sagesse, qui me fait mal.	Es ist dieser untere Zahn, obere Zahn, Vorderzahn, Hinterzahn, Backenzahn, Eckzahn, Weisheitszahn, der mir weh tut.
One of my teeth is decayed. Is it possible to save it? Can you fill (or stop) it?	Une de mes dents est cariée. Est-il possible de la conserver? Pouvez-vous la plomber?	Einer meiner Zähne ist hohl. Läßt er sich noch retten? Können Sie ihn füllen oder plombieren?
A nerve is exposed. Can you destroy it?	Un nerf est exposé. Pouvez-vous le détruire?	Ein Nerv ist freigelegt. Können Sie ihn töten?
You are hurting me. It (what you are doing) hurts.	Vous me faites mal. Cela me fait mal.	Sie tun mir weh. Es tut mir weh.
I should like gas, a local anaesthetic.	Je voudrais avoir du gaz, un anesthétique local.	Bitte betäuben Sie mich mit Gas, Bitte geben Sie mir örtliche Betäubung.
My denture (or plate) is broken. Can you repair it?	Ma denture artificielle est cassée. Pouvez-vous la réparer?	Mein künstliches Gebiß ist zerbrochen. Können Sie es reparieren?

Soffro di nevralgia nella mascella, di nevralgia facciale.	Padezco de neuralgia de la quijada, de la cara.	Ik lijd aan zenuwpijnen in mijn kaak, in mijn gezicht.
Ho un dolore. Gli occhi mi dolgono.	Tengo un dolor. Me duelen los ojos.	Ik heb pijn. Mijn ogen doen pijn.
◄Ho un po' di reumatismo	Estoy un tanto reumático.	Ik heb lichte reumatiek.
Soffro di nausea.	Padezco de náuseas.	Ik ben misselijk.
Non ho dormito bene ieri notte.	No dormí bien anoche.	Ik heb niet goed geslapen vannacht.
Ho male alla gola, la faringite. Soffro di raucedine.	Tengo mal de garganta o Me duele la garganta, Tengo faringitis. Padezco de ronquera.	Ik heb keelpijn, een ontstoken keel. Ik ben hees of schor.
Avete un remedio contro le punture di zanzare?	¿Tiene usted un remedio para aliviar los picazones de mosquito?	Hebt U een middeltje tegen muggebeten?

Dal dentista	En casa del dentista	Bij de tandarts
◄Un chirurgo dentista.	Un cirujano dentista.	Een tandarts.
Ho [il] mal di denti, uno straziante mal di denti.	Tengo dolor de muela, un dolor rabioso de muela.	Ik heb kiespijn, razende kiespijn.
Vorrei levarmi un dente.	Quiero que me saquen una muela o un diente.	Ik wil een tand laten trekken.
È questo dente di sotto, dente di sopra, dente davanti, dente in fondo, [dente] molare, [dente] canino dente del giudizio, che mi duole o mi fa male.	Me duele esta muela (o este diente) de abajo, de arriba, de delante, de atrás, esta muela, este colmillo, esta muela del juicio.	Het is deze ondertand, boventand, voortand, zijtand, kies, hoektand, verstandskies, die pijn doet.
Uno dei miei denti è cariato. È possibile salvarlo? Potete impiombarlo?	Tengo una muela picada. ¿Será posible salvarla? ¿Puede usted empastármela?	Een van mijn tanden is rot. Kan hij gered worden? Kunt U hem vullen?
◄Un nervo è scoperto. Può Lei ammortirlo?	Está descubierto un nervio. ¿Puede usted destruirlo o matarlo?	Er ligt een zenuw bloot. Kunt U die doden?
Mi fate male. Mi fa male.	Me está usted lastimando. Eso me duele.	U doet me pijn. Het doet pijn.
Vorrei avere il gas, un anestetico locale.	Quisiera tomar gas, un anestésico local.	Ik zou graag gas, plaatselijke verdoving hebben.
La mia dentiera è rotta. Può Lei accomodarla?	Se me ha roto la dentadura postiza. ¿Puede usted reparármela?	Mijn gebit is gebroken. Kunt U het repareren?

WEIGHTS AND MEASURES

(more exact equivalents are given in decimals)

A **kilo**[gramme] (1000 grammes) = about 2 lbs 3 oz. (2.2 lbs).

A **gramme** = about 15 grains (15.43 grains). 15 grammes = about 1/2 oz.

1 **ounce** avoirdupois weight = a little over 28 grammes (28.35 grammes).

1 **ounce** apothecaries and troy weight = a little over 31 grammes (31.1 grammes).

A **litre** = about 1 3/4 pints (1.76 pints).

A **centilitre** (100th of a litre) = 7/100ths of a gill (0.07 gill).

1 **fluid ounce** apothecaries measure = about 3 centilitres (2.84 centilitres).

A **metre** = about 3 feet 3 inches (3.28 feet).

A **centimetre** (100th of a metre) = about 2/5ths of an inch (0.39 inch).

A **kilometre** (1000 metres) = about 5/8ths of a mile (0.62 mile). To convert kilometres to miles, approximately : multiply kilometres by 5 and divide by 8. To convert miles to kilometres : multiply by 8 and divide by 5.

A **square centimetre** = about 1/7th of a square inch (0.155 sq. in.).

A **square metre** (10000 sq. cm.) = about 1 1/5th square yards (1.2 sq. yds.).

A **hectare** (100 ares or 10000 square metres) = about 2 1/2 acres (2.47 acres).

MONEYS

(Values in foreign currency according to the exchange of the day.)

GREAT BRITAIN   A **pound** = 100 pence.

UNITED STATES OF AMERICA : A **dollar** = 100 cents.

FRANCE : A **franc** = 100 centimes.

BELGIUM   A **franc** = 100 centimes.

SWITZERLAND : A **franc** = 100 centimes.

GERMANY : A **mark** = 100 pfennig.

AUSTRIA : A **schilling** = 100 groschen.

ITALY : A **lira** = 100 centesimi.

SPAIN : A **peseta** = 100 centimos.

HOLLAND : A **guilder** = 100 cents.

24-HOUR CLOCK SYSTEM

Continental transport and postal services are worked on the 24-hour clock system.

8.30 = 8.30 a.m. 8.30 p.m. is stated as 20.30.

Midnight is zero hour.

Thus :—

12-hour system		24-hour system
12.0 midnight arrival		24.00
,, ,, departure		0.00
12.10 a.m.		0.10
11.55 a.m.		11.55
12.0 noon		12.00
12.15 p.m.		12.15
1.1 p.m.		13.01
11.20 p.m.		23.20

THERMOMETERS

	Fahrenheit	Centigrade or Celsius	Réaumur
	(F.)	(C.)	(R.)
Water freezes at	32°	0°	0°
Water boils at	212°	100°	80°

To convert :

F. to C. :	Subtract 32°, multiply by 5, and divide by 9.
F. to R. :	Subtract 32°, multiply by 4, and divide by 9.
C. to F. :	Multiply by 9, divide by 5, and add 32°.
R. to F. :	Multiply by 9, divide by 4, and add 32°.
C. to R. :	Multiply by 4, and divide by 5.
R. to C. :	Multiply by 5, and divide by 4.

PINTS INTO LITRES

(for reckoning quantities of oil)
(To the nearest 1/4 litre)

1/2 pint	=	1/4 litre
1 ,,	=	1/2 ,, (or, more exactly, in decimals, 0.568 litre).
2 pints	=	1 1/4 litres
3 ,,	=	1 3/4 ,,
4 ,,	=	2 1/4 ,,
5 ,,	=	2 3/4 ,,
6 ,,	=	3 1/2 ,,
7 ,,	=	4 ,,
8 ,,	=	4 1/2 ,,

GALLONS INTO LITRES

(for reckoning quantities of petrol)
(To the nearest 1/4 litre)

1/2 gallon	=	2 1/4 litres
1 ,,	=	4 1/2 ,, (or, more exactly, 4.546 litres).
2 gallons	=	9 litres
3 ,,	=	13 3/4 ,,
4 ,,	=	18 1/4 ,,
5 ,,	=	22 3/4 ,,
6 ,,	=	27 1/4 ,,
7 ,,	=	31 3/4 ,,
8 ,,	=	36 1/4 ,,
9 ,,	=	41 ,,
10 ,,	=	45 1/2 ,,
11 ,,	=	50 ,,
12 ,,	=	54 1/2 ,,

---

5 litres (petrol is sold per 5 litres) = about 1 gallon and 1 pint.

TYRE PRESSURE

1 lb. per sq. inch = 0.0703 kilogramme per square centimetre, *written on the Continent as 0,0703, the decimal point being indicated by a comma.*

20	lbs	per	sq.	inch	=	1.41	kilos per sq. cm.		
21	,,	,,	,,	,,	=	1.48	,,	,,	,,	,,
22	,,	,,	,,	,,	=	1.55	,,	,,	,,	,,
23	,,	,,	,,	,,	=	1.62	,,	,,	,,	,,
24	,,	,,	,,	,,	=	1.69	,,	,,	,,	,,
25	,,	,,	,,	,,	=	1.76	,,	,,	,,	,,
26	,,	,,	,,	,,	=	1.83	,,	,,	,,	,,
27	,,	,,	,,	,,	=	1.90	,,	,,	,,	,,
28	,,	,,	,,	,,	=	1.97	,,	,,	,,	,,
29	,,	,,	,,	,,	=	2.04	,,	,,	,,	,,
30	,,	,,	,,	,,	=	2.11	,,	,,	,,	,,
31	,,	,,	,,	,,	=	2.18	,,	,,	,,	,,
32	,,	,,	,,	,,	=	2.25	,,	,,	,,	,,
33	,,	,,	,,	,,	=	2.32	,,	,,	,,	,,
34	,,	,,	,,	,,	=	2.39	,,	,,	,,	,,
35	,,	,,	,,	,,	=	2.46	,,	,,	,,	,,
36	,,	,,	,,	,,	=	2.53	,,	,,	,,	,,
37	,,	,,	,,	,,	=	2.60	,,	,,	,,	,,
38	,,	,,	,,	,,	=	2.67	,,	,,	,,	,,
39	,,	,,	,,	,,	=	2.74	,,	,,	,,	,,
40	,,	,,	,,	,,	=	2.81	,,	,,	,,	,,

1 kilo per sq. cm. = 14 1/4 lbs per sq. inch, or, more exactly. 14.223 lbs per sq. inch.

INDEX

Printed in Great Britain
by Unwin Brothers Limited
The Gresham Press, Old Woking, Surrey, England
A member of the Staples Printing Group

ISBN 0 7100 1674 3